SURVIVING GLOBAL CHANGE?

Non-State Actors in International Law, Politics and Governance Series

Series Editors:
Math Noortmann, Erasmus University, Rotterdam, The Netherlands
Bob Reinalda, Radboud University Nijmegen, The Netherlands
Bas Arts, Radboud University Nijmegen, The Netherlands
Peter Willetts, City University, London, UK

The proliferation of non-state actors in the international system over the last three decades has increased the need for a broader theoretical analysis and empirical validation. The series explores the capabilities and impact of non-state actors, such as privately-based transnational corporations, non-governmental organizations (NGOs), international criminal oganizations, and liberation movements, as well as intergovernmental organizations (in which NGOs often participate). The series seeks to address this need and to deepen the knowledge and understanding of non-state actors by scholars, practitioners and students in the fields of international law, politics and governance. By emphasizing legal, political and governance aspects of non-state actors' activities at the international (global or regional) level, the series intends to transcend traditional disciplinary and organizational boundaries.

Also in the series

**The Romani Voice in World Politics: The United Nations
and Non-State Actors**
Ilona Klímová-Alexander
ISBN 0 7546 4173 2

Non-State Actors in International Relations
Edited by Bas Arts, Math Noortmann and Bob Reinalda
ISBN 0 7546 1848 X

**Agents of Altruism: The Expansion of Humanitarian NGOs
in Rwanda and Afghanistan**
Katarina West
ISBN 0 7546 1839 0

Surviving Global Change?
Agricultural Interest Groups in Comparative Perspective

Edited by
DARREN HALPIN
The Robert Gordon University,
Aberdeen, Scotland

Routledge
Taylor & Francis Group

LONDON AND NEW YORK

First published 2005 by Ashgate Publishing

Reissued 2018 by Routledge
2 Park Square, Milton Park, Abingdon, Oxon OX14 4RN
711 Third Avenue, New York, NY 10017, USA

Routledge is an imprint of the Taylor & Francis Group, an informa business

First issued in paperback 2018

A Library of Congress record exists under LC control number: 2004028603

Notice:
Product or corporate names may be trademarks or registered trademarks, and are used only for identification and explanation without intent to infringe.

Publisher's Note
The publisher has gone to great lengths to ensure the quality of this reprint but points out that some imperfections in the original copies may be apparent.

Disclaimer
The publisher has made every effort to trace copyright holders and welcomes correspondence from those they have been unable to contact.

ISBN 13: 978-0-815-39727-4 (hbk)
ISBN 13: 978-1-138-62073-5 (pbk)
ISBN 13: 978-1-351-14832-0 (ebk)

Contents

PART III: NORTH AMERICA

PART IV: CONCLUSION

List of Tables

List of Appendices

List of Contributors

Carsten Daugbjerg is Associate Professor at the Department of Political Science, University of Aarhus, Denmark. His research is mainly within the fields of agricultural policy and environmental policy. He is the author of *Policy Networks under Pressure: Pollution Control, Policy Reform and the Power of Farmers* (Aldershot, UK: Ashgate Publishing, 1998), the co-editor of *Magtens organisering: Stat og interesseorganisationer i Danmark [Organizing Power: State and Organized Interests in Denmark]* (Aarhus, Denmark: Systime Publishing, 1999) and together with Gert Tinggaard Svendsen, he has authored *Green Taxation in Question: Politics and Efficiency in Environmental Regulation* (Basingstoke: Palgrave, 2001). He has also published several articles in Scandinavian and international journals and contributed to several edited volumes.

Wyn Grant is Professor of Politics at the University of Warwick and chair of the Political Studies Association of the UK, 2002-5. He has written on agricultural policy issues for some thirty years and his publications include *The Common Agricultural Policy* (Basingstoke: Palgrave, 1997) and (with William Coleman and Timothy Josling) *Agriculture in the New Global Economy* (Cheltenam: Edward Elgar, 2004).

Alan Greer is Reader in Politics and Public Policy at the University of the West of England Bristol, UK. He is a graduate of Queen's University Belfast, where he completed a doctoral thesis on agricultural policy in Northern Ireland. His main research interests lie in the field of public policy analysis and governance, especially in the areas of agricultural and rural policy. He has written two books and numerous journal articles in this area, including *Agricultural Policy in Europe* (Manchester: Manchester University Press, forthcoming 2005) and *Rural Politics in Northern Ireland* (Aldershot: Ashgate, 1996).

Darren Halpin is Lecturer in Public Policy at The Robert Gordon University, Aberdeen, Scotland. He was formerly a Post Doctoral Research Fellow at both Central Queensland University and Edith Cowan University in Australia. Prior to these appointments he was also a Leverhulme Visiting Research Fellow in the Politics and IR Department at the University of Aberdeen (Scotland). His research interests include interest groups, political representation, Australian and European public policy and farm politics. He has recently published articles (solely and jointly) on these themes in journals including *Political Studies*, *British Journal of Politics and International Relations*, the *Australian Journal of Political Science*, the *Australian Journal of Public Administration* and *Sociologia Ruralis*.

Eduardo Moyano-Estrada has a PhD in Rural Sociology (University of Cordoba). He is Deputy Director of Institute of Advanced Social Studies (IESA) belonging to Spanish Council for Scientific Research. His scientific work is in the fields of collective action in the farming sector and rural society, and the participation of organized interest groups in the decision-making process. He has led some research projects on farm interest group systems in Latin American countries (Brazil, Argentina and Mexico) and Morocco, and is a member of the European research network on farmers' unions.

Christilla Roederer-Rynning is Assistant Professor at the University of Southern Denmark, Odense. Her research focuses on the institutional aspects of CAP reform and EU enlargement and on the politics of farm protest in France. She is currently working on the EU's food safety regime. Her previous publications include 'Impregnable Citadel or Leaning Tower? Europe's Common Agricultural Policy at Forty,' in *SAIS Review* (Winter-Spring 2003), 'From "Talking Shop" to "Working Parliament": The European Parliament and Agricultural Change,' in *Journal of Common Market Studies* (March 2003), and 'Farm Conflict in France and the Europeanisation of Agricultural Policy,' in *West European Politics* (July 2002).

Grace Skogstad is Professor of Political Science at the University of Toronto. Her research focuses on the politics of agriculture, agricultural trade, and food safety policies in North America and the European Union. She is a past president of the Canadian Political Science Association.

Graham K. Wilson is Chair of the Department of Political Science, University of Wisconsin. He is the author of many books on interest groups, bureaucracy and public policy including 'Business and Politics' (Chatham, N.J.: Chatham House, Third Edition 2002) and 'Only in America?' (Chatham, N.J.: Chatham House, 1998).

Foreword

Debates about globalization have placed more emphasis on NGOs (non-governmental organizations) and transnational social movements, or in more general terms *promotional* interest groups, than on *sectional* interest groups. This volume in our series on non-state actors in international law, politics and governance gives the floor to a debate about sectional interest groups. It discusses the fate of a particular group of national industry associations under conditions of global change, i.e. agricultural interest groups. The volume's strong focus on *national* interest groups in a comparative perspective of states does not make it irrelevant for the issue of non-state actors in the international economy and related governance structures. On the contrary, the volume discloses how important national interest groups have remained in a period characterized by globalization and liberalization. The strong and vehement debates about ongoing protectionism in the case of agriculture, as can be heard against the World Trade Organization and the European Union, underline this relevance given the many references to 'organized interests'.

Global Change: From a State-Assisted to a Market-Liberal Paradigm?

Agriculture is a most interesting case because after the Second World War modern Western nation-states 'partnered' with agricultural interest groups to aid the successful modernization of their domestic agricultural sectors. Special arrangements, referred to as 'agricultural exceptionalism', considered the agricultural sector as hazardous (unstable weather and market conditions) and salient (contributing to crucial national policy goals). These assumptions justified special treatment which included various forms of governmental assistance. This special treatment resulted in national policies and supportive arrangements, such as income policies for farmers and their families, government assistance to marginal producers and the promotion of technology transfer in order to increase the sector's efficiency. The position of agricultural interest groups within their national political systems is often referred to as a 'corporatist' alliance, in which governments give interest groups access to, and influence in, national decision-making procedures in exchange for their contribution to achieving national goals. The interest groups managed to contribute thanks to such capacities as encompassingness, independent research facilities, information provision and facilitation of sectoral consensus. This situation of national embeddedness and of groups representing territorial interests explains why *international federations* of national organizations operating at the global or regional levels remained relatively weak. The International Federation of Agricultural Producers (IFAP) and the

Committee of Agricultural Organizations in the European Union (COPA) for the most part are aggregations dominated by national groups. Their major function consists of light coordination in order to form a united front at international forums.

Internationalization and globalization processes during the last quarter of the twentieth century enhanced the international competitiveness of national industries amidst liberalizing world markets. The reduction in impediments to economic activity across the globe, plus the rise in stronger forms of multilevel governance through international regimes and institutions, have resulted in:

a.   the necessity for national governments to learn to play 'two-level games', in which they have to deal with both national preferences and interests (within their national political systems) and international or regional commitments (within such international arrangements as the General Agreement on Tariffs and Trade, the World Trade Organization, the European Union and the North American Free Trade Agreement);

b.   the restructuring of domestic agricultural industries with declining farm numbers, increasing farm size, and stronger concentration of ownership; and, most relevant for our topic,

c.   challenges to the partnerships between governments and national interest groups. Globalization in this case focuses on the reduction of activism of the nation-state in the conduct of agriculture and a concomitant rise in the importance of the market in settling issues of production, price and farm survival.

The editor of this volume, Darren Halpin, raises the question of whether the *state-assisted* paradigm will be replaced by a *market-liberal* paradigm, which treats the agricultural sector as any other economic sector. Such a shift would imply that agricultural producers become fully dependent on market forces. It also implies a challenge to the position of the agricultural interest groups, for instance by weakening their position in the political system and by opening up the original partnership to a broader range of players, including consumers or environmentalists, and thus reflecting the increased complexity of modern agricultural production and consumption. With regard to the position of interest groups in national political systems, the question arises as to whether the state remains supportive of the partnership or that it needs the interest groups less, as is suggested by the shift towards a market-liberal paradigm.

It can also be asked whether changes in the constituencies of the interest groups following the restructuring of agricultural industries have made the interest groups less capable of generating resources and undertaking the governance functions that the political system is expecting. If the state needs the interest groups less, this can be seen as a challenge from above; in case the interest groups themselves weaken substantially, this can be seen as a challenge from below. These challenges may also be discussed in the terms of Streeck and Schmitter, who in the 1980s developed a framework on the logics of influence and membership. Streeck and Schmitter presented interest groups as actors facing ongoing challenges with respect to exerting political influence and organizing their constituencies. The editor and his collaborators have adopted this approach.

With regard to challenges facing agricultural interest groups in a globalizing era Halpin puts forward two theses. One is the *decline thesis* which states that interest groups will decline, because they cannot survive in the changed environment where the state needs them less (for instance because of the stronger global and regional forms of governance), nor can they survive in their own constituency, which is weakened as a result of agricultural restructuring. The other is the *resilience thesis*. It states that the interest groups, although weakened, are still strong enough to have an ongoing partnering role with the state. In this case the nation-state remains central to governing, albeit in a multi-level world in which governments need to play two-level games. Associative processes of governance, such as corporative partnerships, also remain crucially important in this context, in particular in assisting national economic sectors to adapt to global change.

Embedded Institutions and their Capacity of Resilience

What do the chapters in this volume show about the fate of agricultural interest groups under conditions of global change as discussed above? The shift from a state-assisted to a market-liberal paradigm has indeed reshaped the conditions of the partnerships between governments and national agricultural interest groups that originated in post-war Western nations. According to the researchers of this volume, the shift altered the attitude of the state to globalizing pressures; it changed the organizability of the farm base and expanded the capacities required for groups to be valuable. In fact, the attitude of the state towards globalizing processes and adequate policy goals is regarded as one of the decisive factors in interest group decline and resilience. More precisely, it shows that national agendas and imperatives heavily influence the economic processes of liberalization, as they are being politically discussed within regional and global intergovernmental organizations. This implies that the orientation of national governments to market liberalization proves decisive in structuring the environments in which interest groups participate. The fact that governments under conditions of globalization need to play two-level games, with both domestic imperatives and international commitments, at least leaves room to manoeuvre for national interest groups to prove their resilience. This volume maintains that interest groups will be most resilient when they can retain, or create, conditions that approximate those of the original partnerships. Hence, nationally embedded institutions also try to survive when the conditions of national arrangements are redefined in an interplay between national and international politics. This conclusion is in line with research about the fate of the nation-state under conditions of internationalization at the end of the twentieth century, which argues that the significance of the nation-state will not be lost. While it is true that the nation-state is delegating authority to international institutions and that this internationalization is limiting national policy autonomy, the state is also finding new forms of cooperation and coordination, both nationally and internationally, in order to preserve and even to strengthen its power and autonomy (cf. K. Van Kersbergen, R.H. Lieshout and G. Lock, Eds, *Expansion and Fragmentation. Internationalization, Political Change and the Transformation of the Nation State,*

Amsterdam: Amsterdam University Press, 1999). The authors of the volume now show that interest groups aware of these trends will be active participants in finding these new forms of coordination and cooperation.

The changes in the conditions of the original partnerships between governments and national interest groups have not only challenged the national interest groups with regard to the logic of influence, but also with regard to the logic of membership. Agriculture is undergoing significant restructuring with declining farm numbers, increasing farm size and more dimensions to the production processes (such as environmental consequences and consumers' preferences). This implies that interest groups have great difficulty in maintaining the size and coherence of their memberships. This has consequences for the resources available to them, for their ability to provide valuable agricultural expertise and information, and for their capacities to play their roles in the partnership.

The chapters in the volume show, with regard to the decline and resilience theses put forward by Halpin, that notwithstanding the fact that agricultural interest groups have faced challenges and shown evidence of decline, they have by and large been resilient. Or, to put it differently, they have survived in an era of global change. National interest groups have been active in generating general support for agriculture and in renewing sectoral-state relations in order to adapt to new state priorities and thus renew the logics of influence. They have also renewed the logics of membership by establishing a stable membership base that provides sufficient resources, can be effectively represented and creates group capacities that allow the interest groups to fulfil their functions with regard to expertise provision and facilitation of sectoral consensus in the context of a partnership between state and interest groups.

This national survival also means that the international federations of agricultural interest groups, such as the IFAP and the COPA, have remained weak. Due to the domination of the national interest groups little room is left for the international federations. According to Halpin there is little evidence of transnational activity beyond coordination of national activities with other agricultural groups on a basis that reflects trade alliances, such as those of the EU or the CAIRNS group. National agricultural interest groups remain predominantly territorial actors, notwithstanding some transnational relations with non-farm interest groups. This is also true for the European agricultural organizations, which is dealt with in a special section of the volume. These European federations have 'europeanized' to a large extent, but nevertheless have remained without stronger influence. The positions held in the EU were not the result of a previous strategy of their coordination, but rather of the construction of a consensual position of national interests. It explains, according to Moyano-Estrada and Rueda-Catry, the presence in Brussels of numerous representatives of national farmers' organizations and their relatively autonomous behaviour within the EU institutions.

The current volume in our series thus informs about the relative non-strength of international federations of agricultural interest groups at the beginning of the twenty-first century and about the ways in which sectoral interest groups that have a corporatist relationship with the state have reacted to the impact of global change.

Bob Reinalda

Preface

This book emerged from a discussion I had with Wyn Grant at the 2002 UK Political Studies Association Annual Conference (held at Aberdeen University, Scotland). We discussed the absence of a comparative literature on agricultural interest groups in the same tradition as a compilation put together some time ago by Clive Thomas (1993) *First World Interest Groups: A Comparative Perspective*, Westport, CT: Greenwood Press. Wyn encouraged me to generate a proposal for such a book and under his guidance to solicit contributors.

In the second half of 2002, having taken up a Post Doctoral position at Edith Cowan University (Perth, Australia), I recruited a group of scholars to contribute a chapter to such a book. As you will see, the mix of contributors has made for a rich and productive engagement. In the meantime, Ashgate agreed to include our collection it its series on Non-State Actors. With the assistance of the Series Editor, Bob Reinalda and Ashgate's Commissioning Editor, Kirsten Howgate, we narrowed in on the theme of the fate of national level agricultural interest groups amidst global change.

After circulating draft chapters, the group of contributors met in December 2003, at Edith Cowan University (Perth, Australia), for a week-long meeting to review the chapters and to discuss the findings. We had a very vigorous and enlightening discussion, in the process learning a great deal about the nuances of each national situation. This peer reviewing process has, in our view at least, made this book a much better and a more tightly structured product. In the six months after the meeting, individuals revised the chapters, and several versions of the introduction and conclusion were revised based on the comments of contributors. The volume is the result of this exhaustive process.

In its broadest sense, the book may contribute to the literature on the fate of associative forms of industry governance in what has been labelled a 'globalizing' world. More specifically, we seek to update the literature on agricultural interest groups in developed nations and to do so in a comparative perspective. There is still a significant gap in our knowledge of agricultural groups in developing countries, and particularly in Eastern Europe, Asia, Africa and South America. Work in this area would be most welcome. We hope this volume stimulates additional scholarship in the area, and particularly that of a comparative nature.

Darren Halpin
Aberdeen, Scotland

Acknowledgements

This book would not have been possible without the support and mentorship of Prof. Wyn Grant. He has provided advice and acted as a sounding board throughout this project. Prof. Grant Jordan and the 'politics' team at Aberdeen University continue to encourage and challenge me, and are responsible for introducing me to the European and US political science community for which I am grateful.

Thanks must go to the contributors to this volume who were extremely patient and obliging in shifting the emphasis of their chapters as we built on the original prospectus. Many also provided detailed comments on the introductory and concluding chapters for which I am grateful. In this respect, Wyn, Alan, Carsten and Grace were particularly active. Eduardo and his team provided much of the material for the appendices. The support of the team at Ashgate and of the Series Editor is also appreciated. I would like to thank the anonymous reviewer, particularly for the comments on the final chapter.

I also need to acknowledge the contribution made by the ECU Visiting Scholars Program through which the attendance of contributors at the December 2003 meeting was largely made possible. The project was also supported by my previous and current employers, each of which has provided me with the time to complete the final drafting and editing of the volume.

Last but not least, thanks to my wife Jenny who patiently reassured me I was on the right track as I drafted, redrafted (and redrafted) parts of the book. She helped with organizing the December 2003 meeting and accepted the loss of many a weekend and evening in the name of completing this volume.

Chapter 1

Agricultural Interest Groups and Global Challenges: Decline and Resilience

Darren Halpin

Introduction

What challenges do national industry associations face in the 21st century? What is the contemporary fate of such organizations? National industry associations in western developed nations have often been credited with partnering the state in mid 20th century efforts at reconstruction and development. They are said to have formed close knit partnerships, or 'associational governance', with the state to modernize a range of national industry sectors (Coleman, 1997c). Like labor, professional and welfare client interest groups, these industry associations 'developed' or were 'revitalized' by post-war interventionist policies (Grant, 2000, p.2). The value of such groups to the state resided in their national coverage, ability to generate sectoral consensus and independent information gathering and analysis capacities.

At the beginning of the 21st century, the environment confronting national industry groups appears to be vastly different. It has been argued that national economies have entered a 'globalizing era' (Coleman and Grant, 1998), one in which establishing the international competitiveness of national industries amidst liberalizing world markets is a key state imperative. The value of such 'associative' arrangements in a globalizing era, along with the capability of national groups to retain the abilities long valued by the state, is the subject of some contention.

Adherents to strong versions of globalization may be tempted to see reductions in national sovereignty as evidence that decisions have moved out of reach of national group-state partnerships. It has more generally been noted that in responding to global challenges national governments seem to increasingly favor market arrangements and institutions as modes of governance; viewing groups as self interested rent-seekers rather than valuable partners (Marsh, 1995). Finally, market change and restructuring is often viewed as undermining the cohesiveness and organizability of industry sectors, rendering industry associations less valuable and capable (Coleman, 1997c). These are all causes for pessimism about associational governance and the contemporary fate of national industry associations.

However, there is a thread in the literature that finds a valuable contemporary role for groups – albeit too infrequently recognized by governments – in assisting nation states to address global challenges like international competitiveness (e.g. Marsh, 1995; Weiss, 1998). Others are more optimistic still, arguing that associative arrangements with a long standing history tend to be resilient to challenges arising from global change (Coleman, 1997c). There is even the talk of a revitalization of neo-corporatism (even macro-corporatism) in the European context (e.g. Rhodes, 2001; Schmitter and Grote, 1997). But there is less attention on how groups who may participate in such arrangements have fared amidst global change.

In engaging with this debate, interest group scholars can make a valuable contribution by elaborating the contemporary challenges facing groups and enunciating their links with global change. In a modest way, this book takes up the task and examines the fate of national industry associations in the 21st century amidst global change.

Global Change

Almost all spheres of social scientific and political scholarship have been touched by discussions of the scope and impact of processes referred to as 'globalization'. While there is a degree of debate over what this term refers to specifically,[1] characteristics of *global change* or a *globalizing era* surely encapsulate; the partial deterritorialization of governance; the emergence of multi-layered or multi-level governance with potential divisions of authority, autonomy and sovereignty; the ascendancy of a form of liberal globalization (a push for a reduction in impediments to economic activity across the globe); and the development of multilateral institutions to facilitate these economic programs (see Held *et al.*, 1999 and Scholte, 2000, for excellent summaries).

Not surprisingly, talk of these global changes has sparked a debate about the role of the nation state. Some argue that the impact of global change implies the decline of the territorial nation-state; its sovereignty and authority displaced by emerging global actors and multilateral institutions. Others argue that there is little new in 'globalization'; that these 'global' forces amount to economic 'internationalization'. Here nations are authors rather than victims of 'internationalization' (Weiss, 1998). Wary of perpetuating exaggerated claims about global change, perhaps a more balanced view is that, '… states survive under globalization, but governance has become substantially different' (Scholte, 2000, p.22). These global changes require nation states to balance both domestic (territorial) and global (non-territorial) interests and to recognize and work within non-territorial forms of transnational (regional or global) authority and sovereignty. While the nation state is still a prominent player, it shares its authority 'upwards', to regional and international organizations and 'downwards' to sub-national government. Governance in global terms also involves a range of new players apart from the nation state, including non-state actors like transnational business, multilateral institutions and global social movements (O'Brien *et al.*, 2000, p.2). Concepts such as multi-level governance or multilayered governance seek to capture the essence of this emerging pattern of activity (see for example Hooghe, 1996; Marks, Hooghe and Blank, 1996).

Much of what is referred to as global change is about reorganizing global economic affairs or (trade) liberalization. Indeed, some argue that 'contemporary globalization' amounts to 'neoliberal globalization' (Held *et al.*, 1999, p.431; Scholte, 2000, p.135). This aspect of global change is about eliminating national borders as an impediment to free trade and facilitating the unfettered flow of capital through the convergence of national policies and approaches. Key multilateral institutions, like the World Trade Organization (WTO), pursue these goals through promotion of principles like 'harmonization', 'de-regulation', 'world best practice' and 'transparency' (Braithwaite and Drahos, 2000). As such, key tools used by nation states in promoting domestic industries, raising revenue and managing balance of payments issues, like tariffs and price subsidization, are today under high levels of scrutiny and regulation by bodies like the WTO and through regional trade agreements (NAFTA, EU single market) (Held *et al.*, 1999, p.187).

While these governance structures dedicated to liberalization may be read as constricting the autonomy of nation states, the role of the state in influencing the pace of national integration into global economic activity should not be underestimated. Caution is required in 'reading off' state decline from assertions about global change. The absence of policy convergence across states points to the varying levels of adherence to neoliberal patterns of economic regulation (Held *et al.*, 1999, p.441). As Scholte notes, different states clearly have differing capacities to respond to global change, to exhibit autonomy and to exert influence in these global spaces (2000, p.135). Deploying a familiar set of categories, Woods (2001, p.293) contrasts 'weak' and 'strong' states, with the former shaping the 'rules and institutions which have made a global economy possible', continuing with high protective barriers in the face of global change, and able to 'control – to some degree – the nature and speed of their integration into the world economy'. In a globalizing era nation states occupy a precarious position between serving *both* 'internal' (territorial domestic) interests and 'external' (supraterritorial/global) interests (Scholte, 2000, p.140). States are able to resolve this 'precarious position' in different ways and in so doing exhibit different capacities.

This discussion and debate cannot be adjudicated upon here, although it is fair to say that most contributors in this volume are cautious in embracing strong theses of global change and exaggerating (or reading off) its impacts. Nevertheless, this discussion invites interest group scholars to (re)consider the contemporary fate of groups in what has been argued is a globalizing era. It has been argued that the capacity of nation states to reorganize and modernize their domestic industries during the 20th century (but particularly the depression and the post second world war years) was assisted by close 'partnerships' with equally capable national sectoral interest groups (Coleman, 1997c). But what is the fate of such governing arrangements amidst global change? Are such partnerships important in managing the present day task of integrating national industry sectors with the international economy? Most importantly for this book, where does this leave national sectoral interest groups? How do global changes impact on the ability of industry associations to generate the requisite capacities to remain capable partners?

While much has been said about the implications of global change for nation-states, very little has been said about the fate of national general sectoral industry associations and, by extension, associative governance in a globalizing era. Much *has* been said with respect to the emergence of transnational or global social movements, Euro-groups, International Non-Governmental Organizations (INGOs), global civil society and transnational advocacy networks as evidence of the scaling up of mobilization (see for example O'Brien *et al.*, 2000; Arts, Noorman and Reinalda, 2001; Keck and Sikkink, 1998). But, the issue of the fate of national sectoral interest group in the face of global change warrants renewed attention.

Have Industry Associations 'Weathered the Global Storm'?

Coleman (1997c) has set out to examine whether national general sectoral groups and associative governance is able to stand up to global change. His implicit reference point for this examination is the close bargaining between industry associations and the state that was the hallmark of post Second World War economic development in many national industry sectors of developed nations. Where and when it was established, this partnership required groups 'to order and coordinate complex information and activity' and to 'be able to rise above the short-term, particularistic interests of its members' (Coleman, 1997c, pp.129-30). In short, they were encompassing, able to generate sectoral consensus and had substantial information and data gathering capacities. They operated within a commitment to pursuing an insider strategy with its implicit norms of responsible political behavior. Adopting a framework developed by Schmitter and Streeck (1981, 1985), Coleman explores the impact that contemporary global change may have on the capacity of industry associations to organize their constituency and exert influence (logics of membership and influence).

At first blush, the contemporary evidence about encompassing industry groups and global change is that i) nation states need groups less, and, ii) that the groups themselves are less capable of undertaking key governance functions. In respect of the first plank of this argument, globalized regimes of governance and a preference amongst national governments for market based (neoliberal) modes of governing logically reduce the basis for exchange between collective organizations and the state, particularly where industry 'sponsoring' branches of the public service are disbursed (Coleman, 1997c, p.132, pp.140-41). With respect to the second plank of the argument, it is proposed that international competition, and trade liberal policies have shrunk and restructured 'mature' industries, like agriculture. Consequently, the newly restructured industry sector is less fertile ground for associational activity. Not only are collective positions harder to find but individual motivations for association memberships are also reduced which in turn cuts the financial resources available to the groups through membership subscriptions (Coleman, 1997c, pp.130-31). As Coleman (1997, p.132) states;

Generally speaking, the processes involved in the internationalization of economic activity do not appear to favor associational governance. They promise to destabilize memberships, possibly to the point that the association may be forced into mergers or even defined out of existence. They favor developments in the policy process that may undermine cooperative behaviour between the state and collective interests. As cooperation decreases, associations will lose their access to some information, may cut back on their own policy research, and thus may become less autonomous from members. Without this policy expertise and autonomy, they become less able to exercise a governance role.

Collectively, these contemporary trends act on groups from above (reconstituting state-group relations) and below (reconstituting group-constituency relations). As Coleman (1997c, p.147) colorfully puts it, 'As an actor, the association takes on the image of a dinosaur – old, lumbering, and soon to be extinct'.

Yet, Coleman finds counter trends, arguing that '...not all evidence supports this thinking about the relationship between globalization and associational governance' (1997c, p.132). With respect to the states need for groups he argues that shaping economic and industry policies in the emerging liberalized world may be assisted by a '*redefinition* and *strengthening* of the role of associations' (Coleman, 1997c, p.142, *italics added*). The ongoing importance of associations is attributed in part to the technical and complex nature of policy making: they have information, expertise and implementation capacities that the state still needs. Interest groups are said to be particularly important where government may proceed with 'anticipatory' forms of policy. That is, proactively adapting to global change by formulating long term industry plans and involving associations in identifying weak sections of the industry and facilitating rationalization (Coleman, 1997c, pp.146-7). The continued relevance of groups is also evident where market mechanisms seem unable to deal with 'externalities', such as environmental harm, socio-economic distress and inequality (Coleman, 1997c, p.128).[2] On this basis, there is ample counter evidence to suggest, as Lofgren (2001, p.80, *emphasis added*) argues, that amidst global change there has been 'no decline in *the states need* to draw on organized interests for policy deliberation, design, implementation and legitimacy'.

But quite apart from a residual *need* the state may have for industry associations, there is the second issue of the residual *capacity* of the groups themselves. That is, the state may need groups but are they still up to the job? What types of groups do national governments need to form partnerships with? After all, according to Coleman, general sector wide groups are likely to confront reduced resources and shrinking and heterogeneous constituencies, all in the context of rapid processes of industry adjustment, which is not likely to be conducive to promoting group capacity. In this respect, Coleman argues that interest groups often hold considerable adaptive capacities.

As an autonomous actor in its own right, [a group] is able to pursue the redefinition of its domain or the merger with other groups that is necessary to embrace a membership more consistent with reshaped markets. ....It is also in a strong place to convince the state that necessary adaptations are being made. (Coleman, 1997c, p.148).

The point made by Coleman is that groups are able to renew their capacities by pre-empting, anticipating or adapting to their changing circumstances. He argues that '[a]ll these factors assist the association to weather the storm of market liberalization prompted by the globalization of markets' (Coleman, 1997c, p.148).

The Case of Agriculture

This general synopsis of 'associations facing global challenges' provides the backdrop against which this edited collection examines national general agricultural interest group organizations. Agriculture provides a good case to examine these issues for at least two reasons. Firstly, in many western nations, agricultural interest groups, both general and commodities based, have, at various points in the 20th century, been credited with 'partnering' the state to aid the successful modernization of domestic agricultural sectors. Secondly, agriculture has been the subject of intense activity aimed at facilitating liberalization and establishing global economic governance. As Coleman (1997c, p.142) notes,

> Both general farm organizations and more specialized commodity associations have often been part of corporatist policy networks in many OECD countries. As the era of expanding agricultural production and rapid modernization began to end in the late 1970s and early 1980s, governments were forced to reconsider the objectives of agricultural policy and to look at new ways to implement these policies.

In this volume we ask how these groups have fared amidst global change. The volume adopts a comparative perspective of groups in Western European (Denmark, France, Ireland, United Kingdom, and Spain), North American (US and Canada) and Australasian (Australia) nations. Such a mix of national cases provides the opportunity to examine the fate of groups operating in nations that are both differentially integrated in the global agricultural economy and more/less influential in steering global change (weak vs strong states). We anticipate that this may be a key variable in setting up the dynamics of any group-state partnership in a 'globalizing era' and, hence, the fate of national agricultural interest groups. As such, this collection connects with and extends past work on national agricultural interest groups (see for example, Grant, 1983; Manzetti, 1992; Roche, Johnston and Le Heron, 1992) and comparative studies of agricultural interest groups within Europe and beyond (see for example, Ball and Millard, 1985, Chp 5; Just, 1990; Moyano-Estrada, 1990 and 1995).

Initially this chapter will set out key definitions and the scope of the book. Subsequently it will elaborate the central question of the book, creating a generalized account of the forces defining the challenges presented to national agricultural interest groups in the 21st century, a 'globalizing era'. Finally it will provide an overview of the structure of the book and a synopsis of the national chapters.

Definitions and Scope

Before proceeding much further it is important to define the focus of our analysis and in so doing set out what is and is not included in the scope of the book.

What is an Agricultural Interest Group?

Interests can be organized to seek public policy influence in a range of ways. These can include electoral power, via political parties, through own account lobbying, systemically through social or political institutions or through interest organizations (see Salisbury, 1991; Halpin and Martin, 1999). This volume is specifically concerned with analysing one form of 'interest organization' – *national level agricultural interest groups*.

Like all terms it is open to diverse interpretation. So what do *we* mean by this term? The general term *interest group* is used in the academic literature to denote a multitude of different types of organizations. While interest groups are unproblematically differentiated from political parties by the fact that the former do not seek to attain formal political office, it is more difficult and contentious to differentiate between interest groups and other types of politically active organizations.

In this volume, following Jordan, Halpin and Maloney (2004), the term *pressure participant* is adopted to refer to *all* those actors involved in seeking to influence the public policy process. Within this overall category, organizations with a unitary character – those that Salisbury (1984) would call 'institutions' such as a company, lobbyist or governmental agency – are referred to as *policy participants*. The term *interest group* is reserved for organizations with multiple members (whether individual members are citizens or institutions) and whose reason for being is to exert influence over public policy and exercise the political representation of their membership. Therefore, for the purposes of this book, the term *agricultural interest group* refers to associations that have as their primary purpose the collective political organization and representation of individual farmers or agricultural primary producers.

The membership of an *agricultural interest group* is composed of individual farmers or farm businesses. Consequently, organizations excluded from the definition of an agricultural interest group in this book are i) individual business firms operating directly in the political process (e.g. supermarkets or agri-business firms); ii) *dedicated* social clubs (such as young farmers' unions); iii) not-for-profit organizations *dedicated* to service provision (such as cooperatives); iv) government or quasi-government institutions (such as marketing boards or departments of agriculture), and; v) individual lobbyists. Clearly, some of these excluded organizations may be equally as important in terms of farmer political activism, representation and influence. Whilst these organizations will not be the focus of the book, their importance is acknowledged in chapters where that is relevant. For instance, farm cooperatives would be considered important elements in the agricultural group system in some European nations (see discussion in Just, 1990). As such, Moyano-Estrada deals with these in his chapter on Spain.

The book is specifically concerned with *general* and *national* farm interest groups *and not with commodity or regionally specific organizations*. For federal nations, national agricultural interest group organizations will often have a federal structure made up of commodity and/or regionally based organizations. In these cases, this book will focus on the national federations. In some EU nations, the division between smaller or peasant farmers and larger commercial farmers is expressed in separate agricultural interest group organizations, such as in Spain. But, as will become clear in this volume, finding a truly national or encompassing group has proven more difficult than the definitions imply. For example, even the National Farmers' Union in the UK, often thought of as the quintessential peak industry association, is arguably not a peak nor a national group at all. British devolution has created a quasi federalist structure, with no real formalized peak. In Canada, the two groups draw membership from different commodity and regional strengths, which makes their claim to be national and general difficult to sustain. To accommodate this complexity, this book examines those groups that make a *claim* or have *aspirations* to be a national agricultural interest group *and* that are taken by national governments to represent *a voice* for the nation's farmers. The sum of agricultural interest groups operating at all levels within each nation state is, for the purpose of this book, referred to as the *agricultural interest group system*.

Scope

The agricultural interest groups that are given consideration in this book are listed in Table 1.1. As is evident, in some nations, such as Australia and Denmark, the agricultural interest group system includes all the groups affiliated with a dominant peak or umbrella group. Yet, in some cases, most notably the US, UK, Canada and Spain, the agricultural interest group system implies a more complex range of discrete organizations that may be in varying levels of cooperation or competition with one another.

Why Focus on National General Agricultural Interest Groups?

As referred to earlier, national agricultural groups formed close relationships with the state in the post Second World War period in many developed nations. Accounts of agricultural policy are replete with references to these partnership arrangements. Global change *implies* a challenge to these groups. On this basis we believe that reviewing the contemporary challenges, and then the fate, of these *particular* types of groups will tell us something important about agricultural governance in a globalizing era.

Table 1.1   National general agricultural interest groups included in this volume

Country	Group
Canada	• Canadian Federation of Agriculture (CFA) • National Farmers' Union (NFU)
US	• American Farm Bureau Federation (AFBF) • National Farmers' Union (NFU)
United Kingdom	• National Farmers' Union of England and Wales (NFU) • NFU Scotland (NFUS) • Farmers' Union of Wales (FUW)
Spain	• Asociacion Agraria-Jovenes Agricultores (ASAJA) • Union de Pequenos Agricultores (UPA) • Coordinadora de Organizaciones de Agricultores y Ganaderos.-. Iniciativa Rural (COAG - I.R.)
Ireland	• Irish Farmers' Association (IFA) • Irish Creamery Milk Suppliers Association (ICMSA)
France	• Fédération Nationale des Syndicats d'Exploitants Agricoles (FNSEA)
Denmark	• Dansk Landbrug (Danish Agriculture)
Australia	• National Farmers' Federation (NFF)

There are, however, many groups operating and coordinating action beyond national borders. The Committee of Agricultural Organizations in the EU (COPA) provides an EU collective voice (joined more recently by European Farmers Coordination – CPE, recognized by the Commission in 1998) (See Appendix 1 for a review of these European farm groups). At the international level, the International Federation of Agricultural Producers (IFAP) provides a voice for agricultural producers from the 'north' and 'south' (See Appendices for a list of member groups of COPA and IFAP). But for the most part these are aggregations of national groups representing territorial interests. Taking the EU as an example, national groups lobby their governments to form joint positions to be pursued at the EU level, they influence groups like COPA, and they act as own account actors direct to the EU apparatus. Even groups that appear more global in style, such as Via Campesina, are movements made up of national groups. Their membership is composed largely of national or sub-national farmer, peasant or farm worker organizations. In sum, the (historic?) bedrock of agricultural representation and policy making in a multi level process – whether it be at international, supranational, national or sub-national levels – are groups operating as national general agricultural interest group.

The Case of Agriculture: State-Group 'Partnership' and Post-war Agricultural Modernization

The discussion above about the challenges global change presents encompassing industry associations organizing 'mature' industries maps well onto the case of agriculture and national level agricultural interest groups.

The study of agricultural policy and politics has generated the concept of agricultural exceptionalism, which captures the 'special' arrangements that underpinned post Second World War agricultural 'modernization' in most western countries. First and foremost 'agricultural exceptionalism' relates to a set of ideas, held both by policy makers and society at large, which justify the treatment of agriculture as a 'special case' (Skogstad, 1998). As a set of ideas, agricultural exceptionalism reflects the view that special attention is necessary because agriculture i) is a uniquely hazardous enterprise, with unpredictable and unstable weather and markets, and/or ii) contributes as a sector to broad national goals (Skogstad, 1998, p.468). These ideas provided the rationale for the post war state-assisted policy paradigm. This paradigm was founded on the principles that 'the agriculture sector contributes to national policy goals and therefore merits special attention [and] ... the price mechanism is a sub-optimal means of achieving an efficient and productive agricultural sector' (Coleman et al., 1997a, p.275). This paradigm employed the proposition that the income derived from production should be enough to sustain a farm family, technology transfer should contribute significantly to any increase in efficiency and marginal producers deserve government assistance to become commercially viable.

This set of ideas found expression and shaped 'exceptional' administrative arrangements and policies. In the first respect agriculture was typically afforded a dedicated ministry to administer the policy area and advocate on behalf of the sector in a clientelistic fashion. In the second, agricultural policy resulted in the transfer of relatively large proportions of taxpayers'[3] funds to farmers in a pattern of support not repeated for other sectors of the economy or community (Grant, 1995, pp.168-9). National policies typically amounted to state intervention aimed at rebuilding national agricultural industries. For the most part this meant the support of farmers through import barriers, orderly marketing schemes and internal subsidy.

National agricultural associations, both general and commodity specific, have been accorded a central role in agricultural development in western nations, particularly in the post Second World War era (Coleman, 1997c, p.142). Agricultural groups are said to have taken on a semi-autonomous role mediating state or national goals (like food security, self-sufficiency, and export development) with those of their farmer members (Cox, Lowe and Winter, 1987, p.74; Moyano-Estrada, 1990, pp.193-95). As Goodman and Redclift put it, during the post war period, particularly in Western Europe but also elsewhere, '... national structures of negotiation and legitimation emerged based on the corporatist alliances of the State, farm unions, commodity associations and agroindustrial interests' (1989, p.9). Partnerships of this type require a group with specific capacities: encompassingness, independent research capacity and information provision and the ability to facilitate sectoral consensus. Groups are given access and influence by government in exchange for exercising these capacities.

Given this role it is no wonder that the study of agricultural public policy or politics in almost any western nation tends to deploy terms like 'iron triangle', 'neo-corporatism', 'sub-government', and 'closed policy community'. The early work on agricultural interest groups focused upon the close links between farmer and state.[4] For political scientists, almost regardless of nationality, agricultural policy making became the textbook example of a tightly bound farmer dominated sub-government. For this reason, agriculture has often been used as a canvas for illustrating more general theoretical arguments about policy making. In the US, studies include those of Lowi (1979, chp4), McConnell (1966, chp7) and Olson (1965), while in the UK Self and Storing (1962) is the classic example.

While one must be cautious about generalizing to all western nations, and we acknowledge that the precise patterns of associative governance are likely to differ between nations, this narrative of 'partnership' serves as a reference point for our analysis of the contemporary fate of agricultural interest groups. Analysis of the contemporary challenges facing groups is made meaningful by comparing it with this era, where policies and governing arrangements were focussed upon addressing national priorities of food security and production, where the modus operandi was state assistance and where there was general societal acceptance that agriculture played a pivotal economic and social role. The agriculture sector in western nations confronts a 'globalizing era' (Coleman and Grant, 1998) which at face value appears to interrupt this supportive group environment and present a number of challenges to national general agricultural interest groups. The extent to which this turns out to be the case, and the fate of groups in such an environment, is a matter for the empirical analysis that follows in this volume.

National Agricultural Interest Groups: Points of Challenge in a Globalizing Era

In elaborating the contemporary challenges confronting these types of groups and forms of partnership, three general trends seem defining features of the group environment: emerging patterns of global and supranational agricultural regulation; the restructuring of domestic agricultural industries, and; challenges to agricultural exceptionalism and agricultural policy change. These processes combine to create what, at face value, appears a challenging contemporary environment for agricultural interest groups. It is important to note that some of the forces shaping the environment of groups are long standing forces that may, at most, simply be exacerbated or pushed along by global change or merely more prominent in a globalizing era. There may be more continuity than change in these trends. Nevertheless, recalling the general points about associational decline made by Coleman (1997c), these challenges imply impacts on both the capacity of industry associations to organize their constituency and exert influence (logics of membership and influence).

Regionalized, Internationalized and Globalized Agricultural Governance

There is evidence to suggest that nation states have become less preoccupied with the post Second World War questions of national food security and productive capacity and slowly shifted attention to managing the link between domestic production and world trade. The costs to national budgets of farm assistance (for both production and the disposal of surpluses), the generation of national surpluses and questions about mechanisms for their disposal have acted as catalysts for introducing agriculture into intergovernmental venues dedicated to facilitating the liberalization of world trade, such as the Organization for Economic Co-operation and Development (OECD) and General Agreement on Tariffs and Trade (GATT) (Coleman and Chiasson, 2002, p.175). This move is said to coincide with a decline in the power of the interventionist nation-state (Bonanno *et al.*, 2000, p.455). In its place, it is argued, come strengthened globalized and regionalized forms of agricultural trade and food regulation coordinated through both intergovernmental institutions and increasingly active transnational capital.

A form of multi-level governance is said to have emerged whereby patterns of agricultural and food production are shaped by a mix of global, supra-national, national and sub-national regulations and institutions (see Jones and Clark, 2001, pp.2-8). At the regional level trade agreements like the North American Free Trade Agreement (NAFTA), and institutions like the European Union (EU), regulate market access. Globally the parameters for agricultural production and trade are increasingly settled in intergovernmental fora, such as the World Trade Organization (WTO) and the Codex Alimentarius Commission (see discussion by Braithwaite and Drahos, 2000, pp.399-417). The 'global food restructuring' and 'food regimes' literature emphasizes not only intergovernmental institutions but also the role of inter- and intra-firm coordination by transnational corporations (TNCs) in global food regulation (Friedmann and McMichael, 1989; McMichael, 1994; Bonanno, 1994; Bonanno *et al.*, 2000). It is argued that TNCs bring about a 'deterritorialization' of agriculture, by organizing their activities to both 'influence and avoid the regulatory actions of nation-states' (Bonanno *et al.*, 2000, p.440). And further, that increasingly the price paid for commodities and the costs of farm inputs used to generate agricultural products are heavily influenced by international companies. Whereas nation-states are constrained by their national boundaries, TNCs are able to operate globally. In essence, it is argued that 'the growing power of capital to organize and reorganize agriculture undercuts state policies directing agriculture to national ends, such as food security, articulated development and the preservation of rural/peasant communities' (Friedmann and McMichael, 1989, p.95).

But there is reason to be somewhat cautious about drawing the conclusion that global change has inevitably weakened the role of the nation state in the world economy (Buttell, 1996, p.26). Firstly, the WTO acts as a secretariat for member nations, reflecting the positions bargained amongst member nation states. Nation states need to sign onto these agreements: they can and do walk away from multilateralism or find more suitable bilateral approaches. In a multi-level system, these international venues can *enable* national governments to disarm domestic resistance by 'blame shifting' to international fora (Coleman *et al.*, 1997b, p.480). Secondly, while transnational corporations, in particular retailers and processors, have a large role in regulating modes of agricultural production (quality and quantity), nation states still remain crucial in that they facilitate conditions that support the smooth operation of global commodity chains. Regardless of whether policies are national programs of protection or GATT/WTO inspired commitments to trade liberalism they '...require state intervention to maintain them and to legitimize their outcomes to the general population' (Bonnano, 1994, p.260).

While the nation state remains an important actor in the internationalized agricultural economy it can be argued that their role has changed substantially from the post Second World War era. At a minimum, global change means that national governments have to set about regulating national agricultural priorities, not only with national ends like food security, rural development and environmental care in mind, but also with an eye to meeting international governmental agreements and global market requirements (e.g. in setting and harmonizing food quality standards and establishing transparency in assistance measures). Although, as was noted earlier, some nations are in a stronger position than others to meet international priorities on their own terms (i.e. to ensure that their domestic priorities shape international ones). What were essentially domestic processes of consensus building are now bound up in two or three levels of international decision making and bargaining (Coleman *et al.*, 1997b). In the EU context, Coleman, Atkinson and Montpetit (1997, p.469) have argued that such processes hamper efforts by 'domestic-level producer groups in EU member states' to retain support. This suggests that any industry-state partnerships will form on the basis that they facilitate the transformation of domestic agriculture to meet emerging global conditions and/or ameliorate the negative domestic impacts of this transformation such as rural restructuring, regional economic decline, and rural environmental damage.

It is important to note that in a 'globalizing era' we are not seeing the creation of world agricultural markets (they have long existed), but rather an attempt to reduce the activism of the nation state in the conduct of agriculture and a concomitant rise in the importance of the market in settling issues of production, price and farm survival. Before moving onto national policy developments, we look at agricultural sector restructuring.

Patterns of Agricultural Restructuring

As with other 'mature industries' built on post war expansion (see Coleman 1997c), the emergence of more liberalized world agricultural markets (and more importantly the policy reactions of national governments to that potentiality) has contributed to or reinforced existing patterns of agricultural industry restructuring in advanced western nations. Overall farm numbers are declining (although these are somewhat compensated for by the increase in part-time farmers), farm size is increasing, and ownership is becoming more concentrated (Albrecht, 1998, p.51; Bonnano, 1990). Agriculture tends to be a declining contributor to national GDP and overall employment generation. A more 'dualistic' or 'polarized' structure is emerging in agriculture, where a small number of large farmers are responsible for the majority of the production (Bonanno 1990, p.2; Lawrence *et al.*, 1992). There is a rise in pluri-activity (the increasing importance of off-farm sources of income) and a general decline in those communities dependent on agriculture (Lawrence, 1996; Albrecht, 1998). More broadly, agricultural commodity production is being replaced as the centrepiece of many local rural economies. Counter-urbanization in some areas has changed the structure of local 'farming' communities and tourism or recreational activities in rural spaces both challenge the 'productive' and suggest 'consumptive' uses for farming areas. Overall agricultural production and productivity has increased due to technological innovation and economies of scale.

While these may constitute general trends and patterns evident in most western nations, they manifest themselves in different ways at national levels. For instance, in the UK context, terms like 'post-productivism' or 'consumption countryside' have been used to imply that contemporary restructuring is occurring in ways that depart from a productivist emphasis on mass commodity production for a single undifferentiated global market (See Marsden, 1999; Ilbery and Bowler, 1998; Halfacree, 1997). This same concern is encapsulated in the European term 'multifunctionality'. Some dispute the applicability of these descriptors of change to the UK and to Europe more broadly (Hoggart and Paniagua, 2001, p.55), while antipodean authors are not convinced of the applicability of these terms to account for the 'colonial experience' (Le Heron and Roche, 1996). Some point out that Australasian patterns of agricultural activity still largely reflect export-led productivism (Burch *et al.*, 1999; Argent, 2002). Overall trends, and impacts from trends, also often vary from region to region within nation states (Marsden, 1999).

It is this type of 'industry restructuring' that Coleman noted would make collective positions harder to find and reduce individual motivations for group membership, with an overall diminution in the level of resources available to any industry association. In relation to agricultural interest groups, the most immediate impact of restructuring is the loss of overall farm numbers, and with that the reduction in subscription income and resources. Indirectly, the reduction in farm numbers, economic importance and contribution to employment, reduces the 'structural' power of the agricultural lobby. These processes of restructuring, or rationalization, generally tend to be accompanied by a high degree of economic hardship for sections of the farming constituency. As such, this process is also likely to catalyse heightened, often short term, demands for political solutions from farmers, which agricultural interest groups will have to contend (see Grant, 2001).

At a more fundamental level, these agricultural restructuring processes suggest negative impacts on the organizability of farmers as a constituency. The multivalent manner in which agricultural and rural space is being remade is reflected in the debate amongst rural scholars about the ongoing empirical utility of concepts such as 'rurality' and 'agriculture' (Friedland, 2002, p.351). This highlights the way in which restructuring has challenged 'traditional' notions of what it means to practice agriculture and indeed who agriculturalists are. Is a farm tour operator a farmer or a tourism operator? Is a vertically integrated winery an industrial firm or a farm enterprise? Is a landowner running sheep in an extensive manner for environmental subsidies a farmer or a government environmental contractor? Essentialist constructs of the family run farm confront the fact that those self-identifying as 'farmers' may include hobby farmers, long time farm families and retirees, all operating vastly different enterprises for vastly different reasons. This ambiguity hints at the type of emerging organizational problems facing general agricultural interest groups.

Already, nations with diverse agricultural production bases present general agricultural associations with difficulties in reconciling heterogeneous positions. In this regard the classic division is between grain and livestock producers over grain prices. However, as farming communities are becoming increasingly diverse and heterogenous groups, 'farmers' may well be expected to develop significant internal divisions of interests and identity. The most likely cleavage is between smaller part-time farms and agribusiness and larger farmers. The concerns of the former may be centred on lifestyle and amenity issues, while the latter remain vitally interested in maintaining an efficient and competitive industry environment. While managing diversity has been a longstanding task of farmer organizations, we should expect an increasing 'plurality of positions' to emerge reflecting the increasing complexity of farming and rural society. This not only makes it difficult for governments to assess the representativeness of agricultural groups but also challenges the groups to adapt to the more complex contours of rural and farming society (Moyano-Estrada, 1995, pp.350, 361).

In sum, to the extent that this pattern of industry restructuring occurs in a nation it *implies* a reduction in the resources available to established agricultural organizations, an overall decline in the political and economic power of agriculture more generally and a fragmenting constituency. We could logically expect this to negatively affect that group's ability to generate the capacities (encompassingness, independent research functions, and ability to foster internal consensus) that make it valuable to the state and other policy interlocutors. However, this restructuring may also be viewed as strengthening (or restoring) the capacity of groups. A lower number of members may reduce financial resources, but if the decline in members signals the removal of 'marginal' producers (those who often tend not to be group members), then it may increase overall membership density, make for a more homogenous membership and increase its capacity for representativeness.

Policy Change and Challenges to Agricultural Exceptionalism

As would be expected, there are signs that western nation states are reconsidering long standing policies of state assistance, examining how to align domestic priorities with international commitments for market liberalization, and deliberating over the question of compensating for the pain of restructuring. This process is, in contrast to the post war era, characterized by *challenges* to agricultural exceptionalism, in its ideational, administrative and policy forms at the national level.

Consistent with the international initiatives of the OECD and GATT/WTO outlined above, it has been argued that a general shift from a 'state assisted' to a 'trade liberal' paradigm of agricultural policy is taking place in most western nations (Coleman *et al.*, 1997a). There has been a growing consensus in almost all developed nations that the 'state-assisted' paradigm needs a fundamental rethink. This has been prompted by high levels of overproduction, escalating and unsustainable levels of governmental expenditure, international trade tensions (both between developed nations and between the 'north' and 'south') and negative environmental impacts and food safety scares associated with the 'state-assisted' approach. The 'market-liberal' paradigm has been promoted as an alternative. This paradigm has four central tenets. Firstly, agriculture is to be treated as any other economic sector. Secondly, a competitive market should be the source of a producer's income. Thirdly, only producers who can earn an income from this competitive market should remain active. Finally, individual producers should be responsible for protecting themselves against adverse natural conditions through private insurance markets.

The challenge to the state-assisted paradigm also indicates a parallel challenge to the ideas expressed by agricultural exceptionalism (Skogstad, 1998, p.471). This shift in values has had a flow on effect into 'exceptional' policy and administrative arrangements. There has been an across the board reduction in the level of public payments to the world's farmers (see OECD, 2002). Similarly, the administration of agricultural policy is increasingly being stripped from dedicated departments of agriculture, shared with other agencies or agricultural departments are being merged into larger entities, with responsibilities for a mix of consumer affairs, rural development or environment. Venues for agricultural policy are being shifted and recast. A challenge to agricultural exceptionalism (in its ideational, administrative and policy forms) *implies* a weakening of the dominance of agricultural interest groups and the inclusion of previously excluded groups into what were formerly agricultural policy communities. This shift is reflected in the move away from categorizing agricultural policy making in terms of relatively closed agricultural policy communities (e.g. meso-corporatist) to increasingly open issue networks that involve a broader range of actors (see for example Jordan *et al.*, 1994; Daugbjerg, 1998). There is evidence of heightened activity by environmental, consumer, and animal welfare groups in what were once dedicated agricultural policy domains. The increased focus on value adding and 'food' as opposed to 'mass commodity' production in western democracies, suggests that agribusiness, up-stream processors and retailers may also be more active in agricultural policy networks. Evidence of this shift of dominance can be found in a change in policy image, where what were formerly presented as 'farm management' issues are increasingly cast as 'agri-environmental', 'rural development' and 'consumer' issues. There is also evidence, across most developed nations, of a rise in the deployment of 'capacity building' efforts whereby the state seeks to elevate the skills base of farmers so that they will be better able to compete in a liberalized environment. State involvement may be largely about facilitating and enabling farmers to rationally respond to imperatives set by global regulatory standards, supermarket specifications and post-material consumer values.

But what does this imply in terms of the fate of national agricultural groups? A shift to a trade liberal policy, as Coleman noted, 'would logically reduce the basis for exchange between collective organizations and the state'. We would expect the decomposition of state-assisted approaches to be associated with a decline in the role for national level agricultural interest groups. We would expect agriculture to have lost its special 'policy rights' (Le Heron, Roche and Johnston, 1992, p.270) and for its dedicated policies to be aligned with those operating for the rest of the business sector (Montpetit, 2002, p.1). If the ability of national general agricultural interest groups to deliver general price increases through state-support to the farming constituency was the glue that leaders used to contain internal conflict, as some have argued, then we would also expect this paradigm shift to partly unpick group solidarity (Roederer-Rynning, 2002). This suggests a decline in group capacity.

However, the evidence is that this process is taking unpredictable and divergent paths between different nations, and in turn suggests differing potential impacts on the capacities of general agricultural interest groups and the states willingness to form partnerships with them.

Firstly, there is much evidence to suggest that the paradigm shift has not been as neat as indicated, with a decline in a state-assisted paradigm not necessarily meaning a turn to trade liberalism. If there is an increasing commitment to market liberal ideas, as pursued through global institutions such as the OECD and GATT/WTO, then we should witness a convergence as exemplified by 'common policies with a similar market liberal content, delivered through similar policy instruments' (Coleman and Grant, 1998, p.225). But of course this is far from the case. Indeed even the commitments to market liberal ideals 'wax and wane' between nation states, even under the discipline of the EU system (Sheingate, 2000). This diversity and equivocation hints at the underlying power of nations states (weak vs strong) in setting their own pace for integrating with the global agricultural economy.

Some nations, like Australia and New Zealand, have moved ahead and implemented a program of reforms that closely adhere to a trade liberal approach. Although even here there is much more enthusiasm for liberalizing 'world' trade than for loosening farmer control of domestic marketing boards with their statutory export monopolies (see Curtis, 2001, p.32, for New Zealand case). However there is more intense debate and speculation over the patterns of change emerging in the US and European Union. Moyer and Josling (2002, pp.31-2) have argued that 'although the "old" paradigm may have broken down in Europe, it is not being replaced by the same new paradigm that appears in the US policy debate'. In the European Union context, the term 'multifunctionality' has come to signify attempts to elaborate a distinctively European model of agriculture. From a 'mutlifunctionality' perspective, '... agriculture is viewed as a provider of public goods in addition to, and in many ways more important than its role as a producer of raw materials for the food industry' (Moyer and Josling, 2002, pp.34-6). While some would view it as an alternative to either fully embracing trade liberalism or persisting with state assisted approaches, others argue it is merely the state-assisted paradigm in all but name (see Swinbank, 1999).

The emerging EU position around multifunctionality and the fact that the US position is straying from the trade liberal position, suggests a breakdown in the smooth transition between paradigms as presented by Coleman *et al.*, (1997a). This does not diminish the overall hypothesis that existing encompassing national agricultural associations face challenge. But it does suggest that agricultural interest groups, perhaps newly defined and recast, *may* find opportunities in contributing to the elaboration, implementation and legitimation of what could be more accurately referred to as 'post state-assisted paradigms'.[5]

Secondly, while policy may be changing it is not always the case that this equates with a decline in agricultural exceptionalism. This has implications for group relevance. The rationale for agricultural policy reforms in some cases holds within it opportunities to re-establish a justification for exceptionalism, but on new foundations. Reforms in the US come under the weight of domestic budgetary pressures and the need to cut overproduction, but are aimed at enhancing international competitiveness. They rest on the principle that markets and not the state provide an income for farmers. According to Potter and Ervin (1999, p.54) the '...onus [is] on protectionists to make the case for a reinstatement of agricultural support'. In the EU, however, moves have been made to 'decouple' assistance from production levels and productivity and to *replace* them with payments from the state for the provision of public goods (not just food self sufficiency) such as environmental care and rural development. While the US and third countries may still provide special policy support or administrative arrangements to agriculture, they have *largely* dispensed with justifying it on the basis that it meets national goals or that agriculture is an especially difficult business enterprise. In contrast, the support for EU agriculture shows signs of reaffirming exceptionalism, albeit for 'new' public ends (Skogstad, 1998). This suggests a renewed basis for state-group relations if groups can adapt their message.

Thirdly, there is evidence that even in those countries where trade liberal approaches have taken overt hold, such as Australia and New Zealand, this has not led to the end of state intervention (Gray and Lawrence, 2001). Indeed, the state is re-regulating agriculture in ways necessary to establish, reproduce and stabilize global agriculture production or 'global commodity chains' (Le Heron and Roche, 1999, p.204). This is particularly apparent in activities aimed at guaranteeing food safety, consumer health and environmental care. This type of activity may not involve the same closed clientelistic relations between the state and farmers characteristic of state-assisted paradigms, but it necessarily involves relationships with collective farmer organizations.

Finally, there is no reason to suppose that the partnership between group and the state will be broken across the entire agricultural policy domain. The policy process is both multi-level and multi-stage, and influence may be expected to vary between these stages and levels. We could surmise that agricultural interest groups may well be weakened over a limited number of 'newer' or 'controversial' policy issues, yet retain dominance over the more technical policy areas.[6] Similarly, they may give up influence in agenda setting for control over implementation. Finally, they may be weakened at some levels but retain dominance at others. Overall, it is quite likely that the challenge to agricultural exceptionalism, as conceived of in public policy and interest group terms, may be a partial process. In turn this suggests sufficient scope for continued agricultural group dominance and partnership where and when groups can generate those capacities the state values, and where the state provides capable branches of the public service able to sponsor industry development.

Challenges Facing Agricultural Interest Groups in a Globalizing Era: Decline, Resilience, Adaptation and Transformation?

In terms of speculating on the fate of groups, the trends reviewed in the preceding section serve the purpose of helping us establish the general nature of the operating environment for national agricultural interest groups. As with the analysis offered by Coleman for national associations representing 'maturing' industries, viewed collectively they suggest an environment that holds considerable challenges for national general agricultural interest groups. While these trends are not likely to be equally evident in all western nations, and some national particularities could undoubtedly be added, this serves as an overall statement of a generalized group environment and a review of the types of possible impacts in terms of a group's ability to organize its constituency and exert influence.

Recalling the argument set out by Coleman (1997c) at the outset of this chapter, two points of challenge were noted for business associations in a globalizing era. In terms of being *challenged from above*, the question is whether the policy environment, including the state, remains supportive of 'partnerships' and the 'insider' orientated groups they encourage. This shapes the logic of influence of the group. In terms of being *challenged from below*, the question is whether changes amongst the farming constituency have affected the ease by which they are organized, and the capacity for groups to generate resources and capacities valued by the state. This shapes the logic of membership. The evidence in the preceding section provides us with mixed expectations and some key questions to explore in the national case studies presented in this book.

From the generalized account of the group environment, and bearing in mind Coleman's analysis, we can create two 'ideal type' accounts of contemporary group challenges and opportunities to guide our subsequent comparative discussions. The decline thesis adopts the strongest statement of these trends and the resilience thesis adopts a weaker account.

Decline Thesis

When stated in their strongest terms, these trends would appear to create an environment within which groups would confront challenge unsuccessfully and, by extension, decline. In sum, from *above*, it was said that the state would need them less, while from *below* industry restructuring would lead to a loss of significance amongst the constituency and a diminution of those capacities that the state saw as valuable.

From *above*, the emergence of *global and regional forms of agricultural governance* would logically reduce the role of the nation state, which in turn would reduce the role of national interest groups. Markets would govern and regulate unfettered world trade monitored by multilateral institutions. We could hypothesize that this would prompt groups to become either more transnational in their focus or withdraw to more local levels of organization and action. In relation to *policy change* and *challenges to agricultural exceptionalism,* the shift to a trade liberal paradigm would remove the need for encompassing peak groups to bargain with the state over assistance levels and assist with implementation. The broad social and political currency of arguments that supported the special treatment – both in policy substance and administrative terms – of farmers would in turn reduce the dominance of agricultural groups in key policy making venues and their control of policy image. We could hypothesize that groups would exhibit a loss of policy dominance and influence, operate in increasingly pluralized networks and face an escalation in the number of issues with which they had to deal across two or three levels of governance.

From *below*, *global agricultural restructuring* would fatally affect that ability of groups to generate the capacities (encompassingness, independent research functions, and ability to foster internal consensus) valued by the state and that underpin established partnerships. Patterns of *agricultural restructuring* would likely have an uneven impact on farming communities further promoting heterogeneous and diverse sets of interests. We could hypothesize that this would likely lead to more difficulty in reaching encompassing positions, lead to enhanced demands for immediate and short term remedial action by group leaders, and the potential for a splintering of otherwise 'organizationally mature' agricultural interest group systems. This would be exacerbated by declining state assistance levels which would likely remove one factor cohering diverse commodity sectors together.

Global change is unlikely to have left the capacities required by groups in partnership with the state unchanged. Thus, it is not simply a matter of whether groups are able to *continue* to generate capacities required in the post war period, but whether they are able to generate the new ones demanded of them in a globalizing era. In this respect, the escalation in the range and complexity of issues considered in some way relevant to agricultural producers (e.g. the environment, consumer affairs, food safety, global trade rules) would require a vastly greater group research capacity than was necessary in the postwar era. This implies that the groups that assisted in earlier partnerships, namely general agricultural farm interest groups, like Coleman's 'associational dinosaurs', may lack capacities desired by the state.

Resilience Thesis

The alternative end of the spectrum is to argue that such a reading of global change is too extreme, and that more caution is warranted. A resiliénce thesis would contend that, *from above*, the nation state remains central to governing agriculture, albeit in a more complex and multi-level world, and that associative processes of governance remain important in assisting national economic sectors to adapt to global change. Further, *from below*, that while the social base of groups is being remade it is not fatal to the generation of resources and capacities necessary for groups to have an ongoing partnering role with the state. Indeed, it may even renew capacity and make organizing easier.

In terms of *challenges from above*, the evidence from *policy change* and *challenges to agricultural exceptionalism* are that groups remain relevant. There is evidence of a decline in a state-assisted paradigm, consistent with emerging global preferences, but the replacement paradigm(s) are polyvalent and defy categorization as simply 'trade liberal'. Even where groups are operating in trade liberal environments, the state still intervenes, albeit in a different guise from administering special payments. Further, and more importantly, the rationale for the emergence of post state-assisted agricultural policy is heavily contested, with non-agricultural interests (such as consumers, and environmentalists) seeking to shape future agendas. Evidence that this *policy shift* is less than pervasive suggests a basis for state-group relations. Consequently, groups may demonstrate continued relevance to the state by administering 'anticipatory' policies – managed industry rationalization – or by administering state assistance for public goods. Similarly, while *agricultural exceptionalism* may be under challenge in most nations; the drivers behind the challenge, including the degree of broader societal pressure mounting against agriculture's special treatment, differ significantly. As such, we would expect groups to renegotiate new bases for exceptionalism. In so doing, they may experience only partial competition in policy networks, as they quarantine some issue areas from 'external' interests, or give away dominance in agenda setting for a continued influence over policy implementation. Further, the technical and complex nature of agricultural policy acts to protect a decline in farmers' influence, even if control over the policy agenda is lost. Groups may be able to revive partnership where and when they can summon the resources sought by the state. However, where it has occurred, the reorganization of formerly 'clientelistic' state bureaucracies is surely an impediment to resuming this kind of partnership.

In terms of *challenges from below*, *agricultural restructuring* will clearly reduce the financial resources available to groups from member subscriptions as overall farm numbers decline. However the decline of numbers does create certain opportunities. Where those leaving the industry are marginal farms, the restructuring process may end up establishing a more business-minded constituency that is easier to organize and represent. Further, the density of the group may rise if those leaving farming are typically non members of farm organizations. Regardless, groups have flexibility to create viable constituencies that reflect salient cleavages within their national context.

Adaptation and/or Transformation?

Absent from the discussion so far is the issue of group agency, expressed through groups adapting to their environment. We do not assume that this environment – however constituted – determines the fate of groups. This volume anticipates, rather than discounts, the ability of groups to adapt to challenging conditions. While Coleman argues that agricultural interest groups seem to have been particularly successful and resilient (1997, p.132), that is a matter for empirical research that follows in this volume. A related issue is that of *transformation*. National general agricultural interest groups may not merely adapt to new conditions, but fundamentally transform their existing structures, roll-over into new structures or be taken over or subsumed by new or existing groups. If *adaptation* is the logical consequence of a *thesis of resilience*, then *transformation* is the logical partner of a *thesis of group decline*.

In respect of the question of *adaptation*, it is likely that groups may see agricultural restructuring as an opportunity to adjust the definitions of whom it is they seek to organize and represent. This would turn around the fall in group income as well as better reflect salient political constituencies, such as rural business. The change in the policy paradigm and challenges to exceptionalism suggest groups may need to recreate a basis for relevance to the state and a new basis for exceptionalism. In this respect exceptionalism based on environmental care and rural development priorities seem likely strategies. Global and regional patterns of agricultural regulation provide opportunities for groups to better acquaint themselves with operating in a multi-level manner in pursuing their influence activities. The generation of new policy venues may not inevitably lead to a diminution of their influence despite their status as representatives of domestic territorial interests. But this will be determined by their ability to adapt to the multi-level type games generated by multi-level forms of governance.

There is also the possibility that the state may require a different type of group in a global era, which in turn suggests *transformation*. Coleman and Chiasson (2002) have argued that two types of groups may be necessary in a global era. The first are groups capable of organizing horizontally in the cross-sectoral manner, and able to operate with consumers and environmentalists, required to address the 'externalities' of agricultural production (horizontal multipartite corporatism). The second are commodity based groups able to organize vertically (including the post farm gate supply chain) and which are necessary to create tailored plans for domestic integration with world markets (vertical bipartite corporatism). It raises a question mark over the suitability and capacity of national general agricultural interest groups to contribute in the way required by nation states in a globalizing era. As such it suggests *transformation*. Some contemporary developments provide support for the idea of a more substantive *transformation* of groups in the face of a challenging environment. There is an apparent rise of the importance of interprofessional associations in European agriculture (see Coleman *et al.*, 1997b, p.477).[7] These groups include all aspects of the supply or value chain in a particular nation, but again, tend to involve *existing* national professional bodies. These bodies may be on the rise particularly as they can come to assume some of the market coordination responsibilities formerly undertaken by nation-states under the state-assisted paradigm. On a different tangent, groups like the 'Cream Club' which involve 100 producers world-wide in comparing production techniques and data under the banner of the International Farm Comparison Network (IFCN), illustrate the type of vehicle through which global changes in production systems can be coordinated and facilitated. In relation to horizontal cross-sectoral groups, the UK Soil Association (constituting farmers, environmentalists and consumers) is a robust example. Likewise, FARM emerged to bind together a coalition of similar groups to advocate agri-environmental and rural development policies in the UK (see Wyn Grant in this volume).

In the balance of this book we seek to answer the following general questions. How do these trends manifest themselves in different nations (or groups of nations) to create a group environment? What evidence is there of challenges from above and below? How does this support a thesis of decline or resilience in the case studies examined? Are groups able to adapt or are they being fundamentally transformed and new groups on the ascendancy? In addressing these questions we examine the fate of contemporary national general agricultural interest groups in the 21st century, a 'globalizing era'.

Structure of the Book

In structuring the book, there were a number of ways that it could logically be presented. One could have looked at the prevailing agricultural trade policy position of each country. However, this would be to overstate the coherence amongst EU nations in their attitudes to trade liberalization (see Sheingate, 2000, p.345). In the end we have decided to present the volume in continental groups. The reason being that this would likely reflect the interests of individual readers, who we assume are likely to be more interested in nations of a particular geographic region. The book is structured in three parts, with each focussing on a continent.

Part One focuses on activities in European Union member nations, with chapters on United Kingdom (Wyn Grant), Ireland (Alan Greer), Denmark (Carsten Daugbjerg), France (Christilla Roderer-Rynning) and Spain (Eduardo Moyano-Estrada). Australasia is the subject of *Part Two*, with a contribution on Australia (Darren Halpin). *Part Three* focuses on North America and has contributions for the United States (Graham K. Wilson) and Canada (Grace Skogstad). *Part Four* contains the final chapter which concludes with an overview and analysis of developments as reported in individual chapters.

Notes

[1] In particular there is robust debate over whether global change is internationalization or globalization (see for example Scholte, 2000, pp.44-46).

[2] The concept of 'transformative capacity', promoted by Weiss (1998), captures well the idea that state-and associational actors are a key component of the capacity for nation states to respond to the international economy.

[3] High price policy also ensured that the money was redirected from consumers to the farming sector.

[4] There is stiff debate about the distinctiveness of corporatism versus existing versions of pluralism; with some preferring 'corporate pluralism' to stand for the routine and structured consultation of groups by government in a sectoral context (e.g. Jordan and Richardson, 1987).

[5] In the UK context, Jones and Clark (2001) have illustrated how the NFU has expanded agrarian notions of 'trusteeship', normally promoted in a productive capacity, to encompass environmental stewardship roles, hence maintaining a policy role and agricultural primacy in the emerging agri-environmental area. Again this is a point at which national level agricultural interest groups can gain access to this process of paradigm elaboration.

[6] This is based on the assumption that a very small minority of issues attract an overwhelming amount of policy activity and competition (Baumgartner and Leech, 2001) and that groups typically stick to narrow issue niches (Browne, 1990; Jordan et al., 1994).

[7] For instance, a nation interprofessional pig organization was recently formed in France. In addition to primary producers, it includes butchers, processors, traders, wholesalers, abattoirs and feed producers. It was founded to address issues such as traceability, export strategies, crisis management and promotion activities. Notably it does not include industry adjustment, rationalization or 'redundancy' amongst its issues to be addressed ('New French pig organization formed', *Agra Europe*, June 21, 2002 p.N/4(1)).

References

Albrecht, D.E. (1998), 'The Industrial Transformation of Farm Communities: Implications for Family Structure and Socioeconomic Conditions', *Rural Sociology*, Vol. 63(1), pp.51-64.

Argent, N. (2002), 'From pillar to post? In search of the post-productivist countryside in Australia', *Australian Geographer*, Vol. 33(1), pp.97-114.

Arts, B., Noortmann, M., and Reinalda, B. (eds.) (2001), *Non-State Actors in International Relations*, Ashgate, Aldershot.

Ball, A. and Millard, F. (1986), *Pressure Politics in Industrial Societies*, Macmillan, London.

Baumgartner, F. and Leech, B. (2001), 'Interest Niches and Policy Bandwagons: Patterns of Interest Group Involvement in National Politics', *Journal of Politics*, Vol. 63(4), pp.1191-213.

Bonanno, A. (1990), 'Introduction', in A. Bonnano (ed.), *Agrarian Policies and Agricultural Systems*, Westview Press, Boulder, pp.1-8.

Bonanno, A. (1994), 'The Locus of Polity Action in a Global Setting', in A. Bonanno, L. Busch, W.H. Friedland, L. Gouveia and E. Mingione (eds.), *From Columbus to ConAgra: The Globalization of Agriculture and Food*, University of Kansas Press, Kansas.

Bonanno, A. Constance, D.H. and Lorenz, H. (2000), 'Powers and Limits of Transnational Corporations: The Case of ADM', *Rural Sociology*, Vol. 65(3), pp.440-60.

Braithwaite, J. and Drahos, P. (2000), *Global business regulation*, Melbourne, Cambridge University Press.

Browne, W.P. (1990), 'Organized Interests and Their Issue Niche: A Search For Pluralism in a Policy Domain', *Journal of Politics*, Vol. 52(2), pp.477-509.

Burch, D., Goss, J., Lawrence, G., and Rickson, R.E. (1999), 'The Global Restructuring of Food and Agriculture: Contingencies and Parallels in Australia and New Zealand', *Rural Sociology*, Vol. 61(2), pp.179-85.

Buttell, F.H. (1996), 'Theoretical issues in global agri-food restructuring' in D. Burch, R. Rickson, G. Lawrence (eds.), *Globalization and Agri-food Restructuring: Perspectives from the Australasia Region*, Avebury, Aldershot, pp.17-44.

Coleman, W.D. and Skogstad, G.D. (1995), 'Neo-Liberalism, Policy Networks, and Policy Change: Agricultural Policy Reform in Australia and Canada', *Australian Journal of Political Science*, Vol. 30, pp.242-63.

Coleman, W.D., Skogstad, G.D., and Atkinson, M.M. (1997a), 'Paradigm Shifts and Policy Networks: Cumulative Change in Agriculture', *Journal of Public Policy*, Vol. 16(3), pp.273-301.

Coleman, W.D., Atkinson, M.M, and Montpetit, E. (1997b), 'Against the Odds: retrenchment in Agriculture in France and the United States', *World Politics*, Vol. 49(July), pp.453-81.

Coleman, W.D. (1997c), 'Associational Governance in a Globalizing Era: Weathering the Storm', in J.R. Hollingsworth and R. Boyer (eds.), *Contemporary Capitalism: The Embeddedness of Institutions*, Cambridge University Press, Cambridge, pp.127-53.

Coleman, W.D, and Grant, W. (1998), Policy Convergence and Policy Feedback: Agricultural Finance Policies in a Globalising Era', *European Journal of Political Research*, Vol. 34, pp.225-47.

Coleman, W.D. and Chiasson, C. (2002), 'State power, transformative capacity, and adapting to globalisation: an analysis of French agricultural policy, 1960-2000', *Journal of European Public Policy*, Vol. 9(2), pp.168-85.

Cox, G., Lowe, P. and Winter, M. (1987), 'Farmers and the State: A crisis for Corporatism', *The Political Quarterly*, Vol. 58(January/March), pp.73-81.

Curtis, B.M. (2001), 'Reforming New Zealand Agriculture: The WTO way or farmer control?', *International Journal of Sociology of Agriculture and Food*, Vol. 9(1), pp.29-42.

Daugbjerg, C. (1998), *Policy Networks under Pressure*, Ashgate, Aldershot.

Friedland, W.H. (2002), 'Agriculture and rurality: Beginning the "final separation"?', *Rural Sociology*, Vol. 67(3), pp.350-71.

Friedmann, H. and McMichael, P. (1989), 'Agriculture and the State System: The rise and decline of national agricultures, 1870 to present', *Sociologia Ruralis*, Vol. 24(2), pp.93-117.

Grant, W. (1983), 'The National Farmers' Union: The Classic Case of Incorporation?', in D. Marsh (ed.), *Pressure Politics: interest groups in Britain*, London, Junction.

Grant, W. (1995), 'Is agricultural policy still exceptional?', *The Political Quarterly*, Vol. 66(July/September), pp.156-69.

Grant, W. (2000), *Pressure Groups in British Politics*, Macmillan Press, Basingstoke.

Grant, W. (2001), 'Pressure Politics: From "Insider" Politics to Direct Action?', *Parliamentary Affairs*, Vol. 54, pp.337-48.

Gray, I. and Lawrence, G. (2001), 'Neo-liberalism, individualism and prospects for regional renewal', *Rural Society*, Vol. 11(3), pp.283-98.

Halfacree, K. (1997), 'Contrasting roles for the post-productivist countryside', in P. Cloke, and J. Little (eds.), *Contested Countryside Cultures*, Routledge, London.

Halpin, D. and Martin, P. (1999) 'Farmer Representation in Australia: Avenues for Changing the Political Environment', *Australian Journal of Public Administration*, Vol. 58(2), pp.133-46.

Held, D., McGrew, A., Goldblatt, D. and Perraton, J. (1999), *Global Transformations: Politics Economic and Culture*, Polity Press, Cambridge.

Hoggart, K. and Paniagua, A. (2001), 'What rural restructuring?', *Journal of Rural Studies*, Vol. 17, pp.41-62.

Hooghe, L. (ed.) (1996), *Cohesion Policy and European Integration: Building Multi-Level Governance*, Oxford, Oxford University Press.

Ilbery, B. and Bowler, I. (1998), 'From agricultural productivism to post-productivism', in B. Ilbery (ed.), *The Geography of Rural Change*, Addison Wesley Longman, Harlow, pp.57-84.

Jones, A. and Clark, J. (2001), *The Modalities of European Union Governance*, Oxford University Press, Oxford.

Jordan A.G. and Richardson, J. (1987), *Government and Pressure Groups in Britain*, Oxford, Clarendon Press.

Jordan, G., Maloney, W.A., and McLaughlin, M. (1994), 'Characterizing Agricultural Policy-Making', *Public Administration*, Vol. 72, pp.505-26.

Jordan, G., Halpin, D. and Maloney, W. (2004), 'Defining Interests: Disambiguation and the Need for New Distinctions?', *British Journal of Politics and International Relations*, Vol. 6(2), pp.195-212.

Just, F. (1990), *Cooperatives and farmers' unions in Western Europe*, Esbjerg, Sydjisk Universitet Center Press.

Keck, M.E., and K. Sikkink (1998), *Activists Beyond Borders*, Cornell University Press, Ithaca, NY.

Lawrence, G., Share, P. and Campbell, H. (1992)'The restructuring of agriculture and rural society: Evidence From Australia and New Zealand', *Journal of Australian Political Economy*, Vol. 30, pp.1-23.

Lawrence, G. (1996) 'Contemporary agri-food restructuring: Australia and New Zealand', in D. Burch, R. Rickson and G. Lawrence (eds.), *Globalization and Agri-food Restructuring: Perspectives from the Australasia Region*, Avebury, Aldershot, pp.45-73.

Le Heron, R., Roche, M., and Johnston, T. (1992) 'The reregulation of New Zealand agriculture and its implications for a restatement of policy and planning agendas', in A. Gilg, D. Briggs, R. Dilley, O. Furuseth and G. Mc Donald (eds.) *Progress in Rural Policy and Planning*, Vol. Two, Belhaven Press, London.

Le Heron, R. and Roche, M. (1996), 'Eco-commodity systems: Historical geographies of context articulation and embeddedness under capitalism', in D. Burch, R. Rickson and G. Lawrence (eds.), *Globalization and Agri-food Restructuring: Perspectives from the Australasia Region*, Avebury, Aldershot, pp.73-90.

Le Heron, R. and Roche, M. (1999) 'Rapid Reregulation, Agricultural Restructuring, and the Reimaging of Agriculture in New Zealand', *Rural Sociology*, Vol. 64(2), pp.203-18.

Lofgren, H. (2001), 'Business Associations and the Food Processing Industry in Australia: How Neoliberalism has Reinforced Employer Collectivism', *Labour and Industry*, Vol. 12(2), pp.77-95.

Lowi, T.J. (1979), *The End of Liberalism*, New York, W.W. Norton and Co.

Manzetti, L. (1992), 'The Evolution of Agricultural Interest Groups in Argentina', *Journal of Latin American Studies*, Vol. 24(October), pp.585-616.

Marks, G., Hooghe, L. and Blank, K. (1996), 'European Integration from the 1980s: State-Centric v. Multi-level Governance', *Journal of Common Market Studies*, Vol. 34(3), pp.341-78.

Marsden, T. (1999), 'Beyond Agriculture? Towards Sustainable Modernisation', in M.R. Redclift, J.N. Lekakis, and G.P. Zanias (eds.), *Agriculture and World Trade Liberalisation: Socio-environmental Perspectives on the Common Agricultural Policy*, CABI Publishing, Oxfordshire.

Marsh, I. (1995), *Beyond the Two Party System*, Cambridge University Press, Melbourne.

McConnell, G. (1966), *Private Power and American Democracy*, New York, Alfred A. Knopf.

McMichael, P. (ed.) (1994), *The Global Restructuring of Agro-Food Systems*, Cornell University Press, Ithaca.

Montpetit, E. (2002) 'Policy Networks, Federal Arrangements, and the Development of Environmental Regulations: A Comparison of the Canadian and American Agriculture Sectors', *Governance*, Vol. 15(1), pp.1-20.

Moyano-Estrada, E. (1990), 'The Agricultural Professional Organizations in the EC: Theoretical and Practical Aspects', in A. Bonnano (ed.), *Agrarian Policies and Agricultural Systems*, Westview Press, Boulder, pp.180-226.

Moyano-Estrada, E. (1995), 'Farmers' unions and the restructuring of European agriculture', *Sociologia Ruralis*, Vol. 25(3/4), pp.348-65.

Moyer, W. and Josling, T. (2002), *Agricultural Policy Reform: Politics and process in the EU and US in the 1990s*, Ashgate, Aldershot.

OECD [Organization for Economic Co-operation and Development] (2002), *Agricultural Policies in OECD Countries: Monitoring and Evaluation 2002*, Organization for Economic Co-operation and Development, Paris.

Olson, M. (1965), *The Logic of Collective Action: Public Goods and the Theory of Groups*, Harvard University Press, Cambridge.

Potter, C. and Ervin, D.E. (1999), 'Freedom to Farm: Agricultural Policy Liberalisation in the US and EU', in M.R. Redclift, J.N. Lekakis, and G.P. Zanias (eds.), *Agriculture and World Trade Liberalisation: Socio-environmental Perspectives on the Common Agricultural Policy*, CABI Publishing, Oxfordshire.

Rhodes, M. (2001), 'The Political Economy of Social Pacts: "Competitive Corporatism" and European Welfare Reform', in P. Pierson (ed.) *The new politics of the welfare state*, Oxford, Oxford University Press.

Roederer-Rynning, C. (2002), 'Farm Conflict in France and the Europeanisation of Agricultural Policy', *West European Politics*, Vol. 25(3), pp.105-24.

Roche, M.M., Johnston, T. and Le Heron, R.B. (1992), 'Farmers' interest groups and agricultural policy in New Zealand during the 1980s', *Environment and Planning A*, Vol. 24, pp.1749-67.

Salisbury, R.H. (1984), 'Interest Representation: The Dominance of Interest Groups', *American Political Science Review*, Vol. 78(1), pp.64 -78.

Salisbury, R. (1991), 'Putting Interests Back into Interest Groups', in A. Cigler and B. Loomis (eds.), *Interest Group Politics*, Washington, Congressional Quarterly Press, pp.371-98.

Scholte, J.A. (2000), *Globalization: A Critical Introduction*, Macmillan Press, Hampshire.

Schmitter, P.C. and Streeck, W. (1981), 'The Organisation of Business Interests. A Research Design to Study the Associative Action of Business in the Advanced Industrial Societies of Western Europe', International Institute of Management, Berlin, Discussion paper IIM/LMP 81-13.

Schmitter, P.C. and Streeck, W. (1985), 'Community, market, state – associations? The prospective contribution of interest governance to social order', *European Sociological Review,* Vol. 1(2), pp.119-138.

Schmitter, P. C. and Grote, J. R. (1997), 'The Corporatist Sisyphus: Past, Present and Future', EUI Working Papers 97/4, European University Institute, Florence.

Self, P. and Storing, H. (1962) *The state and the farmer,* Allen and Unwin, London.

Sheingate, A.D. (2000), 'Agricultural retrenchment revisited: Issue definition and venue change in the United States and the European Union', *Governance,* Vol. 13(3), pp.350-63.

Skogstad, G. (1998), 'Ideas, Paradigms and Institutions: Agricultural Exceptionalism in the European Union and the United States', *Governance,* Vol. 11(4), pp.463-90.

Swinbank, A. (1999), 'EU Agriculture: Agenda 2000 and the WTO commitments', *World Economy,* Vol. 22(1), pp.41-54.

Weiss, L. (1998), *The myth of the powerless state: governing the economy in a global era,* Cambridge, Polity Press.

Woods, N. (2001), 'International political economy in an age of globalization', in J. Baylis and S. Smith (eds.), *The Globalization of World Politics: An introduction to international relations* (2nd Edition), Oxford University Press, Oxford, pp.277-98.

PART I
EUROPEAN UNION

Chapter 2

An Insider Group Under Pressure: The NFU in Britain

Wyn Grant

Introduction

The system of interest representation in Britain has been undergoing major changes against the background of a transformation of the British state. Moran (2002, p.4) uses language from Marquand to term 'the deep institutional crisis' of the 1970s 'a crisis of club government'. What had existed before the 1970s had been a highly centralized and authoritative system of executive government which provided opportunities for 'insider' groups to interact, originally through the London club system, with civil servants and ministers. Indeed, the National Farmers' Union (NFU), often cited in the literature as the classic example of an insider group, had their own club in their headquarters.

Although the crisis of the 1970s started a long process of the functional and geographical dispersion of authority so that the state became 'hollowed out', and its authority was increasingly challenged as greater transparency revealed the often unsatisfactory way in which decisions were made, this process was long delayed in agriculture. In part this was because the subsidy regime was entrenched in the Common Agricultural Policy (CAP), a politically embedded policy that was difficult for the UK Government to change however much they might want to. Even under Mrs Thatcher this traditional relationship with farmers was little disturbed, with the 'East Anglian mafia' of Conservative farm ministers protecting the interests of the large farmers of their region. With the return of New Labour to office in 1997, the traditional agricultural agenda was challenged by new concerns about food safety and quality and the protection of the environment. Although the traditional insider group relationship with the NFU did not disappear, as was shown by its role in the foot and mouth crisis and the decisions about the implementation of the EU's new Single Farm Payment, it seemed to be less effective than it had been. New 'outsider' groups appeared on the scene to feed on the discontent of some NFU members about their waning influence.

The NFU's response to shift away from its traditional insider status and strategy by deciding to move its offices out of London might seem surprising. Nevertheless, the orthodox system of well-organized and encompassing membership peak groups has been facing difficulties in all sectors of the economy. The Trades Union Congress (TUC) is a shadow of its former self and the Confederation of British Industry (CBI) with a much reduced staff has not always found it possible to respond to the consultation opportunities made available under a business friendly New Labour government. As far as the organization of the state itself is concerned, the sponsorship function has been considerably reduced in size and importance in line with the view that the state's role is an enabling and facilitating one rather than a provider of solutions for business problems.

The System of Farm Interest Representation

The NFU has been the dominant organization in farmer representation in Britain throughout the post-war period. It has worked closely with the National Farmers' Union Scotland (NFUS), organizing 12,000 Scottish farmers and the Ulster Farmers' Union (dealt with in the chapter by Greer), although recently there have been increasing disagreements over tactics with the NFUS. The Country Land and Business Association, originally the Country Landowners' Association (still called the CLA) had about two-thirds as many members (45,000) as the farming membership of the NFU (estimated at 67,000), but has generally been seen as a complementary rather than a competitor organization. Historically, its core membership was seen as the great estates of the aristocratic 'landed interest', but membership has always appealed to smaller scale farm owners because of the comprehensive range of services it offers. The CLA invested greater resources in lobbying activities in the late 1990s, but this move was not seen as a success and effort in that area had to be reduced against the background of financial problems. In Wales, the NFU has had competition since 1955 from the *Undeb Amaethwyr Cymru* (Farmers' Union of Wales, FUW) which has made particular inroads among Welsh-speaking farmers in the rural heartland with a total membership of 12,000. The Tenant Farmers' Association, formed in 1981, serves a niche market with some four thousand members. What has posed more of a threat to the NFU since 2000 is the protest group Farmers for Action (FFA). It is not in competition for members of the NFU as it does not have a formal structure to protect itself against legal action, but it is certainly competing for influence. Its outsider group tactics threaten the insider group strategy of the NFU.

The NFU was founded in 1908, initially principally as an organization of tenant farmers. It was formed against a background of increasing state intervention and growing marketing complexities that encouraged collective action. As Winter notes (1996, p.84) 'The genius of the NFU was to restrict its membership to *bona fide* farmers but at the same time to avoid taking an overt and antagonistic stance regarding the organisations of either landowners or workers.' In the 1920s the NFU's impact on government policy was limited, partly because 'it was slow to develop a clear policy on agricultural support.' (Winter, 1996, p.94). In the 1930s, however, it became much more involved with policy-making:

This was basically for two reasons: to keep the demands of the increasingly powerful Union in bounds, and to gain the support of farmers as the government attempted to deal with the Depression and the preparations for war. Consequently, the government relied on the NFU to help out in a number of ways, including providing agricultural statistics to the ministry and selecting candidates for the marketing boards and commissions (Wilt, 2002, p.134).

The 1947 Agriculture Act institutionalized the position of the NFU in the policy-making process. It provided for the negotiation of guaranteed prices and other forms of support between the government (represented primarily by the Ministry of Agriculture, Fisheries and Food, MAFF) and the NFU. This annual price review formed the centrepiece of agricultural policy-making until Britain joined the European Community (although it survived in truncated form for a few commodities until 1992). Agricultural policy formation was removed from much effective scrutiny within government, let alone in Parliament or by the wider public. 'As a result, the NFU-MAFF axis became so strong that relations between ministry civil servants and NFU officers could be closer than between the civil servants and government ministers' (Winter, 1996, p.106). However, relations between ministers and NFU officials were also based on mutual respect. Tom Williams, the agriculture minister in the post-war Labour Government, recalls of his relationship with Jim Turner, the NFU President, 'We worked together on opposite sides of the table from 1947 to 1951' (Williams, 1965, p.161).

British membership of the European Community changed the way in which subsidies to farmers were delivered. However, if anything, the complexities of the Common Agricultural Policy (CAP) simply reinforced the privileged position of MAFF within Whitehall. The NFU set up a Brussels office. In addition, about a third of expenditure on agriculture was still driven by domestic policies, while the implementation of the CAP was a national task. If anything, the CAP reforms of 2003 have reinforced the element of national discretion.

MAFF remained a very special ministry devoted to the interests of one industry. It was therefore a considerable blow to the NFU and other farming interests when it was replaced in 2001 by the Department of Environment, Food and Rural Affairs (DEFRA). Some farmers complained that the real title of the department should be the Department for the Elimination of Farmers and Rural Activity. However, the first secretary of state, Margaret Beckett, made it clear that she would eventually like to see all subsidies to farmers eliminated and that she also regarded farmers as major polluters. Nevertheless, the view persisted in farming circles that DEFRA's task was to represent the interests of farmers.

Changes in Agricultural and Rural Policy and Politics

The European Union (EU) engages in the most trade distorting policies of any participant in the World Trade Organization (WTO). The measures used, which have a substantial impact on agricultural exporters, particularly developing countries, include high import tariffs and export subsidies as well as extensive domestic support.

Within the EU, the UK has consistently pushed for a more liberal approach to international trade issues in agriculture. However, it has won support from only a limited group of north European countries (Denmark, the Netherlands and Sweden) and has faced effective opposition from France. Nevertheless, the need to reach agreement in the Uruguay Round prompted the MacSharry reforms in 1992 which were the most far reaching reforms to date of the CAP. The need to have a credible negotiating position in the Doha Round greatly influenced the CAP reforms of 2003.

Significant changes have come about in agricultural policy through the broadening of policy networks to include a new range of actors. One area of concern has been conservation and the environment. Agriculture has increasingly come to be perceived as a major source of environmental problems. This has particularly applied to water pollution, but also to biodiversity issues resulting from changes in farming practice, e.g., removal of hedges, increasing trends towards monoculture, more intensive forms of livestock farming etc.

A range of environmental organizations has had an increasing impact on agricultural policy. The Royal Society for the Protection of Birds (RSPB) has been a particularly important actor, building its membership to over one million. Its resources have enabled it to develop and articulate sophisticated alternatives to current agricultural policy. The effects of this increased activity by environmental organizations can be seen in a number of areas of agricultural policy. On the one hand, there has been increasingly effective enforcement of existing regulations, in particular in relation to the pollution of watercourses by dairy farming. On the other hand, new pieces of legislation have been introduced, starting with the Wildlife and the Countryside Act of 1981. Although this was seen as an inadequate piece of legislation by environmental organizations, it was followed by other initiatives. EU initiatives have been of increasing importance. Agri-environmental schemes formed part of the 1992 reform package. The 2003 reforms enshrine the concept of cross-compliance which means that farmers have to meet environmental standards if they are going to qualify for subsidies.

Food safety and food quality issues were originally regarded as highly technical issues that were best left to experts. However, as a result of salmonella, BSE and foot-and-mouth disease, these issues have become increasingly politicized. One consequence was the formation of a Food Standards Agency (FSA), taking away an important slice of MAFF's activities and thereby hastening its eventual demise. It is not just these institutional changes that are significant, but a more general shift of power down the food chain to the retailers. This results from the very high level of concentration in food retailing in Britain, a level of concentration that is likely to increase rather than diminish. In many ways food quality standards are enforced through a private system of retailer led governance rather than by legislation. Farmers who contract directly with supermarkets to supply vegetables find that they have to meet both rigorous quality standards and also pressure on price.

Agricultural 'exceptionalism' has been undermined in many other ways. Agricultural advice services were put on to a fee paying basis and then effectively privatized. The specialist network of agricultural colleges has been eroded through closures and mergers. The specialist agricultural credit body set up by legislation, the Agriculture Mortgage Corporation, was deregulated and then sold to a private bank. Specialist media programmes on farming have been cut back and often replaced by 'countryside' programmes that are often critical of farming practices. As the privileged economic and political position of farming has been eroded, some farmers have clung to a mindset that calls on government to produce 'orderly' and 'planned' solutions to their problems. Attempts have been made to revive food security concerns as a justification for intervention in the context of increased fears about terrorist attacks. Often, agriculture appears to be the last refuge of 'statism', a belief in the benevolence and necessity of government intervention.

The Changing Agricultural Sector

Agriculture in 2003 accounted for less than one per cent of the UK's gross domestic product (0.8 per cent of gross value added). Agricultural employment accounts for 1.9 per cent of the total workforce. The total labour force employed in agriculture in England declined by fifteen per cent between 1990 and 2002. 'It is now widely accepted that agriculture is no longer the main economic driver in rural economies and that the traditional analytical framework that saw rural areas through an agricultural perspective is out of date.' Farming is no longer the 'key rural industry. The mix of industrial sectors in rural areas is now very similar to that in urban areas with the service sector being by far the largest employer' (Roberts, 2002, p.4).

Farm amalgamation started as a major trend in the arable areas of the country, but has now spread to the more pastoral north and west. Renting or whole-farm contracting is a more normal form of expansion than purchase. Companies that farm on behalf of the farmer who owns the land have not expanded to the extent once anticipated and the major player, Sentry Farming, shed contracts and delisted from the stock exchange. More limited contract arrangements can enable the farmer to retain the role of farmer and secure tax advantages.

There has been a continuing increase in part-time employment and part-time farming. Official statistics suggest that there are 178,100 part-time farmers in Britain compared with 157,000 full-time producers. However, these figures may overstate the number of full timers. Part-time farmers are made up of those who diversify out of farming for more income and those who diversify in for lifestyle reasons, sometimes called 'hobby farmers' elsewhere in the world. 'Lifestyle' farms are estimated to make up seven per cent of all farms, a figure anticipated to increase to thirteen per cent by 2007.

Fifty-eight per cent of all farms in England are now involved in some kind of diversified activity. Although large arable farmers in Eastern England were less likely to diversify than livestock enterprises in the West of England, the reduced subsidies available after the 2003 CAP reforms have created a new interest in diversification in predominantly arable areas. Farm diversification now accounts for an estimated forty-three per cent of the total aggregate income of agricultural holdings in England. Farm contracting accounts for more than one in three ventures and accommodation and equine-based enterprises are found on nearly a quarter of all diversified farms. However, research by Exeter University shows that large farms have been much more successful at diversification (*Rural Report*, 2003, p.10). Although 'late adopters' are now joining in, some markets have reached saturation point.

In terms of patterns of farming, 'mixed' farming has become much less common. In part this reflects the increasing cost of specialized capital equipment. Remaining grassland in predominantly arable areas is under considerable pressure, a development that has considerable biodiversity implications. It also means that farmers' interests are more oriented to specific commodities, making it more difficult for the NFU to mediate between the interests of arable and livestock farmers.

Government policy increasingly emphasizes the problem of 'social exclusion' in rural areas. Inward migrants are increasingly affluent and do not need to use local facilities such as village shops and post offices and even public houses. These facilities are then closed and the quality of life of long established residents deteriorates. Bus services to local towns are expensive to maintain. Falling levels of employment in the countryside make it difficult to maintain 'retained' fire services staffed by on call part-timers. It is against this background that Greer argues (2003, p.523) that 'it does make sense to talk of a countryside crisis in the British context'.

The Countryside Alliance (CA) has sought to capitalize on this sense of crisis by organizing two large protest demonstrations in London. However, it is generally believed that the principal agenda of the CA is the threat to field sports, principally hunting with dogs, and its concern over issues such as rural post offices is simply a means of broadening its appeal. The emergence of the CA, alongside FFA, does, however, point to a growing discontent with the 'insider' strategies adopted by the NFU and other principal farm organizations. They have sought to accommodate to existing policy and cooperate with government rather than engage in outright opposition.

Relations between the Associations

The relationship between the principal farm organizations, the NFU, the NFUS and the CLA is broadly a cooperative one. There is also a cooperative relationship with the Tenant Farmers Association (TFA), although it is a much smaller organization and in some respects a potential competitor to the NFU. In 1983 the TFA was officially recognized by the NFU on the understanding that it would confine itself to tenancy matters. The effective working relationship between the different associations is illustrated by the Tenancy Reform Industry Group (TRIG) set up by DEFRA which reportedly in 2003 contained three members from the CLA, two from the NFU, two from the TFA and one from the FUW.

Any new group that hopes to join the national farm interest group system has, in effect, to win the trust of the NFU. The NFU is not slow to slap down any group that it perceives as a rival. Using its near monopoly of influence provided by its symbiotic relationship with MAFF, its strategy has been to freeze out any breakaway groups and hope that they would disappear. The Hill Farming Initiative (HFI) was set up in 1994 by a former NFU county chairman and emphasized that it was not in conflict with the NFU. However, the NFU's response was that the HFI's launch was a slur on the NFU and would weaken the industry's message to government. When the HFI wrote to the then NFU president to seek his cooperation, his reply merely set out how the NFU represented hill farmers. In 2002 a group of farmers and environmentalists set up a group called FARM that claimed that the NFU was too close to government and big business and had allowed big supermarkets and agribusiness to become too powerful. The group was set up with £200,000 funding partly provided by millionaire environmentalist Zac Goldsmith. The NFU rejected the accusation that its effectiveness had been diluted by its links with government and business and said that the last thing the farming industry needed was another pressure group. In fact, the real threat to the NFU could come not from an externally established organization, but from an internal breakaway, as will be discussed later in the chapter.

The NFUS has traditionally worked closely with the NFU in England. It cannot match the resources of its English counterpart and the creation of a Scottish Assembly and Executive has meant that it has had to devote a lot of attention to the policies of the devolved administration. Historically, the NFUS might make a special contribution to discussions at European level where it has special expertise, e.g., hill farming. The relationship has come under more strain in recent years as the NFUS has tended to adopt a more militant stance than its English counterpart. In September 2002 the NFUS organized a blockade of the Grangemouth depot of leading reatiler Asda (owned by Wal-Mart). The union's president warned that future demonstrations would not be as friendly. This greater enthusiasm for outsider strategies is perhaps in part because of internal tensions that are discussed more fully below.

The BSE crisis also produced tensions between the two unions. Scottish farmers claimed that the English union was preoccupied with the dairy sector whereas beef production was more important in Scotland. The NFUS leadership rejected claims that it was being ruled by the English union, drawing attention to the battle it had had with the NFU over the introduction of the selective cull and certified herds scheme. The union's vice-president commented, 'We try to work with our colleagues in the south. But when Scottish interests conflict with those in England then we fight our own corner tooth and nail' (*Farmers Weekly*, 13 June 1997). The NFUS has also taken a somewhat different stance on relations with FFA.

There has been a long history of tension between the FUW and the NFU with a number of merger attempts ending in failure. 'The formation of the FUW in

1955 was occasioned principally by the dissatisfaction of hill sheep farmers and small marginal dairy farmers with an NFU perceived to be dominated by larger lowland arable farmers' (Winter, 1996, p.117). The development of the FUW has been closely related to the development of Welsh nationalism and its core support is among Welsh speaking farmers in the rural heartland, although it is believed that some farmers belong to both organizations. The FUW has 'espoused a populist ideology, defending family farming as economically, politically and morally superior to large-scale capitalist agriculture' (Winter, 1996, p.117). For twenty years the FUW was very much an outsider group until it was officially recognized by the Labour Government in 1978 at a time when the government lacked a Parliamentary majority and support from Plaid Cymru MPs was necessary for its survival.

Attempts were made to unify the two organizations in 1972 and 1979 and foundered on the FUW's demand that a single union must be independent and not controlled by the NFU's London headquarters, though some form of federation with the English union was thought to be acceptable. In 1987 Peter Walker, then Secretary of State for Wales, suggested that it might be sensible to have one organization representing Welsh farmers. Two years later, against a background of rising costs and falling membership, merger talks began under the chairmanship of a senior Welsh Office civil servant. These talks broke down and an 'honest broker' attempt by a farmer in 1991 also failed.

The formation of the Welsh Assembly in 1998 prompted another attempt at merger, this time on the basis of a proposal put forward by the Wales Federation of Young Farmers Clubs. In 2001 there was another public and heated row over which organization best represented Welsh farmers. The NFU in particular criticized the FUW for failing to continue a dialogue with the Welsh executive when Christine Gwyther, a vegetarian, was Welsh farm minister. It seems likely that the two organizations will continue competing for members and influence, particularly since the election of a NFU president from Wales in 2004. It would seem that NFU Cymru-Wales is the slightly larger organization with around 15,000 members as against 12,000 in the FUW. Given their role in attempting to promote a merger, it is interesting that in 2003 the Wales Federation of Young Farmers Clubs announced that they were thinking of breaking away from the English federation.

The CLA is essentially concerned with property rights and has been seen as a more defensive organization with a narrower focus than the NFU. 'Although it began as an élitist gentleman's club it has transformed itself into a successful modern parliamentary pressure group and in so doing adapted itself to the growing convergence between estate-owners and farming owner-occupiers' (Newby, 1979, pp.56-7). The larger-scale landowners that form the core of its membership had broadened its appeal by cross-subsidizing an extensive range of services that appeal to smaller-scale owner occupiers. Thus, for example, the writer knows of one seventh generation Welsh speaking farmer who belongs neither to the NFU or FUW, but to the CLA because of its services. The CLA is, however, very active on policy issues, but tends to concentrate on those where its members have a special interest such as taxation, access rights and forestry. It therefore complements the work of the NFU and has an effective working relationship with it. It has also re-named itself as the Country Land and Business Association in an effort to represent all sectors of the rural economy including tourism.

Group Structures and Resources

All the three main organizations (NFU, NFUS, CLA) have a regional structure with branches below that level in the case of the NFU and the NFUS. The NFU has eight regions and the NFUS nine (which replaced twenty-eight areas in a streamlining operation at the end of the 1990s). Despite the existence of these regional and local structures, all the organizations remain highly centralized. There are full time staff members at local level whose main job is supposedly to sell insurance. In practice, there is considerable cross subsidization that helps the NFU and the NFUS to maintain services to members. A typical local secretary reported that 'About half my time is spent solving problems on the NFU side – which pays a mere £190 a year – and the other half selling insurance for the Mutual' *(Farmers Weekly*, 16 January 1998). In addition to financing the local group system, the NFU Mutual also provides direct financial support to the NFU running into millions of pounds a year. Other services the NFU provides to members include discounted private health care, discounts on personal computer systems designed to meet farmers' needs and an energy advice and consultancy service.

As the farming population has shrunk, the organizations have sought to broaden the basis of their membership. The NFU offers 'NFU Countryside' membership to 'all who share a practical passion for the countryside'. (http://www.nfu.org.uk/ 7 July 2003). It has over 70,000 countryside members out of an estimated total of 130,000 members. The CLA has re-styled itself as the Country Land and Business Association, claiming 'the rural economy is our business'. The NFUS seems to have made less of an appeal to a broader membership. Its website does, however, offer potential members a 'ready reckoner' to calculate the direct benefits of membership. Faced with a declining membership base, it has attempted to broaden the range of services offered to members, but lost money on NFUS Assist, a farm office service (Halpin and Jordan, 2003, pp.12-13).

The NFU has the largest staff of any of the organizations, but six hundred of these are group secretaries who provide important services to members but are not directly involved in representation or policy-making. This leaves around two hundred staff members working at the London headquarters. In 2003 the CLA, which has had financial problems, announced that it was making ten to fifteen of its ninety-eight staff redundant. It was also considering moving out of its London office. The NFUS has a headquarters staff of thirty, backed up by forty-five group secretaries. It faced a financial crisis in 1998 when there was a cumulative loss of £314,000 from 1996 and headquarters salary costs had to be cut by twenty per cent. The FUW has ten headquarters staff and twenty-five local secretaries. The TFA has a head office staff of just four, backed up by nine regional secretaries.

The emphasis in all the organizations, but especially in the major ones, is of a professional staff working closely with a carefully selected leadership. This has, however, led to complaints that some of the organizations are insufficiently internally democratic. A persistent charge made against the NFU has been that larger scale arable farmers from Eastern England have dominated its leadership, in part because they have the time to devote to NFU activities. The NFU has already tried to balance the interests of its larger and smaller and arable and livestock farmers through its elaborate committee structure. This did not prevent office holding horticulturalists and potato producers in the NFU openly dissenting from the organization's stance on the Single Farm Payment which was harmful to their interests. Internal dissent and the threatened formation of breakaway organizations have become increasing problems for the NFU and the NFUS, although the NFUS's response has been somewhat different from that of the NFU.

The Management of Internal Dissent

Tensions have appeared within the NFU about its internal democratic arrangements, in particular its method of indirect election. County branches elect part of the 92 (the figure varies) members of the national Council (although the majority are still not the result of a membership election) which in turn elects the principal office holders. Two recent elections have enhanced controversy about the voting system and illustrated the difficulty dissenting members have in getting elected to senior posts.

Richard Haddock is a militant farmer from Devon whose advocacy of direct action has made him popular with NFU grass-roots members. He was voted *Farmers Weekly* personality of the year in 1999. In 2000 he considered running for the post of NFU president against the incumbent Ben Gill but pulled out of the contest despite receiving 81 per cent of the votes in a poll conducted by *Farmers Weekly*. He did stand for a vacancy as vice-president that arose later in the year following the death of an office holder. He was defeated in the vote by a Council member who served on the policy committee and also chaired another committee.

In 2002, a well-known Norfolk farmer, Marie Skinner, tried to become the first woman senior office-holder in the NFU, standing for deputy president with the backing of twenty influential farmers. Her qualifications were impressive. Trained as a biologist, she was a senior member of the Home Grown Cereals Authority, a new government Rural Affairs Forum and the East England Development Agency. As a self-defined radical candidate, her platform was one of modernizing farming, adapting to a world where government subsidies will no longer guarantee farmers' income and environmental protection will be a high priority. She also urged the NFU to put more effort into coalition building with other organizations such as the Council for the Protection of Rural England and the RSPB, rather than just lobbying government. In a different election system, she might have done well. However, the conservative NFU Council was not impressed. In accordance with the rules, she was not even allowed to address the meeting and she was not elected.

County branches have attempted to bring the issue of one member, one vote before the annual general meeting. The largest county branch, West Yorkshire, tried unsuccessfully to place the issue on the agenda for the 2000 meeting. In 2001 resolutions from Yorkshire and Somerset calling for direct elections were diverted to the internal 'Meeting Members Expectations' review. The NFU's secretary argued that the organization's election procedures 'are similar to those used in most other membership organisations. The system is designed to protect the democratic process by allowing council members to use their judgement after considering the views of the farmers they represent' (*Farmers Weekly*, 14 April 2000).

The outcome of the Meeting Members Expectations review was a disappointment but not a surprise to the advocates of change. What the NFU presented as a series of significant changes to its democratic structure in fact emphasized organizational efficiency before membership representation. The establishment of a board to oversee the daily running of the NFU was designed to give a much greater strength to its direction. There was a proposal to increase the directly elected proportion of the Council, but no mention of one member, one vote. Going down that route could well lead to changes in leadership that would disturb the NFU's well honed insider strategy.

If members are denied the option of exit, they may well resort to exit with voice.

The strength of the NFU rests on its claim to represent all types of farmers. Given the prominence of arable farmers in its leadership, it is somewhat paradoxical that it was from this core group of the membership that the threat of a breakaway organization developed in 2002. Arable farmers had become discontented with the NFU because its preoccupation with the foot-and-mouth disease crisis had led to some neglect of the very low prices experienced by arable farmers. The main backer of the scheme was a prominent Essex farmer, Guy Smith, who had supported Marie Skinner's campaign to become deputy president. He and his colleagues were undoubtedly disillusioned by the re-election of the existing NFU leadership, showing the relationship between a lack of voice and exit. He used his column Smith's Soapbox in *Arable Farmers* magazine to canvass support among its 20,000 readers for his plan. The advocates of a breakaway organization had been directly influenced by the more commodity-based structure of farm representation in the United States and that a perception that single issue groups outside farming are successful because they are more focused. There was also a subtext about arable farmers becoming more efficient and better able to adapt to a life without subsidies, but not wanting environmentally linked subsidies that might be more acceptable to livestock farmers. Although nothing eventually came of this breakaway proposal, it was a warning to the NFU leadership.

Large-scale farmers may make use of informal club-like organizations to define and articulate their interests. The writer addressed one such grouping in Lincolnshire, an area of very large scale enterprises, in which membership was restricted to fourteen members. The Commercial Farmers Group (CFG) has just seventeen large farmers in membership, but it has taken a strong stand in favour of genetically modified crops and published an influential discussion paper in favour of import protection.

The NFU leadership has not faced the humiliation of being forced out of office by discontented members. In 1997 the president of the NFUS, Sandy Mole, was forced to resign after losing the confidence of his members over his handling of the European Union ban on British beef. Members began to take direct action at ports against cheap imports of beef and he received a frosty reception at a picket at Stranraer. Jim Walker, one of the organizers of the Stranraer protest and a NFUS official for south-west Scotland commented that 'He had to go for the sake of the union. Had he remained, the NFU would have torn itself apart.' *(Financial Times,* 10 December 1997).

Influence Activities

The farming organizations have used an 'insider' strategy which has concentrated on relations with the executive, although backed up by parliamentary links with the CLA having particularly strong connections in the Lords. The NFUS and the FUW have replicated similar strategies at regional level following the development of the devolved administrations. The NFUS remains a central participant in a more diverse policy network in Scotland that has emerged through a new emphasis since devolution on rural policy frames (Halpin and Jordan, 2003, p.17). The success of these strategies has never been dependant on the party in office. It was a Labour government that passed the 1947 Agriculture Act and some of the best settlements under the old price review system were obtained from Labour governments.

This is not to say that there was not a close relationship between farmers and the Conservative Party. Larger scale farmers overwhelmingly voted Conservative and were often active in local constituency associations. One study found that in the four general elections between 1964 and February 1974, 95 per cent of East Anglian farmers with holders of over a thousand acres consistently voted Conservative (Newby, Bell, Rose and Saunders, 1978, p.289). Livestock farmers in western and northern Britain are, however, more likely to support the Liberal Democrats or to some extent the Nationalist parties in Wales and Scotland, e.g., the highly rural constituency of Carmarthen East and Dinefwr containing many marginal farmers was won by Plaid Cymru from Labour in the 2001 general election. In Ceredigion in west Wales in 1971, the votes of those engaged in farming were split 29 per cent Liberal, 27 per cent Conservative, 18 per cent Labour and 8 per cent Plaid Cymru (Madgwick, Griffiths and Walker, 1973, p.196).

Farm ministers under the Thatcher and Major governments were sometimes referred to as 'the East Anglian mafia' because of the location of their constituencies. Nevertheless, there was an erosion of the traditional relationship between the Conservative Party and the farmers as the party became more urban in its orientation and composition. In 1987 the NFU passed a motion of no confidence in Michael Jopling, then minister of agriculture. One Conservative MP commented, 'The Thatcher years have been anti-corporatist years and we have seen a diminution of all interest groups. The farming lobby is the greatest Conservative interest group, but it has been immune from that process' (*The Independent*, 24 December 1988). However, when John Major appointed Gillian Shephard as agriculture minister he asked her to work 'to bring the farmers back on side' (Shephard, 2000, p.107).

The 1997 general election saw a considerable surge in the number of rural constituencies held by the Labour Party and the balance changed only marginally in the 2001 election with a net loss of two rural seats. Defining a 'rural' constituency is notoriously difficult, but a careful analysis by Woods shows that New Labour won seven out of fifty-five agricultural constituencies (where agricultural employment was five times the national average) in 1997; sixteen out of twenty-five constituencies in small manufacturing towns with rural hinterlands; and five out of eighteen Scottish rural constituencies. (Woods, 2002, p.214). He also notes that 'The more tightly the definition of rural areas is drawn, the lower Labour's share of the vote falls, to the benefit not just of the Conservatives, but also of the Liberal Democrats and the nationalist parties.' (Woods, 2002, p.216). Attempts to mobilize rural voters against Labour on issues such as hunting, farming and fuel prices appeared to have little effect in the 2001 election, in part because the biggest movements of votes occurred in seats already held by the Conservatives and in part because affluent rural incomers often held very different views on issues such as hunting wild mammals with dogs. New Labour has also sought to forge a new non-conservative rural coalition by highlighting issues such as rural poverty and social exclusion and deficient public services (Woods, 2002, p.226).

Maintaining an insider strategy has always depended on a careful balance between satisfying the demands of the membership for vigorous action and not offending the government. This has opened the NFU's leaders to the criticism that they 'all too often [sound] like MAFF spokesmen' (*Farmers Weekly*, 20 October 2000). Lord Plumb, a former president of the NFU, has written about the difficulties inherent in the balancing act required of its leadership. 'It would have been easy to swing open the floodgates of protest …but I had to consider the end result in the long term, and the effect it would have on future negotiations with the Government.' From his perspective, 'Militant action would undoubtedly be counterproductive and inflict damage on ourselves. One way or another, however, it was imperative to show solidarity' (Plumb, 2001, p.64). This meant demonstrations that were kept under the control of the NFU leadership and were used to create media publicity to reinforce policy messages being relayed to government.

However, this was always a perilous strategy with the possibility that control of events would slip away from the leadership. In 1974 there was a crisis in the beef sector as a result of the loss of the old guaranteed price/deficiency payment system at a time when the protection of the new European Community system was not fully operative. By the end of October Welsh farmers were massing at Holyhead to prevent the unloading of Irish beef. The demonstrations later spread to other ports at Fishguard and Birkenhead and a flying picket of Midlands farmers was reported ready for action. On the one hand, the demonstrations brought home to the public at large the extent and depth of the farmers' fears. Sir Henry Plumb commented, 'What has been done in Anglesey helps the cause' *(Farmer and Stockbreeder*, 9 November 1974). However, as long as the demonstrations continued there was always the danger that the Union's leadership might lose control of the situation with consequent damage to their credibility with government. The NFU was placed 'under fearsome stress' as its own journal remarked: 'The Union leadership has ... been in a slightly delicate position – unable to advocate anything which could be interpreted as illegal ... but anxious not to discourage spontaneous demonstrations.' The chairman of the Union's Welsh Council commented 'In Wales, we have kept the initiative but only just.' *(Farmer and Stockbreeder*, 23 November 1974). Once a negotiated settlement had been achieved, Sir Henry Plumb warned his members not to engage in further demonstrations before giving the new arrangements a chance to work.

The NFU's pursuit of its insider strategy was always assisted by its 'extremely close' (Smith, 1989, p.93) working relationship with MAFF. 'Not only was it this partnership that gave the unions a genuine opportunity to influence policy; the well publicized closeness of MAFF and the farmers' unions gave farmers the feeling that their subscriptions to the unions were well spent, and that joining any other farmers' organizations was futile' (Wilson, 1975, p.300). Agricultural policy-making was not subject to much scrutiny from elsewhere in government, particularly by the Treasury so that MAFF and the NFU could pursue their shared goals of 'high support and high production' (Smith, 1989, p.93). As Shephard recalls (2000, p.22), 'the Minister was left alone for the most part to get on, which is certainly in its way a form of power. It worked particularly well with the Treasury, whose clever officials knew nothing about agriculture, and usually gave in during the course of public spending rounds, simply out of boredom.'

The NFU and the other leading farm organizations have enjoyed considerable success in influencing government policy. For example, during the foot and mouth disease episode, the NFU had a considerable influence on the government's decision not to resort to a policy of vaccination. The sums paid out in compensation to farmers far outweighed those available for tourism and other rural businesses. However, there is considerable membership dissatisfaction with the performance of the farm organizations. Farmers have seen a substantial fall in their income and the profitability of their businesses, a downturn that has hit hill farmers and smaller livestock farmers particularly hard. They have also seen their perceived standing and status in society decline. This has opened up a space for more radical organizations, notably FFA. The NFU for its part decided in 2003 to move its headquarters from London to Warwickshire. Although this was partly motivated by financial considerations, it was also seen as an attempt to move the organization away from DEFRA and make it more market oriented. Although a small Parliamentary staff will be retained in London, the NFU is moving away from its traditional insider status. Its members increasingly consider that they need business solutions to their problems rather than political interventions which they often see as being far from beneficial.

The Challenge of an Outsider Group: The FFA

Robinson has drawn attention to the increasing marginalization of the agricultural sector in the UK. 'Since the mid-1990s marginal groups (typically small-scale hauliers and farmers) who have been hit particularly hard by political and economic changes have broken away from their representative organisations, becoming policy outsiders; as a result they have begun to adopt the tactics of direct action and extra-legal activity increasingly resorted to by outsider groups' (Robinson, 2001, p.61). In March 2000 *Farmers Weekly* published a list of over three pages of direct actions taken by farmers over a five year period including blockading supermarket distribution depots and closing roads and bridges. A particularly important episode in the development of this repertoire of protest was an incident in 1997 when more than seven hundred Welsh farmers dumped forty tons of Irish beef burgers into the sea after intercepting an Irish lorry at Holyhead. Although in part they acted on their own initiative, 'the protesters drew on the repertoire of French farmers made familiar by TV news and, for some, by direct contact with French farmers' (Doherty *et al.*, 2003, p.9). Comparisons were made between the French farming unions and the alleged uselessness of the NFU.

These actions assumed a more organized form with the formation of FFA at a meeting at a motorway service station in March 2000. The farmers who were present were annoyed at being excluded from the Downing Street summit on agriculture. The NFU's presence at the summit was an indicator of its insider status, but the dissident farmers claimed that they would be poorly represented by the main farm organizations. One of the participants commented, 'Farmers are fed up with hearing that the NFU and [FUW] are holding meetings that achieve nothing. We have proved that direct action brings results' *(Farmers Weekly*, 9 June 2000). A leaked report on a subsequent meting between the Dairy Industry Federation (DIF) (representing processors) suggested that the farmers' union was 'disconcerted by the apparent willingness of supermarkets to meet [FFA] representatives'. For its part the DIF was said to be 'fully supportive of the NFU in giving the unofficial protesters no encouragement' *(Farmers Weekly*, 9 June 2000).

A somewhat closer relationship appears to be developing between the FFA and the NFUS. In 2002 the then president of the NFUS, Jim Walker, was telephoned by senior NFU officials urging him not to attend a meeting between FFA and Robert Wiseman dairies. The NFU was anxious to minimize positive publicity for FFA, but Mr Walker declined to comply with their request. He commented, 'The NFU in the south does not control NFU Scotland, and it most certainly does not control me. People can agree or disagree with Farmers for Action's tactics, but everyone involved in that organisation is totally committed to our industry and they see no other way to get people to listen' *(Farmers Weekly*, 16 August 2002). The NFUS followed this up by calling for a campaign of milk distribution depot blockades, hoping that the protests might encourage the English NFU to join them.

The president of the NFUS, by then John Kinnaird, and the leader of the FFA, David Handley, met in May 2003. The NFUS also joined a blockade of a retailer's depot. Mr Handley commented that being able to talk to the NFUS was in stark contrast to FFA's relationship with the NFU. 'To say we are distant is an understatement, and that will continue until the current president goes' (*Farmers Weekly*, 30 May 2003). However, personalities aside, the NFU is unlikely to support the FFA's plan for a body like the Trades Union Congress to bring together the various organizations speaking for farmers. The NFU would then be downgraded to one of many organizations.

The FFA was actively involved in the fuel price protests of September 2000. Although farmers can purchase 'red' diesel that attracts a lower rate of duty, its price increased by 9p a litre in the summer of 2000. 'Haulier-farmers ... were important in linking the networks of farmers and hauliers.' (Doherty *et al.*, 2003, p.9). The protests did not achieve major changes in policy. 'Farmers began to complain that other issues in farming were being neglected in the concentration on fuel prices. Fuel was less important for farmers than for hauliers.' (Doherty *et al.*, 2003, p.6).

In 2001 the FFA claimed the credit for an increase in in-store milk prices announced by retailers in January 2001, but the retailers responded that the decision was driven by an economic decision to restore margins. When they targeted nine milk distribution depots later in the month, the police took a tougher line than usual, threatening them with arrest if they tried to prevent lorries leaving the depots. In August 2002 FFA attempted to organize a one day national strike by farmers, but only one in five farmers took part.

In 2003, however, FFA had a major success with the German owned supermarket chain, Lidl, a ruthless discounter of prices in its shops. First, FFA blockaded its distribution depots after it failed to pass on a price increase to processors. After Lidl gave way on this issue, it was subsequently prevented from going ahead with a proposed 1.3 per litre cut in milk prices. This was a substantial victory for the advocates of direct action. Subsequently, the chair of the NFU's milk committee sought a meeting with FFA to see if the two groups could find common ground to tackle problems in the dairy sector. It is unclear if the NFU's leadership approved this move, although they can hardly have been unaware of it. It suggests that the NFU may be at least considering a more cooperative approach towards the FFA. However, this could not go too far without the NFU surrendering the insider strategy that has been the key to its success. As the FFA has stated, 'the difference between them and us is that we are not too close to government' (http://www.farmersforaction.org/ press release 16 August 2002).

Future Prospects

The leading farm organizations are successful on at least two criteria. They continue to be well run, highly professional, generally respected organizations that are financially stable, even if they have had to make some reduction in staff. Despite the decline of the importance of farming in the economy, they continue to enjoy contacts in government up to prime minister level and exert a substantial influence on policy, although the replacement of MAFF by DEFRA is a setback. The CAP continues to deliver high levels of subsidy and protection to farmers. Recent moves towards renationalization of the CAP give greater scope for the exercise of influence at domestic level, e.g., the NFU's request for the complete decoupling of subsidies.

Where they do less well is in terms of member satisfaction despite all their evident successes. Farming in Britain has gone through a difficult period, but there are deeper problems. It is evident from the farming press that many farmers are still trapped in a productionist mindset where whatever they produce will be purchased, regardless of the market or consumer preferences. Many farmers still hanker for an environment in which there is an 'orderly' market underwritten and regulated by government. One indicator of this is the way in which some farming commentators have seen the events of September 2001 and subsequent concerns about terrorism as a means of reviving traditional food security discourses and hence reducing exposure to foreign competition. Farming leaders see discourses about 'multifunctionality' as a means of preserving subsidies that would be more in tune with contemporary public opinion. However, a comment made by the director of the Ramblers Association in 1990 still applies today: 'We think the NFU is one of the most effective pressure groups in the country but they are prisoners of their backward-looking members who have not kept abreast with changing public opinion' (*Farmers Weekly*, 16 March 1990).

The membership base of farming organizations has declined, and become more diverse, but the NFU and the CLA have responded to this challenge in innovative ways. Internal organizational unity has been maintained and there has been an effort to relate to changing public opinion. The perception that insider strategies are no longer working leads to a demand for more radical forms of action that has been met by FFA. As FFA has become more successful, the dilemmas it has produced for the established organizations have become more acute. The NFU has pursued a strategy of attempting to deny it legitimacy, but has become increasingly difficult to maintain. To the dismay of the NFU, the NFUS has gone down a different route of establishing a dialogue with FFA and the NFU now appears to be making tentative steps in that direction. The NFUS has also emphasized establishing a dialogue with environmental and conservation bodies (Halpin and Jordan, 2003, p.20).

The underlying problem is that many smaller farmers feel economically and psychologically vulnerable (stress is high in rural areas on a range of indicators). They can see that trade liberalization and other globalizing forces, along with changes in public attitudes, are changing the context in which they work, but their traditional values and mindsets give them little guidance on how to respond. One possible, but not very positive, response is to assert those traditional values more forcefully and demand a return to protected domestic production. However, power is not going to flow back down the food chain from retailers as surrogate representatives of consumers, nor are forces pressing for agricultural trade liberalization going to disappear. In these circumstances, the vigorous rhetoric and dramatic actions of the FFA offer to many a more appealing response to crisis than the apparent timidity and collusive tactics of the NFU, even though they have earned substantial policy concessions. However, one of the constraints of being an 'insider' is that you have to limit your demands to what is achievable in the current political climate. That may seem inadequate to a farmer whose livelihood is threatened.

It is difficult to predict what the outcome of the present state of flux in farmer representation in Britain will be. The emergence of more broadly based rural organizations with a rural policy focus in response to changing government priorities is one possibility, but the internal heterogeneity of such organizations might prevent them being credible participants in the policy process. Despite the threat of breakaways, and the emergence of shadowy formations like the CFG, the NFU is likely to survive as the voice of bigger farmers. It will also continue to attract many small farmers, if only because of the services it provides. However, the FFA is not going to disappear. The NFU and the CLA may undergo a slow decline in influence because of other political forces in society, but the FFA will not supplant them. What one is seeing played out in the farming arena is part of a set of wider changes in British pressure politics in which, against the background of changes in the nature of the state, insider strategies are no longer seen as necessarily the best way of being politically effective.

References

Doherty, B., Paterson, M., Plows, A., and Wall, D. (2003), 'Explaining the fuel protests', *The British Journal of Politics and International Relations*, Vol. 5, pp.1-23.

Greer, A. (2003), 'Countryside Issues: a Creeping Crisis', *Parliamentary Affairs*, Vol. 56, pp. 523-42.

Halpin, D. and Jordan, G. (2003), 'Resiliency and Adaptation Amongst Agricultural Interest Groups: Strategies for Survival Amongst Scottish Agricultural Organisations', unpublished working paper, University of Aberdeen.

Madgwick, P.J. with N. Griffiths and V. Walker (1973), *The Politics of Rural Wales: a study of Cardiganshire*, London, Hutchinson.

Moran, M. (2003), *The British Regulatory State*, Oxford, Oxford University Press.

Newby, H. (1980), *Green and Pleasant Land? Social Change in Rural England*, Harmondsworth, Penguin.

Newby, H., Bell, C., Rose, D. and Saunders, D. (1978), *Property, Paternalism and Power: Class and Control in Rural England*, London, Hutchinson.

Plumb, H. (2001), *The Plumb Line*, No location, Greycoat Press.

Roberts, S. (2002), *Key Drivers of Economic Development and Inclusion in Rural Areas*, London, DEFRA.

Robinson, N. (2002), 'The Politics of the Fuel Protests: Towards a Multi-Dimensional Explanation', *Political Quarterly*, Vol. 73(1), pp.58-66.

Shephard, G. (2000), *Shephard's Watch*, London, Politico's.

Smith, M.J. (1989), 'The Annual Review: the Emergence of a Corporatist Institution?', *Political Studies*, Vol. 37, pp.81-96.

Williams, T. (Lord Williams of Barnburgh) (1965), *Digging for Britain*, London, Hutchinson.

Wilt, A.F. (2001), *Food for War: Agricultural Rearmament in Britain before the Second World War*, Oxford, Oxford University Press.

Wilson, G. (1975), 'The Policy Making Process in British Agriculture' in D. Murray, R. Thomas, W. Grant and N. Smith (eds.) *Decision Making in Britain: Agriculture, Parts 6-9*, Milton Keynes, Open University Press.

Winter, R. (1996), *Rural Politics*, London: Routledge.

Woods, M. (2002) 'Was There a Rural Rebellion? Labour and the Countryside Vote in the 2001 General Election', in L. Bennie, C. Rallings, J. Tonge and P. Webb (eds.) *British Elections and Parties Review*, Volume 12, London, Frank Cass.

Chapter 3

Farm Interest Groups in Ireland: Adaptation, Partnership and Resilience

Alan Greer

Introduction

This chapter considers the nature of farm interest group politics in Ireland, focused primarily on farm interest structures in the Republic of Ireland – notably the Irish Farmers' Association (IFA) and also the Irish Creamery Milk Suppliers' Association (ICMSA). The chapter begins with an overview of the interest group system, set within an overall economic, political and ideological framework. The history, internal governance, objectives and core policies of the main farmers' organizations, and the pattern of their interactions with the state, are then discussed. Of particular importance is their response to contemporary policy debates about globalization, agricultural policy reform and trade liberalization. One important aspect of farm interest systems in Ireland concerns the relationships between associations north and south of the border, particularly between the IFA and the Ulster Farmers' Union (UFU). This is viewed in the context of the institutional innovations for cross-border cooperation introduced as part of the 1998 Belfast Agreement. The relative success of farm interest organizations and their response to the pressures they face – their resilience or decline – is then evaluated in the light of contemporary opportunities and challenges.

Similar Conditions, Different Institutions

Farm interest group systems in Ireland reflect the fundamental political cleavage between unionism and nationalism, which led to the creation of separate political and administrative systems after partition in 1921. Two parallel interest worlds developed, based around institutional structures for agriculture operating in Dublin and Belfast. A major difference is that interest aggregation in Northern Ireland took an essentially regional character. So whereas governments in the Republic of Ireland identified the promotion of the agri-food sector as a national priority, the interests of Northern Ireland always have been mediated through a UK prism, even when there is a locally elected government. Because farming interests are less politically salient for British governments, there are frequent complaints that, in terms of state support, the agri-food sector in Northern Ireland suffers by comparison with its counterpart in the south. Indeed it has been argued, usually by nationalists, that the interests of Northern Ireland farmers would in the past have been better protected by the policy priorities followed by the Irish government, particularly on CAP issues (Greer, 1996, pp.166-70).

Crucial to such arguments is that the basic political divide does not reflect socio-economic or structural differences. A temperate climate and the proximity of the British market promoted the development of a grassland-based, export-oriented, system of livestock production. Land reform in the late nineteenth and early twentieth centuries produced an agricultural sector dominated by relatively small owner-occupied family farms. This structure still persists, despite long-term trends to fewer and larger holdings. Since 1970, agricultural employment (including hunting, forestry and fishing) in the Republic of Ireland has fallen from twenty seven per cent of total civilian employment to just seven per cent in 2002. The Republic of Ireland has around 142,000 holdings with 114,000 individuals for whom farming provides the primary source of income; Northern Ireland has an agricultural labour force of 54,000, working in just over 28,000 farm businesses. Of these, around sixty per cent (34,000) are farmers and partners, of whom fifty seven per cent are full time. Forty four per cent of holdings in the Republic of Ireland are smaller than twenty hectares, seventeen per cent larger than fifty (although these account for forty five per cent of total agricultural area). In the north, around half of farm businesses are classified as very small and unlikely to provide full-time employment or an adequate income solely from farming activities.

The political centrality of agriculture is underpinned by its 'disproportionate contribution to the local economy, balance of trade and employment' (Collins, 1995, p.664). In both cases, the agri-food sector contributes around ten per cent of total employment and eight per cent of GDP. Both are heavily dependent on external trade, for example accounting for seven per cent of total exports from the Republic of Ireland. So while overriding political imperatives produced separate institutional arrangements, the socio-economic structures of the agri-food sectors are very similar. Consequently it is often noted that there is a 'commonality of interest between farmers in the Republic and in Northern Ireland' that has 'profound implications both for policy and for the way in which policy is developed' (British-Irish Inter-Parliamentary Body, 1999, para. 50). In recent years this assumption about commonality has underpinned the development of cross-border institutional structures in the agri-food sector, notably as a result of the 1998 Belfast Agreement.

Farm Interest Groups in the Republic of Ireland

Farm interest group systems in both parts of Ireland have been dominated by a small number of farmers' associations, which aspire to horizontal representation across a wide variety of product sectors. Alternative 'outsider' organizations at times articulate a critique of the established policy paradigms on which the programmes of the dominant groups are built. There are also some sub-sectoral associations, especially in the milk sector but also in newer production niches such as organic farming. For example three organizations represent the organic agriculture community in the Republic, the biggest of which is the Irish Organic Farmers and Growers Association (Greer, 2002; Tovey, 1997). Farmers' co-operatives remain important too, represented by peak associations such as the Irish Co-operative Organisation Society and the Ulster Agricultural Organisation Society.

The roots of agricultural organization in Ireland were put down during the First World War, when state control of food production prompted the creation of structures for farm interest representation, for example the Dublin-based Irish Farmers Union (IFU). However this proved ephemeral, partly because of its initial emphasis on party political activity as the best vehicle for promoting agricultural interests. Although the IFU's own machinery, the Farmers' Party, won around ten per cent of the vote in early elections to the Irish parliament, it attracted the support of only a small number of farmers. Instead agricultural interests were mediated primarily through the main political parties. So Fine Gael, which absorbed the rump of the Farmers' Party in the early 1930s, became the voice of the more commercially oriented livestock producers reliant on the British market (who had dominated the IFU). Fianna Fáil, politically dominant from the 1930s, drew on the support of more marginal peasant-type farmers and the 'landless', but it also presented itself as the 'national' party, capable of appealing to all parts of society.

A combination of social, economic, political and cultural factors produce a favourable environment in which farm interest groups operate. The public, representatives, parties and governments are all generally sympathetic to the agri-food sector. This does not mean that there are no disagreements; however it does provide a structural advantage that helps to underpin the resilience of farm interest groups in the face of challenges. Agriculture remains crucial, both because of its economic importance and of its symbolic appeal. Elements of rural fundamentalism, including a positive attachment to the maintenance of a large number of family-owned farms, still persist and 'for many, farmers and non-farmers alike, land is by no means simply a resource to be exploited and managed' (Chubb, 1992, p.13). The Single Transferable Vote (STV) election system and localist political culture ensure that agricultural issues remain influential in electoral politics. The political cleavage, where large livestock farmers identify with Fine Gael, smaller farmers with Fianna Fáil, still helps to shape voting patterns, and farmers make up a particularly sizeable element in support for Fine Gael. Twenty-one of the 166 Dáil deputies (TDs) elected in 2002 were farmers (thirteen per cent). Indeed the number of farmers elected 'has remained unaltered despite the shrinking number of farmers in the workforce, and farmers remain a significant force in both the Fianna Fáil and Fine Gael Dáil groups' (Gallagher, 2003, pp.114-15). For both main parties, the promotion of the agri-food sector is a core priority, and neither is likely to go into an election pledged to abolish export subsidies or cut farm spending. The high salience of agricultural and rural policy in Irish politics is also reflected in the frequency with which questions in the Dáil deal with the CAP and the structural funds' (Laffan, 1996, p.303). A high profile in one of the main farmers' associations can facilitate a political career. For example, Tom Parlon, ex-President of the Irish Farmers' Association, was elected as a Progressive Democrat TD in 2002, having initially flirted with Fine Gael (Gallagher *et al.*, 2003, pp.40, 45). Farm organizations may try to influence electoral politics by mobilizing the rural vote. In a bitter dispute with the government over the implementation of the EU Nitrates Directive in 2004 for example, one body pledged to 'make every effort to ensure that this issue moves into the spotlight for the European and local elections' and urged farmers 'to ascertain where each and every candidate who comes to their door stands on this issue' (www.icmsa.ie).

Origins

The two core agricultural organizations in the Republic of Ireland emerged in the 1950s – the Irish Creamery Milk Suppliers' Association (ICMSA) and the Irish Farmers' Association (IFA). Both had their roots in the Young Farmers' Clubs formed in 1944 (now known as *Macra na Fierme*), which emphasized progress through education, training and development (Breen *et al.*, 1990, pp.202-3). A National Farmers' Association (NFA) was established in Dublin in January 1955 to create an organization that could present a coherent national voice for all Irish farmers on all issues. In 1971 the NFA merged with several smaller associations (the Irish Sugar Beet Growers' Association, the Irish Commercial Horticultural Association, Leinster Milk Producers and Cork Milk Producers) to establish the Irish Farmers' Association. Today the IFA is the largest and dominant organization with around 85,000 members.

With a membership of around 40,000, the Irish Creamery Milk Suppliers' Association was founded in 1950. As its name indicates, ICMSA emerged initially to mobilize dairy farmers against low milk prices. It too brought together several small regional farmers groups (such as the Cavan Milk Suppliers Association) to combine their efforts in a larger and stronger 'national' organization. Initially it represented around 100,000 dairy farmers from all over the country but subsequently broadened its appeal to livestock producers generally.

Internal Governance

Two themes underpin the structure for internal governance operated by the IFA and ICMSA: democracy and professional expertise. These are embodied in the overlapping relationship between members and employees. The IFA regards its structure as central to its success and development, allowing it to 'function as an effective voice for Irish Farmers as an entirely democratic organization' (www.ifa.ie). The basic building blocks of both associations are their members, and an annual financial subscription paid by individual farmers provides the bulk of financial resources. In ICMSA for example, some ninety four per cent of total income is obtained in this way.

To allow the views of members to be reflected in policies and operations, structures have been developed that draw on the basic principle of democratic election. In the IFA, members are organized in over 900 local branches and 29 County Executives (the basis for a system of commodity committees), each with their own elected leaders. Some 3000 elected voluntary staff 'work with branches to ensure well thought and democratically decided policy is pursued'. At the apex of the structure stands the President, elected by the membership at the annual general meeting. A 68 member National Council is made up of a representative from each of the County Executives, chairs of the National Commodity Committees and Sections, and the National Officers Board (including the President and four Regional Vice Presidents). This is the governing body and meets around ten times per year. A smaller National Executive meets six times a year, often to discuss issues that concern more than one commodity committee before final decision in the National Council. Essentially much of the day-to-day work of the IFA is carried out in twenty-two committees and sections. These mainly are commodity based (milk, sheep etc) but also include horizontal bodies such as those for 'Rural Development' and the 'Farm Family'.

ICMSA describes itself as 'a democratic, non-denominational, non-political body'. A democratic organizational structure 'enables farmers to voice their opinion at branch level which leads to their view being echoed by their representatives at county, regional and national levels'. The result is that 'the aims and aspirations of the grassroots membership can be reflected in the policies adopted by the Association'. Much of the work of ICMSA is carried out at local level where members organize regular meetings and seminars. The 25 County and Area committees are drawn from local branches and these elect representatives onto the 61-member National Council, which is the principal policy-making body, meeting approximately eight times a year. Among its primary roles is the election of the President and the Administrative Committee, which meets approximately every month and manages the day-to-day affairs of the organization. Six functional committees cover the main policy themes: dairy, beef, sheep, tax, farm services, and rural development.

Parallel to the democratic membership structure is the full-time and part-time appointed staff. Both are headed by a General Secretary (also known as the Chief Executive Officer in the IFA), who has a central role in co-ordinating policy and organizational resources, the communication, coordination and implementation of policy decisions, and managing the day-to-day affairs of the organization. ICMSA has around fifteen staff, which it describes as 'professional'. The larger IFA has a more extensive professional, executive and administrative apparatus of over fifty. Around half of these work full-time in the association's Dublin headquarters, and are described by the IFA as 'highly motivated and experienced', with 'strong links with the relevant Divisions in the Department of Agriculture and in the European Commission and with their counterparts in other farm organizations across Europe' (www.ifa.ie). For example the Economics Section, led by a full-time Chief Economist, provides 'detailed analysis and research on national, EU and international farm and economic policy developments. This work is critical to the success of IFA's negotiations and representations at all levels and in all commodity sections'. Twenty-five development officers/administrators staff twelve regional offices and three sub-offices, working closely with the locally elected branch officers. Their main functions are to maintain the membership and income support structures of the IFA and to provide vital assistance to members on matters such as grant applications, as well as maintaining close contact with the local media.

Aims, Functions and Policies

As organizations dedicated to the welfare of their members, the IFA and ICMSA combine several vital functions ranging from representation to specific member services and benefits. These include policy development, representation of farmers' interests 'outside the farm gate', the provision of advice and the supply of other membership benefits. Expertise and advice for example is provided on problems concerning CAP payments, taxation, and on the complex regulatory requirements attached to environmental, animal welfare and food safety interventions. The IFA stresses the vital importance of its expert advice and professional back up functions, for example monitoring prices and assisting with credit problems. Membership incentives take the form of a comprehensive package of benefits for fully paid up members. These include personal accident cover, discounted insurance, tax advice, IT/telephone facilities, and a variety of leisure and holiday benefits such as free travel insurance and discounts on Irish Sea ferry crossings.

While many officials probably spend most of their time providing advice to members, the public face of farmers' organizations is their policy work. Generally the IFA describes itself as an effective organization, which is acknowledged by a wide range of policy actors at local, national, European and international levels, including the Irish government, the European Commission and political parties. It argues that it has played 'a central role' in the 'spectacular development' of the Irish agriculture and food industry since the 1950s. ICMSA too stresses its communication/information and expert/advisory functions, for example on matters such as taxation, rural development and farm services. Membership benefits include discounted insurance and access to a highly professional staff. According to ICMSA it 'quickly became a powerful lobbying force' and remains an 'effective lobbying body from ground to national level' with a 'proven track record of delivering for Irish farmers'. Delivering its policy priorities such as fair farm incomes requires,

> ... an active and a well-funded organization to constantly bring forward policies to overcome obstacles and to harness opportunities. ICMSA today has the ability and the confidence to lobby effectively at local, national and European level in the interest of the family farm. We are an organization driven by commitment, concern, and realistic well researched policies.

Farm associations are repositories of beliefs and values that inform their public policy stances, for example about the social and economic importance of agriculture and the rural world. Essentially the dichotomous network pattern in Ireland is not constructed on structural differences or policy preferences. For both organizations the defence of rural life equates with a primary concern with the level of farm incomes, which is reflected in policy priorities at all levels. The IFA stresses the desirability of using state intervention to underpin the maintenance of the maximum number of farm families on the land with appropriate incomes. 'Fair incomes' for the maximum number of family farms is the 'core objective' of ICMSA also. However, in its public rhetoric at least, it puts more emphasis on the defence of 'family farming', especially the need to ensure the viability of small and medium-sized farms. According to its own publicity, ICMSA 'became renowned for its staunch defence of all farm families, so much so that over the years it became known as the Family Farm Organisation'. It argues that its credibility derives from its consistent record in fighting for the family farm structure, which is 'a positive and valuable system that should be developed and not undermined'. To this end there should be no diminution in the contribution made by agriculture to the national economy and the 'greatest injustice done to the farming community is the withdrawal of incentives for marginal farm families to remain working and earning a living from the land'. Consequently 'the biggest challenge' it faces is to 'convince the Government to introduce policies aimed at stemming the exodus from farming'.

So although there are variations in emphasis, there is little substantive difference between ICMSA and IFA on many important high policy issues. Regulation, especially in relation to cross-compliance with environmental, food safety and animal welfare requirements, is increasingly important to both, not least because 'unnecessary red tape' compromises farmers' ability to increase incomes by restricting the development of 'progressive' agriculture. On the implementation of the EU Nitrates Directive for example, the proposals for which were published in spring 2004, both organizations were extremely critical of the approach adopted by the government. The IFA 'rejected out of hand' the strict nitrogen limits proposed because it would 'shackle our best farmers for no benefit to the environment' and pose a 'serious threat to the viability of our farming sector' ('IFA Rejects Strategy on Nitrates Directive', www.ifa.ie). Similarly ICMSA argued that the enforcement of low nitrate application rates would 'force over 13,000 farmers to reduce production to a level that will drastically reduce their incomes' and accused the government of 'sabotaging progressive farming in Ireland'. The government's 'absolutely unacceptable' approach would 'place a complete block on the development of farming – particularly dairy farming' and indicates that it 'no longer seems to care for the welfare or future of farming' ('Progressive Farming in Ireland has been Sabotaged', www.ICMSA.ie).

The glue that has held together the policies of farm interest organizations in Ireland is the defence of agricultural exceptionalism and of the state-assisted paradigm. Historically their ability to do this has been greatly assisted by the priority attached to the agricultural sector by the state. At the end of the 1960s, Irish agriculture was still small-scale and relatively under-modernised. The development of 'progressive' farming through state-assisted' modernization has dominated agricultural policy throughout Ireland since then, and the Irish state has accorded agriculture 'a special status, both for its own strategic importance and as a key industry for the promotion of economic growth' (Adshead, 1996, p.604). The dramatic transformation, attributed largely to the positive benefits of EU membership, helps to explain the continued popularity of the CAP among large sections of the Irish public, not just in rural areas. Indeed the net budget advantage from the CAP in 2002 has been estimated at over €1.4 billion (Irish Department of Agriculture and Food, 2003). Moreover the CAP has never been regarded simply as a sectoral policy for agriculture but a way to increase national wealth overall and of 'securing the socio-economic cohesion of rural Ireland itself' (Lowe *et al.*, 1999, p.4).

The major Irish farm organizations elaborate at least two linked responses to challenges to agricultural exceptionalism: resistance to trade liberalization and an effort to maintain firewalls between agriculture and other issues. The defence of protectionism and resistance to extensive agricultural trade liberalization are fundamental policy values. Consequently CAP reform episodes are amongst the most important issues they face. It has been fiercely critical of notions such as co-financing, decoupling (breaking the link between support and production), and modulation (shifting resources to the rural development pillar). Essentially the IFA tries to preserve the advantages that the CAP brings to Irish agriculture, usually by adopting a rejectionist stance on reform proposals, especially those that would impact adversely on the livestock sector. For example the IFA argued that its activities helped to roll back the severity of the initial Agenda 2000 proposals in three crucial areas – discriminatory allocation of milk quota, failure to provide full compensation for price cuts, and the imbalance between extensive and intensive beef production.

Opposition to substantial trade liberalization is a corollary of the defence of the CAP. A basic stance is the rejection of a link between CAP reform and the wider trade context. In particular, another re-negotiation of the CAP in the WTO talks is unacceptable because it would mean that Europe would 'pay twice' to secure an agreement. Specific policy preferences include the retention of export subsidies, and the 'blue' and 'green' boxes, in which some protectionist measures are exempted from tariff reduction commitments. In May 2004 for example, the IFA objected to a renewed EU initiative (made jointly by the Agriculture and Trade commissioners, Fischler and Lamy) to phase out export refunds and allow extra beef imports. For the IFA this offer exceeded the negotiating mandate agreed by the Agriculture Council in early 2003 but also would 'damage Ireland most' because of its small domestic market and high export dependence. Overall the proposal was 'a move too far and a sell out of agriculture for little or no gain'. It was 'not acceptable that farmers are being asked to foot the bill again for a WTO deal', having already 'paid a very heavy price' under Agenda 2000 and the Mid-term review. Agriculture 'simply cannot take any further cuts on refunds or imports' ('Ireland could be greatest loser from Fischler export refund proposal', press release 11/5/2004, www.ifa.ie).

A second response to the challenge to agricultural exceptionalism is the attempt by farm organizations to maintain firewalls between agriculture and other sectors, most notably those relating to the environment, public health and wider rural development. Essentially this involves trying to perpetuate long-established closed policy network structures that privileges the IFA and ICMSA as the dominant sectoral organizations. In recent years however, this pattern has been challenged from within the sector and from outside. The IFA is a strong defender of the established approach that emphasises the primary vocation of farmers as food producers operating in a commercial and market environment – what is referred to as 'progressive' farming. To this extent its vision is for an agriculture that is efficient, competitive, responsive to consumer and market demands but which also provides the bedrock for prosperous and thriving rural communities. However this vision has been challenged from within the sector itself, undermined by the crises in the CAP, the environmental critique, and by high profile food scares and outbreaks of animal disease such as BSE and FMD. The effect has been to produce a greater politicisation of agricultural policy, linked to an (admittedly limited) opening up of the network to a wider range of participants, many of whom are critical of the 'productionist' paradigm. So while the Irish agricultural policy community is characterized by the 'effective exclusion of alternative farming interests' (Adshead, 1996, p.598), some smaller groups advocate different visions of rural life and forms of production. At times, organizations representing marginal, 'non-viable' producers such as the United Farmers Association (UFA) articulate a 'small scale rural populism' that is critical of the commercial orientation of the CAP (Flynn and Lowe, 1996, p.4). Such groups, including those representing the organic sector, are more open to proposals that challenge the granting of subsidies for large intensive farmers and are more sympathetic to compensatory social and environmental policies. Indeed some even suggest that the environment is beginning to re-open the 'myth of unity between Irish farmers' (Flynn and Lowe, 1996, p.13). However groups such as the UFA have been unable to challenge the established network, not least because the core value about progressive agriculture also is at the heart of government policy.

Broader issues related to trade, the environment and integrated rural development also has challenged the 'agricultural' vision of the IFA and ICMSA. Trade unions, industrial leaders and even some agri-business concerns have been critical of protectionism, arguing that Ireland is 'first and foremost an industrial trading nation with a very open economy' that will benefit from liberalization (Flynn and Lowe, 1996, p.4). In Ireland generally the environmental critique of agricultural policy was slow to emerge. Until very recently agriculture has been widely regarded as making a positive contribution to the environment, buttressed by the 'much touted "green" image' (Flynn and Lowe, 1996, p.9). However the dissemination of this 'green' international image, linked to natural and quality food, is informed more by a concern to retain the valuable export markets threatened by crises such as BSE than by environmental considerations. Increasingly also organic farming has been reinterpreted as a valuable element of the broader commercial vision rather than a critique of industrial production methods (Greer, 2002).

In both parts of Ireland the dominant agricultural policy community has therefore been relatively successful in containing environmental issues within the productivist agricultural framework. This is also evident in the area of rural development. Although policy pays lip service to its multifaceted character, rural development has been subverted and redefined to the agricultural paradigm in which market responsive and efficient production is the core objective. So while the economic and social development of rural areas may no longer be synonymous with farming, agriculture is still regarded as the most important component of policy interventions designed to underpin the fabric of the countryside. This points to tensions at the very heart of the idea of multifunctionality or the 'European model' of agriculture. If this denotes the contribution that farming makes to a wide range of public goods as well as food production, then its logic is a weakening of the boundaries between agriculture and other concerns, not the maintenance of the firewalls advocated by the dominant farm organizations. For them, however, the notion of multifunctional agriculture is simply a contemporary version of the long-established state-assisted paradigm that has its roots in cultural assumptions about the importance of farming in underpinning social cohesion, and even of national unity itself.

Group-State Relations

The creation of functional departments of agriculture allowed policy issues to be managed within a relatively insulated bureaucratic structure. Relatively few public actors are involved in agricultural policy in the Republic where the Department of Agriculture is 'unrivalled as the formal governmental core' of the policy network (Collins, 1995, p.667). On the other hand the relative importance of agriculture means that rural issues often become matters of high politics, whose handling involves other key actors in the political system. Crucially this functional bureaucratic structure facilitates the development of close links with farm organizations. Historically the state has influenced the development of the farm interest systems. In the north, for example, the regional government sponsored the Ulster Farmers' Union because it wished to enlist the support of 'progressive' farmers in a programme of agricultural modernization. The Irish government formally recognized the IFA in the late 1960s because the state again saw the benefits of working alongside an established and representative farmers' association. Consequently the pattern of interest intermediation between the state and farmers' associations has taken a meso-corporatist form, typically described in terms of closed policy communities (Adshead, 1996; Collins, 1995; Greer, 1994).

However the early years of farm interest mobilization in the Republic of Ireland were characterized by hostile relationships between groups and the state. Militant tactics and demonstrations were commonplace. In 1953 for example, ICMSA organized a sixteen-day milk strike and in 1966 around 450 of its members were jailed as a result of a campaign on milk prices. The NFA also used direct action in an effort to establish its effectiveness. This was encapsulated when a 'Farmers' Rights march' in Dublin in 1966, followed by a mass rally of 30,000 farmers and a twenty day 'siege' of government buildings, demanded the right to negotiate directly with government. In 1967 farmers organized machinery blockades, a commodity strike and a rates strike. The response of the state was to jail farmers, threaten to ban the NFA and its journal, and to confiscate livestock, machinery and household furniture from demonstrators.

The hostile attitude of government prevented the NFA from achieving its main early priority – recognition by the state as the representative body for Irish farmers. In the late 1960s, however, influenced by imminent EC entry, the Taoiseach, Jack Lynch, recognized NFA as the voice of farmers. Since then, relations between farm organizations and governments have been largely consensual, and crucial policy issues are managed through close consultation at the national level. The construction of consensus is facilitated by the localism of the political system, personal ties and informal patterns of interaction between relatively small political and professional elites. Agricultural policy-making in the Republic of Ireland also takes place within an over-arching system of national socio-economic management, based upon agreement between the state and the 'social partners', which emerged in the late 1980s. Breen *et al.* note for example, that farmers have 'become more involved, both formally and informally, in the corporatist arrangements of the Irish state' (1990, p.202). As made explicit in the sixth programme – 'Sustaining Progress: Social Partnership Agreement 2003-05' – social partnership is viewed as a dialogue and 'problem solving process' that provides 'a coherent and focused strategy for managing the interlocking elements of the economy and the behaviour of economic and social policies' (Department of the Taoiseach, 2003, chap. 1.4). It embodies the recognition that 'problems can best be solved in modern governance only with the active involvement of the relevant stakeholders'. In this arrangement, the government 'has a unique role in the partnership process. It provides the arena within which the process operates. It shares some of its authority with social partners. In some parts of the wider policy process, it actively supports the formation of interest organizations' (Department of the Taoiseach, 2003, chap. 1.4).

These programmes provided the opportunity for the IFA and ICMSA to embed themselves into interest intermediation structures at the national level. So under the farming element of the Programme for National Recovery negotiated in 1987 the IFA achieved the status of social partner alongside government, employers and trade unions. ICMSA also can be viewed as a core element of the agricultural policy network, but although it is incorporated into these structures, it is the IFA that is regarded as the crucial social partner for rural interests. The IFA has a good working relationship with the agriculture department based on mutual respect, trust, credibility and consensus. Indeed formal meetings often 'sew up loose ends already decided upon in informal meetings' (Adshead, 1996, p.593). On the Agenda 2000 proposals for example, the Irish Ministry of Agriculture set up four consultative groups on beef, milk, cereals and rural development. There were regular consultations, often informal, with the IFA and other main farm organizations. The Minister commented that he had 'shared all the proposals and our papers in relation to them with the social partners, farmers and their representative associations.' Consistent also with the advantages of network arrangements, the Minister added that he found such consultation arrangements 'very helpful in enabling me to gauge the strength of opposition to these proposals by Irish producers and the Irish agriculture industry' (*Dáil Debates*, 17 February 1999).

Nonetheless such mechanisms are prone to occasional rupture. According to the Taoiseach, while the IFA has 'established itself as one of the leading forces in Irish society', this does not rule out trenchant criticism of government policy. Indeed the government is 'well aware that the IFA is an organization that will always speak clearly and fearlessly on behalf of its own members' (Department of the Taoiseach, 1999b). In 2004, ICMSA interpreted the government's tough stance on the implementation of the Nitrates directive as a breach of the 'Sustaining Progress' agreement, and its President 'reluctantly' recommended to the National Council that the Association withdraw from the agreement. Indeed it tried to appeal over the heads of departmental ministers by writing directly to the Taoiseach, 'strongly urging him to take a direct and personal involvement in securing the changes necessary for the survival of progressive farming in our country' ('Progressive Farming in Ireland has been Sabotaged', www.ICMSA.ie).

Farm Interest Groups in Northern Ireland and Cross Border Cooperation

Greater cooperation between organizations in the Republic of Ireland and Northern Ireland provides a potential avenue for the strengthening of farm interest representation in Ireland as a whole. In the north, unionist hegemony after 1921 militated against the emergence of farmers' parties. The main vehicle for the representation of agricultural interests became the Belfast-based Ulster Farmers' Union (UFU), established in 1917 as a general association to represent producers across all production branches. The UFU identifies its central objective as the promotion of the interests of farmers and growers in Northern Ireland both at home and abroad through professional lobbying. Although resource pressures threatened its continued existence at times, it emerged as a dominant monopolistic representative body for farmers, bolstered by the development of a close relationship with the regional government. Indeed while party political neutrality was presented as a formal value by the UFU, its influence derived in reality from its close connections with the dominant Ulster Unionist Party, which governed the province between 1921 and 1972 (Greer, 1996, 1994).

The UFU remains at the core of the policy network in Northern Ireland and retains very close links with the regional Department of Agriculture, often lubricated by personal contacts. It also has a history of working closely with its partner associations in Britain (NFU, NFUS), especially in the context of national UK policy prior to EU entry. Recently however these relationships have become increasingly strained, for example on high profile issues such as BSE and FMD but also because financial retrenchment has made it difficult to accommodate differences on important issues. For many years, the UFU's structural relationship with the state helped to prevent the formation of a viable rival association, despite several attempts to mobilize marginal producers around an alternative structure in the 1960s. Perhaps not coincidental with wider political upheaval in the early 1970s, notably the collapse of the regional government and entry into the EU, the Northern Ireland Agricultural Producers' Association (NIAPA) was set up in 1975. Despite its emergence however, the UFU has continued to dominate agricultural interest representation in the north. Recently moreover the influence of NIAPA has waned as a result of major internal tensions that have threatened its continued existence.

The UFU-NIAPA division reflects a religious cleavage – NIAPA is based in the western counties where smaller catholic farmers predominate, the UFU represents mainly protestant farmers in eastern counties. However it primarily encapsulates a structural cleavage between commercial and stewardship orientations (viability/non-viability), and between a commitment to end-price and to the maintenance of family farms as the bulwark of rural areas. The UFU has a similar set of high policy concerns and priorities to the IFA. It advocates commercial production and the retention of as many farming families on the land as possible. Its stance on major issues can be characterized as generally lukewarm about radical reforms to world agricultural trading structures and to the CAP, especially in areas such as modulation, degressivity and the dairy sector. NIAPA mainly represents hill farmers in marginal areas and tries to develop links with other small farmer organizations, including through *Coordination Paysanne Européenne* (CPE). It challenges the dominant vision articulated by the UFU, arguing that the productivist approach sacrifices small farmers on the altar of globalization. Indeed the emphasis on 'structural adjustment' is regarded simply as a euphemism for a continued contraction in the number of farmers.

The policy work of the UFU is structured by the requirement that it works within the UK context, not least because the British government establishes the negotiating position on issues such as trade liberalization. Generally this agenda, notably on radical agricultural policy reform, is less sympathetic to the core concerns of the UFU and presents it with a set of problems not experienced by its counterparts in the Republic (although also the advantage of having its interests advocated by a large EU state). So, unlike in the Irish Republic, farming interests in Northern Ireland normally are faced with governments who do not share some of their basic policy priorities. Because of the overarching UK context in which Northern Ireland exists, and the perceived importance of the agri-food sector to the regional economy, the construction of regional consensus has always been of crucial importance to local political elites. This enables the UFU to incorporate its values into a regional agricultural policy framework that reflects its priorities, although it also provides an opportunity for alternative voices to become included in consultation processes. For example, under the leadership of Ian Paisley, the agriculture committees of the Northern Ireland assemblies (1982-86, 1998-2002) emphasized openness to all points of view and tried to generate and co-ordinate a coherent regional policy network by incorporating the main regional farmers unions' and rural development bodies into their work.

Cross-border Cooperation

Collaboration in the agri-food sector is generally accepted as desirable for reasons of efficient and effective policy delivery. However this is cross cut by political tensions. Irish nationalists regard cooperation as a political imperative; on the other hand, after partition unionist leaders' emphasis on the importance of economic ties between Northern Ireland and the rest of the UK far outweighed the desirability of cooperation with the Republic. Indeed until the 1960s north-south relations were characterized by hostility and mutual suspicion. In recent years the main impetus for increased cooperation has been in the context of the search for an overall settlement to the political problems in Ireland. The institutional machinery developed as a result of the 1998 Belfast Agreement to link the Irish political system with devolved institutions in Northern Ireland has the potential to completely refashion the relationship between north and south in agricultural policy. This in turn is likely to stimulate much greater and more intensive cooperation between the respective farm associations.

Crucial in the agricultural sphere are the north-south implementation bodies established in December 1999 (although in abeyance since late 2002 as a result of the wider political stalemate). Of six areas identified for common policy implementation through all-island institutions, the Special European Union Programmes Body (SEUPB) and the Food Safety Promotion Board (FSPB) are directly relevant to agriculture. Agriculture also is one of six designated 'areas of cooperation' where collaboration is to be developed through existing institutional machinery but with separate implementation. Meetings in agricultural format of the North/South Ministerial Council (NSMC, established to oversee the development of cross-border co-operation in policy formulation and implementation) bring together the ministers and departments from the Irish Government and the Northern Ireland Executive. At a meeting of the NSMC in October 2001, ministers noted the 'shared concerns' that emerge from the similarities in agricultural structures. The first plenary meeting of the NSMC in December 1999 agreed that enhanced co-operation in agriculture should focus on the CAP, animal and plant health policy (including an all-island animal health strategy), and research and rural development.

Partition also directly influenced the nature of farm interest structures in Ireland. In 1919 for example there was a failed attempt to create a federal structure that would incorporate both the UFU and the Irish Farmers' Union. Subsequently, practical and political considerations militated against extensive and regular collaboration, exacerbated by the absence of a strong representative farmers' organization in the south that could develop contacts with the UFU. Parallel to the thaw in political relations in the 1960s, some cooperation developed on common policy concerns between the UFU and the NFA, for example on animal disease and EU entry. The overarching policy framework provided by the CAP provided a further imperative to cooperation. Regular informal meetings between the UFU and IFA take place, particularly between commodity committees, facilitated by common membership of COPA. The two organizations recognize each other as representing the vast majority of effective farmers in their respective areas and make joint approaches on CAP and other matters where advantageous. In 1995, in the context of the 'peace process', the UFU and IFA made a joint submission on the future development of agriculture on the island to the Forum for Peace and Reconciliation established by the Irish government.

Generally, relations between the UFU and IFA are characterized by pragmatism, with co-operation justified in terms of its practical benefits rather than in political terms. For the UFU, however, the unionist sympathies of most of its members impose a basic political constraint on cooperation, particularly through formal institutional mechanisms. There is also an ever-present tension in the UFU between advocating a more sympathetic agricultural policy for the UK as a whole, advancing arguments for special treatment for Northern Ireland, and exploiting the advantages of greater north-south cooperation. NIAPA on the other hand sees collaboration across the border as a factor that helps to differentiate it from the UFU and which appeals to its many catholic members. In the early 1990s NIAPA even mooted merger with the southern-based United Farmers' Association (UFA), prompted by a desire to pool resources to meet the expenses of working at the Brussels level. It also has developed links with ICMSA, for example in June 1998 they jointly launched the Cross Border Agricultural Forum to promote the interests of farm families in all parts of Ireland.

Overall the effect of the development of cross-border policy institutions as a result of the Belfast Agreement is likely to increase the incentives for collaboration between farm interest organizations. In January 2001 for example, Bríd Rodgers, Minister for Agriculture and Rural Development in Northern Ireland, met a joint delegation from the UFU and IFA to discuss the potato sector. Unsurprisingly, given her nationalist political identity, she stressed that the 'interests of the agricultural industry in Ireland are common and today's meeting is another milestone in building contacts and co-operation on agricultural issues throughout the island'. Farm associations are especially concerned about the potential disadvantages that might result from different policy approaches. Negotiations in areas such as policy reform and trade liberalization are viewed as crucially important for the future of agriculture throughout Ireland, and requires close liaison to agree negotiating priorities that ensure 'outcomes impact fairly' and do not cause distortions in north-south trade. The UFU especially emphasizes the importance of north and south harmonization of the implementation of CAP reform measures, for example on issues such as modulation and especially in co-ordinating discretionary spending to avoid distortion of the market.

Decline or Resilience?

The influence of farm organizations, and their ability to respond to changing circumstances, depends upon a number of factors including representativeness (the proportion of the total potential membership mobilized), financial resources, expertise and organizational effectiveness, and their level of access to policy institutions. On these criteria the main farmers' associations in the Republic of Ireland, and to a lesser extent in Northern Ireland, have proved resilient in the face of increasing challenges. Representativeness underpins this continued resilience. Whilst the trend in the absolute number of members is downwards, reflecting the continued contraction of the numbers engaged in the industry, the membership density of farmers' associations is stable if not upward. The IFA and ICMSA increasingly represent a *higher proportion* of their *potential* farmer membership. So expressed as a percentage of the 114,000 people in the Republic of Ireland who have farming as their primary source of income, the IFA mobilizes around 75 per cent of Irish farmers; ICMSA approximately 20-25 per cent. In the north, the UFU historically has found it difficult to mobilize even a majority of farmers. Typically however it has always claimed to represent the vast majority of 'progressive' producers, i.e. those who are viable and commercially oriented. UFU membership accounts for just over a third (36 per cent) of the 35,000 full and part-time farmers, excluding spouses, in Northern Ireland. However when calculated on the basis of 20,000 full time farmers, this figure rises to around 70 per cent. In addition the UFU claims to represent more small farmers than NIAPA, with 13,000 farm families as members (which they argue equates to 50,000 individuals), compared to 6,000 in NIAPA.

Farmers' associations are active across a wide range of activities that encompass membership services and policy work. To overcome some of the problems of collective action, members are offered a range of benefits such as insurance discounts and financial services. The administrative complexity of agricultural policy also allows farmers' unions to appeal to potential members on the basis of their expertise, especially assistance with bureaucratic procedures such as form filling and grant applications. The self-image of the IFA is as 'a highly professional, well-resourced, lobby organization whose record of delivery is the envy of many other representative bodies at home and in Europe'. ICMSA is regarded as less ambitious but well organized and respected (Flynn and Lowe, 1996). However there is a continual need to adapt structures to meet changing circumstances. Increasingly the IFA extends the benefits of membership to a wider range of stakeholders, reflected in the development of several different targeted packages, for example covering 'retired', 'associate business', 'farm family', 'forestry', and 'countryside' members. In the Farm Family category, spouses, sons and daughters (over 18 years) of fully paid up members can avail of IFA membership at a special subscription rate. This confers full voting rights, coverage under IFA's personal accident insurance and other benefits. Crucially moreover, the IFA has broadened its range beyond primary agricultural producers, mirroring the approach of other European farm associations. Associate Business membership for example is aimed at businesses who service the industry; IFA Countryside also has been introduced in an effort to mobilize rural dwellers generally, even if they are not farmers (but without full voting rights). For the IFA such developments are a pragmatic response to broader changes in rural society, including the continued fall in the number of producers but concomitant increase in the number of countryside dwellers not engaged directly in the industry.

In April 2004 the IFA also launched a major review of its resources, structures and operating procedures, to be carried out by private consultants with close contacts to the agri-food sector. The key objective of the review, to be completed by July 2004, was a strengthening of the IFA's structure, procedures and communications. Other main terms of reference included an 'assessment of activities and methods against stringent cost benefit analysis', enhancement of 'strategic policy formation, negotiating capacity and delivery of tangible benefits for farmers by equipping the organization to deal effectively with the wide range of institutions and bodies it must engage with', to 'streamline structures and increase efficiency', to 'improve communications with members', and to 'develop existing services and exploit new opportunities for IFA members'. For the IFA President, the central driver of this review was the 'huge challenges for Irish farmers' posed by fundamental reform of agricultural and trade policy at the EU and world levels. Against this backdrop, the time was appropriate 'to put in place improved structures and procedures, capable of meeting the challenges now facing the organization arising from the far-reaching changes in farming'. However, the review was presented not as a panic response from a position of weakness but as prescient incremental reform of a healthy organization, whose membership was at a high level and which was in a strong financial position. The review, according the General Secretary, was intended to ensure that IFA 'continues to be both effective and efficient in meeting the needs of its members and the challenges facing the farming and agricultural sector' ('IFA commences organisational review to meet challenges facing farming sector', press release 28 April 2004, www.ifa.ie).

As this review highlights, with the important international and supranational dimensions to agricultural policy, the resilience of farmers' associations in the face of external challenges depends in part on their effectiveness at these levels. Here the focus of the IFA and ICMSA is on obtaining the best possible treatment for Ireland under the CAP and WTO. At the international level, the IFA and UFU cooperate with other national farm organizations through the International Federation of Agricultural Producers (IFAP). Recognizing the importance of the CAP to Ireland, the IFA set up a permanent office in Brussels and established a 'European Involvement Fund' to provide the necessary resources to fund its growing European activity. It also is the Irish member of COPA, represented on 20 official EU Advisory Committees in addition to 25 COPA Committees. Indeed EU entry strengthened the position of the IFA relative to its rivals because it is the only body with the resources needed to employ full time representatives in Brussels. At the supranational level, groups such as the IFA have 'evolved an informal, yet highly sophisticated network of political contacts, which relies heavily on close personal relationships and a mutual respect between policy actors' (Adshead, 1996, p.597).

However, the crucial factor in the resilience of the IFA is its partnership with the Irish state. The fundamental feature of the Irish agricultural policy community is the high degree of consensus between government and farming interests on the main elements of agricultural policy. This enduring pattern may have something to do with the late modernization of Irish agriculture, driven forward through partnership between 'progressive' farming interests in both civil society and the state. The relationship became especially crucial with EU entry, when it became increasingly necessary to develop common positions that could then be advanced in multi-national negotiations. Indeed for the Taoiseach, the IFA has 'fully grasped the importance of the European and international dimension that is now so important in agriculture policy, and has fully engaged with this process in a sophisticated and effective manner' (Department of the Taoiseach, 1999b).

Essentially the negotiating priorities of the Irish government on high policy issues broadly reflect the dominant values of the IFA. Irish agricultural policy discourse has focused on the defence of the CAP, including opposition to phasing out of export subsidies in WTO negotiations. The net budget advantage from the CAP and the relative economic importance of the agri-food sector underpin a broad consensus on agricultural policy. The benefits gained from the CAP 'encourages co-operation and consensus between the Department of Agriculture and the recognised farming interests' (Adshead, 1996, p.601). A crucial feature is the attempt by governments and interest groups to forge agreement on policy issues. For Irish governments of all political hues, unanimity between the state and rural interests is a core requirement for the defence of the national interest in agricultural negotiations at supranational and international levels. The response of the Irish agricultural policy community to the pressures exerted by WTO negotiations and further CAP reform is to attempt to strengthen the agri-food sector and to manage gradual structural change. In some cases the farm organizations have led the way, for example on the decisions taken about the implementation of the CAP reforms agreed in June 2003. While the Irish government was one of those who argued for flexibility in the Mid Term Review (MTR) negotiations, once the approach had been agreed, farming opinion swung firmly behind full and immediate decoupling. Despite its opposition to decoupling in the negotiations therefore, after consulting with the social partners on the model best suited to Irish requirements – defined as maximizing efficiency, competitiveness and protecting the rural economy – the government announced in October 2003 that Ireland would fully decouple all payments from production from 2005.

So although there are occasional disagreements on specific elements of policy, the IFA and the Irish government are brought together in 'social partnership' and by shared understandings about the importance of the agri-food sector. The relationship between them is one of 'mutual respect and trust'. Indeed for the Taoiseach, Bertie Ahern, the IFA is a key social partner which has played a central role 'in creating a new, positive and effective set of relationships that lie at the very heart of our economic achievements of recent years. It is a model other countries now study as an example of how things should be done' (Department of the Taoiseach, 1999b). So the IFA, according to Ahern, has 'a good and effective working relationship' with the Department of Agriculture 'in working towards a common goal of achieving what is best for Irish agriculture' (Department of the Taoiseach, 1999b).

The IFA remains what Chubb once described as 'without doubt one of the country's most effective pressure groups' and also 'among the most vociferous' (1992, p.113). Both it and ICMSA (and the UFU in the north) share dominant values that centre on the promotion of a modern and viable agriculture and the support of farm incomes, and they tend to take a similar line on major issues such as CAP reform. Within this framework, one way in which farm interest representation in Ireland might be strengthened is through a process of merger. IFA and ICMSA were themselves initially the products of merger between several smaller groups and their integration in a single organization would produce a larger and better-resourced body. However personal and organizational tensions have 'inhibited the development of a single body to speak for all agricultural interests' (Chubb, 1992, p.113). So despite occasional suggestions for merger, rivalry between ICMSA and IFA, which itself emphasizes the need for 'strength in unity', remains 'an important feature of the network' and public exchanges are 'frequently less than friendly' (Collins, 1995, p.672). The large degree of policy consensus so far has proved insufficient to overcome the barriers to merger, several attempts at which over the years have failed.

In terms of cross-border relationships, north-south mergers are clearly a long way off. Nonetheless greater cooperation is likely. The advantage for both the IFA and UFU is that a common policy framework for Ireland as a whole will be predicated on the core elements of their shared 'progressive' agricultural vision. This includes a continued justification for agricultural exceptionalism, portrayed in terms of the multifunctional European model in which the CAP is defended and trade liberalization resisted. On the other hand, one of the main challenges to the IFA and UFU is likely to concern their ability to articulate an inclusive agricultural vision that all farmers can buy into, irrespective of their scale or production orientation. For Breen *et al.* a notable feature of the Irish policy network has been the ability of the IFA to negate internal differences amongst farmers. This is attributed to several factors including the still pervasive ideology of the family farm and the common heritage of most farmers in the land struggle that was central in the national independence movement (1990, pp.206-7). However tensions resulting from further CAP reform and world trade liberalization may exacerbate internal divisions within farm organizations, with some producers increasingly advocating greater commercial freedom. For example it has been suggested that views on trade liberalization in Ireland may be more positive than often assumed. There are competitive and agri-business elements in the agricultural sector for whom the liberalization agenda is appealing, for example with 'growing disgruntlement' among younger farmers about the restrictions of milk quotas (Flynn and Lowe, 1996, p.10). So there is a strand of opinion that views further liberalization of the CAP 'as unavoidable and probably advantageous to the more commercial, export-oriented sectors of Irish agriculture' (Lowe *et al.*, 1999, p.14). A two-speed agriculture may be emerging, in which a small number of highly competitive producers operate at close to world market prices, albeit within environmental constraints, alongside a sector of small niche producers supported by direct payments for tourism, alternative enterprizes, and environmental stewardship. For general farmers' associations the problem is how to reconcile such tensions, especially in times of financial retrenchment. Accordingly the main challenge for groups such as the IFA, ICMSA and UFU, who until now have proved remarkably resilient, may become their ability to articulate a single voice in an increasingly fragmented agricultural world.

References

Adshead, M. (1996), 'Beyond clientelism: agricultural networks in Ireland and the EU', *West European Politics*, Vol. 19(3), pp.583-608.

Breen, R., Hannan, D. F., Rottman, D. B., and Whelan C. T. (1990), *Understanding contemporary Ireland: state, class and development in the Republic of Ireland*, Basingstoke, Macmillan.

British-Irish Inter-Parliamentary Body (1999), Report on Reform of the Common Agricultural Policy (Agenda 2000) (Doc. 67, July 1999). www.biipb.org/biipb/committee/commb/6701.htm

Chubb, B. (1992), *The government and politics of Ireland* (3rd ed.), London, Longman.

Collins, N. (1995), 'Agricultural policy networks in the Republic of Ireland and Northern Ireland', *Political Studies*, Vol. 43(4), pp.664-82.

Department of Agriculture and Food (2003), Annual Review and Outlook for Agriculture and Food 2002-3. Dublin. www.agriculture.gov.ie/publicat/review02-03.

Department of the Taoiseach (2003), *Sustaining Progress: Social Partnership Agreement 2003-05*, Dublin, The Stationery Office.

Department of the Taoiseach (1999a), Statement by the Taoiseach Mr. Bertie Ahern, T.D., in advance of the opening of negotiations on Agenda 2000; press release, 'Agenda 2000 Negotiations - Taoiseach sets out Ireland's Stance', 22 February, 1999.

Department of the Taoiseach (1999b), Speech by the Taoiseach Mr. Bertie Ahern, T.D., at the IFA AGM, in the Irish Farm Centre on Wednesday 3 February, 1999.

Flynn, B. and Lowe, P. (1996), European perceptions of the CAP and its impact on the countryside and natural environment: a national report for the Republic of Ireland.

Gallagher, M. (2003), 'Stability and Turmoil: Analysis of the Results', in M. Gallagher, M. Marsh and P. Mitchell (eds.), *How Ireland Voted 2002*, Basingstoke, Palgrave Macmillan, pp.88-118.

Gallagher, M., Marsh, M. and Mitchell, P. (eds.) (2003), *How Ireland Voted 2002*, Basingstoke, Palgrave Macmillan.

Greer, A. (2005, forthcoming), *Agricultural Policy in Europe*, Manchester, Manchester University Press.

Greer, A. (2002), 'Policy networks and policy change in organic agriculture: a comparative analysis of the UK and Ireland', *Public Administration*, Vol. 80(3), pp.453-74.

Greer, A. (1996), *Rural politics in Northern Ireland: policy networks and agricultural development since partition*, Aldershot, Avebury.

Greer, A. (1994), 'Policy networks and state-farmer relations in Northern Ireland', *Political Studies*, Vol. 42(3), pp.396-412.

Laffan, B. (1996), 'Ireland', in D. Rometsch and W. Wessels (eds.), *The European Union and Member States: Towards Institutional Fusion*, Manchester, Manchester University Press, pp.291-312.

Lowe, P., Flynn, B., Just, F., Valadas de Lima, A., Patricio, T. and Povellato, A. (1999), *National perspectives on the greening of the CAP: a comparative analysis*, University of Newcastle, Centre for Rural Economy.

Tovey, H. (1997), 'Food, environmentalism and rural sociology: on the organic farming movement in Ireland', *Sociologia Ruralis*, Vol. 37(1), pp.21-37.

Websites
Irish Creamery Milk Suppliers' Association, www.icmsa.ie
Irish Farmers Association, www.ifa.ie
Ulster Farmers' Union, www.ufuni.org

Chapter 4

Uniting to Meet Challenges: Danish Farm Interest Groups in the 21st Century

Carsten Daugbjerg[1]

Introduction

The farm industry in Denmark is still considered one of the country's important export industries, although its share of total Danish exports has declined over time. Up until the 1960s the farming industry was the largest export industry accounting for more than 60 per cent of total exports. In 1992, the share had declined to 21 per cent and in 2002 it was only 12 per cent (Hansen, 1993, pp.37-39 and own calculations). In 2002 the farming industry exported 68 per cent of its produce. The major export items are cereals, pigmeat, butter and cheese. 58 per cent of the agricultural produce is exported to EU countries and 42 per cent goes to non-EU countries (mainly Japan and the US) (Landbrugsraadet, 2003). This means that the farm sector is vulnerable to changes in international trade rules and developments in the world market for food. For instance, restrictions on the use of export subsidies laid down in the GATT agreement of agriculture and the failed attempt to reform the EU's dairy policy in the Agenda 2000 reform of the Common Agricultural Policy have restricted Danish dairy exports to the world market.

As a highly export-orientated industry the Danish farm sector is affected by globalization. This has put some pressure on farm interest groups and was one of the reasons why the two major groups merged and formed the federation, *Danish Agriculture*. Nevertheless, compared to international trends, domestic developments remained the more important driving forces behind the decision to merge.

This chapter pays special attention to the Farmers' Federation – *Danish Agriculture*. It has a pivotal position within the farming sector as it organizes 90 per cent of farmers. However, it cannot be analyzed in isolation from the broader agricultural interest groups system. Agriculture is perhaps one of the best organized industries in Denmark. All aspects of the industry have found organizational expressions and well-integrated organizational systems have been developed to coordinate the views of various types of farm and farm cooperative interests. The main coordination body is the Agricultural Council, of which *Danish Agriculture* is a leading member. The other members of the Council are farmers' cooperatives and some specialized branches and commodity groups. In most political issues, *Danish Agriculture* coordinates its policy positions with these associations.

In this chapter, it is argued that there are no organizational threats to *Danish Agriculture* in the near future. It is *the* spokes group for Danish farm interests and has managed to adjust to the declining number of farmers and the increased difficulties in exercising influence on domestic political decisions.

Overview of the Danish Farm Interest Group System

Roughly speaking, the Danish farm sector can be divided into three main sectors. These are pig production, dairy farming and cereals production (including oil and protein crops and seeds). The first-stage food processing industry is organized as cooperatives, owned and controlled by farmers. Over the past three decades there has been a dramatic decline in the number of cooperatives in the abattoir and dairy sectors. There are only two cooperatives left in the abattoir sector [Danish Crown, which slaughters close to 90 per cent of all pigs (19.5 million) and a smaller one (Tican) which slaughters 6 per cent (1.1 million)]. The dairy sector is dominated by one large dairy cooperative (Arla Foods) which buys 93 per cent of all milk produced in Denmark. The dairy sector also consists of a limited number of locally based small dairies.

The organizational system in agriculture is not the result of a rational process of organization building. Rather, it is the result of historical traditions and compromise among political and economic interests.

Almost all important agricultural interest groups are affiliated to the Agricultural Council (*Landbrugsraadet*) (founded in 1919) which is an umbrella organization for the Federation of Danish Farmers – *Danish Agriculture*, farmers' cooperatives[2] and a number of commodity groups and specialized branch associations. It is the Agricultural Council's prime objective to coordinate agricultural interests in relation to the European Union, the Government, the Danish Parliament, the state administration and domestic and international trade organizations.

The interests of farmers as primary producers are represented through *Danish Agriculture*, which is a relatively new association. It was founded in 2003 through a merger of the Danish Farmers' Union (*De danske Landboforeninger*) and the Family Farmers' Association (*Dansk Familielandbrug*) (previously the Danish Smallholders' Union (*Danske Husmandsforeninger*). The Farmers' Union was established in 1893 and was an association of regional farm associations, which, in turn, was an association of local farm unions. It was not until a central organizational office was established in Copenhagen in 1917 that the national association was able to gain some autonomy from the regional farm unions. In 1971 an organizational reform gave local farm unions a much more important role at the expense of regional associations, as the local unions became members of the national association. The Farmers' Union represented medium-sized and larger farmers.

The first local Smallholders' Union was established in 1896 and in 1910 a national association was formed. Traditionally, the Union has represented the interests of small farms mainly based on livestock production. The Smallholders' Union was considered one of the established agricultural associations and thus granted access to participate in negotiations with the government on agricultural policy. The agricultural crises of the early 1930s motivated the Union to join the Agricultural Council in 1932. In 1939 disagreement over grain prices meant that the smallholders withdrew from the Council; however, cooperation continued as the Union remained a member of the export committees set up to regulate exports. Cooperation also continued on a more informal basis in other policy areas. To enable a better coordination of the Danish position in European Union agricultural policies, the Smallholders' Union again became a member of the Agricultural Council in 1976 and has remained so ever since.

The largest farmers' interests were represented by the Country Landowners' Association (*Tolvmandsforeningerne*) which was formed in 1923. Later on, it changed its name to the Commercial Farmers' Association (*Dansk Erhvervsjordbrug*). However, this interest group was of minor importance because it did not have its own advisory service, was not represented independently in negotiations with the government and represented only 1 per cent of Danish farmers (Just, 1991, p.189). To ensure that the interests of the largest farms were represented politically, the association joined the Farmers' Union and became a section within it. The section chairman was a permanent member of the governing board of the Farmers' Union.

The Federation of Danish Farmers – *Danish Agriculture*[3]

Danish Agriculture is the association representing Danish farmers' interests at the national level. The association is for all farmers, including part-time farmers, though they are definitely not its core constituency. *Danish Agriculture* is an amalgamation of the Danish Farmers' Union and the Danish Family Farmers' Association. The new association was formed in January 2003 as an attempt to strengthen the national voice of farmers in agro-politics. The vast majority of agricultural policy issues are dealt with by the national government.

There were a number of reasons for merging the two farm groups. Perhaps most importantly, was the fact that the number of farms was decreasing and with that, the number of members. External political pressure, and new challenges nationally and internationally, were also important reasons. Finally, the two groups already cooperated closely and thus it was a logical step to merge. Interestingly, the amalgamation of the two farm groups has only taken place at the national level. At the regional and local levels, the two farm groups continue to exist. The members of *Danish Agriculture* are 50 local farmers' unions and 13 regional family farmers' associations. These represent about 60,000 members in total – of which approximately 42,000 are active farmers. The remaining 18,000 are passive members, mainly retired farmers. The local unions vary significantly in size; the smallest ones have about 100 members and the largest have more than 3,000 members. The membership density is about 90 per cent.

Danish Agriculture has subsumed two minority groups. The section for large-scale farms was formed in January 1997 as a result of the amalgamation of the Commercial Farmers' Association and the Farmers' Union and continued to exist within the new association *Danish Agriculture*. The amalgamation of the Farmers' Union and Family Farmers' Association resulted in the formation of a section for small farms, named the Family Farmers' Section. This section has a special position within the new federation in that it has the right to give minority statements, a privilege that the large farmers section does not have (Dansk Familielandbrug and Landboforeningerne, 2002, p.9).

The highest authority of *Danish Agriculture* is the annual national meeting of delegates. This meeting gathers around 500 farmers appointed by the local and regional unions and functions as a 'farmers' parliament'. It formulates political goals and makes policy decisions.

The delegates elect the governing board and appoint the president and three vice presidents. The board is constructed in a way in which both regional and specialized interests are represented. To ensure the influence of special interests within the federation they are given seats in the governing board. Six members are elected by the section of family farmers, ten by the farmers' unions and one by the section of large-scale farmers. The chairmen of the committee for part-time farmers, the committee for organic farming, the Danish Cattle Federation and National Committee for Pig Production are permanent members of the governing board. The section of family farmers has the right to appoint one of the three vice presidents. The two others are elected from among the other members (Dansk Familielandbrug and Landboforeningerne, 2002, pp.20-21).

The national office of *Danish Agriculture* is situated in the 'Axelborg' building in Copenhagen, the same building in which the Agricultural Council is located. The national office has a staff of about 50, most of them agricultural economists and agronomists educated at the Royal Veterinary and Agricultural University. The president, the vice presidents and the national office maintain close relations with the government, the political parties and the ministries. They are also responsible for financial administration, contact with other agricultural associations and take care of the daily contact with the local and regional unions, the national agricultural advisory centre, and the Federation's publishing house. The publishing house publishes a farmers' weekly magazine (*LandbrugsAvisen*) which is the most important communication link between *Danish Agriculture* and its members. It also publishes four specialized monthly magazines. A more important factor linking individual farmers to the Federation is its agricultural advisory service. It is organized as a two-level system. The National Agricultural Advisory Centre, which is located in Aarhus, provides technical know-how and service to 60 local advisory centres. These centres, which are owned and managed by the local and regional farm unions, offer an advisory service within most fields of agricultural production. In total, they employ approximately 800 agronomists and agricultural economists, 500 workers with a shorter agricultural education and 1500 others conducting administrative and practical functions. The advisory centres vary considerably in size from 10 to 100 employees.

New farmers are offered membership of the farm groups when they buy their farm. Since taking over a farm requires economic and tax advice, new farmers are brought into close contact with the advisory centres right from the beginning of their career as self-employed farmers. Membership of the local/regional unions is associated with certain benefits such as reduced prices for services offered by the advisory centre. This provides a selective incentive to join the local union.

Danish Agriculture had a budget of 70.5 million Danish *kroner* in 2003. This income arises from membership subscriptions (41 million), interest on its own capital (13.5 million) and interest on funds (18 million). The largest expense is the running of the national office. It costs 31 million Danish *kroner*. Contributions to the National Agricultural Advisory Service amount to 14 million, the publishing house costs 12 million, board meetings, committees meetings and the annual meeting cost 10 million. In 2003, 3.5 million was spent on the amalgamation.

There is no public funding for *Danish Agriculture*. There is, however, some public support for the advisory service but this has decreased over time and further reductions are continuously subject to political discussion during the formulation of the state's annual budget.

Competition and Cooperation within the Farm Interest Group System

When analyzing farm interest groups in Denmark one cannot focus solely on *Danish Agriculture* because the agricultural interest groups system is well-integrated. Therefore, it is necessary to include the Agricultural Council, which is an umbrella organization for all the established agricultural organizations. For a large number of policy issues of major concern for farmers, it speaks for the whole agricultural sector.

Danish Agriculture mainly speaks for farm interests related to primary agricultural production but when these affect the interests of other types of agricultural associations the Agricultural Council becomes involved. Since many policy issues affect various types of interest groups within the agricultural sector, *Danish Agriculture* is the sole spokes group in only a limited number of policy fields. The most important of these are agri-environmental policies, agricultural law (which for instance regulates farm sizes) and farm tax policies. Major policy fields affecting agricultural interests, other than primary producer interests, such as food safety policy, animal welfare policies, and the Common Agricultural Policy, are handled by the Agricultural Council. In practice, Council decisions are made by the use of deliberations aimed at reaching broad agreement, although, formally speaking, votes can be called. This informal norm for consensual decision making means that decisions can only be made if all members of the Council with a vital interest in a question agree (personal communication Agricultural Council, June 2003). Nine standing committees have been set up under the Council to handle coordination.

The fact that the Agricultural Council deals with many of the policy fields important to farmers does not imply that farmers' interests are downgraded. Farmers' influence is well-entrenched as the representatives of *Danish Agriculture* account for 20 of 49 seats in the Council and the president of the Council is always the chairman of *Danish Agriculture*. Most importantly, with the exception of one, all Council members are farmers.

Although the member associations of the Agricultural Council rarely enter into public discussions about their interest jurisdictions, there are a number of tensions. Until the mid-1960s the organizational structure was fairly straight forward. The two farm unions, the Farmers' Union and the Smallholders' Union, represented the broader interests of farmers while food processing and export interests were represented by the cooperative food processing industries. The most important of these were the Dairy Board and the Bacon and Meat Council.

The Farmers' Union and the Smallholders' Union represented primary producers which, in general, produced more than one type of agricultural commodity. Most farms had milk, beef and pig production and perhaps also production of arable products for sale. From the late 1960s up until now, most farms have specialized in the production of one main commodity. This has put pressure on the farm unions because their members have changed from a fairly homogeneous group to various groups of members with narrow, well-defined and specific interests, which in some situations may be conflicting. In attempting to represent all specialized interests the farm unions would risk that some member groups could feel that their interests are not sufficiently defended or promoted. This would be a threat to the farm unions because these members might form specialized commodity groups (Buksti, 1983, pp.198-201; Just, 1991).

To some extent, this has happened. A number of commodity groups have been established. Some of them are integrated in the established organizational system, while others are in direct opposition. Undoubtedly, the most important of the commodity groups is the National Association of Pig Producers, which was formed in 1974. The commodity groups did not become a major threat to the farm unions for two main reasons. Firstly, the farm unions were able to respond to the dissatisfaction with the lack of specialized agricultural advisory service through the amalgamation of local advisory centers, so that they could provide highly specialized and professional advice to specialized farmers. Secondly, the established farm unions and the cooperatives were able to co-opt the most threatening and well-organized of the commodity groups into the established system of agricultural organizations. For instance the National Association of Pig Producers was given the right to appoint one of the members of the powerful National Committee for Pig Production (Just, 1991, p.196). In 1990, a former leader of the National Association of Pig Producers was appointed chairman of the committee. In 1996 he became president of the Meat and Bacon Council. This co-option of the National Association of Pig Producers did not mean that its profile was watered down. It still has a high profile in the media and continues to exist as an independent group. Just (1991, p.196) refers to this type of integration as 'accepted independence'.

The specialization of farmers has blurred the borderline between *Danish Agriculture*, the Dairy Board and the Bacon and Meat Council. This means that it is not always clear who should speak for farmers in various issues (see Buksti, 1983, p.201). Occasionally this causes tensions. The Dairy Board explicitly states that one of its major aims is 'to safeguard the interests of Danish milk producers in relation to national and international policies, including EU policies' (Mejeriforeningen, 2003, *author's translation*). The Bacon and Meat Council expresses similar objectives, however, not quite as explicitly as the Dairy Board (Danske Slagterier, 2003).

Commodity groups were not the only type of oppositional groups developing outside the established agricultural organizational system. In 1981, the National Association for Organic Farming was formed. In 1986, the association made an agreement with the Smallholders' Union for the provision of specialized advisory service for organic farmers. It was natural for the smallholders to establish cooperation with organic farmers because, at that time, organic farming was viewed as a small scale farming technology. Perhaps more importantly, the Smallholders' Union was losing members because the number of full-time small farmers was declining rapidly. In that context, organic farmers were an attractive new group of potential members, especially because the Farmers' Union had no interest in them. However, this changed in the late 1980s when the leaders of the Farmers' Union realized that agri-environmental problems were not a short term political problem. Organic farming was then seen as a way of demonstrating environmental awareness and, as a result, the two farm unions each formed committees for organic farming. In 1997 the Organic Farmers' Association became a member of the Agricultural Council (Michelsen *et al.*, 2001, pp.63-70; Ingemann, 2003).

In a policy sector in which the established agricultural associations are deeply integrated into the policy process, implying a corporatist decision making style (see below), agricultural crises may trigger the formation of oppositional groups wanting a radical political strategy. This happened in the early 1980s and early 1990s when the number of bankruptcies increased dramatically and many younger farmers with livestock production experienced hard times. In both periods, protest groups were formed but they vanished again after a short period. They criticized the established agricultural associations for giving too much away when negotiating policy measures to relieve farmers from the crisis. Furthermore, they criticized the government for doing too little. There are a number of reasons why these farm groups remained short lived. Just (1994, pp.94-6) argues that, since they were short of financial resources, they relied on their leaders' voluntary and non-paid activities. This was their major weakness. Secondly, they compensated for the lack of resources by using the media as a channel of influence, but this strategy was counterproductive because the media required events, in this case protest events, to cover the farm groups. This forced them into continuing protest events (which compared to those of French farmers, were very moderate). This turned out to further distance them from the established farm groups and politicians. Thirdly, the leaders of the protest groups had very limited organizational and political experience (Just, 1994, pp.86-7).

Influence Strategies of Farm Interest Groups

The agricultural associations apply a fairly wide range of influence strategies. Traditionally, they have relied on well-established contacts with the Ministry of Agriculture and to political parties. More recently, influencing the political agenda through the media has become more important to them.

An important arena in which farm interests can exercise political influence is the agricultural policy network which has a core and a periphery. The core consists of the agricultural associations affiliated with the Agricultural Council and the Ministry of Food, Agriculture and Fisheries (MFAF).[4] These actors share an interest in maintaining the international competitiveness of agricultural production in order to uphold a high level of export earnings and of employment in the agricultural sector, especially in the food processing industry.

The process through which Danish positions in EU agricultural policy making are formulated centers around the so-called Article 2 Committee. The committee has 24 members and advises the Minister of Food, Agriculture and Fisheries ahead of the meetings of the European Union's Council of Farm Ministers, and also on the administration of the Common Agricultural Policy in Denmark. It consists of representatives from the MFAF, the agricultural associations, organic farming and food processing associations, horticultural associations, the Ministry of Economic and Business Affairs, the Confederation of Danish Industries, the Danish Chamber of Commerce, the Economic Council of the Labour Movement, the Consumer Council, the Nature Preservation Society and the Danish Outdoor Council (Lovbekendtgørelse no. 967, 2002). The committee is, first of all, a forum in which members express their official positions. Decisions are often made in a complex, continuous system of informal contacts and in various types of ad hoc working groups which usually consist of civil servants from the MFAF and/or its agencies and officials from the agricultural associations. Access to these working groups are open to the other members of the Article 2 Committee but they only participate on an occasional basis because they have no interests at stake in the specific and technical issues discussed (Daugbjerg, 1998a, p.151; 1999, p.115).

The non-agricultural interest groups represented in the Article 2 Committee have not been able to position themselves centrally in the agricultural policy network and therefore they form the network's periphery. The Consumer Council plays a minor role within the network and complains that the agricultural associations dominate the meetings and that the MFAF and the agricultural associations make deals before the meetings. Moreover, they hold that the Ministry is mainly concerned with agricultural interests (Daugbjerg, 1998b, p.152; 1999, pp.113–8). Although membership of the Article 2 Committee does not in itself lead to political influence, the fact that the Nature Preservation Society and the Danish Outdoor Council recently have been given seats in the Committee may strengthen non-agricultural interests in the policy process in the future. However, it may also be the institutional manifestation of a trend which started earlier on. As argued below, the agricultural associations have lost control over the agenda in agri-environmental policy, but still have considerable influence over the formulation of policy measures. The lost agenda control has put agricultural exceptionalism (as expressed by dominance in policy networks) under pressure but has not yet dismantled it.

Agricultural and national interests are closely linked. Since Denmark has had a net economic benefit from the budget and trade effect of the Common Agricultural Policy (Ackrill, forthcoming, pp.37-42), it has been in the national interest to uphold a high level of agricultural production. The close link between national and agricultural interests means that, in the European arena, the Danish state and farmers consider themselves partners. In fact, the MFAF and the agricultural associations have traditionally gone to Brussels together to get the best possible deal (see Bregnsbo and Sidenius, 1993, p.193).

In national policies assigned to the MFAF the decision making process is more formally organized. A large number of committees and boards are set up to deal with various technical issues in policies administered by the Ministry and its agencies. Yesilkagit (2003, p.20) has examined these boards and found that in 2000 the Ministry had 53 boards of which 89 per cent had members from agricultural interest groups. Most of the boards were advisory (83 per cent).[5] However, in practice, their advice is likely to be followed by the Ministry since the issues they deal with are highly technical.

Farm groups also exercise influence through contacts with the political parties. Since the first decade of the 20th century, farm groups have relied on close ties with two parties, namely the Liberal Party (*Venstre*) and the Radical Liberal Party (*Det radikale Venstre*), which is a social liberal party. The Liberal Party has been closely connected with the Farmers' Union and the Radical Liberal Party with the Smallholders' Union. Since the 1960s the Radical Liberal Party has detached itself from smallholders' interests and receives only few farm votes (Daugbjerg, 1998a, pp.173-5). In the 1998 election less than 2 per cent of farmers supported the party (Andersen and Jensen, 2001, pp.115-16).

Thus, the Liberal Party is now the main agrarian party. During the 1990s it received about two-thirds of farmers' votes and in the 1998 general election it was able to attract 70 per cent of the farm vote (Andersen and Jensen, 2001, p.119). The party has close links to farmers. For instance, in 1998, 24 per cent (10 of 42) of the liberal members of parliament were farmers. If those with a family background, such as sons and daughters of farmers, are included 43 per cent of the liberal MPs have a farming background. In 2001, the share of liberal MPs who were farmers had decreased to 16 per cent. But, when including those MPs who are daughters and sons of farmers, the liberal MPs with a farming background accounted for 45 per cent. Another indication of the strong linkage between farmers and the Liberal Party is the fact that half of all full-time farmers are members of the party (*Landsbladet*, 15 December, 2000).

Although farmers only account for 1-2 per cent of the electorate, they made up 7 per cent of the liberal votes in 1994 and 1998. An analysis of the 1994 election shows that farm votes may count much more than this because 24 per cent of the party's voters have a family background in the agrarian class. Thus, almost a third of the liberal voters can be considered farm class votes. A further factor underlining the argument that farm interests are still crucial to the Liberal Party is farmers' long term loyalty to the party. With the exception of higher-level employees in the private sector, the other voter groups' support is fluctuating over time. For instance, during the last three decades the percentage of those who are self-employed voting liberal has fluctuated between 8 and 35 per cent (Andersen and Jensen, 2001, pp.117-18).

However, the Liberal Party has changed during the last decade, making it a less reliable defender of agricultural interests in parliament. As Andersen and Jensen (2001, p.127) conclude:

> In both the 1994 and 1998 elections, Venstre [the Liberal Party] secured nearly one-quarter of the votes and took on a very different appearance from being the class party of the farmers. The party has been notably successful in attracting higher-level employees in the private sector, and this group may well become a new core group for Venstre, replacing farmers. More surprisingly, the party also has unusually large support among blue-collar workers, at least when compared with other non-socialist parties, and it has been keen to retain this support by toning down its anti-welfare state rhetoric.

Perhaps Andersen and Jensen overstate the possibility of the higher-level employees in the private sector replacing farmers as a core group of the Liberal Party. In the long term they may perhaps do so, but in the short and medium term, farmers will remain an important core group because farm interests are strongly entrenched in the party.

Within the parliamentary arena, the Liberal Party has had a strategic position in periods of liberal-conservative coalition governments because it has been one of the two major governing political parties in such coalitions. This ensured that agricultural interests were not disregarded by the other government parties. However, during the 1990s, the party developed a broader profile and this weakened farm interests somewhat, in particular in agri-environmental policy making. The party has had to strike a balance between urban middle class voters, who tend to hold green attitudes, and farmers, who wanted to limit environmental intervention. While the Liberal Party was strongly supportive of farm interests during negotiations for the first aquatic action plan in 1986 and 1987, farmers strongly criticized the party for giving into environmental interests during the negotiations on the second aquatic action plan in 1998. The then party leader, Uffe Ellemann-Jensen, confirmed that there had been a change in the Liberal Party's policy position, saying that the party, to a large extent, had developed into an urban party and therefore it was natural that environmental policy would play a larger role for the party (*Miljø-info*, no. 3, 13 February, 1998).

This change in party profile is clearly indicated in the change in farm groups' contacts with the political parties in parliament (see Table 4.1). In 1980, agricultural associations, to a large extent, relied on contacts with the Liberals; 71 per cent of the liberal MPs had contact with the agricultural associations at least once a month. In 2000 the pattern of contact had changed significantly. Contact is more evenly distributed among the parties and only 48 per cent of the liberal MPs have contact with agricultural organizations once a month or more frequently.

Table 4.1 The percentage of Danish MPs who have monthly or more frequent contact with agricultural associations, by party[6]

Year	Left wing	Soc. Dem.	Centre parties	Cons.	Lib.	Right wing	Total
1980	10	12	29	18	*71*	17	24
2000	18	23	33	42	*48*	38	34

Source: Christiansen and Nørgaard (2003, p.194)

The development in the patterns of contact is striking because, in both 1980 and 2000, Denmark had social democratic minority governments or minority governments led by the Social Democratic Party. Thus, the change in contact patterns cannot be explained by the nature of the governing coalition. However, the change in contact patterns may not only be explained by a change in the Liberal Party's profile, but perhaps also by the increasing intervention of the political parties in agricultural affairs, particularly in agri-environmental policy and food safety policy.

During the last two decades the media has become more important to the agricultural associations as a channel to influence the political agenda. *Danish Agriculture* has an information section but the major media effort is carried out by the Agricultural Council. It has set up the Agricultural Committee for Public Relations and a press office which coordinates contact and dialogues with the press and the public. The purpose of the media strategy is to create a positive image of farmers and their businesses and to make the public aware of the agricultural sectors' importance to Danish society by attempting to set the agenda of the media and to react to news affecting agricultural interests. Agenda setting is considered the more important aspect of media relations. Activities aimed at improving the public image of farming includes an introductory course for new journalists covering agricultural and food issues, one-day school visits on farms and 'Green Sunday', which involves the opening of selected farms to the public.

The Council's press office produces press releases and articles and is in daily contact with the media. It edits an internet database which provides factual information on agriculture and it has set up surveillance of the media outside ordinary office hours in order to be able to react quickly to news (Landbrugsraadet, 2002, pp.29-32). The public relations section of the Council employs 15 full time employees which is a considerable number considering that only 24 deal with agricultural and food policy issues (Raadet, 2002). Though the Council spends considerable organizational resources on influencing the agenda of the media, it very often ends up in a defensive position in the national media, reacting to issues put on to the agenda by others. The agri-environmental problems of the 1980s and the food safety problems of the 1990s gave farmers a negative image in the national media and it has been difficult to reverse that development.

Policy Change, the Role of Farm Interests Groups and Impacts

In EU agricultural policymaking Denmark belongs to a group of member states favoring liberalization of the CAP. A broad majority in the Danish parliament agrees that the government should work for a long term phasing out of direct payments and in the medium term a phasing out of export subsidies and price support (Folketinget, 2002).

Traditionally the Minister of Agriculture and the agricultural organizations coordinate their views on the CAP and engage in concerted action in Brussels. During the Mac Sharry reform of 1992 and the Agenda 2000 reform of 1999, the Minister of Agriculture and the agricultural associations had similar views on the direction of reform but there were different views on some of the details (Daugbjerg, 1999, p.119). In the recent debate on the future on the CAP there has been overall agreement on the need to liberalize the CAP and phase out support. For a while there seemed to be complete consensus between the farm unions and the minister. The president of the Agricultural Council, Peter Gæmelke, who was also the chairman of the Farmers' Union, said in his report to the annual Council meeting in May 2001:

> There is a need for new reforms. ... Danish farmers want a gradual and equal reduction of the subsidies within the World Trade Organisation, WTO. Should there be any doubt in this assembly on how the Danish farmer wants to secure his income, then I can assure you that most of all he would like to sell his products in straight, fair and equal competition rather than struggling for his income through intricate and non-transparent support schemes (Gæmelke, 2001, pp.9-10, *author's translation*).

Commenting on a Farmers' Union report on the impacts of liberalization of the CAP the chairman highlighted that Danish farmers would survive liberalization provided that there was a long transition period, that liberalization of agricultural policies was a global, and not just a European, project and that Danish government restrictions and taxes were aligned with those abroad (Landboforeningerne, 2002). This optimism was clearly a result of the fact that Danish pig producers had overcome the crisis resulting from the decline in pig meat prices in the late 1990s and experienced good prices in 2001.

The president of the Agricultural Council repeated his position in the 2002 annual meeting (Gæmelke, 2002, pp.3-4) but a little later that year he became more cautious as it appeared that pigmeat prices would decrease more than expected. Although EU support for pig production is limited pig farmers would be hurt by general reductions in support levels in the arable sectors. In order to have sufficient land for disposing of manure pig farmers farm large areas of land and therefore reductions in direct area payments would affect them significantly. Referring to previous CAP reforms the president claimed, at the 2003 annual Council meeting, that the reform pace was too fast. As he said: 'There are some who think that support reductions are moving forward too slowly. But for farmers, who must live from farming, things are developing too fast' (Gæmelke, 2003, p.7, *author's translation*). The Minister of Food, Agriculture and Fisheries disagreed, saying that liberalization had to be global, and provided that this requirement was fulfilled, she found no reason to slow down (*Andelsbladet*, no. 11, 23 May 2003, pp.240-41).

Although recently the agricultural associations have become more cautious in agricultural policy reform, they are still a pro-reform group in a European context. It may not seem logical that Denmark is a pro-reform country given that it has a clear net economic benefit from the Common Agricultural Policy. Indeed, Denmark is an outlier in that respect, because net benefiting EU member states tend to be opposed to reform (Ackrill, forthcoming). There are two reasons for this. Firstly, in trade policy Denmark has traditionally belonged to a group of liberal European countries and this may effect the overall agricultural policy position. Secondly, there seems to be a belief among Danish farmers that basically they do not need support, but because all other countries support their farmers, Danish farmers need it to ensure fair competition. They support international liberalization because they believe that Danish farmers are internationally competitive in a liberalized world market (Gæmelke, 2003, pp.6, 10).

In national agro-politics farm interest groups are more reluctant to change. Since the mid-1980s farm interest groups have increasingly come under pressure since new policy issues have been put on to the agro-political agenda. In the political discussions on policy measures to resolve the new problems appearing on the agro-political agenda, farm groups have attempted to limit state intervention because they have feared that restrictions on farm practice would increase production costs and thus damage international competitiveness. Therefore, they have attempted to avoid the introduction of compulsory policy measures which have been perceived as costly.

Agri-environmental problems have made up the most sustaining pressure on farm groups. To a large extent, farm groups have lost control over the policy agenda in these issues. In the mid-1980s the Environmental Protection Agency, supported by the Society for Nature Preservation, managed to put agri-environmental issues on to the political agenda. The core conflict concerned the question of introducing fertilizer taxes. Farmers strongly opposed green taxes, and succeeded in avoiding them, and persuaded politicians to adopt a highly complicated regulatory instrument which requires farmers to work out fertilizer and crop rotation plans and fertilizer accounts. These are subject to inspection by the Ministry of Food, Agriculture and Fisheries. Both farm unions accepted this alternative, except its emphasis on inspections. In fact they had suggested this regulatory approach themselves (Daugbjerg, 1998a, pp.85-97; 1998b, pp.287-9; 1999, pp.120-22).

Pesticide use was the other major agri-environmental item on the agri-environmental agenda but it was not until the 1990s farm groups lost control over the agenda. In 1986 a pesticide action plan was adopted. It stated that the use of pesticides should be reduced by 50 per cent by 1997. A number of measures, such as strict rules on registration of new and old pesticides, compulsory education of farmers and information campaigns were introduced. These measures were acceptable to farm groups but they decreased pesticide use by less than they had hoped for. In 1995 the social democratic led coalition government introduced a tax equal to 37 per cent of the retail price on insecticides and 15 per cent on fungicides, herbicides and crop growth-regulating chemicals. The revenue would be reimbursed by suspending the state's share of the regional land tax. The tax scheme would only involve minor redistribution in the farming community. This is an important reason why the farm unions perceived the pesticide tax as a tolerable measure, although they would have preferred not to have it (Daugbjerg, 2000; Daugbjerg and Svendsen, 2003, pp.91-2). During 1996 and 1997 waterworks authorities throughout the country detected new pesticide residues in the drinking water and many people, including scientists, environmental officials, water companies and politicians, feared that the situation would deteriorate further and threaten public health unless something radical was done. The response of the government was a doubling of the pesticide tax in June 1998. This was opposed by the farmers' unions but within half a year they succeeded in persuading politicians to reduce local land taxes as a measure to reimburse tax revenues (Daugbjerg and Svendsen, 2001, pp.94-5). At the same time a committee consisting of a variety of interest groups, including environmental and agricultural groups, somewhat surprisingly reached agreement on a new action plan on pesticides, which, by and large, was adopted by the government (Daugbjerg, 2000, pp.9-11).

In the 1990s food safety was put onto the political agenda and this put farm groups on the defense. Salmonella in poultry, eggs, and later also in pigmeat, was the most salient food safety issue in the 1990s but not the only one. Until the early 1990s food safety was a non-issue in Danish politics. Danish food production had a positive image to politicians, the media and the public, and those who dared to question the quality of Danish agricultural food products were given a hard time (Justesen, 2002, pp.51-58, 100). In particular, the salmonella problems changed the public's and many politicians' views on Danish agricultural food production. From being a political non-issue it became a hot political issue. The problems were, to a large extent, put down to the production process itself, in particular the specialization and concentration of production (Justesen, 2002). Despite being under pressure, the agricultural associations succeeded in damage limitation in the policy formulation process. For instance, they persuaded the state to share some of the costs of combating salmonella in eggs but not as much as egg producers had hoped for (Larsen, 2002).

These national policy developments demonstrate that farm groups had lost control over the agenda in these two new policy areas. They could no longer control what issues were discussed and when. It took some time before they realized this; it was not until the early 1990s that farm unions shifted towards a cooperative strategy in environmental and food safety policy making. However, this shift in strategy came too late. Farmers had lost their credibility within the public domain and this spilled-over into other policy issues, constraining farmers' ability to control the public and political agenda. Despite this loss of agenda control farmers were able to utilize the agricultural policy network and their political contacts to influence policy formulation. They had a considerable say on the way in which public and political demands on regulation were transformed into specific policy instruments. Thus, the role of farm groups in national policy change is damage limitation rather than agenda control.

Farmers seem to demand more than this achievement. A survey undertaken among the members of the Farmers' Union in 2000 showed that only 27 per cent were satisfied with the way in which the Union represented their interests (*Landsbladet,* 15 December, 2000). However, this dissatisfaction cannot be explained by the Union's lack of skills; rather it is the result of unrealistically high expectations among farmers (Daugbjerg, 2001). Although dissatisfaction exists, it has not, in any way, threatened *Danish Agriculture's* position as *the* spokesman of farmers' interests. Member density remains high and farm protest groups have shown to be short-lived. This indicates that dissatisfaction is superficial.

During the last three decades the structure of farming has changed dramatically in Denmark. Farms are increasing in size and have become more specialized. The number of farms that are less than 50 hectares in size has decreased dramatically while the number of medium sized and large farms has increased.

Table 4.2 Changes in Danish farm structure

	1968	1978	1988	1998	2002
Total number of farms	161,142	125,521	84,093	59,761	53,489
Less than 5 hectares	25,285	17,167	2,560	1,900	1,848
5-50 hectares	127,816	97,451	66,364	39,942	33,978
50-100 hectares	6,552	8,967	12,027	12,001	10,662
More than 100 hectares	1,489	2,026	31,41	5,917	7,001

Source: Danmarks Statistik (1983, 1995, 2003)

Further, while 75 per cent of all farms had both dairy and pig production in the late 1960s, only 7.6 per cent had this type of production in 2002.

A state commission set up to analyze this development in farm structure concluded the changes could hardly be put down to public policies. It concluded that neither the developments in the Common Agricultural Policy nor national agri-environmental policies could account for the developments in farm structures. However, the commission recognized that, on the one hand, some agri-environmental measures seemed to influence farmers to acquire more land but, on the other hand, other agri-environmental measures seemed to put limits on farm sizes (Just, 1998). The commission concluded that the most important factor influencing structural development is economies of scale. As it was stated: 'A decisive factor in the structural development is thus that the larger farms have lower cost per unit produced' (quoted in Just, 1998, *author's translation*).

Conclusion: Danish Farm Interest Groups in the Future

Globalization of agricultural policy, through the adoption of stricter trade rules within the GATT Uruguay Round Agreement on Agriculture and the Doha Round negotiations, has put pressure on EU agricultural policy. Reforms of the Common Agricultural Policy to comply with the trade agreements and to put the EU in better positions in international negotiations on agricultural trade has put some pressure on Danish farm interest groups. However, as this chapter has demonstrated, domestic pressures have been the more important factor influencing the farm interest group system. In particular, new policy issues such as pollution and food safety and the declining number of farmers have forced farm groups to reconsider the ways in which they organize themselves and pursue their interests. The formation of the federation *Danish Agriculture*, through the merger of the Farmers' Union and the Family Farmers' Association, is an organizational adjustment to the declining number of farmers and the increased difficulties in exercising influence on political decisions.

Although farm groups have lost control over the agenda in relation to these new issues, they have managed to remain influential in the process in which policy tools are designed. This influence is maintained through strong and resourceful interest groups that are able to coordinate members' views, and influence policy makers, through a well-established and well-integrated policy network. Furthermore, traditionally, farm unions have had well-established contacts with influential political parties, in particular the Liberal Party. However, during the last decade the Liberal Party has detached itself somewhat from farm interests in order to reach middle class voters. Farm groups have reacted to this by broadening their parliamentary contacts to other political parties and by emphasizing political agenda setting through the media. However, the latter strategy has only had limited success.

In the long term a declining number of fulltime farmers might become a problem for *Danish Agriculture* because it is likely to force farm leaders to undertake further organizational adjustments. However, *Danish Agriculture* will remain well-resourced and powerful for two reasons. Firstly, as with most other interest associations within the established agricultural interest groups system, *Danish Agriculture* has considerable funding which is independent of members' contributions. This makes them less vulnerable to a decrease in membership due to development in farm structures. Secondly, since agriculture will remain to be considered an economically important industry in Denmark in the future, a declining number of full-time commercial farmers is unlikely, in itself, to cause a decline in political influence. The economic importance of agriculture will ensure farmers' political influence, though unwillingness to accept new policy agendas has put them in a defensive position. As long as the vast majority of domestic and overseas consumers prefer standardized food products, farms groups will remain reluctant to introduce further environmental, animal welfare and food safety measures.

To conclude, there are no organizational threats to *Danish Agriculture* in the near future. It is *the* spokesman for farm interests in Denmark and will remain so in the future.

Notes

[1] I am grateful to Tina Klejs Jensen for assisting with data collection.

[2] Traditionally, the Federation of Cooperatives represented the interests of cooperatives in the Agricultural Council. In December 2003, the Federation of Cooperatives merged with Agricultural Council and the cooperatives became directly represented in the Council.

[3] A draft for this section was prepared by Tina Klejs Jensen. The sources of evidence for this section are mainly personal communication with members of staff of *Danish Agriculture* and the National Agricultural Advisory Centre, unpublished memos, and unpublished manuscripts for presentations.

[4] By January 1, 1997, the Ministry of Agriculture and Fisheries was reorganized and became the Ministry of Food, Agriculture and Fisheries (MFAF).

[5] Also includes a very limited number of boards dealing with fisheries.

[6] Also includes fishermen's associations. Unfortunately the data set does not allow one to exclude these.

References

Ackrill, Robert (forthcoming), 'The Common Agricultural Policy', in P. van der Hoek (ed.), *Handbook on Public Administration and Policy in the European Union*.

Andelsbladet, (2003), no. 11, 23 May 2003.

Andersen, J.G. and Jensen, J.B. (2001), 'The Danish Venstre: Liberal, Agrarian or Centrist?', in D. Arter (ed.), *From Farmyard to City Square? The Adaptation of the Nordic Agrarian Parties*, Aldershot, Ashgate, pp.96-131.

Bregnsbo, H. and Sidenius, N. C. (1993), 'Denmark: The National Lobby Orchestra' in M. C. P. M. van Schendelen (ed.), *National Public and Private EC Lobbying*, Aldershot, Dartmouth.

Buksti, J.A. (1983), 'Et enigt landbrug? Landbrugets organisationsforhold – specialisering, konkurrence og politisk indflydelse', in Dubgaard, A. (ed.), *Landbrugets placering I samfundsøkonomien – en foredragssamling*, Copenhagen, Statens Jordbrugsøkonomiske Institut, pp.197-216.

Christiansen, P.M. and Nørgaard, A.S. (2003), *Faste forhold – flygtige forbindelser: Stat og interesseorganisationer i Danmark i det 20. århundrede*, Aarhus, Aarhus Universitetsforlag.

Danmarks Statistik (1983), *Landbrug 1982: Statistik om landbrug, gartneri og skovbrug*, Copenhagen, Danmarks Statistik.

Danmarks Statistik (1995), *Landbrug 1994: Statistik om landbrug, gartneri og skovbrug*, Copenhagen, Danmarks Statistik.

Danmarks Statistik (2003), *Landbrug 2002: Statistik om landbrug, gartneri og skovbrug*, Copenhagen, Danmarks Statistik.

Dansk Familielandbrug and Landboforeningerne, (2002), *Fusionsaftale for Dansk Landbrug og vedtægter for Dansk Landbrug*, Copenhagen, Dansk Familielandbrug and Landboforeningerne.

Danske Slagterier, (2003), 'Danske Slagterier, (DS)', http://www.danskeslagterier.dk.

Daugbjerg, C. (1998a), *Policy Networks under Pressure: Pollution Control, Policy Reform, and the Power of Farmers*, Aldershot, Ashgate Publishing.

Daugbjerg, Carsten, (1998b), 'Linking Policy Networks and Environmental Policies: Nitrate Policy Making in Denmark and Sweden 1970-1995', *Public Administration*, vol.76(2), pp.275-94.

Daugbjerg, C. (1999), 'Landbrugspolitik: Stabilitet eller forandring?' in Blom-Hansen, J. and Daugbjerg, C. (ed.), *Magtens organisering: Stat og interesseorganisationer i Danmark*, Aarhus, Systime, pp.106-27.

Daugbjerg, C. (2000), 'Landbruget og miljøpolitikken: Konfliktløsning gennem forhandlinger med landbrugets organisationer?', *Økonomi og Politik*, Vol. 73. (3), pp.2-14.

Daugbjerg, C. (2001), 'Magt eller afmagt i landbruget?', *Jyllands-Posten*, 2 March, 2001.

Daugbjerg, C. and Svendsen, G.T. (2001), *Green Taxation in Question: Politics and Efficiency in Environmental Regulation*, Basingstoke, Palgrave.

Daugbjerg, C. and Svendsen, G.T. (2003), 'Designing green taxes in a political context: From optimal to feasible environmental regulation' *Environmental Politics*, Vol. 12(4), 2003, pp.76-95.

Folketinget, (2002), 'Forespørgsel til fødevareministeren om EU's midtvejsevaluering af landbrugspolitikken og om en afvikling af EU's landbrugsstøtteordninger', http://www.ft.dk/samling/20021/forespoergelse/f11.htm.

Gæmelke, P. (2001), *Landbrugsraadets årsmøde, tirsdag den 15. maj 2001*, Copenhagen, Landbrugsraadet.

Gæmelke, P. (2002), *Landbrugsraadets årsmøde, onsdag den 15. maj 2002*, Copenhagen, Landbrugsraadet.

Gæmelke, P. (2003), *Landbrugsraadets årsmøde, torsdag den 15. maj 2003*, Copenhagen, Landbrugsraadet.

Hansen, H.O. (1993), *Landbrugets placering i samfundet*, Frederiksberg, Jordbrugsforlaget.

Ingemann, J.H. (2003), 'The Evolution of Organic Agriculture in Denmark' draft working paper, University of Aalborg.

Just, F. (1991), 'Producentforeninger i dansk landbrug' *Tidsskrift for landøkonomi*, Vol. 178(4), pp.187-198.

Just, F. (1994), 'LR 80 og Landbrugets Græsrødder', *Bol og By*, part 2, pp.78-100.

Just, F. (1998), 'Landbrugets strukturudvikling – hvor går vi hen?' *Tidsskrift for landøkonomi*, Vol. 185(3), pp.95-102.

Justesen, A.H. (2002), *Fra jord til politikernes bord – fødevarer på den politiske dagsorden*, Master dissertation Department of Political Science, University of Aarhus.

Landboforeningerne (2002), 'Landbruget vil overleve liberalisering i EU', http://www.landbo.dk/main.jsp?o_id=2789.

Landbrugsraadet (2002), *Landbrugsraadets beretning 2001/2002*, Copenhagen, Landbrugsraadet.

Landbrugsraadet (2003), *Tal om landbruget 2003*, Copenhagen: Landbrugsraadet

Landsbladet, (2000), 15 December 2000.

Larsen, Morten (2002), 'Fødevareministeriet: fra erhvervets forlængede arm til forbrugernes beskytter', *Politica*, Vol. 34.(2), pp.150-67.

Lovbekendtgørelse (2002). 'Lov om ændring af lov om administration af Det Europæiske Fællesskabs forordninger om markedsordninger for landbrugsvarer m.v. med flere love', *Lovtidende A 2002/03*, Copenhagen.

Mejeriforeningen (2003), 'Mejeriforeningen', http://www.mejeri.dk.

Michelsen, J. *et al.* (2001), *Organic Farming Development and Agricultural Institutions in Europe: A Study of Six Countries*, Organic Farming in Europe: Economics and Policy, Vol. 9, University of Hohenheim, Stuttgart.

Miljø-info, (1998), no. 3, 13 February 1998.

Raadet (2002), 'Ressourceanvendelse i landbrugets organisationer', November 2002, Raadet 36/02, Copenhagen.

Yesilkagit, K. (2003), 'Delegation and Administrative Organization in Corporatist Democracies: The Case of Agriculture and Fisheries in Denmark and the Netherlands' unpublished paper, Dept. of Political Science, Aarhus University.

Chapter 5

France's FNSEA: A Giant on Clay Feet?[*]

Christilla Roederer-Rynning

Introduction

Can the FNSEA today escape the doom that struck its predecessor, the *Confédération Générale de l'Agriculture* (CGA), fifty years ago? On 28 November 1953, the organization that had officially represented farmers since 1946, the CGA, was indeed dissolved after a protracted and highly publicized conflict with its five constituent groups. Chief among these groups was the national federation of farm unions, the *Fédération Nationale des Syndicats d'Exploitants Agricoles* (FNSEA), created in 1946. Freed from its ties to CGA, the FNSEA became one of the most powerful interest groups in post-war France, at any rate the single-largest farm union and the only official voice of farmers in policy-making in the next three decades.

The proximate origin of this conflict lay in the legacy of World War II and the experiment of the Vichy regime to organize the traditionally highly fragmented French peasantry within a single, hierarchic, peasant corporation.[1] The CGA represented the post-war socialist government's response to Vichy corporatism, a farm unionism still based on monopolistic representation but inspired by Socialist ideals. Above all, farmers' *fronde* against CGA revealed their distrust of urban and political elites and their desire to build farm unionism on an apolitical and professional basis (Wright, 1953). To politicians eager to instrumentalize peasants' concerns, FNSEA president Lepicard declared: 'we will not allow the meddling of any political party, be it a peasant party' (*Rassemblement*, 1 April 1954). They saw in this motto the best guarantee for maintaining the unity of farm unionism.

Two factors appeared decisive in FNSEA's spectacular rise to power.[2] First, the FNSEA was directly in contact with the rank-and-file. This situation placed the CGA in a double dependency vis-à-vis FNSEA: first, in terms of legitimacy, as the FNSEA alone could credibly pretend to speak on behalf of the grassroots; and second, in financial terms, as it was the FNSEA, which collected farmers' dues. Second, the FNSEA received the support of the specialized commodity groups, notably the most influential sugar beet producers' confederation (*Confédération Générale des Planteurs de Betteraves* / CGB), and the wheat producers' association (*Association Générale des Producteurs de Blé* / AGPB). Predating the creation of the FNSEA, these two commodity groups had grown powerful financially and, in particular the sugar beet producers, also politically (Barral, 1968, p.222). In the conflict opposing the CGA and the FNSEA, the support of commodity groups proved decisive when some of the local farm unions attempted to go their own way and create an alternative organization in defense of small- and medium-sized holdings. On these two feet, the FNSEA grew into a formidable giant, shaping the agricultural paradigm in close concertation with policy-makers and organizational counterparts at home and abroad.

Today, the FNSEA's membership rate has fallen to 42 per cent,[3] and the union must compete for the official status as representative organization of the farming community with two rival farm groups: *Confédération paysanne* on the left, and *Coordination rurale* on the right (Lemétayer, 2003, p.56). The farm interest group system has become openly competitive. At the same time, the organization is torn apart between the diverging interests and visions of commodity groups.

How significant are these trends? On the face of it, there is little new. From the beginning, the FNSEA was doomed to a life of endless compromises between small and large farmers, cereal producers and livestock growers, southern and northern regions, left and right wings.[4] In several cases, local farm unions were excluded for challenging too overtly the federal line, and other seceded to establish dissident farm federations on the left and the right of the political spectrum.

Yet, the context in which the tensions play themselves out is new. CAP reforms and international trade negotiations have exposed the contrasts between a commercial and a social agriculture while preventing the FNSEA from activating the traditional leverages of internal peace-making. The state itself has begun scrutinizing its role and mission in French agriculture under the pressure of escalating public deficits and emerging citizen concerns about the environment and food safety. In sum, the FNSEA must think through its role anew if it is to avoid the misfortune of the CGA fifty years ago.

The objective of this chapter is to evidence the dynamics linking organizational change in France and paradigmatic shift in the European Union. The analysis proceeds at three levels in order to pin down the effects of: 1) European – international; 2) national – governmental, and 3) societal dynamics. Part one describes the tensions built into the FNSEA's structure and the traditional 'recipes' the union used to alleviate them. Part two investigates the impact of international trade negotiations and CAP reforms on the FNSEA and the efforts of the latter to influence these negotiations. Part three discusses the reorientation of the state's role in agriculture and its consequences for the FNSEA's access to public resources. Finally, part four examines the role of non-farm actors in the contemporary agricultural debate in France and FNSEA's response to retain control of the agenda.

FNSEA's 'Thirty Glorious Years', 1958-1988[5]

Conflict has been a permanent feature of the life of the FNSEA. Even in the heyday of the organization's hegemony, groups vied for control of the agenda, and occasionally formed dissident farm organizations. These tensions were reflected in the federation's structure and political line. To maintain the balance, however, the FNSEA leadership had several leverages at its disposal. These recipes worked well until the late 1980s.

Legitimacy of Numbers and Legitimacy of Means

Wright's speculation in 1953 that French 'agrarian syndicalism is likely to be hampered for years to come by the diversity of the base upon which it rests' turned out to be prophetic (Wright, 1953, p.415). If *legitimacy of numbers* is defined as the mobilization of 'a significant number of internally disciplined people committed to seeking an alternative distribution of power' and *legitimacy of means* as the ability to 'convinc[e] the public that [the group] is an appropriate vehicle to achieve its constituent's goals' (Useem and Zald, 1987, p.280), then the dilemma facing FNSEA leaders was couched in the following terms: how to build the legitimacy of numbers (i.e., casting as wide a net as possible) without sacrificing the legitimacy of means (i.e., defining goals and strategies acceptable to all)?

The heterogeneity of farm structures has been an increasing problem. Even though much has been written about the divide between 'small' and 'big' farmers, not two but three or four sizeable groupings crystallized in the three decades following WWII (see Table 5.1). Together with agricultural specialization, patterns of farm structures have yielded pronounced income disparities (Duby and Wallon, 1977, p.265)[6] and entrenched poverty in the sector (see Colson and Blogowski, 1993, p.58; Brageon and Jégouzo, 1995, p.83).[7] Whether these fault lines are most aptly captured by farm leader Michel Debatisse's 'three agricultures' or historian Moulin's four 'peasantries' is open to question (see Debatisse, 1963; Moulin, 1988, p.252). The point is that they constrained the extent to which a strong, independent organization could develop to federate French farmers.

Table 5.1 French farm structures, 1955-1985

Size of land-holdings (in ha)	Percentage of landholdings		Evolution in percentage points
	1955 (mean: 15 ha)	1985 (mean: 28 ha*)	
< 1	6.6	7.4	+0.8
1 - 5	28.3	17.6	-10.7
5-20	44.4	29.9	-14.5
20-50	16.5	29.9	+13.4
50-100	3.3	12.0	+8.7
>100	0.9	3.1	+2.2

*1988 figure.

Source: Moulin (1988, p.259); Lemétayer (2003, p.37); own calculations

The organization of the FNSEA bore witness to the difficulty of its leadership to transcend the diversity of the farm base. The imprint of diversity materialized in the set of horizontal and vertical relationships tying the FNSEA to local farm unions and commodity groups, respectively. Both local farm unions and commodity groups pay dues to the union, and both are involved in policy-making even though formally, only local farm unions are members of the FNSEA. Articulating preferences across sectors and regions has been a catch-22 for the national leadership.

The horizontal layering is the most readily visible organizational parameter. The FNSEA is a peak-organization modeled after the administrative structure of the state, i.e., bringing together farm unions formed at the levels of: *cantons, départements,* and *régions.* Today, the FNSEA brings under one umbrella 20,000 local unions, although formally, as well as substantively, the key échelon is that of the *département,* which is embodied by one *Fédération Départementale de Syndicats d'Exploitants Agricoles* (FDSEA) by *département,* i.e., 94 FDSEAs. The FDSEAs are the official members of the FNSEA, and they have functioned as the transmission belt between the grassroots and the national level. Two mechanisms are to guarantee a certain degree of cohesion between the different levels: the electoral accountability of the national leadership before the general assembly of the FDSEAs,[8] and participation of the local representatives in policy-making via the federal council. Yet, the grassroots have recurrently criticized the effectiveness of the federal council's input, and called into question the fairness of the electoral system. Occasionally, these disputes have surfaced in the media. In 1954, FNSEA's president thus bluntly qualified the electoral system of the FNSEA as 'unfair,' as it granted northern farm unions only 47 per cent of the seats in the national executive board, although these unions contributed 67 per cent of the federation's budget (Table 5.2) (*Rassemblement,* 1 April 1954).

Bringing commodity groups under one structure – the vertical dimension of the FNSEA – has proven no less difficult. When the FNSEA was created in 1946, twenty-six commodity groups 'affiliated' themselves with it, both at the national and at the local level. The peculiar character of this affiliation is seldom explicated. Although the commodity groups are represented in the general assembly, the executive board, and the local branches of the FNSEA and pay dues to the FNSEA, they are independent associations, endowed with their own statutes and resources.

This peculiar form of cooperation has had two consequences of paramount importance. First, the division of labour between commodity groups and the FNSEA has rested essentially on the goodwill and converging needs of commodity groups. Within the FNSEA, a so-called 'commission of coordination of specialized associations' was set up to discuss and aggregate the position of the commodity groups at the national level. The FNSEA envisioned this commission as the natural motor of policy-making on 'political' issues concerning the farming sector, leaving the 'technical' field to commodity groups. However, this conception of the division of labour was not grounded in any formal delimitation of competences, and thus remained vulnerable to an adverse interpretation by commodity groups. Second, the financial contribution of richer – but numerically weaker – commodity groups (e.g., cereal growers) has provided them with leverage vis-à-vis both the FNSEA and less well-off but dense commodity groups. On paper, the FNSEA's situation vis-à-vis commodity groups was not terribly different from that of the CGA vis-à-vis the FNSEA in the immediate post-war years.

Table 5.2 Regional asymmetries in the FNSEA, 1954

	Northern France	Southern France
Average size per holding	20 ha	20 ha
Share of French farmers	40	60
Share of farmers affiliated with the FNSEA	47	53
Share of the dues paid by the FDSEAs	67%	33%
Average due paid by an individual farmer affiliated with the FNSEA	93 francs	43 francs
Dues paid by two departments of same size (in terms of number of unionized members) but of different wealth	Oise 1,896,000 francs	Savoie 290,000 francs
Number of administrators representing the department in the national executive board	12	16
Number of administrators representing the commodity groups and the local sections	7	5
Total number of administrators in the national executive board	19	21
Number of seats in the secretariat (17 in all)	7	10
Number of representatives of the two departments in the national assembly	Oise 4	Savoie 4

Source: M. Lepicard, *Rassemblement*, 1 April 1954. Note the difference between tables 5.1 and 5.2 regarding the average size per holding in the mid-1950s

The Formula of Success

It is thus remarkable that a *modus vivendi* emerged and solidified in this sector in spite of all expectations to the contrary. Commodity groups by and large accepted the FNSEA's ambition to speak on behalf of French farmers. Instead of disputing the authority of the FNSEA, they lobbied it actively to capture representation and make their views prevail. The commission of coordination of specialized associations became one of the prime sources of policy-making at the national level. Certainly, grassroots discontent in the *départements* both within the FNSEA-CNJA sphere,[9] and without.[10]

Two factors crowned the supremacy of the FNSEA. First at the national level, an unprecedented partnership emerged between the state and professional farm organizations. The motivations of state and farm elites have been analyzed elsewhere in detail (Muller, 1984; Keeler, 1987); suffice to note here that this partnership marked a unique period in the history of farm organizations in France, which contrasted with the climate of mutual reservations both in the post-war years and in the 1980s and laid the foundations for the most spectacular success in the history of farm unionism in France. The decisive engagement of the state in agriculture coincided with the coming to power of general de Gaulle in 1958 and the establishment of a new political order within the Fifth Republic. Three political figures illustrated the engagement of the Gaullist state in agriculture (see Barral, 1968, p.318): Michel Debré, prime minister from 1959 to 1962, and chief author of the 1960 law of orientation for agriculture; Edgard Pisani, agriculture minister from 1961 to 1966; and Edgard Faure, agriculture minister from 1966 to 1968. They pursued the vision of a modern agriculture, restructured around farms large enough to boost the productivity and competitiveness of French farm products. Ironically, it was not the FNSEA but its sister-organization created in 1957, the CNJA, which seized the chance of power. Political considerations beyond farm policy played a role in this curious partnership: the FNSEA was still influenced by conservative and traditionalist milieus hostile to de Gaulle (Barral, 1968, p.319), while the CNJA represented a new generation of farmers, influenced by the progressive Christian youth organization *Jeunesse Agricole Chrétienne* (JAC) and led from 1958 to 1964 by the reform-minded Michel Debatisse. Tight cooperation between the CNJA and the state generated the 1960 law of orientation and its complementary laws in 1962 and 1964, which created the main instruments for modernizing farm structures. The FNSEA joined the club several years later, when a new generation of leaders, coming from the CNJA, brought with them their habit and experience of power. Partnership with the state then developed into full-fledged neocorporatism, whereby the FNSEA-CNJA, now acting in concert, became the sole interlocutors of the state and the administrator of agricultural policy.

Partnership with the state provided the FNSEA with two powerful instruments to fight factionalism. The first was representational monopoly. The FNSEA was the only group seated at the negotiation table, and was entrusted with a great deal of policy implementation. The second was access to public financing. A significant share of the FNSEA's budget came from the state in the form of support from the farm development program *Association Nationale pour le Développement Agricole* (ANDA) and the educational program for interest group leaders *Promotion Sociale Collective*. These tools were used to reward members with the provision of a wide range of technical services vital to the profession and threaten recalcitrant members with the unenviable prospect of exclusion. As Keeler has shown in his superb account of farm neocorporatism in France, over time the material gains derived from partnership with the state often became decisive to the upholding of the hegemonic position of the FNSEA in the face of growing intragroup tensions.

From the late 1960s on, the crystallization of the European agricultural policy regime supplied the FNSEA with another powerful lever to discipline its members. The Treaty of Rome providing for the establishment of a Common Agricultural Policy left the issue of the means of intervention open. As it is well-known, agreement was finally reached in favour of a policy of universal, but commodity-differentiated price support. Nearly all farmers, regardless of their income or size, benefited from support; commodity was the only basis of differentiation of price support. Although the hierarchy of support was a potentially important source of discord between commodity groups, all could gain from price policy as long as livestock producers were able to secure ever-higher prices for the input costs generated by high-price cereals (Delorme, 1990, p.43). In other words, the organizational cohesion of the FNSEA postulated price inflation. One aspect of this *modus vivendi* materialized in the notorious though unofficial distribution of the top positions in the FNSEA. Livestock producers were granted the presidency of the FNSEA and the CNJA in exchange for conceding cereal growers the vice-presidency of the two organizations and, crucially, the presidency of the commission of coordination of specialized associations (see Bretonnière *et al.*, 1997; Petit *et al.*, 1987; AGPB, 1974, p.65).

In sum, the engagement of the state in 1958 marked the beginning of a glorious age for farm unionism in France, which reached its apogee in the 1970s under the implementation of price support. This age is now over. Reform at the European and international levels and state disengagement have changed the terms of existence of the FNSEA in the last fifteen years.

FNSEA and CAP Reform: Strategic Split Intermediation or Gridlock?

The EU's agricultural paradigm has been under siege during the last fifteen years. Two reforms have had special significance for French farm unionism: the MacSharry reform in 1992; and the midterm review in 2003. The MacSharry reform introduced direct payments in the form of compensation for price cuts. These payments *de facto* lost their compensatory character following the decision of the twelve member-states in 1995 to extend them to the three new EU members – Austria, Finland, Sweden – and shortly became the single-most significant CAP instrument in budgetary terms. The midterm review provided for the decoupling of these payments from production by creating a single farm payment. The FNSEA overtly resisted every single attempt to end price support, fearing the political and organizational consequences of such a shift.

The FNSEA's attitude in the reform of 1992 and its sequels is well-known: it consisted of a vehement public denunciation of the proposed orientations and an outright refusal to engage in the negotiations with Commission officials. Its preferred mode of operation has been to try to block the reform packages put together by the Commission by lobbying the French government and, secondarily, the Council of Ministers (see Roederer-Rynning, 2002).[11] Two issues are less well-known, or disputed: to what extent this strategy has been freely elected, as opposed to being imposed upon the FNSEA by circumstances beyond its control; and to what extent commodity groups have followed the line of the FNSEA.

Resistance or Impotence?

Public statements by the FNSEA during the negotiations of the MacSharry reform and the midterm review suggested that the strategy of resistance is the logical and accepted consequence of a fundamental opposition to these reforms. FNSEA President Jean-Michel Lemétayer thus justified its refusal to negotiate with the Commission on the midterm review on the grounds that negotiating aspects of the package would amount to legitimizing the whole reform exercise. As late as in May 2003, president Jérôme Despey of the CNJA (now renamed *Jeunes Agriculteurs* / JA) explained that 'negotiating on individual items of the package is to give the green light to Fischler' (*Le Monde*, 23 May 2003). However, confrontation reflects perhaps to a greater degree the growing autonomy of the Commission in formulating policy and choosing its interlocutors. The MacSharry reform notoriously caught farmers by surprise with regard to both its timing and content. The reform came without warning as a very small team of top civil servants in Directorate-General for Agriculture devised it in isolation from external interference. In the negotiations on the midterm review, on the other hand, the Commission had announced early on the broad spirit of the reform and hinted at the concrete forms that it might take. In both reforms, the Commission acted independently and used leaks to the press as a strategy of communication during the formulation phase, supplemented by consultation with a few carefully chosen interlocutors. In the later stages of the negotiations, the Commission simply ignored the most confrontational opponents of reform, like the FNSEA, and relied on more cooperative farm groups to fine tune the package components. These exchanges involved two types of interlocutors. Some were members of COPA. In 1992, a few groups had singled themselves out by cooperating with the Commission: the Italian *Confcoltivatori*, the British National Farmers' Union (NFU), and Dutch farmers. By 2003, only German farmers adopted a position of resistance similar to that of the FNSEA. Commodity groups were the other interlocutors of the Commission. For the FNSEA, failure to influence the Fischler reform was all the more complete since the spirit of the reform was clear from the outset.

Commodity Groups Go to Brussels

That French commodity groups engaged in the negotiations is not surprising given the issues at stake, but it presents the observer with an interesting puzzle given the ambiguous status of these groups – both branches of the FNSEA and independent organizations – and the FNSEA's proclaimed ambition to speak on behalf of commodity interests. Did commodity groups act by virtue of an implicit norm of split intermediation? To be sure, the FNSEA President himself has argued that 'the anglo-saxon model of unionism shows that there is no contradiction between confrontation and concertation. A union must all at once propose, take action, and negotiate' (Lemétayer, 2003, p.60). Such a model could serve to justify a tacit division of labour between the FNSEA (resisting) and commodity groups (proposing). Two arguments could buttress this thesis: pressure from grassroots activists and from rival farm unions in the last two decades had placed the FNSEA leadership in a situation of brinkmanship; commodity groups could then operate as submarine negotiators on behalf of the FNSEA. On the other hand, discontent had been brewing among the commodity groups who had embraced a more forward-looking strategy. The confrontational line of French farm unionism had also nourished a debate worth noting within the FNSEA itself, between on the one hand the professional staff, articulating the logic of resistance, and on the other hand, the salaried personnel of the FNSEA, reluctant to relinquish not only agenda-setting capacities but also crucial bargaining power in the phase of implementation of reforms. This issue came in sharp relief during the midterm review, where refusal to negotiate with the Commission *de facto* placed the FNSEA in a position of dependence on the expertise of commodity groups on all key aspects of the reform except for the issue of conditionality, where it could build on its own related work on integrated farming.

To be sure, CAP reforms did not create farm conflict; they structured it and exposed it. The era of price support enabled the FNSEA to remain unspecific regarding the ends of agriculture policy and carry out a pragmatic two-gear policy, encompassing the economic and social functions of agriculture. Policy standards were external to the farm sector (e.g., average income in other sectors); market instruments were undifferentiated: all concurred to conjure up images of a unified and cohesive farming community. The shift to direct payment accomplished something akin to tarification in international trade, by making support both visible and quantifiable. This move rendered the pursuit of pragmatism doubly problematic. In the short term, direct payments conversions exposed disparities of support across sectors. In the long term, the scarcity of resources raises the question of what type of farmers should benefit and to what ends, and therefore the challenge of developing a more principled policy. As one observer put it, 'as long as price support was the major agricultural policy instrument, large and small farmers shared the same interests [...] Reinstrumentation of agriculture policy towards direct payments make this coalition weaker and redistributional conflicts among different groups of farmers more pronounced' (Rabinowicz, 1999, p.405).

The year 1997 epitomized the tensions unleashed by the shift to direct payments. By that point, it was clear that the payments created in 1992 to compensate for price cuts had become a quasi-permanent instrument of the CAP, extended without debate to the three new members joining the EU in 1995 and now representing 60 per cent of the entire CAP budget. At the same time, the prospect of a new enlargement, this time eastwards to countries with large and often antiquated agricultural sectors, raised the odds of yet another reform of the CAP undoubtedly with possibly new price cuts and cuts in direct payments. An authentic cultural revolution took place that year in the 51st annual congress of the FNSEA in Toulouse (18-20 March). The leadership proposed to replace the existing price support and direct payments with one single payment encompassing all productions and accompanied by a regulation of land acquisition (FNSEA, 1997, pp.47-8). With hindsight, it is not just the substance of the proposal that is surprising given the stubborn opposition of the FNSEA to direct payments, but also the fact that it was put forward one year after the spectacular resignation of two of the top figures of the FNSEA, Gérard Lapie and Michel Tesseydou, who had actively promoted the single payment. A crisis broke out between on the one hand livestock producers from regions of extensive production (i.e., dominated by suckling cow farms) and on the other hand cereal growers and intensive livestock producers. Cereal growers in AGPB and intensive livestock producers in FNB saw in the single farm payment scheme a self-serving proposal on the part of milk producers to integrate dairy products into the system of direct payments. Lapie, Tessedou, and their followers on the other hand blamed the FNSEA for favoring a liberal course and neglecting the social functions of agriculture.

The resolution of this crisis displayed the incapacity of the FNSEA to strike an effective balance among commodity interests. In Toulouse, the FNSEA executive board adopted the single payment proposal with the notable abstention of AGPB President Henri de Benoist, and national delegates approved it in the congress. In so doing, the FNSEA actually endorsed a policy course not much different from that which Agriculture Commissioner Fischler put forward in the midterm review and which they spent so much energy combating. Yet, the resolution remained a dead letter owing to the declared opposition of cereal growers and a lack of support from the French government.

It would be an error to reduce tensions to a simple opposition between cereal growers and livestock producers. Intensive and extensive livestock producers were divided on the issue of a single farm payment. A similar split can be found among cereal growers between on the one hand large, intensive growers in the Bassin Parisien and on the other hand, middle-sized cereal growers in the so-called 'intermediary' regions situated along a crescent stretching from Poitou-Charente in the center-west to Alsace in the east.[12] Thus during the whole crisis on the single farm payment, President Henri de Benoist was fighting his own battle *within* AGPB against the intermediary regions to win support in favor of a price cut on cereals. That year, 17 abstentions were recorded during the vote of the AGPB report – a clear warning from the intermediary regions (*Le Monde*, 23 June 1997; see also *Le Monde*, 11 July 1997). These regions have since sought to organize a common platform within the FNSEA, giving birth in 2000 to a working group devoted to their specificities. Concrete results have yet to materialize, though the specter of the degressivity of farm payments and additional price cuts may provide further prods to mobilization.[13]

In sum, it has become increasingly difficult for French farm leaders, in the FNSEA and elsewhere, to reconcile the economic and social functions of agriculture under one pragmatic policy. The 'one model fits all' strategy, which allowed to accommodate all farmers' interest (positive-sum game) under one policy, has reached its limit with the shift away from price support, pressure from the WTO to phase out production-related support, and the scarcity of resources at the European level. The 1997 congress showed the clearest signs of exhaustion of the old model. The internal debate now hinges on clearer zero-sum premises. The current FNSEA president's motto (*'pas de pays sans paysans, pas de paysans sans revenu, pas de revenu sans prix'*) is thus telling of the difficulty to look forward, as it holds on to a reality where guaranteed prices are the cornerstone of agricultural policy.[14]

FNSEA and the State: Who is in Command?

Traditionally, the FNSEA's most effective weapon to counter the reformist spirit of the Commission was the state. State support itself was unproblematic under the conditions of neocorporatism. This situation has changed in recent years, as the state has claimed a more assertive position in agricultural policy. Change has not been linear or unidirectional for it has reflected the influence of individual personalities and the vagaries of governmental coalitions. Yet, the relationship between the state and farm unions has, nevertheless, evolved with respect to the issues of accreditation and the financing of farm unions. If the state remains an ardent protector of the farm cause in EU and international affairs, political alternance at the top between the left and the right have changed the domestic terms of the partnership between state and farmers.

Ending the Representational Monopoly

Accreditation, the mechanism by which the state selects its interlocutor in agricultural policy, was the first issue attesting to a change in the state's strategy. Formal changes took place in the early 1980s, as a result of new-elected Socialist President François Mitterrand's commitment to 'pluralize' farm politics and redistribute wealth and opportunities among farmers. The adoption of proportional representation in the elections to the Chambers of Agriculture was a decisive step in this process as it facilitated the electoral establishment of 'dissident' farm unions, and thereby mechanically strengthened their claim to representative status. The government shortly extended accreditation to four dissident farm unions that had grown on the left and right fringes of the FNSEA. In parallel, Agriculture Minister Edith Cresson set up a series of new public intervention agencies, the so-called *offices par produits* (commodity agencies), to organize commodity markets in a more redistributive manner on the basis of the principle of differentiated price support.

Pluralism and redistribution shortly ran amok, however, under the combined pressure of massive FNSEA-sponsored street protest at home and clashes with the French government's European commitments (Jobert and Muller, 1987, p.97; Servolin, 1990).[15] The *offices* did come to life, but only as pale copies of the original blueprint, now fully compatible with CAP principles. In 1983, Socialist Agriculture Minister Michel Rocard called a truce with the FNSEA, which among other things materialized in a pragmatic interpretation of representativeness, where one of the conditions for gaining representative status was a threshold of at least 15 per cent of the votes in professional elections – a high toll for minority unions. From then on, the position of the state on farm representation reflected an erratic mix of pragmatic and partisan concerns. In 1986, the victory of right-wing parties brought former FNSEA president François Guillaume to the head of the Agriculture Ministry, where he reversed most of the pluralization decrees passed by his predecessors. From 1988 to 1992, the return of the Socialists to power again marked small improvements for minority farm unions. While reaffirming the threshold of 15 per cent, a 1 March 1990 decree softened its implementation,[16] thereby enabling a fifth farm union (*Coordination rurale*) to be officially recognized by the state in 2000.

Informal changes also took place alongside changes in the formal setting of representation, leading to the sporadic and innovative use of concertation between the government and farm leaders. Socialist governments in 1982 set up alternative concertation mechanisms using Socialist Party fora as a platform of discussion with minority farm unions. Right-wing governments persistently reduced concertation to the FNSEA. Socialist governments in the early 1990s practiced a 'two-tier' concertation, which *de facto* excluded minority farm unions (*Le Monde*, 1 November 1991). In yet another variant, socialist governments in the mid-1990s enlarged concertation to all officially recognized farm unions. This last strategy, pursued under Jean Glavany, marked one of the most serious chills in the relations between the FNSEA and the government.

The Power of the Purse

The financing of farm unions has also undergone changes in recent years. In the past, ANDA subsidies represented a significant and stable source of revenue for the FNSEA. ANDA was a semi-public organization (made up by representatives of the state and of the profession), created in 1966 in order to disseminate the results of applied research in the agricultural sector. ANDA receipts stemmed from nine parafiscal taxes levied on farm products according to a logic of solidarity between rich and poor, whereby sugarbeet producers and cereal growers paid proportionally more than other farmers. The agency then redistributed these funds to accredited farm organizations in the form of subsidies for so-called 'agricultural development' actions. The accreditation of minority farm unions in the early 1980s meant that the FNSEA had to share public subsidies with others, which produced new conflicts among farm organizations. On the one hand, FNSEA claimed that minority farm groups were kept artificially alive through the provision of public subsidies, and cereal growers especially grew increasingly dissatisfied with the level of their dues.

Conversely, minority farm groups accused ANDA, where the FNSEA together with its partners possessed a blocking minority, of discriminatory practices.[17]

In the early 1990s, a reform changed the financial rules governing ANDA. The tax base was enlarged to three additional categories of farm products. While more farmers contributed to ANDA, cereal growers then saw their contribution fall by in all 63 per cent from 1993 to 1995. Simultaneously, the principle of juste retour (according to which one gets back a 'fair' proportion of one's financial contribution) was applied, which limited the redistributive impact of ANDA programs. Together, changes in the tax base and in the mode of distribution of funds sealed the last hours of the logic of solidarity. The reform was a failure. Many farmers refused to pay the taxes. Professional organizations lacked the will to enforce it. ANDA was on the verge of bankruptcy as the falling contribution of cereal growers was not matched by alternative resources.

The publication in 1999 of a critical report by the French Court of Auditors set the stage for a second reform, reversing the spirit of the first. The report traced in detail the evolution of the balance of power between the state and the profession:

> The administration has let the profession assume a preponderant role in the determination of [agricultural] development policy, even though article R.822-3 of the rural code attributed this responsibility to the agriculture minister. The profession has attempted to justify this evolution with reference to the fact that ANDA resources stem from taxes paid by farmers or collected in relation to the marketization of farm products. Yet, this levy rests essentially on the exercise of public authority [puissance publique] prerogatives and nothing permits one to regard the product [of these taxes] as the 'propriety' of taxpayers (Cour des Comptes, 1999, chapter 14, p.1).

The Court of Auditors underscored that, in the absence of state intervention, ANDA had turned into an unethical financing instrument of farm unions, paying lip-service to agricultural development.[18] In conformity with this diagnosis, Socialist Agriculture Minister Jean Glavany presented the legislature with a project of reform containing provision for a greater participation of the state in the definition of policy objectives and in the management of the funds and stricter evaluation procedures. The legislature passed the bill on 9 July 1999, and furthermore decided in December 2002 to replace the twelve ANDA parafiscal taxes with one tax on farm sales turnover. The final act came on 14 January 2003 with the dissolution of ANDA.[19]

What will be the impact of these changes? These reforms will presumably promote a more rational and efficient agricultural development policy, guided by concrete policy objectives and more effective evaluation procedures. The greater involvement of the state in the orientation of policy (both politicians and public servants) and the new mode of financing of agricultural development (through the tax on farm sales turnover) make support more visible and are thus likely to politicize agricultural development. The real question, however, concerns the financing of the FNSEA and of the CNJA. At present, it is not clear how much money the FNSEA stands to lose from these changes because statistics on FNSEA finances are difficult to locate. Estimates suggest that public financing represented in 2001 nearly 60 per cent of the FNSEA's budget (i.e., 6.9 million euros out of a total budget of 12 million euros), the remainder coming from the dues paid by the local branches of the FNSEA and the commodity groups. It is more than the level of public financing disclosed by *Le Monde* in 1992.[20] On the other hand, it is much less than the levels of state subsidies received in the past by the CNJA, which 'in some years ... constituted as much as 92% of the total CNJA budget, with dues accounting for a mere 8%' (see Keeler, 1987, p.122). If national farm budgets can be considered as a good measure of state commitment to agriculture, then there is no doubt that the era of public magnanimity is over. Subsidies now come with strings attached, increasingly in the form of project grants. The FNSEA and the CNJA will no longer be the automatic or the exclusive recipients of public money – they will have to compete for it.

Undoubtedly, left and right continue to shape farm politics in France. Yet beyond shifting governmental coalitions, legislation on accreditation and the public financing of farm unions has been redefining the relationship between the *state* and the profession in a way that limits what individual *governments* can do. The 'losers' in these reforms have been the FNSEA and the CNJA. Their lack of influence on CAP reforms as seen in the previous section, but also on some key aspects of the *national* bills accompanying European reforms – traditionally, their ground of predilection – is a patent illustration of the changing balance of power between the state and the profession.[21] The 'winner' has been the state – not minority farm unions, who have been involved only formally in policy-making. Agriculture Minister Glavany's formula, 'in a republic, there is no room for co-management between a democratic government and the corporations' (*L'Humanité*, 15 September 1999), served to enlarge consultation to all farm unions without committing the state to a single organization's agenda, be it that of a left-wing farm union.

'Public Opinion Must Understand ...'

Socialist Agriculture Ministers Louis le Pensec and Jean Glavany openly acknowledged the role of public opinion in their efforts to reform agriculture. Louis le Pensec's unprecedented critique of the time-honored doctrine of *vocation exportatrice* of French agriculture was driven by the publication of an explosive agriculture ministry report showing that EU payments constituted a significant share of the income of French cereal producers.[22] His successor, Jean Glavany, openly acknowledged that to promote a greener and more social form of agriculture, 'the pressure of consumers – not only in Europe but also in America – will be very useful' (*L'Humanité*, 15 September 1999). The slowly loosening relationship between the state and the profession, together with CAP reforms, has coincided with the return of public opinion in agricultural policy. Today like half a century ago, farmers must make their case in the public arena. In the 1950s when French agriculture was still in search of a paradigm and a protector, farmers exhorted their fellow citizens to 'understand that the peasantry needs a policy of long-term regeneration' (*Le Monde*, 16 May 1956). A cursory glance at today's headlines – 'should we continue to support agriculture?' (*Le Figaro*, 30 March 1995), 'farmers face public opinion' (*La Croix*, 8 February 1996), 'farmers' message is blurred' (*La Croix*, 31 January 2001) – evoke the growing weight of public opinion at a time of oscillating political priorities. Complicating the task of farmers, however, is the fact that food scares and production surpluses have robbed agriculture of its virtuousness.

Civil Society Coalitions against the CAP

Undoubtedly, minority farm unions such as *Confédération paysanne* and *Coordination rurale* have cultivated their public image. Both unions have used spectacular disruptive actions which have enabled them to kill several birds with one stone: make themselves known in the broader public; positioning themselves as the 'real' voice of the people, as opposed to the FNSEA 'establishment'; and set the agenda on new concerns and / or tabooed issues. *Coordination rurale*'s nationalist program struck a chord with the wider public hostility to the GATT's Uruguay Round and increasing EU-skeptic sentiments. The organization was particularly adept at staging public events, such as symbolic blockades of the capital city or interviews with French Nobel Laureate in Economics Maurice Allais.

    Confédération paysanne has resorted extensively to collective action, too, its protest activity focusing on the fight against 'junk food,' typically in the form of attacks on McDonald's restaurants and the destruction of GM crops on scientific sites. Unlike *Coordination rurale*, however, *Confédération paysanne* weaved ties to a series of organizations and foreign farm unions, which embedded it in a broad advocacy coalition. Under the charismatic leadership of José Bové, one of the organization's eight founding members, *Confédération paysanne* has conquered a secure place in the public debate at home as well as abroad, causing irritation with the FNSEA (Rogers, 2000). The results of the last two elections to the chambers of agriculture – a commonly used yardstick of farm unions' relative power – indicate the resurgence of farm conflict in France (see Table 5.3). From 1995 to 2001, *Confédération paysanne*'s results rose by more than 6 percentage points between the two elections, thereby becoming the uncontested second-largest farm union in France with one-fifth of the votes, while *Coordination rurale*'s inroads stabilized at around 12 per cent of the votes. The success of these unions reflect in part the role of charismatic personalities (the 'Bové effect'). Yet, some have also seen in these elections the stamp of a new agricultural dualism, 'shaped by the strategies of agri-business and agricultural policy', leading to a clear-cut zoning of union influence: the regions of large, intensive farming in the north-west supporting the FNSEA; the less favored areas, characterized by smaller and extensive farming voting for *Confédération paysanne* (Delorme, 2001).

    It is unclear how *Coordination rurale* fits into the riddle of the reconfiguration of farm politics, but its good results in the 1995 elections, combined with its staying power, won it the official recognition of the government in 2000. Clearly, agricultural policy has been characterized by a growing degree of politicization and a broadening of the policy agenda to new, 'soft' issues. Several voices now speak publicly on behalf of French farmers. For the FNSEA, the challenge is not, in the immediate future, to fight for the control of the loci of power: the fact that it still controls twice as many votes as *Confédération paysanne* grants the effective leadership of a series of powerful local policy-making bodies. It is, rather, to contain discourses on 'socially and ecologically sound... "peasant agriculture"' (Rogers, 2000, p.60) and the parallel development of sub-sectoral networks around organic farming bypassing official channels of representation.

Table 5.3 Elections to the chambers of agriculture, 1995-2001
(constituency of farm owners)

Lists	1995 (%)	2001 (%)	Evolution (% points)
FNSEA-CNJA	59.79	52.42	-7.37
Confédération paysanne	20.07	26.39	+6.32
Coordination rurale	12.17	12.38	+0.21
MODEF	4.64	2.90	-1.74
Other lists	3.33	5.91	+2.58
Turnout	57.00	61.4	+4.4

Source: Data from the French Ministry of Agriculture, available on
http://www.terre-net.fr/dossiers/election_chambre_agri/resultats_2001/default.asp

Learning to Love Industry

While minority unions have turned to the public opinion as a last resort instance, the FNSEA and commodity groups have opted for a different partner: the industry. On the face of it, these two strategies are opposite. However, a closer examination of the motives of the FNSEA reveals a more complex picture as the industry itself has in the last decade climbed on the bandwagon of civic agriculture. Hence, the FNSEA has used partnerships with the industry to enhance the commercial value of farm products while controlling communication with the broader public. Two industrial strategies have materialized within the FNSEA and commodity groups.

First, the FNSEA and commodity groups have sought to build sector-wide organizational structures, *filières* in French, encompassing all links in the production chain, e.g., from the production of wheat to the distribution of bread. Such platforms are not easy to set up, as the interests of the actors involved tend to be antagonistic and asymmetric. Nonetheless, the need to communicate to the public about food products and the interest in enhancing the commercial value of these products have provided incentives for cooperation. Sectors have been unequally successful in organizing common platforms, meat and milk producers having succeeded to a certain degree whereas platforms have yet to emerge in the pig and cereal sectors. The efforts to organize sector-wide coordination platforms are not new – they date back to the early 1980s, and have perhaps unintentionally been reinforced by the creation of the *offices* par produits by the Socialists (see Coleman and Chiasson, 2002) – yet, food scares and the internationalization of food markets have lent them an extraordinary appeal. At stake here is whether the FNSEA will be able to preside over the movement of intensification and systematization of this movement, as it is the ambition of its current president. A test-of-strength is bound to oppose the leadership of the FNSEA and that of the more independent-minded commodity groups. At present, it is not obvious whether the FNSEA will come out victorious from this battle. It may then be doomed to the same fate as its Dutch counterpart, where decades of strong neocorporatism have eventually given way to a pillarization along vertical, sectoral lines (see Frouws, 1997; Frouws and Ettema, 1994; Greer, forthcoming).

A second strategy materialized in the beginning of the 1990s with the formulation of the concept of integrated farming, around which a partnership has solidified between industry, farmers, and consumers. At the origins of this initiative lay the willingness to manage communication with the greater public. The idea was simply that in order to exist, one must communicate, or that the biggest threat to one's existence is to let others speak on one's behalf. According to the FNSEA, it was not so much the popular achievements of environmental / consumer groups, or left-wing farm unions, which set integrated farming on track, as it was the increasing success of the agro-chemical industry in blaming pollution and environmental problems on the users of fertilizers, fungicides, or pesticides (i.e., incompetent, careless, or greedy farmers) rather than on the products themselves. The Forum for Environment-Friendly Integrated Farming (Forum de l'Agriculture Raisonnée Respectueuse de l'Environnement, FARRE for short) became the focal point for the development of this farming concept. FARRE's public message was the following: farmers can be both responsible citizens and profit-seeking entrepreneurs utilizing productivity-enhancing technologies. The objective was to promote a 'competitive form of farming which aims to satisfy three key criteria: the financial objectives of farming producers, consumer demands and expectations, and also care for the environment' (http://www.farre.org/versionAnglaise/farre_an.htm).

The agri-chemical industry turned out to be *demandeur* of a partnership with the FNSEA on this issue, probably as a result of the realization that they would not be able to persuade public opinion of the innocuousness of their products if they monopolized communication on this issue. FARRE brought together all the industrial actors involved upstream of agricultural production, not least the producers of fertilizers (Union des Industries de la Fertilisation / UNIFA) and the producers of phytosanitary and biotechnological products (*Union des Industries de la Protection des Plantes* / UIPP), thereby substituting a positive-sum game for the previous strategy of brinkmanship pursued by farmers and industrialists. Even more surprisingly, maybe, *Union Fédérale des Consommateurs* (UFC), the largest consumer organization in France, also proved a reliable supporter of integrated farming. Its president, Marie-José Nicoli, designated integrated farming as a 'balanced and convincing' initiative and developed good working relations with the FNSEA personnel involved in FARRE (*Le Monde*, 14 March 2003). Environmentalists, on the other hand, have considered integrated farming as little more than a manipulative attempt to sell conventional farming under a new name.

A vexing question for the FNSEA, again, has been to discipline its own ranks – the opposition this time arising not from commodity groups but from transformation and distribution cooperatives owned by farmers. Unexpected resistance stemmed from the cooperative branch of the transformation sectors. Though managed by farmers, these enterprises (federated in the *Confédération Française des Coopératives Agricoles* / CFCA) joined in the project only reluctantly after bitter debates with the FNSEA. Two factors were key to CFCA's resistance. First, cooperatives pursue predominantly strategies of market segmentation, involving a given product (labels) or production (organic farming). These strategies are alien to the mass logic of integrated farming whose objective is to apply to the farm sector as a whole, i.e. not just to products or sectors of production. Second, cooperatives have been unwilling to heighten consumers' confusion about food quality by adding yet another referential besides the officially recognized 'quality signs'.[23] Still, a greater challenge to integrated farming has come from the five highly concentrated buying groups that represent 70 per cent to 80 per cent of the sector. Though committing themselves to distributing products from integrated farming, some distributors moved to develop their own products under the description of integrated farming, a move which may undermine the efforts of the FNSEA to monopolize integrated farming and claim for its members a growing share of the final added-value of food products, if it is not checked in time.

In sum, industrial partnerships are not solutions without risks in order to restoring the confidence of farmers in the FNSEA and of the broader public in farming products. The two industrial strategies that the FNSEA has developed present dangers for the organizational coherence of the farm union. However, integrated farming may be one of the tools through which the FNSEA may retain state support and the confidence of the broader public in spite of devastating food scares. It has now developed into a full-fledged political program including: the specification of 98 rules in a national schedule of conditions; the establishment of a national, state-administered process of qualification; and the setting-up of a nation-wide pilot network of 352 FARRE farms. Legislation on labeling is pending. The state has set to the profession the voluntary goal of helping 30 per cent of French farmers to subscribe to integrated farming by 2008. Last but not least, consumer organizations have supported this initiative provided qualification for integrated farming should be administered by the state. The state is thus coming back, but it is a little concession considering the new perspectives of public financing that integrated farming may open up for French farmers in the years to come – not a small feat in a context of mass unemployment and large public deficits.

Conclusion

The FNSEA is the child of neocorporatism at home and the developmental paradigm of agriculture pursued at the European level. Neocorporatism and the developmental paradigm provided the FNSEA with the tools and resources to grow as the most powerful and legitimate platform for the representation of farm interests. Conflicts existed within and without the FNSEA, occasionally materializing in the exclusion of dissidents and in the creation of new farm groups. Yet, 'peasant unity,' if it was a myth in ideological terms, reflected at least the self-perception of a large majority of farmers as a distinctive socio-economic segment in need of a single representative organization. For various reasons, neocorporatism and the developmental paradigm have come under pressure in the last decade. The main challenge now facing the FNSEA is to adapt to a less benevolent context, characterized by: 1) representational plurality and reduced opportunities for pursuing a robust agricultural policy at the national level; 2) the growing visibility, conditionality, and territorial character of public transfers at the European level; 3) the globalization of food markets; and 4) last but not least, the resurgence of a public debate on agriculture. At stake is whether the FNSEA will be able to navigate in this new environment and remain a respected and influential player in farm affairs. This problem has two facets: an external and an internal dimension.

The *external* facet concerns the standards or yardsticks that are likely to shape farm groups' strategies and preferences. The one unambiguous trend points towards a greater role for public opinion. There are fewer and fewer farmers in France. Even if one takes into account the notorious rural bias of 5th-Republic institutions and the rural anchoring of the right-wing UMP, this means that farmers are wielding decreasing political clout on their own – in any case, a far cry from the 1950s when farmers represented 6 million votes out of 25 million, 25 per cent of the population, and 16 per cent of the national income (*La Correspondance Hebdomadaire*, 22 October 1954, E424). At the same time, however, there are still many more farmers today in France than there would be, were agriculture subsumed under the realm of market forces. These developments, together with the growing visibility of farm transfers as a result of the shift to direct payments, suggest that the public agenda will play a greater role in shaping farm policy-making. A key currency of power will thus reside in the ability of farm groups to think through their role in society and advocate their cause in the broader public. In this respect, the multiplication of voices speaking on behalf of farmers is a challenge for the FNSEA, which purports to represent the interest of all French farmers. Yet, opportunities for the FNSEA lie in both the strong resonance of agriculture in French society and the organization's own nascent awareness of its social environment. A more ambiguous development concerns the relative role of the state and EU institutions in the making of agricultural policy. The impact of EU enlargement and of the pending negotiations on a constitutional treaty has yet to materialize but one can speculate about the consequence of a weakening of the intergovernmental features of the CAP through the generalized resort to voting in the Council of Ministers and possibly the extension of the co-decision procedure to aspects of agricultural policy.[24] Importantly, these developments may take place *simultaneously with* a partial renationalization of the CAP through the repatriation of some competences and/or resources at the national level. In this complex picture, the strength of farm groups will reside in their quality to behave as chameleons. Strategic flexibility and swiftness of action are not the hallmarks of the FNSEA, which must constantly articulate diverging interests and which has pursued an exclusively state-tailored strategy. Its biggest trump card, then, is its nation-wide, cross-sectoral network of members which it can mobilize through collective action or through the wide range of provision of services.

The real question, under this circumstance, concerns the *internal* facet of influence: the ability of the FNSEA to remain confidently planted on its two organizational feet – the territorial and the sectoral. Making these two feet cooperate and point in the same direction has been one of the thorniest problems facing the FNSEA leadership since its origins. The FNSEA has constantly been forced to adjudicate between the demand of local branches for more transparency and bottom-up participation in the internal decision-making and the desire of some commodity groups to preserve their independence. Today, this dilemma is compounded by the fact that there are now credible alternatives for dissatisfied local members, and that commodity groups have now become used to negotiating directly in Brussels on big reform packages. Crucially, it is not just sectoral issues that escape the purview of the FNSEA. The organization has had difficulties bringing added-value on key horizontal issues, as illustrated lately with pristine clarity by the FNSEA's conspicuous absence on the decoupling of farm payments, the horizontal issue *par excellence*. The FNSEA leadership is therefore now placed in the unenviable position of having to recognize that: either it does not wield any influence on major parts of the CAP reform, thus facilitating the job of those commodity interests who have grown increasingly skeptical of the FNSEA's *raison d'être*; or, less credibly, that it engaged in a deliberate and controlled game of split-intermediation with commodity groups, in spite of incessant guarantees to the contrary given to its local branches.

Is there a way out of this catch-22? The FNSEA is faced with a choice between turning into a lobby organization and remobilizing the grassroots, the consequences of which are significant. The lobbying track entails a regrouping of the activities and services primarily around the function of production of agricultural goods, and a development of the economic and technical expertise of the union. Remobilizing the grassroots, on the other hand, entails casting a wide net under the banner of ruralism to forge coalitions beyond the 'natural' farm constituencies of the union, and ultimately accepting to transfer some power to consumers, maybe also environmentalists, and development organizations.

The FNSEA seems poised to tread the ruralist path. Ruralism will come at a cost. Some commodity groups may jump off the train at this station. Old, established channels of influence with the state may erode while new political alliances may have to be found – possibly in parliament. Yet, the FNSEA does not have much choice, and it possesses some assets to take up the challenge: still a strong reservoir of goodwill in the broader public;[25] some experience of collaboration with national consumer organizations and local environmental groups; and last but not least, a dense nation-wide network of members, held strongly together by the provision of services and human contact. The 21st-century's motto of the FNSEA may thus well read: 'The thirty glorious years are over; long live ruralism!' But will this move suffice to prevent the ongoing pillarization of farm unionism in France?

Notes

* This research was supported by the Danish Social Science Research Foundation (*Statens Samfundsvidenskabelige Forskningsfund* / SSF). The analysis draws upon research in the press archives of the *Institut d'Études Politiques de Paris*, and upon interviews conducted in the spring of 2003 with civil servants at the Directorate-General for Agriculture of the European Commission and in the fall of 2003 with high officials in French farm organizations. The manuscript also benefited from the constructive input of Darren Halpin and the participants in the book and from the golden editorial experience of Vibeke Pierson. I am grateful for the help that I have received from these individuals and institutions.

[1] Freedom of association, gained in 1884, was abolished in 1940 with the creation of a single corporatist organization named *Corporation paysanne*.

[2] André Barthe, *Le Présent*, 6 December 1952; *La Correspondance Hebdomadaire* (1954), E428.

[3] This figure represents the total number of members in local farm unions affiliated with the FNSEA (320,000 in 2000), out of the total number of professional farmers (763,953 in 2001). The data are from Jean-Michel Lemétayer (2003, p.56).

[4] Hardly had the FNSEA celebrated its victory in 1953 than some evoked the threat of a secession of large farmers "increasingly hostile to a political form of market organization, of which they are aware that they pay the price to sustain the small and unprofitable farms." *La Correspondance Hebdomadaire* (1954), E429.

[5] The phrase is borrowed from Jean Fourastié's book *Les Trente Glorieuses*, published in 1979.

[6] In 1963, gross operating revenues varied from 62 in Massif Central to 230 and more in Bassin Parisien (100 = national average), which reflected regional differences in the distribution of farm structures and in agricultural specialization.

[7] In 1987, one-fourth of French farm holdings operated with a revenue below 4,000 ecus / family worker / year. Brageon and Jégouzo (1995) noted that at the end of the 1990s, roughly 100,000 farm households lived under the poverty threshold.

[8] The representatives of the FDSEAs form the general assembly, which elects an executive board, which in turn elects a secretariat and a president. The federal council brings together four times a year the national leadership and the representatives of the local unions.

[9] In the 1970s, the secretary-general of the CNJA denounced publicly 'the common agricultural policy… which has given more money to the rich in the name of liberalism and economic efficiency.' Quoted in Duby and Wallon. According to Duby and Wallon (1977, pp. 654-5), the establishment of the CAP in the late 1960s materialized in a 40 per cent to 50 per cent income gain.

[10] Three movements crystallized outside of the FNSEA: *Mouvement de Défense des Exploitants Familiaux* (MODEF) created in 1959 to defend small-family farming; *Fédération Française de l'Agriculture* (FFA) created in 1969 in reaction to the modernist ideology of the FNSEA; and finally, the *Paysans-Travailleurs* current in the 1970s resisting what their leaders considered to lead to the proletarianization of farmers.

[11] The Council of Ministers is difficult to lobby. The FNSEA uses the Euro-group *Comité des Organisations Professionnelles Agricoles* (COPA), of which it is a member, to influence it, if need be through the organization of protest actions.

[12] These regions are dominated by a mix of cereal and oilseed crops, hence their designation as SCOP regions (where SCOP stands for '*surfaces en céréales et oléoprotéagineux*').

[13] In 1999, during the negotiations of the Agenda 2000, AGPB President accepted the idea of a degressivity of direct payments under certain conditions (Interview with Henri de Benoist, *La Tribune*, 25 January 1999).

[14] This can be translated as: "no countryside without peasants, no peasants without income, no income without price."

[15] On European constraints, see Jobert and Muller (1987, p.97), and Servolin (1990).

[16] At the regional level, farm groups must meet the threshold of 15 per cent in at least half of the *départements* in order to gain a seat in the regional management committees. At the national level, farm groups must meet the 15 per cent threshold in at least 25 *départements* in order to gain a seat in the national management committees.

[17] In 1986, for example, the board of ANDA (where the FNSEA and the CNJA were the sole organizations representing farmers) decided to cut out subsidies to minority farm unions. This decision coincided with the return of a right-wing government to power, and the nomination of former FNSEA President François Guillaume at the head of the Agriculture Ministry. Minority farm unions have always criticized the mode of distribution of subsidies on the ground that ANDA rules of procedure, requiring a two-thirds majority in the general assembly, give the FNSEA block a blocking minority.

[18] A second report, undertaken by the General Inspectorate of Finance and finalized in 2000, raised openly the question of the utility of ANDA.

[19] An organization has yet to be set up to administrate the new policy of agricultural development; it is to be called the *Agence de Développement Agricole et Rural* (ADAR).

[20] According to *Le Monde* of 7 July 1992, the budget of the FNSEA in 1992 was 56 million francs, 80 per cent coming from membership dues (44.6 million francs), the remainder coming from public subsidies (10 per cent ANDA subsidies; 10 per cent *Promotion Sociale Collective* subsidies).

[21] A good example is the inability of the FNSEA to prevent the government from opting for a modulation of EU payments in 1999, by which 1 billion francs were transferred from large farms to finance rural development initiatives.

[22] The report on EU farm payments (Direction des Affaires Financières et Économiques 1997) was published only a few months after the disastrous FNSEA Congress in Toulouse, where milk producers had rebelled against cereal growers and intensive livestock producers.

[23] One could also add that some farmers, within or outside the cooperative movement, criticized the integrated farming approach for making it harder for farmers to sell their produce to the transformation and distribution industries without guarantees of higher profits.

[24] On the role of the EU Parliament in the CAP, see Christilla Roederer-Rynning (2003).

[25] A *Sofres* opinion poll carried out in December 1994 on the basis of a representative sample of the population reported that 74 per cent believed that agriculture must continue to receive support because it is of utmost importance to retain a rural sector in France (see *Le Figaro* 30 March 1995).

References

Association Générale des Producteurs de Blé et autres céréales (AGPB) (1974), *Livre d'Or: AGPB 1924-1974*, AGPB, Paris.

Barral, P. (1968), *Les Agrariens Francais de Méline à Pisani*, Armand Colin, Paris.

Brageon, J. and Jégouzo, G. (1995), 'Revenu Minimum d'Insertion et pauvreté en agriculture,' *Revue de Droit Rural*, Vol. 230 (février), pp.82-8.

Bretonnière, B, Colson, F. and Lebossé, J. (1997), *Bernard Thareau, Militant Paysan*, Edititions de l'Atelier, Paris.

Bruneteau, B. (1991), *Le Gaullisme et les agriculteurs: Les acteurs et leurs discours face à la modernité*, doctoral dissertation, Université Paris I, Paris.

Colson, F. and Blogowski, A. (1993), 'Des agriculteurs en difficulté,' *Projet* 234 (Été), pp. 55-63.

Coleman, W. D. and Chiasson, C. (2002), 'State Power, Transformative Capacity and Adapting to Globalization: An Analysis of French Agricultural Policy, 1960-2000,' *Journal of European Public Policy*, Vol. 9(2), pp.168-85.

Cour des Comptes (1999), Accessed on internet version www.ccomptes.fr/Cour-des-Comptes/publications/rapports/rp1999/ rp1999_19.htm.

Debatisse, M. (1963), *La revolution silencieuse*, Calmann-Lévy, Paris.

Delorme, H. (2001), 'Élections aux Chambres d'Agriculture: Émergence d'un nouveau dualisme,' *Campagnes Solidaires*, No. 151.

Delorme, H. (1990), 'La politique agricole dans l'internationalisation des échanges,' in Pierre Coulomb, Hélène Delorme, Bertrand Hervieu, Marcel Jollivet, and Philippe Lacombe (eds.), *Les Agriculteurs et la Politique*, Presses de la FNSP, Paris, pp.33-51.

Duby, G. and Wallon, A. (eds.) (1977), *Histoire de la France Rurale*, Editions du Seuil, Paris.

FNSEA (1997), *51ème Congrès Fédéral: 'Des Agriculteurs Acteurs, Un Projet de Société, Une Volonté Européenne Affirmée,'* 18-20 March, Toulouse.

Fourastié, J. (1979), *Les Trente Glorieuses*, Fayard, Paris.

Frouws, J. (1997), 'The manure-policy process in the Netherlands: coping with the aftermath of the neo-corporatist arrangement in agriculture,' in E. Romstad, J. Simonsen and A. Vatn (eds.), *Controlling mineral emissions in European agriculture: Economics, policies and the environment*, CAB International, London, pp. 209-23.

Frouws, J. and Ettema, M. (1994), 'Specialised farmers' associations in the Netherlands: recent developments and perspectives,' in D. Symes and A. J. Jansen (eds.), *Agricultural restructuring and rural change in Europe*, Agricultural University, Wageningen, pp.102-10.

Greer, A. forthcoming (2005), *Agricultural Policy in Europe: Less common? Less About Agriculture?* Manchester University Press, Manchester.

Jobert, B. and Muller, P. (1987), *L'Etat en action: Politiques publiques et corporatismes.* Presses Universitaires de France, Paris.

Keeler, J.T.S. (1987), *The Politics of Neocorporatism in France*, Oxford University Press, New York.

Lemétayer, J. (2003), *Qu'est-ce que la FNSEA*, L'Archipel, Paris.

Moulin, A. (1988), *Les paysans dans la société française*, Éditions du Seuil, Paris.

Muller, P. (1984), Le Technocrate et le Paysan. *Essai sur la politique française de modernisation de l'agriculture de 1945 à nos jours*, Éditions Ouvrières, Paris.

Petit, M., de Benedictis, M., Bitton, D., de Groot, M., Henrichsmeyer, W. and Lechi, F. (1987), *Agricultural Policy Formation in the European Community: The Birth of Milk Quotas and CAP Reform*, Elsevier, Amsterdam.

Rabinowicz, E. (1999), 'EU Enlargement and the Common Agricultural Policy: Finding Compromise in a Two-Level Repetitive Game,' *International Politics*, Vol. 36, pp.397-417.

Roederer-Rynning, C. (2002), 'Farm Conflict in France and the Europeanisation of Agricultural Policy,' *West European Politics,* Vol. 25(3), pp.105-24.

Roederer-Rynning, C. (2003), 'From "Talking Shop" to "Working Parliament": The European Parliament and Agricultural Change,' *Journal of Common Market Studies*, Vol. 41(1), pp.113-35.

Rogers, S.C. (2000), 'Farming Visions: Agriculture in French Culture,' *French Politics, Culture and Society*, Vol. 18(1), pp.50-79.

Servolin, C. (1990), 'La gauche aux commandes,' in Pierre Coulomb, Hélène Delorme, Bertrand Hervieu, Marcel Jollivet, and Philippe Lacombe (eds.), *Les Agriculteurs et la Politique,* Presses de la FNSP, Paris, pp.449-60.

Useem,B. and Zald, M.N. (1987), 'From Pressure Group to Social Movement: Efforts to Promote Use of Nuclear Power,' in M.N. Zald and J.D. McCarthy (eds.), *Social Movements in an Organizational Society*, Transaction Publishers, New Jersey, pp. 273-88.

Wright, G. (June 1953), 'Agrarian Syndicalism in Postwar France,' *The American Political Science Review*, Vol. 47(2), pp.402-16.

Chapter 6

Farmer Unions as Relevant Players in the Spanish Farm Interest Group System

Eduardo Moyano-Estrada

Introduction

In Spain, the interests of farmers are represented by an enormous range of associative forms, making farming the sector with the largest number of organizations within the economy. Cooperatives, chambers of agriculture, farmers' unions, organizations of producers of a specific commodity, irrigation communities, federations of cooperatives and local organizations for farmers of mountainous regions are but some examples of this diversity. Many of these organizations, such as the cooperatives, the chambers of agriculture or the irrigation communities, have their origins in the past. Many date back to the old institutions created in the late 19th and early 20th century which have continued to function uninterrupted despite the political changes taking place in Spain in the last century. Others, such as the organizations of producers were founded in response to the policies of agricultural modernization developed in the middle of the 20th century, especially following Spain's entry into the European Union in 1986. Farmers' unions also have their origins in the early 20th century. In contrast to cooperatives, they were forbidden under the Franco-ist regime (1939-1977), rising again later during democratic transition in the 1970s.

This great diversity of associations can be classified into three broad categories (see Moyano-Estrada, 1990); 1) *farmers' unions*, which are claim-oriented associations aimed at defending and representing general interests of specific groups of farmers (landowners of small or large farms) in the political sphere; 2) *producers' organizations*, which are economic-oriented associations aimed at organizing (on a cooperative model or otherwise) interests of specific commodities or production branches (for example, sugar, wheat, tobacco or pork) in the economic sphere; and, 3) *corporatist associations*, which are compulsory ones aimed at representing the general interests of the farming sector as a whole. All these associations are currently attempting to adapt to the new context of change and CAP reforms by modifying their strategies and organizational models in order to improve efficiency within their specific field of action. Of these three categories of associations, the farmers' unions are the cornerstones upon which the Spanish farm interest group system is founded, acting as the backbone of the agricultural policy community.[1]

The aim of this chapter is to analyze the Spanish farmers' unions. This will be done examining how they perceive the changes occurring in Spanish agriculture (in other words, their ideological discourses) and the way in which they respond to these changes through various forms of collective action (that is their strategies and organizational models). The other two categories of agricultural associations (such as the producer organizations, whose interests are linked to a determined commodity,[2] or the chambers of agriculture, today in decline[3]) will not be analyzed here, although they will be referred to in so far as they are closely bound to the farmers' unions.

The study is divided into five sections. The first section provides a brief introduction to the history of the farm interest group system in Spain and will examine the most significant features that characterize it today. In the second section, each of the three associations that represent the general interests of Spanish farmers, the Agricultural Association – Young Farmers (ASAJA), the Coordinating Committee for Organizations of Spanish Farmers and Livestock Producers (COAG) and Small Farmers' Union (UPA), will be analyzed. The third section examines the current context of change occurring in Spanish agriculture that serves as a framework of reference for farmers. In the fourth section the impact that this process of change is having on the discourses, strategies and organizational models of Spanish farmers' unions will be analyzed. Finally, we will assess the role that these organizations play in the decision-making processes when defining and implementing agricultural and rural policy at the European, national, regional and local levels.

An Overview of the Spanish Farm Interest Group System

The processes by which interests have been organized in Spanish agriculture differ greatly from those occurring in the founding countries of the European Union (EU) (Hervieu and Lagrave, 1992). Unlike these countries, agriculture in Spain has not experienced a historical continuity in the process of interest representation. The great diversity and wealth of farming associations existing in Spain in the early 20th century, which gave rise to numerous unions and cooperatives, was brought to a halt when a corporative system of compulsory representation was introduced in 1939 by Franco-ist regime following the Civil War (Moyano-Estrada, 2000). Until that time, Spanish farmers' unions and cooperatives were no different from those of neighboring European countries. However, if the political climate had been more favourable, the Spanish farm group system would likely have undergone a process of development similar to that occurring in the rest of European democratic countries after the Second World War.

The long hiatus of Franco's dictatorship (1939-1977) and the lasting presence of the corporative structures linked to it (mainly chambers of agriculture), prevented the creation of a farm group system on a par with other European countries; a phenomenon that was closely associated in those countries to the processes of modernization occurring in the fifties and sixties. In these countries close relations were forged between the departments of agriculture and the farmers' unions in order to facilitate the implementation of policies for agricultural modernization. With this aim, farmers' unions were granted institutional recognition and provided with the necessary resources for their real and effective participation in the decision-making process.

In the case of Spain, however, the agricultural modernization of the sixties was not the result of a domestic process of social consensus between state authorities and organized interest groups, but the despotic implementation of top-down policies by Franco-ist political elite without the effective participation of the farming sector.[4] Consequently, Spanish agriculture was unable to achieve similar levels of social articulation nor to experience the neo corporatist decision-making procedures that were so successful in other European countries. With the re-establishment of the democratic regime and the right to free association in 1977, the Spanish farm interest group system began a new era, which, following Spain's entry in the European Union (EU) in 1986, allowed it to consolidate structures of representation equivalent to those already existing in other European countries (De la Fuente, 1991).

Today, the farm interest group system in Spain is no different from that of other European countries. There is a single federation of cooperatives: the CCAE (*Confederación de Cooperativas Agrarias de España*) (Spanish Confederation of Agricultural Co-operatives), as usual in the majority of European countries (Just, 1990, and Moyano-Estrada *et al.*, 2001). There are now a variety of farmers' unions available to farmers such as the ASAJA, COAG and UPA. Similar to what occurs in other countries[5] and in the EU institutions – where two representative bodies are recognized as intermediate players: the COPA (Committee of Agricultural Professional Organizations) (Lagrave, 1993) and the CPE (European Committee of Peasantry)[6] – these three Spanish farmers' unions reflect a diversity of ideological discourses: some of which are oriented towards the market and production, others which are concerned with issues related to family farm, labour and the territory, and yet others that stress the professional aspects of farming. The organizational models are also disparate: there is a mixed federation of territorial (regional) unions and commodity associations (ASAJA), a confederation of territorial (regional) unions (COAG) and a national association with non-autonomous regional offices (UPA); models which have their equivalent in other EU countries. Representation of farming interests is measured through several different ways as well. In some regions, such as in Catalonia, Aragon, Castile and Leon, Murcia, Extremadura and Asturias, it is measured by the election results to the chambers of agriculture,[7] while others apply a combined criteria including membership rate, amount of services provided or number of territorial offices (as in Andalusia). Similar systems of measurement can also be found in other neighboring countries of Europe. For example, in France and some German Länders representation of farming interests is measured by election results, while other countries, like the Netherlands or Portugal, use diverse criteria.

Furthermore, the Spanish farm interest group system is socially and politically legitimated to actively participate in decision-making processes regarding agricultural policy, albeit with certain limitations at each of the levels where these dynamics take place, as will be discussed below. According to the study by Gómez-Benito and González-Rodríguez (2000), more than 50 per cent of Spanish farmers attribute representation and defence of their interests to the three farmers' unions mentioned above. Likewise, more than a third of the farmers highly or somewhat highly trusts in the farmers' unions, a percentage of confidence that is only surpassed by the trust placed in cooperatives. To put it another way, farmers' unions are the institutions that, alongside cooperatives, are least mistrusted by farmers. This is especially significant if we take into account the fact that public opinion polls in Spain state that unions, together with political parties, tend to be viewed quite unfavourably on the whole. This would seem to suggest that farmers identify more closely with their farmers' unions than does the general public with unions. This fact is further reflected in membership rates. According to the data of the above study, one out of every three farmers surveyed stated that they are affiliated or have been affiliated at some time to a farmers' union, a percentage that is relatively high in regions such as Valencia (around 60 per cent) or Andalusia (almost 50 per cent). That farmers closely identify with their unions is further corroborated by data regarding levels of participation in elections to the chambers of agriculture. In the majority of Spanish regions, participation in the last elections (2001) was greater than 50 per cent, with over 60 per cent participation in regions such as Navarra, Rioja or Extremadura.

Clearly, in the last ten years Spanish agriculture has consolidated a sound, well-structured union structure around three farmers' unions (ASAJA, COAG and UPA), in addition to a unitary federation of cooperatives (the above mentioned CCAE). In contrast to what occurred during the democratic transition and before Spain entered the EU in 1986, the farmers' unions system is today relatively independent from the political system, giving it greater stability and preventing interference by political parties. The three organizations that comprize the farm interest system are viewed by the farming sector as valid mediators at different territorial levels (i.e. the European, national and regional levels), and this fact is not questioned from within or outside the sector. No longer does recognition hinge upon political events or circumstances, or the political leanings of the government. Instead, nowadays it is the result of an autonomy gained through the high levels of participation in elections to the chambers of agriculture and to the votes won by ASAJA, COAG and UPA, whose regional unions account for practically all of the votes cast. The efforts, conviction and pragmatism of their leaders in the last ten years have, without a doubt, made an enormous contribution to this end at both the national and the intermediate level, since they, without renouncing their demands, have pledged their commitment to collaborating with public authorities and adapted their discourses to the reality of the changes taking place in agriculture and agricultural policy.

Individual National Farm Interest Groups

As mentioned above, three farmers' unions (ASAJA, COAG and UPA) are the cornerstone upon which the Spanish farm interest group system is founded. In this section each one of these associations is analyzed focusing on their historical origins, organizational structure and membership.

ASAJA (Asociación Agraria-Jóvenes Agricultores)

The ASAJA (Agricultural Association-Young Farmers) was created in the early eighties through the merger of three pre-existing organizations: CNAG, UFADE and CNJA.[8] On the one hand, ASAJA brings together the elite of large arable lands in Andalusia, Extremadura and Castile coming from the former CNAG and UFADE and, on the other hand, the modernizing reformism of the CNJA, a young farmers' movement founded upon moderate Catholicism and backed, in its beginnings, by groups linked to the technocratic elite of the Franco regime. Today, ASAJA represents the interests of a heterogeneous group of farmers and is led by the owners of large and medium-sized modernized farms or farms which are likely to become modernized, although it also includes a wide range of family-type farm holders. From an organizational viewpoint, ASAJA is organized into 17 regional associations, each one of them composed of county farmer organizations. Some commodity and national industry specific organizations are also members (for example, sugar wheat, tobacco and pork). In fact, ASAJA is a federation of very strong regional and commodity organizations. That is why each regional and commodity organization is autonomous to fund its administrative and professional staff, and to define their policy strategies. Consequently, ASAJA is an umbrella structure specialized in the intermediation relationship with the national government, and it is a member of COPA in Brussels. In terms of its relationship with other business sectors in Spain, the ASAJA maintains special ties with the CEOE (*Confederación Española de Organizaciones Empresariales*) (Spanish Confederation of Business Organizations), which is the peak organization of Spanish entrepreneurs. This relationship has allowed ASAJA to benefit from the large service infrastructure this business confederation offers and participate through it in forums that are normally off-limits to farm organizations such as social security, labour law or tax issues.

There is no official monitoring of membership data in Spain, which means it is difficult to provide data about the number of farmers who are members of ASAJA or other farmers' unions. An estimate can be constructed from other sources (for example, the results of elections to chambers of agriculture, or some specific surveys). However, it is necessary to consider that ASAJA is a federation of regional and national commodity organizations, and consequently individual farmers are only members of ASAJA through their direct membership of such regional or commodity groups. According to survey data (Gómez Benito et González-Rodríguez, 2000), we can estimate the total number of farmer members of ASAJA's regional organizations at 100,000 (15 per cent of the Spanish farmers). In the last elections for agricultural chambers in 2001, ASAJA was the national farmer organization with the largest vote (45 per cent of votes). From this information, it can be estimated that the supporters (members or not) of ASAJA are around 200,000 farmers.

Regarding the issue portfolios that it claims to address, ASAJA is mainly interested in the following issues: trade, commodity production and EU market policy (see below). Agri-environmental issues have not been important for ASAJA, although the relationship between agriculture and the environment has recently been introduced onto its agenda. In this sense, ASAJA has even established a specific department on this topic, perceiving environment as a productive resource (green capitalism), and emphasizing the economic dimension of sustainability. ASAJA perceives organic farming and integrated production as interesting markets to grow farm incomes. Other issues, such as food safety, have not been introduced onto ASAJA's agenda, since this problem is not yet important in production systems linked to the Spanish large arable lands where this association is hegemonic.

COAG (Coordinadora de Organizaciones de Agricultores y Ganaderos del Estado español)

The COAG (Coordinating Committee for Organizations of Spanish Farmers and Livestock Producers) was created in 1978 as a committee to coordinate a number of regional and local organizations emerging during the democratic transition. These organizations emerged from movements opposed to the Franco-ist compulsory corporatist institutions. Their principal leaders originated from the ranks of left-wing politics, Catalonian nationalism and progressive Catholicism, and their members were family-type farm holders from irrigation areas. In fact, the most important organizations under the umbrella of COAG, namely the unions of Catalonia, Rioja or Aragon, arose from the conflicts with the agri-food industries that took place in the mid-seventies in areas of irrigated family farming. These conflicts, which were known as the 'peasant wars', encouraged small family farmers to take on an increasingly militant role and exert their influence through massive public demonstrations in which thousands of farmers drove their tractors through the streets of Madrid.

Today, however, the COAG is a somewhat decentralized organization, being, in fact, a coordinating committee in which the regional farmers' unions enjoy full autonomy. In effect, COAG is a federation of 17 regional farmers' unions, each one of them composed of provincial farmer organizations. In contrast to ASAJA, commodity or industry specific organizations are not members of COAG. Each regional organization is autonomous to fund its administrative and professional staff, and to define their policy strategies at the regional level. In this sense, COAG is also an umbrella structure specialized in the intermediation relationship with the national government. It is a member of COPA in Brussels, although some of their regional associations (such as those of Pays Basque and Galicia) are members of CPE. However, because of the fact that some of their regional unions are economically and politically weak, the national administrative and professional staff of COAG in Madrid provide important services to them.

With respect to membership, it is necessary to take into account that, such as was mentioned above for ASAJA, the COAG is a federation of regional organizations, and consequently individual farmers are not members. Based on survey work (Gómez-Benito and González-Rodríguez, 2000), we can estimate the total number of farmer members of COAG's regional associations at 80,000 (12 per cent of the Spanish farmers). In the last elections for chambers of agriculture (2001), COAG received the second largest number of votes (40 per cent), which suggest an estimate of about 100,000 farmer supporters (members or not). Although the family farm is considered a distinctive feature of the COAG, its membership is fairly heterogeneous as it brings together family farmers with modern farms as well as small farmers with little chance of making their farms viable.

Regarding the issue portfolios that it claims to address, COAG is mainly interested in trade, and EU rural development policy (see below). Environmental issues are being strongly introduced into COAG, which has promoted the establishment of a specific department on this topic in each one of its regional organizations. In this sense, COAG, contrary to ASAJA, emphasizes the social and ecological dimension of sustainability. In particular, the EU agri-environmental program is perceived by COAG as a new source of social legitimacy for farming activity, and organic farming is viewed as a way to avoid the social exclusion of small farmers. Food safety is starting to be introduced onto the COAG agenda, linking this topic to family farming and quality.

UPA (Unión de Pequeños Agricultores)

The UPA (Small Farmers' Union) was established in 1986, promoted by the old socialist workers union UGT (*Unión General de Trabajadores*) (General Union of Workers), in order to allow the small farmer interests to be articulated in autonomous structures independently of workers. Historically, the UGT had joined agricultural workers and small farmers in the same organizational structure, called FNTT (*Federación Nacional de Trabajadores de la Tierra*) (National Federation of Land Workers). Nevertheless, from the entry of Spain in the EU in 1986, the UGT decided to create a new organizational structure separating the agricultural workers and the small farmers. In the framework of this reform, the UPA emerges as a small and part-time farmer organization which, however, maintains strong links with the UGT and takes advantage of this good relationship to use the services from the UGT's administrative staff. From the time that it gained autonomy as an organization, the UPA has expanded beyond the traditional boundaries of UGT influence, incorporating a variety of small farmers' organizations which were opposed to a lesser or greater degree to the ASAJA and the COAG organizations mentioned above, mainly in the regions of the Duero River or Asturias. Given its centralized structure, and the support it receives from the UGT, the UPA has increased its influence in many areas despite the economic precariousness of its members. According to some survey work (Gómez-Benito and González-Rodríguez, 2000), we can estimate the total number of farmer members of the UPA at 50,000 (7 per cent of Spanish farmers). In the last elections of chambers of agriculture (2001), the UPA received 15 per cent of the votes, which supports an estimate of 75,000 farmer supporters (whether members or not). From the organizational point of view, and contrary to the ASAJA and the COAG, the UPA is a very centralized farmers' union, whose members are individual farmers. That is why in each Spanish region the UPA has got an organizational structure based on offices, which are not autonomous, but they depend on the national staff of Madrid to define policy strategies and to provide services to farmers.

The UPA is interested in the issues of trade, rural development policy and conditions of life in rural areas (see below). As with COAG, environmental issues are being strongly pursued by the UPA, which has established a specific department on this topic in its national office. The UPA perceives environment as an important element of the revitalization of the countryside, and emphasizes the social and ecological dimensions of sustainability. The EU agri-environmental policy is perceived as a new source of social legitimacy for farming activity and as a way to avoid the social exclusion of small farmers. Other issues, such as food safety, are being introduced onto the UPA agenda, promoting relations with consumer movements and ecological associations to encourage debate about the role of agriculture and the emerging population demands in Spain.

In summary, ASAJA, COAG and UPA are farm organizations that show important differences in several aspects. Firstly, their organizational structures are different (ASAJA and COAG are federations of regional organizations, while UPA is a centralized national organization). Secondly, ASAJA's ideology is oriented to enterprise and market, while that of COAG and UPA are oriented to family farms, work and countryside. Thirdly, the collective action of ASAJA is focused on developing an efficient and professional technical staff to provide services to farmers, while COAG and UPA are focused on the mobilization of their members through political demands. Finally, the membership profile of ASAJA is characterized by the hegemony of farmers with large- and middle- farm size, while that of COAG and UPA are characterized by the dominance of family farms and small farmers.

The Context of Change in Spanish Agriculture and Rural Society

Today, Western societies are witnessing an important process of change marked not only by globalization and the liberalization of trade and currency markets, but also by the deep transformation of cultural and political values. In the case of agriculture and rural society in Spain, this current context of change is characterized by a series of interrelated factors whose effects can be felt in economic, social, political and cultural spheres (Moyano-Estrada and Garrido-Fernández, 2003).

Economic Changes

Although Spanish agriculture has declined in economic terms – as demonstrated by the gradual decrease in the number of people employed in agriculture (from 13.2 per cent in 1988 to 6 per cent in 2001) and by the diminishing importance of livestock production to the country's GNP (from 6 per cent in 1985 to 3.6 per cent in 2001) – farming remains key to the revitalization of many rural areas. Many jobs in the manufacturing and service industries depend on the farming sector, namely in machinery factories and workshops, fertilizer and pesticide producers, insurance companies, and agri-food industries. For our purposes, it is important to highlight that the people engaged in these activities come from an urban and industrial background imbued with a business rationale that eschews public subsidies, giving them a much different view of the value of the countryside than that traditionally held by farmers. Thus, while farmers and non-farmers may share a business relationship, they do not necessarily take part in a common system of values when it comes to deciding the fate of the countryside in their local communities (Garrido-Fernádez *et al.*, 2002).

At the same time, advances in telecommunications and improved roadways in Spain have brought rural areas out of their isolation and encouraged non-agriculture oriented industries and services to set up business. This has allowed a new and increasingly large sector of businessmen and independent professionals to emerge; people with a free market background whose values differ from those of farmers. Other jobs, linked directly to the welfare society, are also giving rise to an unprecedented revitalization of the countryside in Spain. These new events are occurring most notably in the spheres of health care, education and social services provided by the government and in areas dedicated to offering leisure and entertainment to the population at large, namely in tourism, the purchasing of second homes, retirement, sport and recreation. The rural population is increasingly engaged in these new forms of employment, offering new and non-traditional ways of integrating society and work (Navarro-Yáñez, 1999).

Rural society in Spain has thus become more complex in both economic and social terms, bringing about a greater internal differentiation and job diversity (Garrido-Fernández *et al.*, 2002). All of this is having a significant effect on local lifestyles by reducing the power traditionally held by landowners and encouraging the rise of a new political elite. A new dynamism is being witnessed at the local level and new opportunities are opening up for political activity; an activity which is marked by either co-operation with or confrontation between the old and the new protagonists depending upon their perception of the changes confronting rural society.

Cultural Changes

In the cultural sphere, two important changes have come about. On the one hand, so-called 'post-materialist' values (Inglehart, 1997) are on the rise as increasingly larger sections of the population are no longer concerned solely with satisfying their material needs, but with their quality of life, that is, the deterioration of natural resources, the loss of biodiversity, the degradation of the countryside, the contamination of rivers, and, more recently, food quality and safety. An important cultural change has also occurred in qualified sectors of the Spanish public opinion as a result of the concept of sustainability put forth in the late seventies in the now famous Bruntland Report. While lending legitimacy to the demands of new social groups, these new changes have also meant that substantial constraints have been placed on farmers regarding how they use their land for agricultural production.

Another significant change which has occurred over the last two decades in Spain in cultural terms is that of the reaffirmation of a 'local identity'; a change that has paralleled the spread of globalization. Although apparently contradictory, when examined more closely these processes are clearly coherent with one another. The rediscovery of rural heritage is a process of recovering identity, a searching for roots and tangible references, of closeness and proximity in a world that is increasingly global and whose physical and social coordinates become weakened as they stretch across the planet. It is within this context that the Spanish people are reaffirming their local identity, reviving the values of their neighborhoods (*pueblos*) and seeking to remain in them. It is a clear attempt to equip them with the necessary resources and to exploit the comparative advantages to be had from the advances in technology and telecommunications that this process of globalization offers. Local development projects are taking place at what some authors have called the *interstices of globalization* (Renard, 1998); projects which attempt to give new meaning to the true value of endogenous resources, while at the same time making different forms of development viable so that rural populations may sustain themselves in dynamic communities. Needless to say, this phenomenon has far-reaching economic and political repercussions and is considered key to revitalizing democracy at the local level (Pérez-Yruela, *et al.*, 2001).

In short, a new cultural context is emerging in Spanish rural society which is characterized, on the one hand, by a re-evaluation of the countryside based on quality of life rather than production, and, on the other hand, by the reaffirmation of local identity (*el pueblo*) as a central framework of reference for the whole population. Consequently, a new opportunity structure has also been created; a structure that is being exploited by the various economic and social players according to their particular interpretation of the changes taking place.

Political Changes

Certain events occurring in the last decade have undeniably affected the perspective from which the problems of Spanish rural society are addressed.

The first of these events were the agreements on the liberalization of agricultural markets that were firstly reached at the GATT (Spring 1996 in Marrakech, Morocco) and later at the World Trade Organization (WTO) (in Doha, Qatar, in 2001). These agreements cut all subsidies for production and establish the system of direct payments to farmers, and have important economic and cultural consequences for the farm sector. From an economic point of view, they introduce a new element of competitiveness that was previously confined to sectors that were not provided shelter under the umbrella of protectionist policies (mainly horticulture and fruit production). Thus, Spanish farmers, cooperatives and agri-food companies in general must now be competitive if they wish to benefit from the opportunities that larger markets offer. Culturally speaking, these political decisions have made it necessary to undertake important changes in the sphere of agricultural education and training as well as in the attitude of Spanish farmers regarding their marketing and business strategies.

Secondly, the process of constructing Europe has important political implications for two main reasons. On the one hand, the enlargement of the EU towards new States members makes farmers and cooperatives modify their economic strategies in a more open market. On the other hand, the process of constructing Europe also implies the implementation of new policies regarding the environment, education, research and development, and infrastructure; measures which will require EU funding. Thus, the above mentioned agricultural policy community is now faced with the predicament of having to compete for available resources with other emerging interest groups in a context where the role of agriculture has changed in the European political and social agendas as enough basic foodstuffs are produced and free agricultural markets are established.

Thirdly, the strategic and geopolitical position of the EU regarding its North-South international relations introduces an issue of great concern to Spain. The growing influx of immigrants from northern Africa is forcing the EU Member States to modify their traditional immigration policies and call for a policy of restricted entry in the short term, and increased cooperative funding aimed at development in the countries of origin in the long term. This cooperation implies the adoption of measures which would open the European market to agricultural and livestock products from non-EU countries, particularly those of the Maghreb. Undoubtedly, these measures will have a significant impact on the Spanish farm sector.

Fourthly, an important element of political change and, perhaps, the most far-reaching in its implications in the medium to long term, stems from the welfare state crisis affecting western countries. The current crisis has forced countries to reassess many of the principles upon which their government policies are founded, including those related to agriculture and rural development. The national budget deficit and, particularly, unemployment and issues related to environmental protection and food safety, are now to be taken into account during the much-needed policy reforms, including the CAP reform. These principles, which have inspired agricultural policy since the fifties, imply a fundamental change in the way farmers view their activity and is the basis upon which future policies are made.

In sum, the debate on the future of rural society and the role that agriculture plays in its development is taking place within the multifaceted context of change described above. It includes the waning importance of agriculture in the economy, the decline of the farming population in rural areas, the diminishing influence of a landed elite in decision-making processes, the diversification and greater structural complexity of employment in the countryside and market liberalization. It must not overlook the recuperation of a local identity and the promotion of local development initiatives nor concerns about food quality, environmental conservancy, the achievement of self-sufficiency in food production, the restrictions imposed by the process of European enlargement or new government policies to overcome the welfare state crisis. This context has given rise to new opportunities for both individual and collective action by the different social and economic actors in the rural areas of Spain. Their actions, however, can be explained not by any structural determinism, but according to our understanding of how they perceive and interpret these opportunities.

The Impact on Farmers' Unions

In this section we will analyze the effects that this process of change is having on farmers' unions in Spain and examine the wide range of discourses and the diversity of their strategies and organizational models.

A Diversity of Ideological Discourses

The changes mentioned above have intensified the diversity of the farming sector in Spain, consolidating the plural system of farm interest representation. In effect, the new orientations of rural and agricultural policies lead, on the one hand, to the recognition of pluriactivity in agriculture and the stressing of environmental implications of farming activity and, on the other hand, to the growing interest of the general population about the quality and safety of foods. Together they make possible the coexistence of different agricultural systems and, consequently, different ways of conceiving the problems of farmers in Spain. This has important implications in the farm interest group system, where a diversity of ideological discourses can be observed. At present, two ideal type discourses are evident (see Table 6.1). The first is the 'enterprise discourse' (oriented to the agri-food industry and the market) which is espoused by the organization that on the whole represents the interests of medium and large scale farms, namely ASAJA. This organization endorses a closer integration of the agri-food industry through the creation of inter-professional structures, and a single sector-oriented model for the organization of agricultural interests in each branch of production. Farmers are encouraged by the ASAJA to adopt new management methods and to continue modernizing production on their farms. However, a detailed analysis of the positions adopted by ASAJA at their meetings and conferences reveals a growing concern about the risks involved in farmers relying exclusively on subsidies; subsidies which are increasingly coming under fire in the EU and are likely to be abolished under the current CAP reform.[9]

The ASAJA holds that agricultural policy should be independent of rural development policy and demands that programs be implemented to provide incentives for farmers to modernize their farms and become integrated into larger commercial networks. Future agricultural policy must, therefore, continue to promote modernization in order to improve competitiveness, particularly in the Mediterranean countries, which are in a less-favourable position than other regions of central Europe. It is for this reason that ASAJA opposes proposals to integrate agricultural and rural development policy, since this would subordinate agriculture to a social rationale based on the creation of jobs; an impossible objective for modern farming given that it is characterized by increased productivity and a reduced labour force.

Table 6.1 Ideal discourses of the Spanish farmers' unions

Discourses / Dimensions	*Enterprise discourse (ASAJA)*	*Neo-peasant discourse (COAG and UPA)*
Concept of farming activity	Market-oriented productive activity	Labour and countryside-oriented activity
Farmer's status	Entrepreneur (professional status)	Farmers with a multifunctional status
Role of the State	Low level of state interventionism (to guarantee market stability)	High level of state interventionism (to guarantee farmers' incomes and correct social and economic inequalities)
Function of agricultural policy	Agricultural policy guided by a production-oriented rationale Direct payments to farmers to compensate for free market competition	Agricultural policy guided by a non-productive rationale and integrated into integral rural development policies Direct payments to farmers based on equity
Relationship between agriculture and environment	Environment is perceived as a productive resource (green capitalism) Emphasis on the economic dimension of sustainability Agri-environmental policy is perceived as a way to supplement farmers' incomes and an incentive to use productive resources more soundly Organic farming is perceived as a viable market to increase farmers' incomes	Environment is perceived as key to revitalizing the countryside Emphasis on the social and ecological dimension of sustainability Agri-environmental policy is perceived as a new source of social legitimacy for farming activities Organic farming is perceived as a way of preventing the social exclusion of small farmers

Source: Moyano-Estrada and Garrido-Fernández, 2003

Finally, although the enterprise discourse does not oppose environmental policies, they are of secondary concern. The problems involved in the relationship between agriculture and the environment are expressed by ASAJA solely in terms of economic sustainability as environmental deterioration represents a threat to natural resources; resources which are key to agricultural production (in other words, 'green' capitalism as mentioned above).

The second ideal type of discourse could be described as a 'neo-peasant' or countryside-oriented discourse in that it stresses the values of a rural society that has undergone a social and cultural renewal and in which the role of the family farm (a renewed and modern concept of peasantry) is central to the revitalization of the countryside. In contrast to the first, this discourse is espoused by organizations representing the interests of small farmers, namely the UPA and the COAG. These organizations back policies that are not only concerned with farm production, but also with the diversification of employment and the countryside.

Thus COAG and UPA support a horizontal, rather than a vertical, model of representation of farm interests and encourage collaboration with other groups in rural society, namely environmentalists and consumer movements. Furthermore, they support a high level of state interventionism to regulate market imbalances and encourage associations that represent small farmers. There is unanimity between the UPA and the COAG based on convenience, but also the need to apply differential criteria in the distribution of CAP subsidies. As a result of the growing restrictions placed on the resources available to regulate the different European CMOs (Commune Market Organizations), aid must be directed to the least competitive farms if small farmers are not to abandon the farming sector. These reforms are also seen as a positive step towards restoring legitimacy to agriculture in the eyes of the general population, which views with surprise, if not indignation, how certain groups of farmers amass large fortunes from CAP subsidies; subsidies which are financed by taxpayers' contributions and handed out for nothing in return and with no clear justification.

The neo-peasant discourse holds that future agricultural policy should be an integral part of rural development and encourage family farms. According to the UPA and the COAG, criteria should be based not on competitiveness but on preventing the exclusion of small farmers who they view as fundamental to rural life. Environmental policies are also considered key to creating new opportunities to enhance farmers' incomes, integrating farmers and countryside into society and granting a new legitimacy to agricultural policy.

In short, the Spanish farm sector has become increasingly diversified as reflected in the different responses, both individual and collective, of farmers and their organizations to the new problems facing them. While it is true that the present process of change is perceived as a crisis by the farming sector as a whole, the responses to this crisis are diverse, as is to be expected in a social structure that has become ever more complex and differentiated.

Effects on the Strategies and Organizational Models

The adoption by an agricultural organization of an ideological discourse involves defining the collective action to be taken and choosing a determined organizational model. However, it is also a fact that changes in the role of agriculture and the limitations set down by agricultural policy are beginning to have an effect on the strategies of the three farmers' unions in Spain, regardless of their ideological discourse. In order to understand these effects, we must first begin by acknowledging that agricultural policy has lost, at least in the process of formulation, a great deal of the autonomy it had as a sectoral policy (see Wyn Grant's (1995) notion of this shift as a decline in agricultural exceptionalism). Instead, the current trend is towards its subordination to the rationale of world economic policy; a policy which is increasingly determined by decisions adopted at supranational forums removed (for example, the WTO rounds) from the specific sphere of agriculture. The emphasis that farmers' unions have traditionally placed on public institutions – that is, to exert their influence in different areas of the public administration – is no longer sufficient as many of the factors that determine the content of agricultural policy increasingly have their origin in decision-making processes that are beyond their sphere of influence. Thus, on the whole, farmers' unions are becoming more and more aware that while this sphere of action should not be abandoned, neither should it continue to be the sole area upon which their efforts at collective action are focused.

Hence, organizations such as the ASAJA, which is guided by a market-oriented discourse, increasingly stress the importance of taking action in the economic sphere. With this aim in mind they have undertaken to improve the services they provide for farmers, develop training programs to facilitate the introduction of new farm production techniques and promote the use of new business management technologies in order to move forward in the process of farm modernization. From an organizational viewpoint, ASAJA proposes greater integration into the agri-food industry through inter-professional structures within each *filiére* and advocates a vertical commodity-oriented model of interest representation to replace conventional horizontal countryside-oriented models (see Table 6.1).

The organizations that subscribe to the 'neo-peasant discourse', such as the COAG and the UPA, continue to mark public institutions as an important area of action that should not be abandoned, given that they believe that the state must continue to play a balancing role to compensate for market inequalities. In their opinion, participation in this political sphere must take place through horizontal countryside-oriented and not vertical commodity-oriented models of representation, as those models are the only ones that provide a global view of the problems confronting agriculture and the rural society. They do advocate, however, a greater emphasis on actions in the sphere of civil society, albeit with a difference from the enterprise-oriented organizations. That is, through dialogue and collaboration with other social groups that share in the rural space (ecologists, consumers, rural youth, etc.) so that rural development policy can be cooperatively designed. In terms of training, these organizations stress the multifunctional nature of farming activity and based on this principle promote a multifaceted profile of farmers that combines the productive dimension with others that are in keeping with society's new demands. Hence they demand that the current training programs be widely reformed to include more diversified modalities which better adapt to the issues of prime concern to farmers (see Table 6.1).

Nonetheless, there is a common feature shared by all of the farmers' unions without exception: the importance that they place upon civil society, bringing them to adopt positions that go beyond a simple matter of strategy. In effect, by changing the priority of their actions they are forced to come up with new organizational structures which are less centralized and more rooted at the local and county levels in tandem with the new setting in which their collective action must be carried out. Thus, ASAJA, COAG and UPA have created specific departments dedicated to rural development in order to channel their participation in the EU Leader program or have set up specialized sections devoted to young people, women and even retired farmers in response to demands by these groups. It has also become common to incorporate agri-environmental issues in their organizational structures, such as has been mentioned above (Garrido-Fernández, 1999; Garrido-Fernández and Moyano-Estrada, 1996).

Farmers' Unions and the Agricultural Decision Making Process

In the general sphere of representation, agricultural decision-making processes take place at four levels: the European Union, nationally, regionally and locally. Each of these settings will be examined below.

The European Union

At the European Union level, the negotiations between national farmer organizations to define the common interests of European agriculture occur in the heart of the COPA (where ASAJA, COAG and UPA are member representatives of the Spanish farmers) and the COGECA (where the CCAE is member representative of the Spanish agricultural cooperatives), a task that is becoming ever more difficult due to the growing number of organizations that comprise these immense structures of representation. In fact, the reports that come out of the COPA and the COGECA are increasingly more generic and less specific in nature as consensus among such a wide range of organizations must be limited to general aspects due to the difficulties involved in reaching agreement. In short, at the European level, intense negotiations occur into the consultative committees among the farmer organizations members to the COPA, the CPE and the COGECA, but consensus is not reached on the CAP, which is, as stated above, the result of negotiations between representatives from the national governments. However, the work of farm organizations should not be underestimated. Their numerous reports and protests have greatly contributed to legitimizing (or de-legitimizing) the CAP process. Nevertheless, it is important to clarify that policy-making decisions in

Brussels are not taken in agreement with representatives of the sector. They are only consulted, meaning that farmers' unions should not be held jointly responsible for the CAP regulations, although certainly they participate in the implementation of such regulations in many EU countries.

The National Level

At the national level, there is greater freedom for genuine consensus to occur regarding agricultural policy. In general, and in the current circumstances, where a large part of agricultural policy is decided by the EU institutions (see above), the decision-making process may occur *ex ante* or *ex post* the passing of European regulations or directives. In effect, prior to the meetings held by the Management Committees or the Councils of Ministers of Agriculture of the EU, the national governments may reach agreement with the farmers' unions and federations of cooperatives representatives of the farming sector in order to put forward a common position that these associations, through the COPA and COGECA, will defend in the farm advisory committees, thus backing national interests in the European institutions. In practice, however, the opportunity for agreement *ex ante* depends on the political goodwill of the governments, as they are not obliged to reach a consensual position with representatives of the farm sector. In Spain, the great diversity of agricultural practices (practically all of the CMOs can be found in our territory, from continental to Mediterranean including intermediate ones), the existence of a diverse union panorama (three large national organizations: ASAJA, COAG and UPA; one large confederation of cooperatives: CCAE, and several important commodities organizations) and the state's quasi-federal organizational structure (with 17 regional governments) make it extremely difficult to reach consensus *ex ante* the negotiations in Brussels. For this reason, the steps prior to reaching consensus, such as the national meetings between the Minister of Agriculture and the agricultural departments of regional governments, or the advisory councils with the farmers' unions, end up being ineffective forums of discussion.

    Ex post consensus is more common, especially with regard to socio-structural policy (included under the so-called second pillar of the CAP). In contrast to the CAP first-pillar policies, which leave little room to decide how these policies should be implemented in each EU member state, the second pillar policies make it more possible for consensus to be reached at the national level between the ministers of agriculture (or their equivalent) and organized interest groups (not only farm organizations and cooperatives, but also ecological organizations or rural development networks as it includes aspects related to production as well as the countryside and the environment). However, problems arise when limitations are placed upon participation by interest groups. For example, in Spain, the Ministry of Agriculture and the agricultural departments of regional governments decide how European regulations should be applied, leaving little opportunity for participation by farmers' unions in the decision-making process at the national level. The same thing occurs when different regional departments (i.e. Agriculture and the Environment) must reach agreement regarding the content of certain policies that have a bearing upon the competence of both (as in the case of certain measures under the agri-environmental program), thereby cutting off any possibility for participation by organizations which represent the interest groups concerned. In these cases, the organizations are invited to participate in a process where policy content has already been set down by the public authorities and which is restricted solely to informing them and perhaps consulting them about procedural aspects or implementation. Thus, while it can be said that discussion usually takes place and consensus may occur at this level, it is hindered by the interference of other players and greatly depends on the good will of the national governments.

The Regional Level

At this level, some policies (such as those of the second pillar, but also some important aspects of market policy, namely the fixing of regional production quotes) are a favorable setting for consensus with farmers' unions. To this we must add the possibility (a reality in some regions such as Catalonia or Andalusia) for regional governments to take initiatives regarding the drafting of laws on issues related to agriculture and rural development, thus paving the way for farm organizations to participate in the decision-making process. In reality, there are fewer limitations at the regional level than at the national or European level for agreement on aspects of agricultural policy that fall within their area of competence. While higher political bodies do not usually interfere at this level, concurrence does occur between departments of the same regional administration (convergence between the departments of agriculture and the environment on agri-environmental issues at the national level as explained above also occurs at the territorial level). Clearly, as the second pillar of the CAP becomes increasingly consolidated, and the principles of modulation and cross-compliance are applied through the first-pillar measures, there will be ever greater possibilities for consensus between regional governments and the organizations representing the farm sector on issues related to agricultural policy and rural development. However, it is also true that as these policies have an increasingly less agrarian focus and are based more on a multifunctional approach, it is likely that a larger number of players, such as ecological associations or networks of rural development, will participate. In short, although opportunities for discussion and consensus exist at the regional level, they depend on each organization's capacity for influence and the political and social recognition that each has to make their voices heard.

The Local Level

Below the regional level (local level is a general term to refer to the municipal, county or community level), it is becoming more common to apply development policy based not on a rural or agrarian approach, but a territorial one (Garrido-Fernández et al., 2002). These policies pave the way for interesting scenarios for social consensus between public authorities and the organizations representing the different groups that comprise the local communities (farmers and non farmers). However, although farmers' unions in this setting are given the opportunity to participate, the problem arises from the fact that farmers' interests are poorly represented at the local level. In Spain, farmers' unions have directed their organizational resources mainly at the regional and national levels (and with a fair amount of difficulty at the European level as well), as until recently this has been where discussion and consensus with public authorities were most visible. Thus their participation in decision-making processes at the local level will depend on whether or not they have a genuine desire and will to do so by strengthening their organizational structures at those levels. If they are to achieve this aim, the farmers' unions must modify their discourse and strategies that have characterized them until now (a discourse based on the perception of farmers as producers) in order to gain access to a wider field of representation (based on a perception of farmers as citizens integrated into a rural community). However, this is not a challenge that all farmers' unions are prepared to face, as it would mean creating more decentralized horizontal structures to the detriment of their current vertical models of organization. In short, great opportunities exist for participation in decision-making processes at the local level, but in order to take advantage of them, the Spanish farmers' unions must make a greater effort to undertake both ideological and organizational changes.

Conclusions

After twenty five years of democracy in the Spanish farming sector the farm interest group system has consolidated its organizational structure following patterns existing today in the rest of the EU countries. It is a plural system of three farmers' unions (ASAJA, COAG and UPA) which are recognized by public authorities to participate in the agricultural decision-making process at European, national and regional levels. The three farmers' unions are well accepted by farmers to defend their general interests and by political parties to act as mediators between the Spanish farming sector and political system. The ideological variety of farmers' unions makes the Spanish farm interest group system relatively independent from political parties. This situation has been achieved because farmers' unions have been able to eliminate important obstacles while managing a relevant place in the farm interest system. Among those obstacles are the following: the long hiatus of Franco-ist dictatorship (1939-1975) where farmers' unions were forbidden; the hegemony of compulsory corporatist institutions (chambers of agriculture) as exclusive channels to represent farm interests; the strong relationship between farmers' unions and political parties in the first years of democratic transition, showing a more political than professional image of them before farmers; the great importance of co-operativism as associative expression of farmers at the economic sphere; and the attitudes of the state authorities, imbued with the despotic culture of the Franco-ist regime with respect to the new democratic culture of farmers' unions. The entry of Spain into the EU in 1986 and the federalization of state administrative structures were two decisive factors in consolidating the role of farmers' unions in the farm interest group system. On the one hand, the three farmers' unions (ASAJA, COAG and UPA) were recognized as mediators to represent the general interests of the Spanish farming sector in preference to the old chambers of agriculture. This recognition as mediators and the opportunities to participate in the decision-making process made farmers' unions shift their ideological discourses and strategies from confrontation towards collaboration with public authorities, and update their organizational structures. On the other hand, the transfer to the regional governments of many important areas of national agricultural policy made farmers' unions increase their relevance as mediators of farm interest at the regional level. In this last sense, the greater political diversity of the 17 regional governments (some regions governed by left parties, others by conservative parties and others by nationalist parties) impelled the three farmers' unions to diversify their strategies and reduce (even eliminating) their former ideological identities in order to generate a more professional image and more independence from the political parties. This explains the growing presence of ASAJA, COAG and UPA in the Spanish farming sector during the last ten years, increasing their legitimacy before farmers together with the federation of cooperatives (CCAE). Besides, the three farmers' unions are showing an important capacity to perceive the changes occurring in agriculture and rural society and to assimilate the new orientations of the CAP, particularly including in their agenda issues such as environment, food safety, and rural development. Finally, it is important to note the role of farmers' unions in the promotion of other associative projects, such as the producer organizations of specific commodities and the inter-professional structures in some agri-food *filiéres* – which demonstrates the strong relation between the farming and industrial sector in Spain – and their participation in rural networks together with non-farmer groups – which shows the diversity of Spanish rural society.

Notes

[1] On the notion of 'agricultural policy community' see Smith (1990). For analysis of the CAP using the notion of 'policy community' and 'policy network' see Frouws and van Tatenhoven (1993) and Daugbjerg (1997).

[2] Commodity organizations are relevant players in Spanish agriculture but they are subordinate to farmer's unions in the farm interest group system (see Langreo, 1995). This mirrors other European countries.

[3] The chambers of agriculture are old compulsory corporative establishments founded in the early twentieth century to provide services to farmers and represent farm interests as a whole. From the democratic regime of the II Republic (1931) to the Franco-ist regime (1939) the chambers of agriculture coexisted together with farmers' unions. During the dictatorship (1939-1977), farmers' unions were forbidden, and chambers of agriculture became the only and compulsory farm interest group in Spain. With the recuperation of democracy (1977), farmers' unions and other farm interest groups were authorized again, and the chambers of agriculture lost their monopoly in the farm interest group system, which became a plural system. In some Spanish regions the new democratic regional governments even suppressed the chambers of agriculture, whereas in other regions these corporative

establishments have continued to exist but with functions reduced to the provision of technical and administrative services to farmers. In such regions the chambers of agriculture are not farm interest groups, but farmers' unions participate in them via representatives voted by farmers in elections each four years.

[4] On farmers under Franco-ist regime, see Moyano-Estrada (2000).

[5] In France four farmers' unions (FNSEA, CNJA, CNP and MODEF) represent general farm interests. In Italy, the Coldiretti, the Confederazione Italiana dei Agricultori and the Confederazione dell'Agricoltura Italiana are the most representative farm associations. In Portugal, the CAP represents the interests of big farmers, and the CNA those of small farmers. In the Netherlands, three farmers' unions (the catholic KNBTB, the christian NCBTB and the KNLC) have represented the Dutch farmers in the Landbouwschap. In Belgium, together with the hegemony of Boerenbond other farmers' unions (such the UPA) participate in the farm interest group system. In Greece, the Paseges is hegemonic among farmers, but the Gedase and Sydase play a relevant role in agriculture (see Moyano-Estrada, 2000).

[6] COPA is the most important institution for representation of general interests of farmers in the EU. Its membership comprises of national farmers' unions who wish to join. Historically, the COPA has been important in legitimising the CAP. That is why in the last decade some farmers' unions opposed COPA and created a European alternative association, called the CPE, whose ideological discourse is aimed to small farmers and oriented towards family farms, the countryside and environment. Recently, the CPE has been recognized as a mediator by the European Commission. For more details on these two organizations see the appendices to this volume.

[7] In some Spanish regions, every four years there are elections for the chambers of agriculture. In these elections, farmers vote for candidates nominated by the farmers' unions. Such elections are used by regional governments to measure the representation of farmers' unions in its region.

[8] The foundation of ASAJA through the merger between three predecessor groups was not the result of low levels of available group resources, but it was motivated by other causes. The most important one was the expectations for large and middle sized landowners to be represented by one strong single organization in Brussels after the entry of Spain in the EU (1986). The process of merging was easy because the three organizations shared an enterprize and market oriented ideology on agriculture and their leaders came from the old Franco-ist corporative establishments.

[9] This internal debate in ASAJA explains the emergence of an autonomous group called GEA (*Grupo de Empresarios Agrarios*) whose members are landowners of large and modernized farms. This group is composed of the ASAJA's current or former members which are critical regarding the leadership of this association and seek a more liberal policy oriented to promoting the competitiveness in farms.

References

Brugge Group (2003), *For a change in European agriculture* (published in Spanish, German, French and English version by several institutions. The rapport can be viewed at www.groupofbruges.com)

Daugbjerg, C. (1997), 'Reforming the CAP: The Roles of Policy Networks and Broader Institutional Structures', *ALF Working Paper*, South Jutland University Centre, Esbjerg, Denmark.

De La Fuente, G. (1991), *Las organizaciones agrarias españolas*, Instituto de Estudios Económicos, Madrid.

Desrues, T. and Moyano-Estrada, E. (1999), 'Límites y posibilidades del Partenariado Euromediterráneo', *Revista Española de Desarrollo y Cooperación*, Vol. 5, pp.35-56, IUDC, Madrid.

Entrena, F. and Moyano-Estrada, E. (1998), 'Reactions of Spanish Farm Cooperatives to Globalization', *Journal of Rural Cooperation*, Vol. 26(1-2), pp.21-36.

Esche, D. (2000), *Le syndicalisme agricole specialisé en France. Entre la specificité des interêts et la besoin d'alliances*, L'Harmattan, Paris.

Frouws, J. and Van Tatenhove, J. (1993), 'Agriculture, Environment and the State', *Sociología Ruralis*, Vol. 32(2), pp.220-39.

Garrido-Fernandez, F. (1999), *Discursos, actitudes y valores de los agricultores y sus organizaciones ante la introducción de métodos sostenibles en la agricultura*, Tesis doctoral, Universidad de Córdoba.

Garrido-Fernandez, F. *et al.* (2002), 'Rural Restructuring and the Effects of Rural Development Policies in Spain', in K. Halfacree, I. Kovach and R. Woodward (eds.), *Leadership and Local Power in European Rural Development*, Ashgate, Burlington, pp.173-202.

Garrido-Fernandez, F. and Moyano-Estrada, E. (1996), 'The European Environment and the CAP Reform. The Case of Spain', in M. Whitby (ed.), *The European Environment and CAP reform*, CAB International, Wallinford, pp.86-105.

Gomez-Benito, C. and Gonzalez-Rodriguez, J. J. (2000), 'Identidad y profesión en la agricultura familiar española', *Revista Internacional de Sociología*, Vol. 27, September-December, CSIC, Madrid, pp.41-69.

Grant, W. and Keeler, J.T.S. (eds.) (2000), *Agricultural Policy*, Vol. I and II, Cheltenham/Northampton, Elgar Publishing Limited.

Hervieu, B. (1997), *Los campos del futuro*, Madrid, Serie Estudios del MAPA (First published in French in Paris, Edit. Boulin, 1994).

Hervieu, B. and Lagrave, R. M. (eds.) (1992), *Les Syndicats Agricoles en Europe*, Ed. L'Harmattan, Paris.

Just, F. (ed.) (1990), *Co-operatives and Farmers' Unions in Western Europe*, Denmark, South Jutland University Press, Esbjerg.

Keeler, J.T.S. (1987), *The Politics of Neocorporatism in France*, Oxford University Press, Oxford/New York.

Lagrave, R.M. (1992), 'La représentation de la représentation', in B. Hervieu and R.M. Lagrave (eds.), *Les syndicats agricoles en Europe*, Ed. Harmatann, París.

Langreo, A. (1995), *Las interprofesionales agroalimentarias en Europa*, Serie Estudios MAPA, Madrid.

Moyano-Estrada, E. (1990), 'The Agricultural Professional Organizations in the EC. Theoretical and Practical Aspects', in A. Bonanno (ed.), *Agrarian policies and Agricultural Systems*, Westview Press, Oxford, pp.180-226.

Moyano-Estrada, E. (2000), 'Farmers' Unions and the Restructuring of Agriculture in Europe', in W. P. Grant and J.T.S. Keeler (eds.), *Agricultural Policy*, Vol. I and II, Elgar Publishing Limited, Cheltenham/Northampton.

Moyano-Estrada, E. and Garrido-Fernandez, F. (2003), 'Social Changes and Interest Groups in Rural Spain', in C. Kasimis and G. Stathakis (eds.), *The reform of the CAP and Rural Development in Southern Europe*, Ashgate, Burlington, pp.117-38.

Moyano-Estrada, E. *et al.* (2001), 'Federations of Cooperatives and Interest Organized in Agriculture. An Analysis of the Spanish Experience', *Sociologia Ruralis*, Vol. 41(2), pp.237-53.

Navarro-Yanez, C. (1999), 'Women and Social Mobility in Rural Spain', *Sociologia Ruralis*, Vol. 39(2), pp.222-235.

Perez Yruela, M. *et al.* (2001), *Nuevos conceptos del desarrollo rural. Estudios de casos,* Serie Politeya, CSIC, Madrid.

Renard, M. C. (1998), 'Los intersticios de la globalización', *Revista Internacional de Sociología,* n. 20, CSIC, pp.35-52.

Smith, J.M. (1990), *The Politics of Agricultural Support in Britain. The Development of the Agricultural,* Aldershot, Dartmouth Publishing Company.

PART II
AUSTRALASIA

Chapter 7

'Digging Deep to Keep their Clout': Agricultural Interest Groups in Australia

Darren Halpin

Introduction

The National Farmers' Federation (NFF) is the undisputed voice of Australian farmers. Yet, despite its dominance and encompassingness, at its 25th anniversary the NFF finds itself at a crossroads. Newspaper headlines like 'Farm groups are digging deep to keep their clout' convey the sense of challenge. In examining the challenges facing the NFF one must address its role in two distinctive accounts of change, both in terms of policy substance and process. The first involves the NFF championing the *dismantling* of agricultural exceptionalism associated with state-supported agriculture. However, as trade liberalism has ascended to policy orthodoxy a more complex policy landscape is emerging. The second account of the NFF involves it in *defending* agricultural exceptionalism associated with the encroachment of other interests in land management, rural development and food safety/quality issues.

This chapter argues that the NFF of today is in many ways the victim of its own past success. The NFF organized its influence strategy and resource levels such that it could play a key role in processes of 'bargained consensus', which legitimated agricultural industry restructuring associated with Australia's efforts to maintain a competitive position in the international agricultural economy. But there is a question mark over its relevance in both pressing home and honing this international advantage and in addressing other emerging 'non-agricultural' issues. The bargained consensus model of government-industry relations, at least at the economy wide level, shows signs of fatigue (challenging the NFFs logic of influence), while contemporary agricultural restructuring threatens to unpick the organizability of the agricultural sector (challenging the NFFs logic of membership). This chapter canvases the challenges the NFF faces and the types of adaptations and transformations it is contemplating to forge a role in this difficult environment. It proceeds in four sections. The first provides an overview of the Australian agricultural interest group system. The next two sections outline the two accounts of the NFFs role, while the fourth considers the success of the NFF, explores the challenges it faces and reviews the various strategies it is employing to survive.

The Australian Farm Interest Group System

Before proceeding too far it is important to gather an overview of the agricultural interest group system in Australia. Australian agricultural organizations emerged in the late 19th century along two lines. There were farmers' and settlers' organizations, composed of small and medium landholders, and graziers' organizations composed of large pastoral operations often owned and operated by wealthy absentee landholders. In the early and mid 1900s they collectively formed the organizational arm of the Country Party, which served as a sectional political party for farmers. The existence of the Country Party led to an overrepresentation of farmers in state and federal parliaments, where they dominated key ministerial positions when in government, typically including Trade and Primary Industries portfolios. By the end of the 1960s this formal association ended and the agricultural organizations formally separated from the Country Party (Aitkin, 1972, p.39).[1] The long-term decline in farm numbers led the Country Party to look beyond the farming constituency for an electoral base and rebadge itself as the National Party. This placed more emphasis on agricultural interest groups for political representation. However, the agricultural organizations of the time were poorly funded, employed untrained staff and were largely devoted to narrow industrial matters (Richmond, 1980).

In July 1979 the National Farmers' Federation (NFF) emerged from a process of amalgamation as the peak interest group for Australian farmers. There had been several prior attempts at a unified national organization but they had failed on all previous occasions (Campbell, 1980, p.198; Connors, 1996, p.113). The formation of the NFF, with its constitution prohibiting any partisan political support, evidenced a clear departure from a reliance on the party political system to effectively transmit the interests of farmers. This is not to say, however, that parties don't matter. When the National Party is in government, it tends to raise (often ill-founded) expectations amongst farmers that their issues will receive special attention.[2] The NFF replaced a plethora of state and commodity based groups with a single federated organization based in the national capital, Canberra. Today the NFF has about 75,000 members through its state member organizations, which suggests a membership density of around 50-60 percent. The NFF is the recognized voice of Australian farming with no other serious competitor.

The NFF is responsible for all issues that affect more than one state or more than one commodity. As the label 'federation' denotes, it does not have individual members, rather it has member organizations. The NFF is fully funded by its constituent state bodies. The NFFs member organizations are State Farm Organizations (SFOs) and Commodity Councils (CCs). At its inception the NFF was a neat package of one SFO for each state, with the exception of two organizations in Western Australia and three in Queensland, and a set of CCs that covered each major commodity sector. The NFF is also a member of the International Federation of Agricultural Producers (IFAP).

The *State Farm Organizations (SFOs)* are the foundation of the NFF family. They pay a contribution in order to be state members of the Federation, as well as a subscription for a seat on relevant CCs. SFOs are the only organizations in the NFF family to have direct farmer members and, hence, the only organizations that generate revenue from voluntary subscriptions. The organizational properties of SFOs vary little from state to state. All have individual members who pay voluntary subscriptions and receive in return a range of benefits and discounts. Although, unlike many European organizations, the SFOs do not operate cooperatives, nor do they provide advisory services (these are provided by government and private consultants). Internal decision making is typically made at annual conferences. The office bearers of the NFF and CCs are delegates of the SFOs, which means the SFOs wield a significant level of power and have traditionally been better resourced. For example, the NFF has 17 staff while the NSW Farmers' Association (NSWFA), admittedly the wealthiest SFO, has 68 staff.

Prior to the NFF the only credible federal agricultural interest groups were commodities-based. It was these groups that 'partnered' the state in developing post war industry assistance policies and institutions. They provided members to sit on a variety of boards, committees and councils that administered assistance and marketing schemes. When the NFF formed, these organizations became *Commodity Councils (CCs)* of the Federation. For example, the Australian Wool Industry Conference (AWIC), formed in 1962, was succeeded by the Wool Council of Australia (WCA) under the new NFF structure. CCs are made up of delegates from SFOs and, as such, become aggregators of state positions on commodities marketing, technical issues and research and development priorities. CCs are funded by a mix of SFOs purchasing seats and funds collected from a compulsory producer levy applied and collected at the point of sale by the federal government.

The NFF structure reproduces the diverse commodity base of Australian agriculture, and reflects the Australian federal system of government, the traditional administration of agriculture on a commodity by commodity basis, and the apportionment of constitutional responsibilities for agriculture to the states (Grogan, 1968, p.297).[3] Given the high degree of interplay and coherence between organizational units, when the term NFF is used it refers to a 'family' of organizations, including the NFF Executive, Council and Committees, and all SFOs and CCs.

Reforming Australian Agricultural Policy and the End of Protectionism

Post World War Two Australian agricultural policy can be usefully considered in two periods: a pre 1970s and a post 1970s era. These two periods are demarcated by the shift from the 'protection all round' policy, synonymous with the Australian

Country Party Leader John McEwen, to free-trade policy. This corresponds with the broad shift, identified in most western countries, from a state-assisted to trade liberal agricultural policy approach (Coleman *et al.*, 1996, p.275). While the direction of policy change in Australia may not be unique, the Australian shift has been both severe and largely depoliticized. The character of the shift owes much to the prevailing institutional policy-making framework (Coleman and Skogstad, 1995), including the relations between agricultural interest groups and the state. In tracing this shift and its impact one can identify challenges for the NFF.

Policy Substance: From 'Protection All Round' to Trade Liberalism

The prevailing post Second World War view was that Australia could buffer itself from the perturbations of the international economy through tariff and other protectionist devices. While a net exporter, and with a long history of linkage to global markets, the fluctuations and distortions of those markets created an environment supportive of protection. In Australia, 'protection all-round' policies were extended to most sectors, albeit in different patterns and forms. However, the 1970s saw this position fall into disrepute. In part, this reflected Australia's 'vulnerable' position in the international economy, arising from its small domestic market, reliance on resource sector exports and need to attract foreign capital and investment (see Castles, 1988). As a price taker internationally, it has had little choice other than to accept global economic change and the need to engage with international market forces (Harris, 1993, p.45). Successive governments of both persuasions have adjusted policies to reflect this view. The first drops in assistance and tariffs occurred in the early 1970s, mostly in agriculture, but similar cuts in other sectors followed in the 1980s. The deregulation of both the currency and financial systems followed in the mid 1980s. Reform continues in the guise of national competition policy, which ensures reforms are implemented by the states such that market forces operate unfettered within the domestic economy. This broad pattern of policy change has been repeated in agriculture.

Direct assistance to Australian farmers emerged during the 1930s and solidified as a practice during the Second World War. It recognized agriculture's long standing role as the primary source of foreign exchange for Australia. Assistance to Australian agriculture up until the 1970s was initially aimed at boosting production, providing stable prices to consumers and subsequently to maintaining and stabilizing farm incomes affected by low domestic prices and/or fluctuating world prices (Throsby, 1972, p.13; McKay, 1972, p.26). Import restrictions/tariffs were used to dampen the import side of the balance of payments. On the export side the government attempted to increase agricultural production through various measures including tax concessions, production controls, government funded research and development, access to cheap finance, accelerated depreciation allowances and generous pricing policies for farmers on the domestic market (Gruen, 1990, pp.20-1; McKay, 1972, pp.23-32). Statutory marketing authorities operated in many industries to collectivize the risk of volatile world prices and to facilitate orderly marketing.

Commencing with the 1972 Whitlam Labor Government, successive federal governments have committed themselves to policies of trade liberalism. The rejection of 'protection all round' was an acknowledgement that large-scale government support was not feasible (financially or politically) given the small size of the Australian economy and the domestic market. Australian agriculture has always been export orientated (starting with the shipment of commodities to Britain in colonial times), and lacks large internal markets to sustain price supports in the way that European countries may. In policy terms this shift translated into the gradual removal of import tariffs, the dismantling of statutory marketing arrangements (which have become publicly listed companies and handed back to producers to operate as 'shareholders'), and the placement of rural industry research and development on a more 'commercial footing' (see Wonder, 1995). These domestic reforms relied (and continue to do so) on a countervailing strategy to strongly pursue the freeing up of world agricultural trade, through multi-lateral and bi-lateral processes (see DFAT, 2003). This has made the pace of international reform in relation to domestic reform a source of constant tension in Australian agricultural politics.

The largest cuts in assistance levels were in the 1970s and early 1980s, since which time overall levels have been largely static. While government support is currently very low by international standards it does still flow to Australian farmers. A recent estimate of combined Commonwealth assistance (budgetary, tariff and pricing/regulatory assistance) in 2000-01 was AUD$873.8 million with an effective rate of assistance of 2.8 per cent (Productivity Commission, 2002, pp.3-7). However assistance has increasingly been allocated to capacity building activities in preference to redistributive payments. Assistance now comes in the form of selective maintenance of statutory marketing arrangements, research and development co-funding, farm skilling programs, tax deductible farm savings plans and drought relief. Government also provides infrastructure, such as water supply, irrigation and the rural services to sustain rural populations, all of which are not normally considered in calculations of government assistance. In a land the size of Australia these are neither insignificant nor inconsequential forms of support and underpin the ongoing competitiveness of the agriculture sector.

Change in the Policy Process

Post World War Two agricultural policies of assistance in Australia emerged from commodity specific bargaining between commodity interest groups, the Department of Primary Industries and the minister (McKay, 1972, p.32; Throsby, 1972, p.9). The influence of commodity groups was further entrenched by their direct hand in nominating those sitting on the plethora of boards, councils and authorities that administered assistance and marketing programs (Warhurst, 1982, pp.16-18). Industry assistance was kept away from parliamentary scrutiny with little in the way of economic assessment and public evaluation of its merit. The dominance of these commodity interest groups during that time is attested to by the Country Party Leader John McEwen's now celebrated comment; 'It is the function of my party to see that the will of those who produce and own the product is carried into legislative and administrative effect' (Hansard – Australian House of Representatives – November 23, 1965, p.3055).

The establishment of the Industries Assistance Commission (IAC) in 1974 commenced a crucial change in the policy process itself. It provided a mechanism to review the levels of assistance for Australian industry, investigating each industry in terms of its capacity to grow the Australian economy and compete in a liberalized international trading environment. Agriculture became just another Australian industry sector where assistance was to be made on the basis of an economic rationale. The IAC broke up the close departmental-interest group relations that had hitherto dominated commodities-based agricultural policy and thwarted the Country Party's use of agricultural policy as a way to shore up electoral support (Warhurst, 1982, pp.20-22). It also impacted significantly on the way agricultural interest groups conducted their affairs. The IAC necessitated the professional presentation of ideas through reasoned economic argument rather than emotion. To generate credible economic argument primary-producer organizations needed to *adapt* by becoming 'professional'. Many started to employ tertiary-educated staff. In contrast with overseas developments, agricultural interest groups in Australia professionalized to *defeat* rather than *defend* protectionism.

The change in Australian farm policy in the late 1970s coincided with the NFF's formation, and it has been key to the managed and unwavering nature with which trade liberalism has subsequently been pursued (Keating and Dixon, 1989; Trebeck, 1990; Connors, 1996). In contrast to the farm groups that preceded it, in its early years the NFF came out stridently in favour of trade liberal approaches;[4] arguing that, while agriculture had endured early cuts, support for secondary industry remained which added to the costs of agriculture. This was in part testament to the domination of the NFFs Secretariat by former employees of the grazier's organizations who were long standing critics of state support (Malcolm, 1989, pp.140, 150). However, it also reflected an overall realization amongst the elites in agricultural organizations and government that British entry to the European Economic Community (EEC) would reduce Australia's privileged access to British markets and, as such, a more radical approach was required to secure the sectors future economic prosperity (Gruen, 1990, p.22).

The election of the Hawke labor government in the early 1980s saw the emergence of a conscious strategy to further accelerate economic reforms (as reviewed above) via 'bargained consensus' (see discussion in Marsh, 1995). This describes a corporatist style process whereby government sought to engage key (economic) interest groups in collaborative arrangements to manage economic restructuring and change.[5] On the basis of the NFF's concurrence with the broad economic aims of government it became an ongoing participant on various quasi-governmental committees and commissions such as the Economic Planning and Advisory Council (EPAC). Through its role in such forums, the NFF supported the reduction in agricultural industry assistance and the deregulatory agenda in return for economy wide reforms, particularly in the areas of industrial relations and transport (Martin, 1989, p.1118). The NFF successfully reoriented itself in such a way as to be influential in the general economic policy area. While the impact of these exercises in consensus building, measured in terms of facilitating (speeding up, anticipating and optimizing) change towards competitiveness, are said to have been limited (Marsh, 1995), the participation of groups clearly smoothed the path for reforms where and when groups could deliver the support of their constituencies. The presence of a strong NFF ensured that early cuts to agriculture were not undone, but rather similar reforms extended to other industry sectors. The 'bargained consensus' term has been used most often to refer to arrangements struck during the Hawke and Keating labor governments. However the practice broadly continues under the present government where the NFF participates in the National Food Industry Strategy along with agri-food industry representatives and government.[6] It also participates in development and review of the existing packages of domestic agricultural policies and programs (referred to later in this chapter).

Patterns of Agricultural Restructuring

As noted elsewhere, the decline in farm numbers, as a result of technological change and related shifts in cost-price relationships, has been a longstanding trend. Yet, in Australia, the post 1970s era witnessed a rapid drop in farm numbers, which was a stark contrast with the stable farm numbers of the 1950s and 1960s (Gruen 1990, p.21, 23), (See Table 7.1). Successive Australian governments have responded to global developments (see above) in ways which have rendered existing cost/price pressures more acute, thereby compounding pre-existing forces driving restructuring. These cuts also exposed the heavily export reliant Australian agricultural sector to volatile global markets *without protection*, which also accelerated patterns of restructuring. Declining farm numbers and expanding farm sizes have produced a farm sector that is not only smaller but one where increasingly a minority of producers generate the majority of the output and the majority of family-run farms survive because of off-farm income. This 'polarization' has been acknowledged by government which notes that 'Structural adjustment is leading towards larger and more capital intensive farms and smaller farms that will likely provide multiple goods and services, including boutique, value-added products' (AFFA, 2003).[7]

Table 7.1 Number of Australian farm establishments over time

Years	Number of Establishments with Agricultural Activity	% change
1955-59	252,438	n/a
1960-69	253,084	0.00
1970-79	217,629	-0.14
1980-89	158,252	-0.27
1990-99	139,610	-0.12

Source: Unpublished data compiled by ABS central office staff from copies of Year Book Australia (various years)

Agricultural restructuring has also stimulated a general decline in the size of the rural population, which has impacted upon overall levels of social cohesion and wellbeing and threatened the removal of already low levels of public service provision (Alston, 2004). The declining terms of trade associated with the post 1970 era has catalyzed a range of farm management measures, including more intensive production, which has had serious repercussions for the quality of rural environments such as reduced water quality, increased soil erosion and salinity (Martin, 1997).

Broad acre production of beef, grain, sheepmeat and wool, have long been the mainstay of Australian agriculture. Post war policies stimulated the expansion of dairy, horticultural, cotton, rice, and sugar industries. The emergence of newly identified export markets has fostered a range of so-called 'sunrise' industries, such as olive, venison and wine production and organic agriculture generally. There has also been a recent upsurge in 'diversification' into farm tourism and on-farm value-adding activities in a bid for small farms to stay viable.

While the agriculture sector is, and always has been, largely export orientated, its direct economic significance has been in steady decline (see Table 7.2). Significantly, over a third of all exports by value are now exported to Japan, United States and China (DFAT, 2003). The United Kingdom, once Australia's primary export market, is now the fourth largest export destination (only 4.2 per cent in 2003). The contribution of agriculture to employment has also declined. In political terms, this decline has eroded the power of the agricultural lobby.

Table 7.2   Farm sector contribution to farm employment and Australian gross product

Time period (Years)	Farm Employment (000)	Contribution to Australian Employment (%)	Average Contribution to gross product (%)
1950/51 to 1959/60	478.4	-	15.27
1960/61 to 1969/70	428.1	8.6	9.43
1970/71 to 1979/80	385.1	6.4	5.59
1980/81 to 1989/90	392.2	5.5	3.93
1990/91 to 1999/00	370.6	4.6	2.95
2000/01 to 2001/02	375.0	4.1	3.02

Source: ABARE (1994, p.2); ABARE (2003, p.1)

It is important to recognize that some sections of agriculture are more or less reliant on export income, which creates differential impacts from global change. For instance, grain, rice, sugar and wool sectors are heavily reliant on exports, while dairy, beef and horticulture are less so, which accentuates vertical distinctions. In addition, commodity sectors break down further into sub-sectors contingent on the specific market they serve, which in turn creates heterogeneous market conditions and economic returns (e.g. the red meat sector contains live export, export feedlot and grass fed domestic elements). Aside from the basic tension around overall farm decline, exposure to corrupt export markets, processes of diversification and polarisation have created new cleavages within the farm base which the NFF has had to manage.

The NFFs Role: Selling Trade Liberal Policy Reform

While the sum of the NFF's involvement in agricultural policy could never be said to equal its role in encompassing economic policy debates, this area has been its explicit focus for much of its existence. The NFF, in contrast to many European and US groups, has been actively lobbying for a shift to a trade liberal policy stance. This approach has not suited everyone and the impact, as outlined above, has fed resentment amongst the farming constituency and created conflicting cleavages in its membership. As such, a large part of the NFFs role has not simply been seeking change in the broader economy through policy advocacy but selling it to its members and maintaining their support.

The NFFs support for trade liberalism was in stark contrast to its predecessor organizations. This change of heart reflected its view that it should support the economically viable farmers (the most productive), but was not indicative of a similar shift amongst its rank and file membership. Not surprisingly, farm militancy and the emergence of some fringe competitor organizations marked the early years of the NFFs support for trade liberalism.[8] These conflicts emerged along well established fault lines, such as distinctions between traditional farmers and those more orientated to 'agribusiness' and between export and domestic orientated commodity sections (Matthews, 1990). In the late 1980s and early 1990s a small number of commodity councils attempted to retain some protection from subsidized imports, which led to numerous disaffiliations (and often reaffiliations a short time later) from the NFF. While this prompted faint calls by the NFF for a stop to rationalization in the farm sector until the pace was picked up in other sectors and overseas, this never amounted to a backwards step. It is important to note that the temptation for opposition to reforms to be mounted at the state level has been curtailed by the tying of competition and economic reforms to commonwealth grant income. Despite the fact that many statutory marketing arrangements are operated under state legislation, this has effectively neutralized the states as a point of leverage for those farm interests opposed to reforms.[9] States have been reluctant to sacrifice grant income for the benefit of relatively small commodity sectors.

The NFF has admitted that its policies, aimed at lowering the domestic cost structure and further liberalizing world trade, provide benefits that will accrue only in the long term and that involve sacrifice amongst its own constituency. The NFF conceded that, 'The campaign by Australian agriculture to be as good as its word, and eliminate tariffs in rural industries, has not come without pain, and some of our people have been forced to restructure to deal with such fundamental change' (Craik, 1998b).

While the NFF was talking about 'pain before gain' many farmers were seeing lots of pain with no tangible gain (as the previous section highlighted). SFOs, those with direct farmer members, have borne the brunt of farmer dissatisfaction, which has included a decline in the membership of SFOs and has heightened levels of public criticism of the NFF. In the face of this internal criticism the NFF has been urged by Government not to retreat from its role of leading the economic debate in Australia (Dick, 1998, p.8). And it has not.

Instead the NFFs approach to its relations with members has been two fold. Firstly, the NFF has committed itself to communicating the individual benefits more effectively with its constituency. Their leaders argue that '... a concerted effort from both industry and government is required to sell the benefits of trade liberalisation, so that families and individuals can see what benefits they have received' (Craik, 1998a). Its second strategy has been explaining its representative role vis-à-vis its members in a way that divests itself of responsibility for the 'pain' and focuses explanations for restructuring on individual farm management abilities. Statements by the NFF have consistently indicated that the farm enterprise takes the bulk of the *responsibility* for adjusting to changes in the economic environment. In its review the NFF stated:

> NFF and state farm organisations generally have seen their role in terms of creating a competitive business framework where individuals can take advantage of such opportunities and succeed according to their ability. It is impossible for farm organisations to guarantee a viable future for all producers, regardless of their commercial ability (NFF, 1996, p.6).

This approach encourages struggling farmers not to seek collective recourse through the NFF but to 'adjust' promptly and quietly. Farmers who wish to criticize the NFF, and seek to force it to renounce their policy positions, first need to overcome this individualizing discourse of representation. The comment by one Australian academic, that 'farm organizations need to be more sympathetic to the situations of their constituents' (Alston, 2004, p.44) testifies to the tough stance adopted by the NFF to the pace and affects of restructuring. That it has not been forced to heed this pleading underlines the strength of its discourses, which have 'naturalized' processes of restructuring. Needless to say, the NFF feels somewhat emboldened by the bi-partisan support for its general approach. This support guards against it being outflanked by rebel groups.

Weathering the Storm: Trade Liberalism as Policy Orthodoxy

While SFOs may have suffered an accelerated loss of members its disciplined approach has maintained the NFFs encompassingness which in turn has been crucial to removing the temptation to roll back cuts in farm assistance and protection. Since formation the number of CCs has increased overall with the few dissaffiliations over time being compensated for with new additions. The NFF has been able to successfully absorb the expanded commodity base of the agricultural sector under its umbrella. All original CCs remain and SFOs have further rationalized. The only sign of direct competition are two 'rebel' commodity groups, the Australian Woolgrowers Association (AWGA) and the Australian Beef Association (ABA). Neither has garnered wide spread support, but they have catalyzed a shift to the direct election of part of the boards of both wool and cattle CCs.

Part of the explanation for the NFF weathering the storm has been its ability to outlast those being 'adjusted out' of agriculture. There are signs that the early period of farm restructuring, marked by a high degree of fluidity, has solidified into a generally polarized farm structure. As a farm representative noted '…there has been a big clean-out in agriculture over the '90s and there has been a polarisation of the farm sector. People have either scaled up or found off-farm income. The middle ground is shrinking and you are moving to those two ends of the spectrum' (Wahlquist, 2004, p.28). The significance here is that this polarization neutralizes the 'disappearing middle' who as a general rule have been both the most resistant to 'market signals' (therefore often experiencing financial and social distress) and the most vocal advocates for state assistance.

In some respects, though, the NFF has become a victim of its own policy success in this area. The 'radical' economic views the NFF advocated have now become policy orthodoxy and it largely remains on a watching brief to guard against any roll back of reform (*in other sectors*). The partnership with the state this monitoring role implies is a much less public one. The NFF's position in support of trade liberalization is now typically pursued through cooperating and advising Australian government as it negotiates multi-lateral and bi-lateral agreements. The NFF trade officer and CC representatives still travel with the Minister and government delegates to important trade venues. However, as NFF resource levels have declined (ironically an artifact of farm adjustment and policy change) its in-house expertise has diminished. Much trade analysis is now conducted by consultants and paid for by Research and Development Corporations funded through farmer levies. The NFF input is now more about mobilizing consent than delivering information and expertise. The NFF's scrutiny of the impact on agriculture from a Free Trade Agreement currently being negotiated with the US is a case in point. While the NFF has been supportive of the FTA process (as long as it is not at the expense of multi-lateral reform), it has been critical of its exclusion of sugar and the long implementation periods for US import beef quotas. The variation in the benefits derived from the FTA by commodity sectors holds the potential for internal dissent within the NFF. But interestingly, the NFF family is holding firm on supporting the thrust of the FTA while also pursuing on behalf of 'losing' sectors, such as sugar, specific industry rescue plans. Beyond the domestic sphere, as part of its leading role in the Cairns Group of farm leaders, it has been pro-active in seeking alliances with EU consumer organizations and transnational actors like the WWF. As one NFF leader put it, 'The core of the proposed new strategy hinges on gaining the support of different groups in the community to put the argument for reform to governments in protected countries' (NFF, 2000).

While mobilizing consent and lobbying internationally are not inconsequential matters, they are roles not easily explained or transparent to members.

Contemporary Agricultural Policy and Politics: Beyond Trade Liberalism

As evident in the previous section the most notable change in Australian agricultural policy has been from a state-assisted to trade-liberal paradigm, which has included an explicit policy of facilitating structural adjustment. However, the 'radical' change in the 1970s and 1980s is now largely viewed as policy orthodoxy and has bi-partisan political support. As such, the issue of trade liberal policy reform (domestically and abroad) has been explicitly subsumed into a broader domestic policy approach. It has not faded from view, but other issues are increasingly moving to the foreground. While the domestic (re)production of trade liberal policy continues, the shift in policy emphasis casts the NFF in a different role and creates a unique set of challenges.

New Policies: Trade Liberalism, Environment and Rural Development ... with a Neoliberal Twist

As one senior civil servant has noted, a broader three pronged approach to Australian agricultural policy has emerged in the 1990s which seeks 'to provide an integrated package of policies and programs that enhance farm profitability and international competitiveness, encourage sustainable agricultural practices and enhance social and economic opportunities for rural communities' (Wonder, 1995, p.2). Agriculture – Advancing Australia (AAA) is the package through which the current conservative Federal government delivers these three threads of Australian agricultural policy. The NFF was closely involved in its development (DPIE, 1998) and subsequent reviews of progress.

The *first* goal of international competitiveness is pursued through a range of programs directed at lifting the efficiency of individual farmers, largely through education and training programs, and through seeding efforts at supply chain coordination. However, some forms of direct assistance are still on offer. For example, assistance is provided to farmers in 'exceptional circumstances', such as in drought. The concept of drought, as with other policy concepts, is an elastic one and farm organizations often frame climatic conditions in terms of drought to avail their constituency of state assistance (Botterill, 2002). Governmental efforts continue to facilitate farm adjustment, with one off payments still made to farmers who leave agriculture: as is evidenced in the recent Sugar Industry Reform Program (SIRP). However, any government payments for farmers *not exiting* are made only where an independent financial assessment indicates good prospects for future viability. In sum, what assistance does flow is made on the basis of a residual notion of exceptionalism – that agriculture operates in conditions other businesses do not – but is coupled to prescribed management approaches, emphasizes capacity building and is not ongoing. Only 'economically' viable farmers are able to access this support.

The *second* goal, to address the environmental sustainability of rural industries, is primarily achieved through the National Heritage Trust (NHT), administered jointly by the Department of Agriculture, Fisheries and Forestry

(DAFF) and Environment Australia. The federal government, through partnership agreements with the states, funds community groups to address environmental issues, many of which are in rural areas or concern externalities of farm production (e.g. dryland salinity, water quality, soil erosion, native flora and fauna). The *third* goal is largely about addressing the impact of agricultural industry decline on regional economies and communities through programs that fund communities to engage in strategic planning processes for economic development.

The AAA package evidences the government's commitment to a neoliberal style of response to global change, whereby government creates a competitive economic environment within which farmers and communities survive according to their own ability and resources (Alston, 2004; Gray and Lawrence, 2001). The Commonwealth Government's own commentary on the AAA Package highlights this orientation. The Minister stated that: 'The 1997 package ... marked an important new direction in the way the Commonwealth Government operated to support rural industries, shifting from short-term subsidy mechanisms towards capacity building and self-reliance in the longer term' (Truss, 2002). This has brought the governments approach into line with that adopted by the NFF: farmers should survive on the basis of individual capacity and ability as determined by market forces rather than expect political guarantees of survival.

Policy Process: New Issues and New Venues

The degree of dominance that agricultural interest groups exercise over this expanded policy area varies considerably. While the NFF facilitated the end of agricultural exceptionalism as it related to domestic assistance, other areas of exceptionalism have remained. Many issues, particularly those related to the practices of food production and land management, have long been the exclusive domain of farmers. As Baumgartner and Jones (1991) have argued, redefinitions of policy image and venue change are important tools in facilitating policy shifts. Control over venue and image as it pertains to what have formerly been regarded as 'traditional' policy areas is what is currently being contested and defended by the NFF.

Exactly what constitutes a 'technical' agricultural production issue, and hence remains the preserve of agricultural interests, as opposed to an 'environmental' issue, 'animal welfare' issue, 'food safety' or even 'consumer'[10] issue, is the subject of considerable debate. Increasingly in Australia what once could be talked about as technical 'agricultural' issues are being successfully reframed, with the consequent impact that other interests are now deemed, alongside farmers, as legitimate stakeholders.

Agriculture and its relationship to the natural environment has been a particularly contested policy area, providing a good example of the broader point about venues and issue definition. While agriculture in Europe has a legitimate environmental maintenance role, the European models of agriculture reproduced in Australia are increasingly accepted as direct threats to the bio-physical environment. As images shift so too does the cast of interests directly involved. In resolving rural environmental issues, environmental, rural community and indigenous groups are common participants alongside farm groups. The venues have also started to change. Issues of rural environmental care were, like macro-economic reform, initially accommodated within the 'bargained consensus' pattern of policy making between peak groups and the relevant government departments (McEachern, 1993).[11] This ensured a dominant position for the NFF. However, more recently government has sought to involve communities *directly* in resolving these issues, constituting new policy venues, often at regional or local levels, that step around interest group structures and operate under new definitions of policy problems (Argent, 2002; Halpin, 2002). This open consultative approach is increasingly being emulated in formulating responses to regional economic and social issues (for example, *Area Consultative Committees* and *Rural Partnership Program* planning forums).

The 're-imaging' of agricultural policy has also led to the expansion of the number of agencies involved in aspects of what may once have been the 'agricultural' policy process. At the Federal level these include the Department of Foreign Affairs and Trade, Environment Australia, the Department of Workplace Relations, Employment and Small Business and the Department of Transport and Regional Services.

NFF Role: Defending Residual Agricultural Exceptionalism

As indicated in part one of the chapter, the NFF finds itself, at least on the economic and industry reform front, purely on a 'watching brief'. The task of domestic industry reform, which has sustained the NFF for the best part of 25 years, is now being tended to by governments who themselves are largely convinced of its national importance. The NFF is now largely valued for its role in mobilizing consent, as the state relies less on it for technical information or expertise in the trade area, instead finding information from within government or from consultants and academics. The foregrounding of issues of farmer capacity building, self reliance and seeding export supply chain development, under contemporary neoliberal modes of agricultural governance, logically reduce the NFF's role even further. Such policies focus on pursuing a more optimal environment in which farmers can exercise their entrepreneurial abilities or indirectly raising the market based abilities and competencies of farmers and supply chain actors. In both areas government is convinced of the importance of the task, but the need for active NFF participation is less apparent. Even in those areas where 'bargained consensus' continues to guide industry policy development, the NFF finds its influence diluted. The National Food Industry Strategy, the only Action Agenda operating in the Agriculture portfolio, involves the NFF as a farm representative, but it is vastly outnumbered by public servants and agri-food industry representatives.

Overall, the NFFs role in the emergent policy environment has been largely contesting the erosion of agricultural exceptionalism. The increasing number of these issues on which the NFF is expected to have a position and the increasing number of well-resourced political adversaries it faces, makes the contemporary policy process increasingly resource intensive. These are points acknowledged by the NFF itself (NFF, 1994 and 1996). The NFFs workload is further exacerbated by the trend for these issues to increasingly be coordinated via a national approach through Ministerial Councils (of Federal and State Ministers). While this means issues being played out nationally, most resources still reside with the NFFs state member organizations.

The difficulties from the changed policy environment are not just resource based. Influence in regional or local policy venues, favoured by governments in terms of environmental and regional policy implementation, relies not so much on monetary interest group resources but on leaders coordinating member's *actions*. Evidence thus far from native vegetation management shows that the NFF will find it difficult to shift their activities from a venue where financial resources are critical in achieving influence to one where member actions are paramount (Halpin, 2002). This will clearly test the SFOs given, like most modern interest groups, they have emphasized membership in terms of an exchange of member subscriptions in return for services which has eroded the vibrancy of local branch structures. To operate successfully within these venues the implication is that agricultural interest groups may need to become more adept at simultaneously managing two quite different types of organization: one professionalized and centralized and the other with strong coordinative capacities between central leadership and regional membership groups.

These issues also rely on harnessing the support of public opinion. In an infrequently deployed strategy, the NFF recently commissioned research to highlight this societal base of support, which confirmed that urban people do indeed see agriculture as an especially difficult business enterprise (Crosby-Textor, 2003). Interestingly, it did so not to legitimate exceptionalism in relation to government assistance (as European groups may do) but to mount defensive efforts against attacks on their environmental credentials and to reaffirm their pre-eminent role in exercising sole management rights over private property.

Given the diverse base there have always been, and always will be, divisions amongst farmers as to what is in their best (economic) interests.[12] However, the contemporary policy environment includes issues that surface latent heterogeneity in the farming constituency in relation to values and beliefs. Tacit agreement about how agriculture *should* be conducted, its *proper* relation to the environment and its *contract* with the broader community remains elusive. The recent debate over a moratorium on GM Canola trials illustrates the point. The NFFs promotion of gene technology, on the basis that it is central to Australia's agricultural competitiveness, has placed it at odds with the Network of Concerned Farmers (NCF), a group campaigning for the banning of GM in Australia. Traditionally, farm leaders could be certain that opposition to 'greenies' or environmental 'urbanites' would tap ideological dispositions and guarantee internal farmer support. While there is still evidence that such an appeal resonates amongst some farmers, this type of discourse is just as likely to divide.

NFF Success: Two Stories, Two Conclusions

Australian farm interest groups have been particularly successful in supporting rapid and radical change in the direction of agricultural policy. That the NFF has a good reputation in Canberra for intervening in economic policy debates based on well-informed arguments couched in 'national' as opposed to 'sectional' interests is largely uncontested. A recent survey of the opinions of federal parliamentarians and journalists concluded that 'The NFF was considered clearly the most effective organization in raising issues in Canberra and particularly successful with the media and Senators' (NFF, 2001). Academic appraisals of the NFF family have tended to concur (Trebeck, 1990; Connors, 1996). The NFF is commended for its activities in advocating and securing a paradigm change in agricultural policy and for attaining organizational amalgamation. The end of protests as a tool of political persuasion and the public displays of disunity are both evaluated as signs of political maturity. For the more critical commentators the policy successes of the NFF are marvelled at in the context of the declining political and economic significance of agriculture (Matthews, 1994; Matthews and Warhurst, 1993; Halpin and Martin, 1999).

The NFF has illustrated incredible organizational resilience. Having initially transformed a plethora of commodity and state groups into a federated encompassing group it has continued to maintain the integrity of that group system. Despite the diverse base of Australian agriculture, the NFFs encompassingness remains intact: it has increased the number of CCs and it still retains an SFO in each state of Australia.[13] It has rebuffed direct competition and militancy and maintains dominance as the authoritative voice of Australian farmers.

However, to some extent this tag of a 'successful' group refers to the NFF of the 1980s and early 1990s. Its primary challenge was to facilitate policy change in broad economic policy making venues whilst defending and championing change amongst its often discontented constituency. On these two scores it has been successful. But, this policy shift is largely over[14] and trade liberalism is accepted as a norm of macro-economic and agricultural policy and enjoys bipartisan support in federal and state politics.[15] As has been established the political terrain ahead is more problematic and there are signs it needs to reposition itself to meet a different operating environment.

Summarizing the Challenges Facing the NFF

Based on this review the challenges confronting the NFF can be said to emerge from (i) the long term trends that diminish farmers' political, economic and electoral significance, (ii) the NFFs support for trade liberal agricultural policy reforms, and, (iii) the complexion of contemporary agricultural policy and politics.

(i) Challenges from long-standing trends The decline in the size, the economic contribution and the electoral significance of the farming constituency continues to make life difficult for Australian agricultural interest groups. These trends place

limitations on the resources available from member subscriptions and continue to slowly weaken the underlying power of the farm sector.

(ii) Challenges from support for trade liberalism The NFFs primary challenge has been to address internal conflict arising from its support of trade liberal policy. While this conflict has largely subsided, the NFFs unwavering support for trade liberal policy has created a somewhat fluid political context. Farmers may not vent frustration at the NFF but this fluidity has prompted farmers to explore forms of collective action with political potential, including flirting with formation of a 'rural' party and forming 'rural' promotional groups (see Halpin, 2003). Domestic policy approaches have accelerated farm restructuring, which has catalyzed further membership decline and reduced income streams for SFOs. Further, the cross cutting cleavages (economic and values based) emerging within the farming constituency have made it increasingly difficult for encompassing agricultural interest groups to arrive at positions.

(iii) Challenges from emerging policy terrain The neoliberal turn in contemporary agricultural policy reduces the NFFs activist role in economic reform to exercising a 'watching brief', which makes its core task more difficult to explain to members. In the areas where agricultural policy is expanding, like environment and rural development, the NFF confronts more competition from other interests and often in more hostile policy venues. The 'bargained consensus' model seems to have found its limits in these policy areas. These venues not only dilute farmer influence but also require the NFF to coordinate the *actions* of members in local forums with its lobbying activities at the state and federal levels. In organizational terms, these issues are complex and require levels of expertise that the NFF does not possess nor can afford to purchase.

The NFF's Future: 'Is it broke ... and does it need to be fixed?'

Despite its apparent resilience there is almost overwhelming acceptance amongst NFF leaders that the organization has outlived its original design. Renewed efforts at reform have been prompted by financial pressures on most state organizations and questions about the ongoing value of the commodity council and federated structure (Morse, 2001a). There is agreement that the *adaptive* strategy of the 1990s, to raise resource levels through more intensive efforts by SFOs at member recruitment, is unsustainable. Membership density will not stave off resource decline nor is it essential to influencing debates in many new issue areas.

A proposal for a unitary organization, called Australian Farmers, to replace the current federated structure was floated in 2001 (Morse, 2001b). The proposal documentation itself acknowledged the irrevocable decline of the farmer subscription base, the struggle to keep up with an expanding and diverse issues agenda, competition from other groups and the decline in staffing and resources to unacceptable levels. It has not, however, garnered the support of the member organizations of the NFF (Morse, 2001b). In the meantime the largest and wealthiest SFO, the NSW Farmers' Association, has shown signs that it may be ready to go it alone despite its protestations that its recent foray into Federal lobbying was to support rather than circumvent the NFF structure (Morse, 2002). Despite the denials there are clearly elements within the NFF structure that support the dominance and autonomy of SFOs and reject models that shift authority and resources towards Canberra.

Debate continues on how best to *adapt* or *transform* the existing structure, with a recent review around the theme 'Is it broke…and does it need to be fixed?'. The emerging compromise is one of *adaptation* of existing structures which would see constitutional change to make it easier for emerging industries to join as associate members (increasing funding and encompassingness), a reduction in the scope of issues pursued (spreading resources less thinly) and a diversification of funding sources (relying less on membership subscriptions for funding). Most significant amongst these changes is the NFFs intention to try and re-establish its image as a hard nosed economic group. One NFF leader noted 'We'll no longer be addressing issues like health, education or women's affairs, which are really not part of our primary charter' (McKenzie, 2003, p.3). This reflects a desire by the current NFF leadership to engage 'productive' farms with elements up the agribusiness supply chain in preference to positioning farmers as 'rural businesses' that are part of a broader rural constituency.

While its member SFOs share the diagnoses of the problems confronting the NFF, a remarkably diverse range of *adaptations* are evident. AgForce, the Queensland SFO, has explicitly asserted a role as the voice for *rural* Queensland (AgForce, 2003). This positioning, presumably aimed at increasing its membership and subscription base, is in direct contrast to that of the NFF. For some, the pursuance of members as the mainstay of organizational funding, especially in the context of an increasingly heterogenous and shrinking constituency, would seem unsustainable. This is reflected in the increasing use of sponsors to supplement member subscription income. In terms of more thoroughgoing *transformations* of the existing group system, the evidence is again diverse. Two SFOs struggling to pay the NFF subscription fees, the WAFF and SAFF, have recently joined forces under the banner of the 'South Western Alliance'. The Alliance is most active on export issues in commodity areas where both SFOs are significant players but, due to financial crises, neither has any representation on relevant CCs (SAFF, 2003). The NSWFA recently announced the creation of the 'Australian Farm Institute', a think tank style research organization. If nothing else, this initiative is confirmation of the growing importance of the weight of argument (as opposed to the weight of numbers) in policy debates and an assessment that the NFFs research capacity is insufficient. A more radical development is talk of an Agribusiness Council. The purpose of such a Council would be to tackle some of the larger 'public interest' issues, like environmental care and animal welfare, which are currently being driven (resisted?) by sectional groups like the NFF who have pursued a property rights agenda. The proposal includes funding a substantial research based secretariat.

One can only speculate about how these collective debates will resolve themselves. However, what is clear is that something more fundamental than simple adaptations, like convincing more farmers to join or increasing levels of financial resources, will be needed to sustain the NFF in the longer term.

Conclusion

A defining feature of the NFFs success has been its capacity to adapt its influence activities to the climate created by 'bargained consensus'. It matched a commitment to research based advocacy, insider strategy and professionalism with an ability to maintain constituency support (or at least a lid on dissent) for its agenda. The place of Australia in the world economy probably means that the policy shifts described in this chapter were all but inevitable. Nevertheless, the NFF contributed towards a managed and sustained change. The signs are that the task ahead is substantially different. While it may have been successful in legitimating the dismantling of state assistance and related forms of agricultural exceptionalism, what is its policy relevance in further developing the sectors competitiveness amidst global change?

Some hint in this respect would surely come from the attitude of the state. The current Federal Agriculture Minister (Truss, 2002) has offered his endorsement of the NFFs contemporary importance:

> A single national voice for the farmers of Australia is especially important at this time. The NFF speaks for Australian farmers. You are the people that we talk to at the federal government level when we want to know farmers' views on issues. So while I know that your organisation faces challenges and difficulties while some State organisations clearly recognise that they've also got a State focus, there are a range of national issues that affect farmers everywhere and we do need to have a capacity to speak to a single body. And let me say we consider that you do that task effectively and well.

At face value it points to the continued belief in government that a group of this type is a necessity. Indeed, government continues to encourage growth in the NFF's encompassingness and continues to support and shield those NFF members that from time to time become the subject of challenge from rebel organizations. But this may be mere polite reassurance. An alternative, if not emotive, view is provided by one commentator who summarizes, 'In the face of a long-term decline in farmer numbers and increasing financial pressures on those who remain, virtually all of the farming organizations including the NFF, are engaged in a battle to remain relevant and appropriately resourced' (Bolt, 2003).

The issue of relevance is an important one. Referring to Australian industry policy more broadly, it has been noted that 'government-industry relationships often survive well after the conditions upon which they were based have changed' raising the issue of 'whether such political relationships can be focused onto other "new growth" agendas' (Wanna and Withers, 2000, p.84). There is a question mark over whether the NFF is a capable or suitable partner to assist the state in meeting the challenges of a more differentiated agricultural policy agenda. The NFFs success relied on matching external conditions shaped by the government's economic reform agenda. Its fate is also likely to hinge on moving with the times and proving a useful partner in efforts to i) facilitate industry capacity building and (re)skilling, ii) develop coordinated export focused agri-food supply chains, and, iii) address the impacts of production on the environment while at the same reassuring (foreign) consumers of our 'clean and green' credentials.

Notes

[1] The party was formed as the Australian Country Party and underwent a name change in 1974 to the National Country Party and finally to the National Party of Australia in 1982.

[2] Recent analysis of budget allocations shows that the percentage of budget expenditure made to agriculture fell under the current Coalition Government.

[3] A point of difference with both US and Canadian federalism.

[4] See its first policy statement *Farm Focus: The 1980s*.

[5] This process has clearly been inhibited by the fragmented nature of business, prompting the characterization of such approaches as 'corporatism without business' (Matthews, 1991). The NFF was a notable exception amongst the Australian business community.

[6] This one of many 'Action Agendas' which serve as focal points for industry government action aimed at raising international competitiveness and market development.

[7] Australian farms tend to be larger than European farms. The average farm size is in the region of 4000 ha, although there are massive fluctuations.

[8] These include the Canowindra Reform Group and the Women's Rural Action Group. In combination with other groups these two formed the Union of Australian Farmers which directly challenged the NFF.

[9] For example, through National Competition Policy the Federal government has brought state governments into line with national policy to end the statutory marketing authorities administered by state legislation under the threat of loss of commonwealth grants income. (e.g. dairy industry). These can only be maintained where market failure of public interest cases can be satisfactorily made.

[10] It is worth noting that the direct 'consumers' of the majority of Australia's commodities are agribusinesses, who in turn supply European, North American and Asian markets. As such, the 'consumers' who tend to carry most weight in Australian agricultural policy debates are those in our vital export market destinations and not Australian consumers. The current debate on GM canola releases provides a clear example of this phenomenon.

[11] This is evidenced by the work between peak interest groups, National Farmers' Federation and Australian Conservation Foundation (ACF), to develop and promote the National Land Management Program (NLMP).

[12] There is the historical division between wealthy free-market graziers and poorer protectionist farmers and the commodity differences such as those between grain producers and beef lot feeders over the costs of grain and between irrigators and non-irrigators in relation to water allocations.

[13] Although at the time of writing the South Australian Farmers' Federation (SAFF) had withdrawn its membership for financial reasons.

[14] Although the NFF pursued an aggressive campaign to remove Union domination of the waterfront in the late 1990s.

[15] Although see the rise of Pauline Hanson in the mid 1990s who, in forming a populist party One Nation, actively opposed trade liberalism and proposed high tariff barriers and fortress Australia.

References

Australian Bureau of Agricultural and Resource Economics (1994), *Commodity Statistical Bulletin 1994*, ABARE, Canberra.

Australian Bureau of Agricultural and Resource Economics (2003), *Australian Commodity Statistics 2002*, Commonwealth of Australia, Canberra.

AFFA (2003), 'AFFA Corporate Plan 2002-2005', www.affa.gov.au/, accessed December 2003.

AgForce (2003), 'History', www.agforceqld.or.au/public/about us/home/html, accessed March 2003.

Aitkin, D. (1972), *The Country Party in New South Wales*, Australian National University Press, Canberra.

Alston, M. (2004), 'Who is down on the farm? Social aspects of Australian agriculture in the 21st century', *Agriculture and Human Values*, Vol. 21, pp.37-46.

Argent, N. (2002), 'From Pillar to Post? In search of the post-productivist countryside in Australia', *Australian Geographer*, Vol. 33(1), pp.97-114.

Baumgartner, F. and Jones, B. (1991), 'Agenda Dynamics and Policy Subsystems', *Journal of Politics*, Vol. 53(4), pp.1044-74.

Bolt, A. (2003), 'Farm groups are digging deep to keep their clout', *Financial Review*, 13 March, p.16.

Botterill, L. (2002), *Government Responses to Farm Poverty 1989-1998*, Report to RIRDC, Canberra.

Campbell, K. (1980), *Australian Agriculture: Reconciling Change and Tradition*, Longman Cheshire, Melbourne.

Castles, F.G. (1998), *Australian Public Policy and Economic Vulnerability*, Allen and Unwin, Sydney.

Coleman, W.D. and Skogstad, G.D. (1995), 'Neo-Liberalism, Policy Networks, and Policy Change: Agricultural Policy Reform in Australia and Canada', *Australian Journal of Political Science*, Vol. 30, pp.242-63.

Coleman, W.D., Skogstad, G.D., and Atkinson, M.M. (1996), 'Paradigm Shifts and Policy Networks: Cumulative Change in Agriculture', *Journal of Public Policy*, Vol. 16(3), pp.273-301.

Connors, T. (1996), *To Speak with One Voice*, NFF, Canberra.

Craik, W. (1998a), 'Issues for NFF', Address to the New South Wales Farmers Association Annual Conference, 22 July, Sydney.

Craik, W. (1998b), 'Taxation and Labour Market Reform', Address to 1998 Australian Agribusiness Congress, 21 July, Albury.

Crosby-Textor (2003), *Community Attitudes to Farmers and Resource Security*, Report Prepared for the NFF, Manuka, ACT.

Department of Foreign Affairs and Trade, (2003), 'Trade in Agriculture: Agriculture and the WTO', www.dfat.gov.au/trade/negotiations/trade_in_agriculture.html, accessed December 2003.

Department of Primary Industries and Energy (1998), 'Action Plan sets out Ten-Year vision for Australian Agriculture', 20 July, DPIE 98/88A.

Dick, A. (1998), 'NFF funding danger. Donges: councils to lose clout', *The Land*, 30 July, p.9.

Gray, I. and Lawrence, G. (2001), 'Neo-liberalism, Individualism and Prospects for Regional Renewal', *Rural Society*, Vol. 11(3), pp.283-98.

Grogan, F.O. (1968), 'The Australian Agricultural Council: A successful experiment in Commonwealth-State Relations', in C.A. Hughes (ed.), *Readings in Australian Government*, University of Queensland Press, St Lucia QLD, pp.297-317.

Gruen, F. (1990), 'Economic Development and Agriculture since 1945', in D.B. Williams (ed.), *Agriculture in the Australian Economy*, Sydney University Press, Australia, pp.19-26.

Halpin, D. and Martin, P. (1999), 'Farmer Representation in Australia: Avenues for Changing the Political Environment', *Australian Journal of Public Administration*, Vol. 58(2), pp.33-46.

Halpin, D. (2002), 'Interest groups and re-establishing stability in policy making: The case of the NSW Farmers' Association and the Native Vegetation Conservation Act', *Australian Journal of Political Science*, Vol. 37(3), pp.489-507.

Halpin, D. (2003), 'The collective political actions of the Australian farming and rural communities: Putting Farm Interest Groups in Context', *Rural Society*, Vol. 13(2), pp.138-56.

Harris, S. (1993), 'The International Economy and Domestic Politics', in I. Marsh (ed.), *Governing in the 1990s*, Longman Cheshire, Melbourne.

Keating, M. and Dixon, G. (1989), *Making Economic Policy in Australia: 1983-1988*, Longman Cheshire, Melbourne.

Malcolm, L.R. (1989), 'Rural Industries Policy', in B. Head and A. Patience (eds.), *From Fraser to Hawke: Australian Public Policy in the 1980s*, Longman Cheshire, Melbourne.

Marsh, I. (1995), *Beyond the Two Party System*, Cambridge University Press, Melbourne.

Martin, P. (1997), 'Saline Politics: Local Participation and Neoliberalism in Australian Rural Environments', *Space & Polity*, Vol.1(1), pp.115-33.

Martin, W.J. (1989), 'Lessons from Australian rural policy reform', Working Paper No.89/7 National Centre for Development Studies, ANU, Canberra.

Matthews, T. (1990), 'Federalism and Interest Group Cohesion: A Comparison of Two Peak Business Groups in Australia', *Publius*, Vol. 20, pp.105-28.

Matthews, T. (1991), 'Interest group politics: corporatism without business?', in F.G. Castles (ed.), *Australia Compared: People, Policies and Politics*, Allen and Unwin, Sydney, pp.191-218.

Matthews, T. and Warhurst, J. (1993), 'Australia: Interest Groups in the Shadow of Strong Political Parties', in C. Thomas (ed.), *First World Interest Groups: A Comparative Perspective*, Greenwood Press, Connecticut, pp.81-95.

Matthews, T. (1994), 'Employers' associations, corporatism and the Accord: The politics of Industrial Relations', in S. Bell and B. Head (eds.), *State, Economy and Public Policy*, Oxford University Press, Melbourne, pp.194-224.

McEachern, D. (1993), 'Environmental Policy in Australia 1981-91: A Form of Corporatism?', *Australian Journal of Public Administration*, Vol. 52(2), pp.173-86.

McKay, D. (1972), 'Stabilisation in Australian Agriculture', in C.D. Throsby (ed.), *Agricultural policy*, Penguin Books, Melbourne, pp.23-32.

McKenzie, D. (2003), 'NFF shake-up looms', *The Weekly Times*, 2 April, p.3.

Morse, C. (2001a), 'NFF investigates restructure proposal', *The Land*, 29 November, p. 5.

Morse C. (2001b), 'State farm organisations meet on NFF revamp proposal', *The Land*, 6

December, p.3.

Morse, C. (2002) 'NSWFA denies attack on NFF', *The Land*, 28 February, p.6.

NFF (1994), *Issues Paper: NFF Review*, NFF, ACT.

NFF (1996), *NFF Strategic Plan*, NFF, ACT.

NFF (2000) 'NFF Calls for Cairns Group – Plus', NR 126/2000.

NFF (2001), 'NFF top issue raiser in Canberra', NR 55/2001.

Productivity Commission (2002) *Trade and Assistance Review 2001-02*, Commonwealth of Australia, Canberra.

Richmond, K. (1980), 'The Major Rural Producer Groups in New South Wales' in R. Scott (ed.), *Interest Groups and Public Policy*, Macmillan, South Melbourne, pp.70-93.

SAFF (2003), 'South-Western alliance boosts export potential 2003/03', Media Release, Tuesday, 21 January.

Stayner, R. (1995), 'Policy Issues in Farm Adjustment', in Department of the Parliamentary Library (ed.), *Australian Rural Policy Papers 1990-95*, AGPS, Canberra, pp.161-98.

Throsby, C.D. (1972), 'Background to Agricultural Policy', in C.D. Throsby (ed.), *Agricultural policy*, Penguin Books, Melbourne, pp.13-22.

Trebeck, D. (1990), 'Farmer Organisations', in D.B. Williams (ed.), *Agriculture in the Australian Economy*, Sydney University Press, Sydney, pp.127-43.

Truss, M. (2002), 'Address to the National Farmers' Federation Annual General Meeting and third conference of Council', accessed June 2003, www.affa.gov.au/ministers/Truss/speeches/adresstoNFF.html.

Wahlquist, A. (2004), 'Dry away those tears', *The Weekend Australian*, April 17-18, p.28.

Wanna, J. and Withers, G. (2000), 'Creating Capability: Combining Economic and Political Rationalities in Industry and Regional Policy', in G. Davis and M. Keating (eds.), *The Future of Governance*, Allen and Unwin, St Leonards.

Warhurst, J. (1982), 'The Industries Assistance Commission and the Making of Primary Industry Policy', *Australian Journal of Public Administration*, Vol. 41(1), pp.15-32.

Wonder, B. (1995), *Australia's Approach to Agricultural Reform*, DPIE, Canberra, accessed December 1998, www.dpie.gov.au/dpie/agriculture/agricultural_reform.html.

PART III
NORTH AMERICA

Chapter 8

Farmers, Interests and the American State

Graham K. Wilson

Introduction: Images of Agricultural Policy Making in the USA

In the not so different past, it was common to interpret the American state as one composed of subgovernments. Mutually reinforcing alliances between government agencies, congressional committees and interest groups produced patterns of public policy that, on the one hand, had the virtue of offering numerous interests a feeling that government was responsive to their concerns and, on the other hand, suffered from the vice of robbing public policy of consistency and purpose. The latter critique inspired Lowi's highly successful book, *The End of Liberalism* (Lowi, 1967). In a sense, of course, the debate replayed celebrated arguments about pluralism. The subgovernment idea both celebrated the responsiveness of the American State to those with a major stake in the policy area and yet also raised concerns about *which* interests actually enjoyed this degree of power and what cost to the public. This was of course a replay of much more general arguments for and against pluralism.

In the last three decades, the subgovernment concept and related ideas such as the 'iron triangle' have fallen into disrepute (Heclo, 1975). It became widely accepted that subgovernment or iron triangles had given way to less bounded, more fluid issue networks. More actors were involved, and relationships within them were neither as permanent nor as mutually reinforcing as the concepts they displaced had suggested. The subgovernment or iron triangle of the Bureau of Land Management (BLM), ranchers and western legislators elected by ranchers gave way to an issue network that also included environmental groups and legislators from the Midwest and East Coast whose constituents wanted wilderness preserved not over-grazed by cattle.

Somewhat oddly, little evidence was advanced to show that the American state was actually composed of subgovernments. Those who used the concept could produce examples but it was of course possible that in the vast world of federal government, these examples were atypical. One might add in fairness that it is equally striking that so little evidence was produced in favor of the issue network idea; one of the most influential arguments for the superiority of the subgovernment over the iron triangle concept contained little in the way of evidence other than some brief examples (Heclo, 1975).

There was, however, general agreement that one policy area fitted the subgovernment concept: agriculture. Agricultural policy was enormously complicated, as little understood as, according to Palmerstone, the Schleswig-Holstein controversy had been in the mid nineteenth century.[1] It was administered by a vast bureaucracy, the US Department of Agriculture (USDA) that was presided over by a Secretary for whom a rural, preferably farming background, was an indispensable qualification. The President gave little attention to the topic. Congress delegated farm issues to Agriculture Committees that were, of course, composed entirely of legislators from rural America plus the odd urban Representative who had been sent there as a punishment for infringing on congressional norms or the authority of its leaders. Both the USDA and Congressional committees were thought in turn to be heavily influenced by the agricultural interest groups, particularly the American Farm Bureau Federation (AFBF.) The AFBF was often cited as an example of one of the strongest of interest groups in the USA. It became the dominant agricultural interest group during the first two decades of the twentieth century, perhaps because it was encouraged by government officials (county extension agents) as a preferable to the more radical National Farmers' Union (NFU). As Hansen (1991) describes, by the time of the New Deal, the AFBF had become recognized as *the* voice of American agriculture. The AFBF played a major role in the creation of the New Deal agricultural programs that in general terms (though not in detail) remained in place until 1996.

Both the AFBF and the NFU consolidated their position in the classic manner recommended by Mancur Olson (1971), namely through providing services to members. The NFU owned and operated a large number of grain elevators in the upper Midwest, perhaps both reflecting and explaining its strength among wheat farmers. The AFBF has operated a very successful insurance business. Particularly in the case of the AFBF, there has been argument about whether the provision of member benefits (in Olson's terms, selective incentives) came to dominate the supposed core activity of representing members to government. AFBF leaders also enjoyed an important degree of leeway in pursuing policies because their members had been attracted to the organization to gain cheaper insurance or discounts on tractor tires rather than because they approved of then AFBF's policies.

In summary, it is easy to see why agriculture appeared to constitute a perfect example of an iron triangle. Policy was controlled by a network of Congressional committees composed of rural legislators, the Department of Agriculture and farm interest groups particularly the AFBF that helped create the programs the Department administered. In reality, however, agricultural politics for fifty years after the Second World War was far more complicated than this picture suggested. In order to appreciate this complexity, however, a little historical background is necessary.

The Legacy of the New Deal

Agriculture had entered a depression as soon as the First World War had ended. Farmers' organizations, particularly the American Farm Bureau Federation (AFBF) had campaigned for government measures to secure a return to 'parity' – the ratio between farm and non-farm income that had prevailed in the last peace time period of farm prosperity in 1911-12. Their campaign was unsuccessful, however. Once the Great Depression hit, the argument that government should stabilize the farm economy (in an era in which 25 per cent of the population still lived on the farm) commanded wider sympathy. Although scholars are divided about the degree to which credit for their creation should be attributed to experts in government or to the farm interest groups, the Agricultural Adjustment Act marked a decisive moment; the US government has never subsequently disengaged from a deep involvement with agriculture.

The actual programs used to support farm incomes have varied from commodity to commodity, however. In some cases, such as tobacco, subsidies have been generated largely through limits on production. Probably the most common technique used was to make payments to farmers conditional on them reducing the acreage they planted with the crop in question. To make matters even more confusing, while the New Deal legislation remained on the statute books until 1996, it was generally recognized to be impracticable and was superceded by legislation that contained sunset provisions. A new Agriculture Act was required regularly, therefore, to prevent a reversion to the permanent but unworkable New Deal legislation.

The fundamental problem in the basic strategy of the New Deal programs – supporting farm incomes through raising farm prices – was that the marginal cost of production of most commodities was falling. Subsidies pegged at constant price levels therefore tended to produce massive surpluses as farmers found it profitable to produce more. The obvious solution to this and several other obvious problems would have been to subsidize farmers for farming, not for producing. This was regarded as too politically dangerous, however, to be feasible. The problem of how to reconcile supporting farm incomes without generating huge surpluses was not immediately apparent because of the vast demand for US products during and immediately after the Second World War. Shortly after the Second World War was over and chronic food shortages around the world disappeared, it became apparent that maintenance of the subsidy programs at a level that would provide farmers with adequate incomes would also result in the production of vast surpluses. Throughout the 1950s, the federal government faced tremendous difficulty in simply storing surplus production and it became apparent that the situation was unsustainable.

The problem of how to support farm incomes without generating huge surpluses generated a bitter division in the agricultural policy network. In general terms two solutions to the problem emerged. These were to pay farmers subsidies but to prevent the emergence of surpluses by limiting the freedom of farmers to produce, for example by restricting the acreage they could plant. There were many practical problems with such approaches, however, including the issues of farmers shifting acreage into less restricted commodities and thus generating fresh surpluses. The alternative was to reduce the subsidies paid to farmers in return for reductions in the controls that government imposed on 'freedom to farm'.

This dilemma produced a major change in the policies of the AFBF. In the 1930s and early 1940s, the AFBF had been closely involved in the development of New Deal farm policies and was firmly attached to subsidy programs. In the late 1940s, the AFBF's leadership changed and it came under the control of extremely conservative people fervently in favor of market liberalization. In general, this shift in ideology was a change from southerners who no doubt shared the South's views on race but who supported government intervention in the economy to midwestern conservatives with a fervent pro-market ideology. The AFBF therefore made a transition later followed by the NFF in Australia towards being more worried about government controls than about maintaining subsidies. The rival National Farmers' Union (NFU) remained firmly in favor of government programs to support farmers' incomes.

The dilemma over how to secure adequate incomes for farmers without producing massive surpluses produced stable and sharply conflicting policy coalitions. One side was anxious to secure adequate incomes for farmers through subsidies with if necessary stringent controls on farmers' freedom to produce as much they wished. On the other side were those determined to end controls, secure 'freedom to farm' and allow market forces to shrink the number of farmers through bankruptcies while hoping that the expansion of markets (for example through free trade) would minimize the hardship of contraction. Most of the Democratic Party and the National Farmers' Union (NFU) fell in the first, pro-subsidy group; most of the Republican Party – including many farm state Republicans and the AFBF fell in the second, as its members would like to say, 'freedom to farm' group. There were clear differences between the policies of Republican and Democratic Secretaries of Agriculture. Truman's Secretary of Agriculture (Brannan) and Kennedy's (Orville Freeman) advanced proposals to establish more effective government controls over production. Secretaries appointed by Republican Presidents such as Ezra Taft Benson (Eisenhower's Agriculture Secretary), and Earl Butz (Nixon's) advanced proposals to phase out subsidies and production controls. These divisions were mirrored in Congress. The House Agriculture Committee was one of the committees with the deepest partisan divisions. Interestingly, perhaps because of the greater likelihood of contested elections than for Representatives, Senators were less bitterly divided and more prone to compromise.

The pendulum swung back and forth over the years in terms of policy proposals.[2] Free market ideas seemed to make progress when Republicans were in power and farmers were relatively prosperous, for example in the early 1970s when farm prices were high due to grain sales to the Soviet Union and the Republicans held the White House. However, no fundamental changes in farm policy were achieved for fifty years after the Second World War. Yet US farm policy was open to several obvious criticisms. First, the policies were economically wasteful generating unwanted production representing a waste of capital, land and labor. Second, because in nearly all subsidy programs the amount a farmer received was determined by the amount he produced, the overwhelming majority of subsidies flowed to relatively few large-scale farmers or 'agribusinesses'. Farm subsidies therefore often constituted regressive income redistribution from consumers and taxpayers to wealthier farmers. Poorer farmers, in whose name the programs were justified, received little. Indeed, subsidies flowing to richer farmers may have increased their economic strength relative to that of the small farmers who were receiving little. Third, the programs were self-contradictory. By raising prices of US agricultural products, they made it harder to sell them on world markets. Fourth, by stimulating production while limiting the acreage in production, the farm programs encouraged highly intensive, environmentally damaging techniques.

In the last ten years, this epic struggle over how deeply government should be involved in agriculture seemed to reach a conclusion. When the Republicans led by Newt Gingrich captured the House campaigning on the basis of a national manifesto, the *Contract With America*, one of the prime targets of these free market reformers were the agricultural policy programs. The 1996 FAIR Act promised a gradual but almost total phasing out of farm subsidies and, in return, government controls. American agriculture would earn its living from the market, not the government. The United States, with allies such as Australia in the Cairns Group, would press internationally for free markets and an end to subsidies. The FAIR Act provided, it was true, an initial increase in subsidies but this was merely supposed to help farmers prepare for a free market. In his outstanding study of US agricultural farm policy, Sheingate (2001) suggests that the FAIR Act provides reassurance that important policy change and innovation is possible in the USA; contrary to common belief, the fragmented US political system does have the capacity to adopt reforms that advance the public at the expense of special interests. The complexity of the US system, far from preventing reform, facilitated it by offering policy makers the chance to by-pass points in the policy process deeply opposed to change. As we shall see, basing optimistic conclusions about the political system in general on the case of agriculture was a little hasty. It is instructive to look at two areas in which agricultural and more general interests have collided, namely in debates over agricultural subsidies and the treatment of agriculture in trade negotiations.

American Farmers in the Global Agricultural Economy

The preceding policy dilemmas reflect the fact that American farmers are crucially but not totally dependent on international markets. Exports vary as a percentage of total sales depending on a large number of factors many of which are not caused by farm factors. One of the most important influences is exchange rate policy; a strong dollar hurts American farm exports and a weak dollar helps. In 2002, the aggregate share of US farm products (by volume) that was exported was 21.9 per cent (ERS 2003). This was sharply down from the proportion exported in 1980-84 (29.2 per cent) There is, of course, also substantial variation in export dependence between commodities. In 2002, only 3.3 per cent of dairy products were exported compared with 46.7 per cent of food grains and 57.6 per cent of tobacco and cotton. In 1980-84, exports of food grains by volume had reached 61 per cent of production. In terms of the aggregate share of agricultural output by value, exports accounted for 21.9 per cent in 1980-84, 16.8 per cent in 1990-94, 16.7 per cent in 1999 and 17.7 per cent in 2002. In brief, American agriculture has been significantly dependent on exports, but not so dependent that farmers instinctively think of international markets as the source of their income. The United States therefore occupies an intermediate position between highly export orientated countries such as Australia and non-exporting countries.

Recent Policy

Subsidies

In practice, events since the FAIR Act have turned out very differently. The FAIR Act passed at a time of relative prosperity for agriculture. Immediately thereafter, world agricultural commodity prices declined while a strong dollar placed US farmers at a competitive disadvantage in international trade. Congress responded with alacrity passing a series of 'emergency' farm bills. In 1998 and 1999, Congress provided over US$14 billion in additional aid to farmers. As the conservative *American Spectator* complained 'Nothing better symbolizes the collapse of Republican principles than the multiple farm bailouts Congress has passed since July [1998] Agricultural subsidies are sky rocketing' (Bovard, 1998, p.72). By 1999, farm subsidies were estimated to be twice as costly as before the FAIR Act was adopted (Carey, 1999). In 2002, Congress revised the FAIR Act placing the 'emergency' farm subsidies on a firmer footing though without accompanying them with serious production controls to raise farm incomes by raising prices. The reforms embodied in the FAIR Act were therefore just an interlude.

The shift away from FAIR came at a high cost. Most obviously, the return to subsidies cost a great deal of money. The shift in policy also brought the United States a great deal of criticism. The ostensible, long-standing commitment to freer trade looked hypocritical when the United States was subsidizing its farmers so lavishly. Exhortations to third world countries to climb out of poverty by relying on market forces rang hollow when farmers in those countries found themselves bankrupted by low prices caused by the dumping of American agricultural surpluses on their markets. Yet the FAIR policy had been abandoned without any substantial shift in the balance of domestic political forces. The proportion of the population employed in agriculture remained tiny – less than 2.5 per cent of the work force – and was shrinking. The Republicans continued to control Congress, with the exception of a brief interregnum of Democratic control in the Senate; the moderate Democratic Presidency of Bill Clinton gave way to the vigorously conservative Presidency of Bush II. If anything the change in the balance of political forces, particularly the advent of Bush, should have worked to strengthen pro-market reforms.

The demise of the FAIR Act and the return to high levels of subsidy was particularly dramatic and puzzling in view of the prevailing political situation. The FAIR Act had been one of the fruits of Newt Gingrich's *Contract With America*, the highly publicized right wing manifesto on which the Republicans had fought and won the 1994 elections. Its free market provisions were in line with American trade policy. Yet within five years of its adoption, the FAIR Act had been abandoned. For all the empirical imperfections of the subgovernment model, as Patashnik (2003) noted, events seemed to show that those who had argued that the American system provided adequate possibilities for policy revisions in the public interest were overly optimistic. Policy makers had failed to establish the 'political sustainability' of reforms. Using a classic 'iron triangle' framework, Patashnik argued that reformers had failed to raise the opportunity costs of reintroducing farm subsidies. The interest groups, sympathetic congressional committees and bureaucrats all remained in place ready to subvert reform. Not even the legitimacy of the interest groups' claims had been undermined in the reform process.

The resilience of the forces favoring subsidies was even evident in the FAIR [Federal Agriculture Improvement and Reform] Act in 1996. As we have noted, Speaker Gingrich was intent on securing significant savings in expenditures on farm subsidies as part of his general campaign for a reduction in domestic expenditures and taxation, a campaign that had been validated in the 1994 midterm election campaigns fought on the unusually national manifesto, the *Contract With America*. Gingrich had also acted determinedly to assert his power as Speaker, perhaps to a degree that was unprecedented since the days of Speaker Cannon. This applied to agricultural policy as well as other areas. One of Sheingate's (2001, p.207) interviewees noted ruefully if not grammatically that "'In the past we done so good protecting [agricultural interests] and we were bipartisan...[the former Democratic Committee Chair] De la Garza allowed no interference from the leadership." In contrast, in 1995 the committee "[suffered] under a very involved leadership"'. Sheingate emphasizes that Gingrich was able to out-manoeuvre the House Agriculture Committee, bedrock of support for subsidies, by transferring the issue to the House Budget Committee, which he himself chaired on crucial occasions when farm subsidies were under discussion. The overlapping, confused jurisdictions of American government thus, Sheingate argues, played a crucial role in facilitating a degree of change in agricultural policy that was not seen in either of the other countries that he studied, France and Japan, in which the policy making process was more formalized and predictable. Sheingate argues that '....because of jurisdictional overlap in Congress, and specifically the rules of the congressional budget process, the House Republican leadership could shift farm policy jurisdiction to the House Budget Committee. In so doing, Gingrich and his allies circumvented recalcitrant farm-state politicians on the House Agriculture Committee'(2001, p.207).

Yet this account over-estimates the degree to which Gingrich triumphed. Far from imposing swinging cuts in subsidies to match cuts made in other domestic programs because of the *Contract With America*, the FAIR Act actually gave US farmers the best of both worlds, although admittedly on a temporary basis. Subsidies increased in the short term, supposedly with the intent of phasing them out in the medium term, that is over seven years. Production controls were relaxed immediately. How was such a pleasing outcome for farmers achieved in a period when ostensibly cutting programs and budgets was the order of the day? The answer, it seems, was that the politics of winning farm state support and Congressional seats was more important than cutting government spending or ideological consistency. Orden, Paarlberg and Roe (1999) argue that Gingrich in fact made the decision to ease off on farmers because he wanted to help legislators from rural districts to fry bigger fish.

> ...it was the relatively large numbers of House Republicans who still cared about farm programs, together with the relatively small savings that agricultural cuts could provide, that finally persuaded the Houses leadership to yield (including even Majority leader Dick Armey, earlier the most vocal opponent of farm programs in the entire Congress.) House Republican leaders knew that the real budget battles of 1995 would take place over the much larger issues of tax cuts, welfare, and health entitlements. To win this large partisan battle, every single rank and file Republican vote would count. This gave Roberts (the Chair of the Agriculture Committee) and the farm district Republicans that he rallied the leverage they needed to face down the Budget Committee and save farm programs (plus a variety of agribusiness subsidy programs) from the cuts for which Lugar was calling in the Senate.

Roberts was aided on his discussions with Gingrich by the importance of rural areas in the electoral realignment that had made Gingrich Speaker. The triumph of the Congressional Republicans in the 1994 midterm elections rested in large part on the working through of a regional realignment that took the South from the Democratic into the Republican Party. Areas that used to send old style Southern Democrats (such as Jamie Whitten, long time chair of the Agricultural Appropriations subcommittee who was from Mississippi) to Congress to defend cotton, tobacco and peanut subsidies now sent Republicans. Roberts contended that this shift had required the Republican Party to shift away from the hostility to subsidies with which it had been associated since Benson. He noted that twenty-four of the thirty-three freshmen Republicans elected in 1994 were dependent on rural support (Orden, Paarlberg and Roe, 1999, p.181).

The FAIR Act had promised to move the United States into a position of moral leadership on farm reforms. After seven years, American farmers would have been operating in a free market without price supports distorting their production decisions. The US Trade Representative (USTR) planned on exploiting this occupation of the high moral ground by resuming the pressure on other countries to create free trade in agriculture, a goal that had been compromised in the negotiations for the Uruguay Round. In practice, no sooner had the FAIR Act passed than it was being abandoned in the face of plummeting farm prices and incomes. By 1999, farm incomes had fallen by 30 per cent since the mid 1990s (Hage, 1999) and, as Congress rushed to help, farm subsidies had doubled to US$14.4 billion (Carey, 1999). In a particularly ironic legislative manoeuvre, legislation to expand farm subsidies was rushed through in 1996 so that under the complicated rules to promote a balanced budget that we have encountered above, savings from cuts in the food stamp program could be applied to extra spending on agricultural subsidies (Hosansky, 1996). While the United States remained slightly below the OECD average in terms of the percentage of GDP spent on farm subsidies (1.2 per cent), it was clearly no longer in a position of moral leadership (*The Economist,* 1999). Indeed, American farm supports were relatively high for a traditionally exporting country and much higher than in Australia and New Zealand, partner members of the Cairns Group of nations campaigning for lower subsidies.

The retreat from *laissez faire* agricultural economics was confirmed in 2002 with the passage of a new agriculture act, the Farm Security and Rural Investment Act of 2002. The act was intended to last six years at an estimated cost of US$248.6 billion over that period. Increased commodity subsidies would account for US$56.7 billion of that increase. Unlike the farm politics of the 1950s and 1960s, the restoration of extensive government involvement in agriculture had bipartisan support. The Democrats had a meager one vote majority in the Senate and close races were expected in Montana, South Dakota, Minnesota, Iowa, Missouri, Arkansas and Georgia. These are all states in which farming has traditionally been important. The parties were naturally eager to prove their loyalty to farmers. The Democratic Senate Majority Leader, Tom Daschle of South Dakota, appointed himself to the conference committee that negotiated the final bill to try to ensure its smooth passage with suitable consideration to the needs of individual Senators. Vermont's Senator Jeffards, whose defection from the Republican Party had given the Democrats their majority was rewarded with a dairy subsidy plan that blatantly discriminated in favor of northeastern dairy farmers at the expense of those in the upper Midwest (Hosansky, 2002). A long-time opponent of farm subsidies, Senator Lugar of Indiana, described the politics of the farm bill accurately if passionately. 'If either party stands in the way of this largess, they risk being labeled the 'anti-farm party' and targeted with sentimental imagery associated with farm failures. Thus, conservative budget hawks and liberal social-welfare advocates alike subordinate their usual priorities to help their parties pay off wealthy farmers regardless of need, justification or even a realistic assessment of how to strengthen small farms' (Quoted in Hosansky, 2002, p.451).

A slightly different dynamic – legislative bargaining – explained events in the House where the Republicans (ostensibly devoted to free markets) held a secure majority. Republican leaders supported a massive increase in government spending on agricultural subsidies because they were anxious to secure votes for fast track negotiating authority for President Bush. Bush had sought fast track authority since his election; Clinton had been denied it throughout his second term. Finding the votes for fast track, in short, was not easy. The House Republican leadership decided that passing a new agriculture act was necessary to consolidate rural support (Rogers, 2001). Rural legislators had threatened to vote against fast track unless farm subsidy legislation was enacted first.

In the event, there were large majorities in favor of the passage of the farm bill. It cleared the House by a two to one margin (280-141) and by almost a solid majority in the Senate (64-35.) House Republicans also supported the bill by a two to one margin (141-73) as did House Democrats (137-63.) Senate support was only slightly less strong (64-35.) The strongest support came from Southern Democrats who backed the measure 48-5 in the House and 7-2 in the Senate. Most of the disagreement that occurred against this backdrop of bipartisanship was focused on issues that involved regional conflicts (such as the dairy program) or the attempts of liberal Democrats such as Senator Harkin (D., Iowa) to limit the amount that would be paid to very large scale, wealthier farmers.

The damage done to the standing of the United States in international trade negotiations by the return to high and permanent farm subsidies was soon evident. The EU no doubt gleefully started to question whether the increase in US actions broke American commitments under the Uruguay Round to limit and reduce subsidies. (The answer probably depended on how subsidies were classified and calculated.) More importantly, American farm subsidies became a staple item of criticism in trade discussions. The International Monetary Fund (IMF) and Oxfam protested that by stimulating over-production that is typically disposed of in food aid, American farm subsidies drove down prices and incomes for poor farmers in third world countries. An article in the *New York Times* provided a telling example. American farm subsidies lead to the production of surplus corn, which is sold on world markets at prices well below long-term marginal cost. Corn from the USA is sold in Mexico at 25 per cent less than it costs to produce. In consequence, poor Mexican farmers are driven into starvation and off the land, as they cannot compete with such prices losing money on every acre that they plant (Rosenberg, 2003). Commentators, politicians and diplomats around the world seized on the issue, no doubt eager to have an example to use against the United States when it lectured them on the virtues of free trade and open markets.

The contradiction between the international trade policy and the farm policy of the United States showed no sign of disappearing. In 2003, the Vice President, Richard Cheney, had to intervene with Congressional Republicans to dissuade them from passing a bill providing a further US$3.1 billion in farm subsidies just as the US trade Representative, Robert Zoellick headed off to Tokyo for trade talks that included agriculture. A representative of the EU in Washington DC noted that passing the bill 'would have further added to the credibility problem between the stated American goals of free trade and their farm policy'. Sophia Murphy of an American think-tank, the Institute for Agriculture and Trade Policy summarized the crux of the matter: 'the continued deep disconnect between America's trade agenda promoted by Bob Zoellick and the agricultural policy promoted by Congress' (Becker, 2003).

Trade Policy

It is generally (though not universally) accepted among economists that free trade results in higher standards of living and economic growth for all countries involved. There is therefore a considerable public interest in successful trade negotiations. This public interest in free trade had been thought by some to also apply specifically to US agriculture. It had become a widespread hope – particularly in the coalition favoring the phasing out of government farm programs – that trade liberalization would enable American farmers to make a decent living without government programs constraining their freedom; open markets would allow highly efficient farmers to sell more.

It is not perhaps surprising that as agricultural policy interests could withstand the onslaught of the *Contract With America* they could also cope with pressures from international trade talks. The making of the North America Free Trade Agreement (NAFTA) is a case in point. NAFTA was negotiated under the 'fast track' authority that is intended to allow the President to negotiate trade agreements over the objection of narrow interests. As these interests typically find their expression through Congress, fast track provides that the trade agreement negotiated by the President will be voted up or down without amendment within a specified time period. This is of course a massive shift in the normal balance of power between Congress and the President and would truly transform constitutional practice if followed more generally. Yet we must remember that at the end of the day, the President still needs at least a majority in the House and Senate (and probably 60 votes in the Senate) to prevail. In short, the incentive to accommodate well-organized factions or interests remains. Even fast track authority itself was accompanied by a requirement that the US Trade Representative have Agricultural Policy Advisory Committees (ATACs) to evaluate the impact of the agreement on specific commodities. Ten ATACs were created and may well have secured a more favorable deal for agriculture. The final scramble for votes in Congress to get NAFTA approved provided agriculture with further opportunities to secure special, favorable treatment. Legislators from Florida demanded protection for growers of the tasteless tomatoes produced in that state against competition from poor farmers in Mexico. The Clinton Administration paid the price. Florida citrus growers were similarly able to secure special treatment. Orden (1996) concluded that

> For agriculture in particular, attaining freer trade with Mexico under NAFTA accomplished only a small percentage of the goals sought eventually through GATT. Progress to be sure, but at a rate as perhaps to be negligible.

The pattern of demanding special treatment for agriculture in trade negotiations continued in the Uruguay Round. The United States entered the Uruguay Round of trade negotiations determined to secure a fairer, more open market for agriculture. This made a great deal of sense in terms of national interest. In the mid 1990s, US farmers accounted for 33 per cent of world exports of wheat, 72 per cent of world trade in corn, 73 per cent in soybeans and 33 per cent in cotton (US Bureau of the Census, 1999, Table 1124). The opportunity to improve on this impressive record was surely attractive to a country that had a chronic tendency to run deficits. One of the best ways for highly efficient American farmers to increase their exports was for the United States to lead other countries into reducing subsidies and removing barriers to trade. Ironically, however, the possibility of trade negotiations worked in the opposite direction. Senator Leahy proclaimed that for the United States to reduce agricultural subsidies would amount to 'unilateral nuclear disarmament'. Drawing on a popular theory about why the Cold War had ended, defenders of subsidies argued that the best way to persuade the EU and other countries to cut subsidies would be to spend freely on support for American farmers. Just as the scale and expense of Reagan's defense build up was supposed to have forced the Soviet Union to realize that it could not continue to compete for world dominance, the scale of American farm subsidies would overwhelm other nations. As Orden, Paarlberg and Rowe (1999) commented,

> The international negotiation was thus producing plenty of synergistic linkage in the United States but it was mostly negative rather than positive from a farm policy reform viewpoint...farm lobbies were instead using the negotiations as an added pretext to avoid domestic subsidy cutbacks and even as a means to seek larger subsidies.

The United States retreated from its pure free market position and in the Blair House Agreement with the EU promised not to seek the abolition of farm subsidies (Bradsher, 1992). Once the Uruguay Round was concluded, US agricultural interests were again able to use Congressional procedures to exert power to protect themselves. The Administration needed to secure passage of legislation ratifying the Uruguay Round before fast track authority expired at the end of 1993. A 'super majority' of 60 was needed in the Senate because of rules adopted to reduce the federal government's deficit: any measure that reduced tax income without corresponding savings from government expenditures needed at least 60 votes in the Senate. The tariff reductions that were part of the Uruguay Round made its approval subject to this 'super majority' requirement. Seventeen of the eighteen members of the Senate Agriculture Committee duly refused to be part of such a super majority unless agricultural subsidies were maintained. Ultimately the Senators received what they regarded as adequate assurances in a letter from the then Secretary of Agriculture and the Acting Budget Director, Alice Rivlin, promising to maintain expenditure levels on agriculture.

The Politics of Agriculture: From Subgovernment to Network – And Back?

i) The Subgovernment Era: 1930s to late 1940s

It is understandable that the period from the First World War until the late 1940s established an image of agricultural policy making as constituting almost the perfect example of a subgovernment or iron triangle. The AFBF had been nurtured by government. The AFBF had campaigned for government subsidy programs. Whether or not it deserved the credit for their creation, the AFBF represented farmers who benefited from them and it enjoyed close relationships with legislators and the USDA who sustained them. It was generally believed that membership in the AFBF secured more favorable treatment from local USDA officials. In short there was a symbiotic relationship between the AFBF and government. This is basically the period described by Hanson in his well-known book, *Gaining Access*.

It is the set of relationships that passed into general political science works such as *The End of Liberalism* as an exemplar of subgovernments and iron triangles.

ii) From Subgovernment to Partisan and Ideological Conflict

Clearly, however, much of the period after the Second World War was not compatible with the normal subgovernment picture of how US government works. The subgovernment idea pictured the interest concerned as represented by a single organization and that the definition of what was in the interest of its members was unproblematic. In reality, several national farm organizations existed and, as we have seen, two of them, the AFBF and NFU differed radically on how to improve the farm economy. The AFBF dwarfed all other groups in terms of membership; even in 2003 after decades of farm contraction, the AFBF clamed five million members on its web site (www.fb.org/about/thisis) and the NFU 300,000. The AFBF figure was inflated by the inclusion of farmers' families, retired farmers and customers of its insurance company who were not actually farmers. The AFBF was generally agreed to be, however, the larger organization. They remained substantial interest groups. However, the often-bitter conflict between the two undermined the credibility of both groups. The impact of the AFBF was further reduced by differences between its national leaders and leaders of state farm bureau branches particularly in the South that continued to favor government production controls and subsidies to raise farm incomes. thus while the AFBF in terms of its membership seemed to dwarf all other groups, in practice its influence on politicians, particularly Democrats, who disagreed with its national leaders' intensely free market ideology was far more modest. An intense farm depression in the 1980s spawned yet another group that claimed nation wide support, the American Agriculture Movement. The AAM is perhaps best thought of as a social movement rather than an interest group. Its formation was a powerful cry of pain but it never really established – and perhaps never really sought – to be a regular player in the policy process preferring to rely on the protests (such as the tractor drive on Washington in 1982) that gave it prominence.

The subgovernment concept pictured legislators from areas where the interest groups had strength as uniting across party lines to help their constituents. In reality, Republican and Democratic Representatives (and, to a lesser degree, Senators) disagreed strongly on the direction that policy should take.

Finally, in the subgovernment view of the world, the relevant executive agency was also committed to what was a widely shared view of the group's interest. In reality, Republican and Democratic Secretaries of Agriculture set out in almost opposite directions as the sort to reform policy. Republican Secretaries of Agriculture placed their faith in expanding markets for American farmers for example through sales to the former Soviet Union or by gaining access to markets in trade agreements. Democratic Secretaries while also pursuing new markers were skeptical about the prospects for phasing out government subsidies.

Adding to confusion of agricultural politics were the existence of numerous commodity organizations and important regionally or commodity based sub-plots within the overall drama of agricultural policy. After the failure of attempts to create a comprehensive agricultural policy in the 1950s and 1960s, agricultural policy makers in the 1970s and 1980s took a narrower approach focusing on individual commodity programs. Browne (1995) has argued that this change in policy was caused by the fragmentation of power in Congress as power shifted from committees to subcommittees. In the case of agriculture, however, the shift in policy following the failure of attempts at comprehensive reform caused (as Lowi would have predicted) a change in politics; the narrower, more limited policy focus on individual commodities given the failure of comprehensive policy making increased the importance of congressional subcommittees at the expense of general farm organizations and congressional subcommittees at the expense of full committees. The inability to make general farm policy in a comprehensive agriculture act naturally raised the profile of farm interest groups representing the producers of specific commodities such as beef, wheat and cotton. Even commodity organizations could be too broad as conflicts emerged between producers in different regions. For example, Wisconsin dairy farmers were understandably outraged by a federal policy that graded subsidies so that the further a dairy farm was from Eau Claire, Wisconsin (the center of that state's dairy industry), the higher the subsidy the farmer received. This curious feature of pre-refrigerated milk transport intended to encourage local production of milk for drinking (rather than for manufacturing into butter or cheese) was zealously guarded by legislators from such implausible dairy states as Florida and California. Only this (the twenty first) century was this bizarre policy ended.

iii) Back to Subgovernment: 1996 to the Present

Yet in the last eight years, the politics of agriculture has changed again. The story that emerged from the recent examples of policy making described above is also clearly not the same as the period of intense division and almost ideological conflict over the role of government in agricultural policy that prevailed for several decades after the Second World War. One of the striking features of the campaign for the 2002 Act was that old enemies such as the AFBF and NFU made joint appeals to Congress to act. The National Farmers' Union has always opposed the FAIR Act and the strategy of phasing out farm subsidies. More surprising was the AFBF's shift to supporting subsidies. Many commodity organizations followed suit. At a critical moment in the campaign to pass the 2002 Act, twenty-six farm groups, including the AFBF signed a letter to the House Republican leadership asking them to bring up the bill for a vote (Hagstrom, 2001b). The chair of the House Agriculture Committee called forty-five farm groups to a meeting to urge them to mobilize support for the Act (Hagstrom, 2001b).

The unity of the frequently divided farm groups was indeed impressive but traces of the old divisions remained. The National Farmers' Union had a relatively simple position. It believed that the FAIR Act had been a fundamental mistake. Only the reintroduction of production controls could secure farmers' incomes. The position of the AFBF was more complicated. On the one hand, it had to acknowledge the pain that its members felt as farm prices and incomes plummeted. On the other hand, the AFBF had long campaigned for exactly the sort of policy change that FAIR represented, namely 'getting the government out of agriculture' and returning to free markets. The AFBF had praised the 'emergency' acts that restored farm subsidies in the late 1990s precisely because they 'kept the Federal government out of farming decisions', a tenet of the FAIR Act and contrary to the policies that had prevailed from the New Deal until 1996 (Johnson, 1998). The AFBF insisted that the permanent subsidy legislation adopted in 2002 maintain a similar approach. While the AFBF accepted the need for government programs to deal with the 'emergency' of rapidly falling prices, its heart was not in the drive for a return to subsidies. Instead a search of quality newspapers and current affairs journals shows the AFBF to have been preoccupied with market building activities such as the lowering value of the dollar, the EU's restrictions on the import of GMO grains, trade liberalization in general, securing permanent Most Favored Nation (MFN) status for China (which it sees a major market opportunity) easing immigration restrictions on migrant workers, ending the trade blockade on Cuba and generally continuing to promote its market based strategies for agricultural prosperity. In short, the largest of the farm groups, the AFBF was not focused on restoring farm subsidies and the second most prominent group, the NFU, failed in its primary goal of securing a return to production controls. The role of agricultural interest groups in securing the current subsidy system should not therefore be exaggerated even though their unity was impressive.

The limited strength of the farm groups is illustrated by the modest degree to which they are players in financing political campaigns. Neither the AFBF nor the NFU are strong compared to other interest groups. Because of the nature of the rural character of the areas in which their members live and vote, neither appears in the list of interest groups paying for political advertisements in major markets. As Tables 8.1 and 8.2 show, neither the AFBF nor the NFU are major sources of campaign finance. They give modest amounts of money. The highest total for contributions by the AFBF was just under US$364,846 in 1996 and for the NFU US$56,250 in 2000. The median contribution to Republicans by the AFBF ranged from US$500 in 1984 to US$833 in 2000. The median payment by the NFU ranged from a meager US$100 in 1984 to US$250 in 2000. This small amount of money, a tiny percentage of the cost of a congressional campaign or of the value of federal farm subsidies (over US$20 billion a year) suggests that both the Bureau and the NFU were paying for access to legislators by its lobbyists rather being a major force in campaign finance. The AFBF made a total of 259 contributions, the NFU 183. The point of making such modest contributions is usually so that an interest group's lobbyists can gain access by being contributors to the legislators' campaigns, even if on a very modest basis. The Table also shows how fully the NFU is committed to the Democratic Party with the share of its campaign contributions going to Democrats never dropping below 90 per cent. The AFBF provides a classic example of an interest group switching its support as the strength of parties shifted; after the Republicans gained control of Congress in 1996, the percentage of AFBF contributions going to Democrats plummeted from just over half (55 per cent in 1994 to 28 per cent in 2000). Thus the major farm interest groups, like many others, should be seen as responding to, not shaping, the balance of political forces.

Table 8.1 AFBF campaign contributions, various years

	Democrat cont	Republican cont	Total cont	Dem %	GOP %	Median cont
1984	$52,075	$28,725	$80,800	64.45%	35.55%	$500
1986	$37,235	$54,380	$91,615	40.64%	59.36%	$500
1988	$69,800	$68,903	$138,703	50.32%	49.68%	$500
1990	$69,750	$88,350	$158,100	44.12%	55.88%	$550
1992	$120,275	$97,786	$218,061	55.16%	44.84%	$500
1994	$135,533	$112,440	$247,973	54.66%	45.34%	$500
1996	$118,260	$236,341	$364,846	32.41%	64.78%	$500
1998	$102,650	$215,738	$318,388	32.24%	67.76%	$500
2000	$75,450	$194,191	$269,641	27.98%	72.02%	$833

Table 8.2 NFU campaign contributions, various years

	Democrat. cont	Republican cont	Total cont	Dem %	GOP %	Median cont
1984	$5,750	$350	$6,100	94.26%	5.74%	$100
1986	$5,307	$0	$5,307	100.0%	0.00%	$240
1988	$5,300	$100	$5,400	98.15%	1.85%	$250
1990	$45,050	$750	$45,800	98.36%	1.64%	$500
1992	$48,425	$1,250	$49,875	97.09%	2.51%	$250
1994	$22,330	$250	$22,580	98.89%	1.11%	$250
1996	$25,400	$500	$25,900	98.07%	1.93%	$250
1998	$29,050	$3,000	$32,300	89.94%	9.29%	$250
2000	$53,000	$3,250	$56,250	94.22%	5.78%	$250

The unity of the farm interest groups had its parallels in Congress. The intense conflict between interventionist Democrats and free market Republicans gave way to a 'farm bloc' alliance reminiscent of the era between the World Wars. There was a bloc of pro-subsidy legislators willing to give or withhold their support on high profile issues on the basis of how agriculture was treated in return. It was particularly important that a significant proportion of the freshman Republicans who had enabled their Party to capture the House for the first time in forty years represented rural areas that had long favored farm programs. As Roberts had claimed, twenty-four of the thirty-three freshmen elected in 1994 were dependent on rural support. As is commonly the case in US politics, their district interest, not a national party platform came first.

Finally, to complete the picture of a return to the old subgovernment or iron triangle days, the Secretary of Agriculture was expected not to question farm subsidies. Ann Veneman, Bush II's Agriculture Secretary, made a notable change in her thinking. Prior to her appointment, she had expressed considerable concern about subsidies. In a book written with J.B. Penn, she criticized farm programs and argued the money could be better spent on conservation, food safety, trade promotion and feeding the hungry. Yet Veneman refused to take a position critical of the 2002 farm bill that placed subsidies once more on a permanent legislative footing. Senator Lugar, prominent critic of farm subsidies, once begged her to take a position on the bill. She refused (*National Journal*, 2003).

Conclusions

What important points emerge from these stories?

Let us start with some general observations about how farmers get what they want in Washington. The stories of the campaigns for a return to subsidizing agriculture and giving it special treatment in trade negotiation appear to confirm the general picture presented by the old subgovernment idea. Farmers have continued to be able to secure policies such as high levels of subsidy and special treatment in trade negotiations even under apparently very adverse political conditions. Farmers, a small and diminishing proportion of the population have overcome such apparently enormous disadvantages as the commitment of strong Republican leaders to reducing the role of government in the economy and reducing domestic expenditures. The easy explanation to offer would be that farmers have particularly strong interest groups. In fact, however, the factors evident in the policy developments we have just examined do not seem to depend heavily on interest groups as such but on a number of other explanations.

American farm interest groups have experienced fluctuating fortunes in the late twentieth century. The story is often seen as a simple tale of the decline of the general farm organizations and the emergence of commodity groups. The reality is more complicated. Commodity groups did indeed gain in importance in the 1970s following the failure of attempts at comprehensive policy making. As politicians narrowed their focus to specific commodities, so their interest in what commodity groups had to say increased. As the focus switched back to general farm policy in the last years of the twentieth century, the lead switched back to general farm groups. In the fifteen years from the passage of the New Deal agricultural legislation until the defection of the national AFBF leadership from it, no single general farm group dominated. The AFBF and NFU were locked in conflict over the general direction that policy should take and were allied with entirely different, ideologically opposed politicians; they diminished each other's standing and influence. There were also very serious divisions in the 1950s and 1960s between the national leaders of the AFBF focused on 'getting the government out of agriculture' and leaders of southern state branches who remained committed to the subsidy programs the AFBF had helped create in the 1930s. Commodity groups were necessarily limited in influence because of the narrowness of their focus. It required politicians to put together the coalitions required to pass farm legislation. In brief, American farm interest groups alone did not possess the power to shape farm policy.

What else, then, has shaped American farm policy? There are a number of explanations.

The first is legislative politics. Agricultural programs often survived because at key moments, legislators from rural areas were able to leverage continued support for farm subsidies by their votes on other issues. Gingrich wanted the Contract with America passed so badly that he was willing to exempt farmers from it. Supporters of NAFTA wanted that trade agreement so badly that they were prepared to exempt much of agriculture from it and the Uruguay Round of GATT. President Bush wanted fast track trade negotiating authority so badly that House Republican leaders decided to buy the votes of rural legislators with an expensive farm subsidy bill that was ironically a major challenge to free trade. Interest groups and the institutional structure of Congress, particularly the Agriculture Committees helped.

A second important general conclusion is that party competition also played a crucial role in shaping farm policy. Political scientists are understandably skeptical about the likelihood that the farm vote – less than 2.5 per cent of the electorate – would actually prove decisive in elections. However, as we have seen, even highly ideological Republican leaders in the House were prepared to make compromises with members of their party representing rural areas in order to safeguard their overall majority. One of the common explanations for the passage of the 2002 agricultural subsidy act was therefore very familiar: 'Only about 2 percent of Americans live on farms today, but farmers are active politically. With both chambers of Congress so evenly divided, Republicans and Democrats are courting the crucial farm vote' (Hagstrom, 2001a). In the United States, at the turn of the 21st century, all of the national, elected institutions – the House, Senate and Presidency – were closely contested by the two major parties. One of the recurring themes in agricultural politics around the world has been the ability of farmers to position themselves as a supposedly strategically crucial group in national elections. This was true, for example, in Britain for some decades after the Second World War. It was true in many American presidential elections after Truman's surprise victory in 1948 was attributed to the farm vote. It was apparently true in American legislative politics in the 1990s and 2000s.

This reminds us that interests can be expressed effectively in politics by means other than by interest groups. It is probably the case that in all democracies, interests are expressed in a variety of ways. After all, both labor and even (at least in their origins) farmers' parties are not unusual. In the United States Congress, numerous interests find expression not only through the work of individual legislators but, as the old iron triangle idea reminds us, through congressional committees and Caucuses such as the Black Caucus (advancing then interests of African Americans) and the Women's Caucus. Some might argue that the interests of certain business interests (such as oil) find direct representation in the Bush Administration.

In short, while agricultural interest groups are indeed active, they are not necessarily the reason why the interests of American farmers continue to be so well protected even at the expense of taxpayers, consumers and general American foreign policy goals such as trade liberalization.

The most important point to note, however, is that the subgovernment picture of policymaking is neither completely right nor completely wrong. It all depends on which period one is discussing. The idea captured the truth of the situation in the 1930s and early 1940s, and was a poor guide to agricultural politics in the 1950s and 1960s. More recently, the subgovernment or iron triangle image seems to describe agricultural policy making fairly well again. Why did these changes occur?

The shift from subgovernment or iron triangle to ideological conflict was occasioned by the apparently inevitable choice that had to be made between subsidies on the one hand and freedom to farm on the other. This coincided with both one of the enduring divisions between Republicans and Democrats, namely belief in an active role for government in the economy. The shift in power within the AFBF from the South to the Midwest shifted it decisively towards the 'freedom to farm' approach.

The shift back towards subgovernment politics since 1996 has both an obvious and less obvious explanation. The obvious explanation is that the crisis in American agriculture was so severe that even interest groups and legislators instinctively opposed to government intervention were forced to accept its necessity in order to avoid mass bankruptcies. The less obvious and more interesting point is the impact of being the majority party on the Republican Party. This impact can be divided into two aspects. The first is that the incorporation of the pro-subsidy South into the Republican Party – and the desire to extend the process by capturing even more Democratic seats in that region compelled it to modify its ideological purity. Changing geographical bases can change party ideology. The less obvious point is that majority parties – in the United States and perhaps in other democracies – always display greater ideological diversity than minority parties. Democrats used to be more ideologically confused when they were the majority party than were the Republicans. Perhaps the situation now is reversing.

The changes in the nature of agricultural subsidy politics that have occurred over the last seventy years or so may well have broader implications for understanding the American State. The image of the American state presented compellingly by critical pluralists such as Lowi lost support in the 1980s. The subgovernment idea needed to be replaced by the more amorphous and less bounded notion of networks. New interests (such as environmental groups) had forced their way into the old closed subgovernment making it a more amorphous but inclusive network. Subgovernments had also lost their autonomy to policy actors more at the center of government including the Office of Management and Budget (OMB) in the Executive Branch or party leaders and the Budget Committees in Congress. The case of agricultural policy suggests, however, that a more fluid situation may prevail. Yesterday's subgovernment (in the 1930s) can give way to a situation in which there are sharply conflicting alternative subgovernments (the late 1940s, 1950s and 1960s) only to reappear in almost classic form (the period since 1996) The agricultural subgovernment is once more under pressure; the EU and United States agreed in principle to reduce farm subsidies as part of the next international trade round (*New York Times*, 2003).

Lowi's insight that policy helps shapes politics often leads us to expect that there will be considerable continuity in the politics of policy areas. In practice, however, as the situation within those policy areas shifts, so too does the form that policy takes. A subgovernment of the past may be gone yesterday and re-emerge tomorrow.

Notes

[1] Only three people had ever understood it; one had died, another had gone mad and the third had forgotten.

[2] This era is described in my first book: Graham K. Wilson (1977), *Special Interests and Policymaking: Agricultural Policies and Politics in Britain and the United States* (John Wiley and Son, Chichester and New York).

References

Becker, E. (2003), 'Republicans Back Down on raising Farm Aid', *New York Times*, 13 February, A5.

Bovard, J. (1998), 'Freedom to Farm Washington', *American Spectator*, Vol. 33(11) (November), p.72.

Bradsher, K. (1992), 'The Trade Accord: Europeans Agree With US On Cutting Farm Subsidies', *New York Times*, 21 November, Section 1, p.1.

Browne, William P (1995) *Cultivating Congress; Constituents, Issues and Interests in Agriculural Policymaking*, University of Kansas Press: Lawrence.

Carey, J.(1999), 'Let Markets Do Their Job', *Business Week*, 28 June, p.33.

ERS (Economic Research Service) (2003), *Amber Waves: The Economics of Food, Farming: Natural Resources and Rural America*, November 03, 2003.

Hage, D. (1999), 'Bitter Harvest', *The Nation*, 11 October, pp.5-7.

Hagstrom, J. (2001a), *Congress Daily*, National Journal Group Inc., 25 April.

Hagstrom, J. (2001b), 'Combest: Farm Bill Will Go To House Floor Next Week', *Congress Daily*, National Journal Group Inc., 26 September.

Hansen, J. M. (1991), *Gaining Access: Congress and the Farm Lobby, 1918-81*, University of Chicago Press, Chicago.

Heclo, H. (1975), 'Issue Networks and the Executive Establishment' in Anthony S. King (ed.), *The New American Political System*, American Enterprise Institute, Washington DC.

Hosansky, D. (1996), 'The Race is on to Complete Agriculture Spending Bill', *Congressional Quarterly Weekly Report*, 27 July, p.2106.

Hosansky, D. (2002), 'Farm Subsidies', *Congressional Quarterly Researcher*, May 17, p.451.

Johnson, D. (1998), 'The Budget Deal: Agriculture', *New York Times*,16 October.

Lowi, T. (1967), *The End of Liberalism*, W.E. Norton, New York.

National Journal (2003), 'Politics: A Drought of Farm Support', *National Journal*, Friday 24 January.

New York Times (2003), 14 August, C1.

Olson, M. (1971), *The Logic of Collective Action: Public Goods and the Theory of Groups*, Harvard University Press, Cambridge MA.

Orden, D. (1996), 'Agricultural Interest Groups and NAFTA', in A. O. Krueger (ed.), *The Political Economy of US Trade Policy*, University of Chicago Press, Chicago.

Orden, D., Paarlberg, R., and Roe, T. (1999), *Policy reform in US Agriculture: Analysis and Prognosis*, University of Chicago Press, Chicago.

Pataschnik, E. (2003), 'After the Public Interest Prevails: The Political Sustainability of Policy Reform', *Governance,* Vol. 16, pp.203-234.

Rogers, D. (2001), 'House GOP Plans Massive Farm-Spending Bill', *Wall Street Journal,* 7 September, A2.

Rosenberg, T. (2003), 'Why Mexico's Small Corn Farmers Go Hungry', *New York Times,* 3 March, A22.

Sheingate, A.D. (2001), *The Rise of the Agricultural Welfare State: Institutions and Interest Group Power in the United States, France and Japan*, Princeton University Press, Princeton.

The Economist (1999), 'Financial Indicators: Farm Subsidies', *The Economist,* 5 June, p. 99.

US Bureau of the Census (1999), *Statistical Abstract of the United States 1999*, Washington DC, GPO, 199, Table 1124.

Chapter 9

The Uphill Struggle to Prevail:
National Farm Organizations in Canada

Grace Skogstad

Introduction

In the early 1990s, a veteran farm journalist described the Canadian Federation of Agriculture as 'a shell – underfunded, indecisive, weaker than its strongest parts, lacking credibility or representation among more than half of Canada's farmers and struggling to control divisions even among those groups it counted as members' (Wilson, 1990, p.142). Rather than being at the centre of important agricultural policy debates, the Canadian Federation of Agriculture was often relegated to the sidelines while its member organizations or non-member specialist commodity groups took centre stage.

This appraisal of Canada's umbrella organization was sobering. Since its creation in 1935 under the name of the Canadian Chamber of Agriculture, the Canadian Federation of Agriculture (CFA) has sought to provide the united voice that would enable Canadian farmers to secure more favourable agricultural policies and improve their social and economic welfare. It had largely succeeded in that endeavour, despite being challenged by commodity organizations and the National Farmers Union, also vying to speak for the particular and general interests of Canada's farmers. Indeed, a decade earlier, this same journalist had described the CFA as 'the most credible, respected, and listened-to farm organization in Ottawa' (Wilson, 1981, p.245). However, events in the 1980s and 1990s de-stabilized the CFA's preeminent position. Commodity groups assumed a more predominant role and the agricultural and food policy community opened to a host of non-farmer groups. Fissures within the farm community were fully exposed and became more pronounced as Canadian agriculture adjusted to changing government goals for the sector and the intertwining of international trade and domestic agricultural policies.

In the early twenty-first century, the CFA nonetheless remains a significant and influential umbrella farm organization. If the leaders of its member organizations are more often the primary interlocutors on commodity- and regional-specific issues than are CFA leaders themselves, the organization still remains at the centre of agricultural and food policy debates that transcend commodities and provinces. It has no national rival, either in terms of its organizational strength or its reputation in government circles. The CFA's influence on national agricultural policy, albeit considerable, is not assured. Its struggle to prevail, like that of the much weaker National Farmers Union, has often required departing from the quiet diplomacy characteristic of organizations that enjoy a partnership role with state officials, to broad-based coalition building and conventional lobbying tactics of mass demonstrations.

This chapter provides a historical and contemporary overview of the coordinating and representational capacities, and consequent policy influence of the CFA and the National Farmers' Union. To do so, it examines both logic of membership and logic of influence factors. Logic of membership factors refer to the attributes of members which dispose them to collective action and render it more or less easy. Logic of influence factors are extraneous to membership characteristics and include principally the structure of the state and its policies (Coleman and Skogstad, 1990, p.23). The logic of membership factors will be examined in the following section on the structure of Canadian agriculture; the logic of influence factors are dealt with here.

Canada's system of multi-level governance importantly shapes the organizational logic and cohesion of agricultural producers, and by extension, the influence of national farm interest groups. The provincial and national governments have concurrent jurisdiction over agriculture. They share legislative authority and expenditure responsibility with regard to a number of agricultural matters, including research, price or income support, credit, and production incentives. On other matters–marketing of agricultural commodities, for example– authority is divided between the two orders of government. The provinces regulate marketing within their borders while the Government of Canada exercises exclusive authority over inter-provincial and export marketing. This legal situation gives incentives for both provincial and national-level organization. On the one hand, there are therefore strong incentives to organize nationally, either as a national commodity group or general farm organization, because the effective redress of many problems, especially those that require instruments of regulated marketing, is impossible without the cooperation of the (ten) provincial and (one) national governments.[1] On the other hand, collective action on a provincial and commodity-specific basis is also promoted by the legal authority of provincial governments and the concentration of certain commodities in particular provinces/regions.

Since the 1970s, several provinces have been aggressive in exercising their substantial expenditure and regulatory powers with respect to agriculture, and demanding more input into federal policies that affect the well being of the agricultural sector. The production and manufacture of food is undoubtedly of greater economic and political significance to a number of provinces than it is to the country as a whole. Whereas the agri-food sector contributes 8 per cent to Canada's GDP and accounts for 13 per cent of total employment,[2] the figures are higher in Alberta, Saskatchewan, Manitoba, and Prince Edward Island. Food processing is the largest manufacturing sector in Quebec and the second largest in Ontario, the two most populous Canadian provinces. Farmers' local economic significance often gives rise to close alliances between provincial farm organizations and provincial agriculture ministers. This partnership has been especially close between Quebec's farm federation and the Quebec government where it has become intertwined with the nationalist aspirations of Quebec governments from the mid-1970s onwards.

The appreciable role of provinces in national agricultural policy and the existence of provincial producer-state alliances have ambiguous effects on national farm organizations' influence in policy making. On the one hand, these provincial alliances can provide added leverage to the CFA vis-a-vis national government officials by demonstrating a broad show of support for its position. On the other hand, alliances between farm groups and the provincial government can undermine the CFA's influence when they result in interprovincial discord and conflicting policy prescriptions and initiatives. (These incompatible policy objectives across provinces are the inevitable result of the differing interests and philosophies of provincial farm federations and commodity organizations as well as their provincial governments.) The CFA's influence is jeopardized in the instance of inter-provincial discord because the Government of Canada is likely to place a higher priority on placating cantankerous provincial governments – who are expected to cost-share transfer programs to the industry – than on keeping a national farm organization onside.

In addition to the opportunities provided by federalism to build alliances with provincial governments, a second institutional factor that directly determines the influence of any national farm organization in Canada is the concentration of decision-making authority in the executive of governments. On matters of expenditure policy, agricultural ministers are beholden to finance ministers, and in the deficit-ridden 1980s and 1990s, Canadian finance ministers narrowed sharply the scope of the state assistance model. This institutional setting – government wide fiscal restraint and strong direction of sectoral policy from central agencies like Finance – means that even the best organized farm lobby, and even one with the confidence of the agriculture minister, can come away empty-handed. And yet, on matters (like regulatory policy) where agriculture ministers enjoy more independence from central agencies, concentrated executive authority can work to the benefit of a cohesive farm lobby. A minister in a majority government who is committed to a farm group's cause has considerable latitude to ignore opposition parties in Canada's Westminister parliamentary system. On that set of issues that do not entail significant fiscal transfers to producers or on which an agriculture minister can act relatively independently of his cabinet colleagues, the cohesion of the national farm associational system can thus be pivotal to its influence.

The Structure of Canadian Agriculture: Six Decades of Rationalization

The structure of Canadian agriculture has an important bearing on the logic of organizational membership. Canada's agricultural community is very diverse, composed of disparate provincial economies. In general, the prairie agricultural economy is based on Canada's major agricultural products – grains, oilseeds, cattle and hogs – all of which rely importantly on export markets. By contrast, some of the most significant commodities produced in the central Canadian provinces of Ontario and Quebec – including milk, eggs and poultry – are sold almost exclusively in the domestic market. These divisions between domestic and export-oriented sectors and regions make it exceedingly difficult at times for Canadian farmers to conceive of their interests – or at least the means to realize common economic goals – in mutually beneficial terms. Other cleavages – between large commercial operators and smaller, less viable farmers, for example – further undermine a logic of membership, but here the effect is equally negative on provincial and national level organizations.

Table 9.1 Canadians living on farms

Year	% living on farms	% change over decade
1931	31.7	-
1941	27.4	13.6
1951	20.8	24.0
1961	11.7	43.8
1971	7.4	36.8
1981	4.7	36.5
1991	3.2	32.0
2001	2.4	25.0

Source: Statistics Canada. Census of Canadian Agriculture, 2001

Like other OECD countries, Canadian agriculture has been in a process of structural change for several decades. The pattern is familiar: 'Labour leaves the sector, farm enterprises increase in size and a large and growing share of agricultural production is produced by a relatively small number of highly specialised farm businesses' (Bowlby and Trant, 2002, p.8). Canadian agriculture underwent considerable restructuring over the period 1950-1980 (see Table 9.1). The number of Canadians living on farms declined decade after decade; by 1981 Canada had 77 per cent fewer farms than in 1951. The trend toward fewer farms continues, as does the increase in their average size (see Table 9.2).[3] As in other OECD countries, the larger commercial farms – 31 per cent – account for almost all production – 87 per cent of all sales – while the 35 per cent classified as small and medium-sized farms account for 12 per cent of sales (Agriculture and Agri-Food Canada, 2001).[4] Not surprisingly, the larger farms are also more viable. Virtually all Canadian farms (98 per cent) are family owned and operated businesses, but an increasing number (37 per cent in 1996) are registered as partnerships or family corporations.

Table 9.2 Changes in Canadian farm structure, selected years

	Total Farms	Total Hectares	Average Hectares per Farm	Rented or Leased Hectares	Average Age
1981	318361	65888916	207	20334571	
1986	293089	67825757	231	24606852	
1991	280043	67753700	242	24792348	
1996	276548	68054956	246	24993993	47
2001	246923	67502447	273	25236740	49

Source: Statistics Canada. Available at:
            http://www.statcan.ca/english/Pgdb/econ124a.htm
            http://www.statcan.ca/english/Pgdb/econ117a.htm

Slightly more land is in production today than 20 years ago. However, more of it is being rented or leased than 20 years ago (Table 9.2). Despite experiencing some of the largest employment declines, the farm labour force has also increased its productivity relative to the goods-producing and service-sectors (Agriculture and Agri-Food Canada, 2001). This increased productivity is the result of more chemical fertilizer use, as well as larger and more efficient farm machinery. Although there continues to be a significant degree of regional specialization of Canadian agriculture – grains and oilseeds in Saskatchewan and Manitoba, cattle in Alberta, dairy in Ontario and Quebec – the pattern is toward more diversification within a region and on individual farm units. The exception is the rapid expansion and concentration of the cattle sector in Alberta.

These structural trends – fewer and larger farms, a minority of farms responsible for the vast majority of food production, a highly productive labour force, greater reliance on off-farm income, more diversified production units – are the result of government policy, technological developments, and responses to market signals. Government subsidized credit has allowed farmers to expand the size of their operations, purchase larger and more efficient machinery, and make more use of chemical fertilizers. The frequent lack of profits in the sector, as farm input costs have risen and market prices have failed to keep pace, has also whittled down farm numbers over time,⁵ reducing the potential membership base for general farm organizations. The decrease in the number of farms and farm families is particularly distressing for the National Farmers' Union since smaller family farms comprise its constituency base.

The Canadian Federation of Agriculture: The Closest Thing to a Peak Association

Since its birth as the Canadian Chamber of Agriculture in the middle of the 1930s depression, the CFA has provided a bridge across producers of different commodities, living in different provinces and regions, speaking two different languages, and operating farm units that over time have come to differ quite significantly in terms of their commercial viability. It is not a direct membership organization, but rather a federation of general farm organizations in the provinces and inter-provincial and national commodity groups. It currently has 21 members and associate members representing 200,000 of Canada's present 250,000 farmers, some 80 per cent.[6] Its members include the ten provincial federations, a base which makes it the only farm organization that can credibly claim to represent producers of all commodities in all provinces. As in the past, the commodity group representing livestock producers (the Canadian Cattlemen's Association) is not a member. Nor is Grain Farmers of Canada (GFC), established in 2000 as a federation of provincial and regional groups representing barley, wheat, canola, corn, and soybean growers who are philosophically committed to liberal markets. GFC claims to represent over 80,000 grain farmers across Canada.

Chronic Limitations to Organizational Development

To coordinate the divergent provincial and commodity interests and policy proposals, the CFA has a democratic structure. An annual meeting of delegates of member organizations sets the policy direction of the CFA and elects the officers of the CFA (a president, two vice-presidents, and a National Council). A Board of Directors, elected from and by the National Council, exercises decision-making powers between meetings of the National Council. Daily direction of the affairs of the CFA is in the hands of an Executive Committee of officers. Despite this democratic architecture, the CFA's capacity to build bridges across the diverse interests of its members, and Canada's farming community has been handicapped by a number of factors.

From the beginning, the CFA (the name it assumed in 1940) lacked the statutory mandate and organizational resources necessary for a fully successful umbrella farm organization. There is no national legislation to allow a general farm organization to extract a compulsory membership due from Canadian farmers. The CFA has relied almost entirely upon voluntary fees paid by its members, which amounted to approximately C$1,000,000 in 2003. This small revenue base provides for a meagre administrative and professional staff; 7.5 permanent staff and a further five on contract in 2003. Its financial structure and small secretariat have required the CFA to lean heavily upon its member organizations to provide it with policy expertise on a host of issues. In this respect it is well served. The Quebec farm union has formidable institutional resources (a budget ten times that of the CFA) and policy capacity – indeed, among the best in the world. Albeit not of the same magnitude, the Ontario Federation of Agriculture's resources also make it an important source of policy expertise. The expertise of long-standing member commodity organizations, like the Dairy Farmers of Canada, the Canadian Horticultural Council, and the prairie pools has also been crucial to the CFA's policy capacity over its lifetime.

Quebec farm organizations have been members of the CFA since its origin. In 1970, the Quebec government passed legislation which allowed a single farm organization to accredit itself as the monopoly voice of Quebec farmers and to extract a compulsory membership fee from every Quebec farmer. The Union des producteurs agricoles (UPA) has been that monopoly voice since 1972, representing some 50,000 producers. Its president serves as one of the two vice-presidents of the CFA. Quebec agriculture is an important component of Canadian agriculture, ranking fourth behind Ontario, Saskatchewan and Alberta in terms of number of farms and farm population. Since 1970, Quebec governments have taken a special interest in agriculture as a sector which represents and reinforces the values of (linguistic) solidarity of the nationalist Quebec state. Pressed by the UPA, Quebec governments have put in place the most advanced model of state assistance in Canada.

CFA's relationship with the UPA, like that with the UPA's predecessor (the Union Catholique des Cultivateurs), is among its most important. For the most part, it has been an effective working partnership and one that has augmented in no small degree the CFA's policy capacity and credibility with the Government of Canada. Provincial federation fees to the CFA are based on the size of the province's farm population and their gross receipts. By virtue of this formula, the UPA's financial contribution to the CFA is among the largest of any member. At the same time, however, the more interventionist stance of Quebec governments in agriculture, relative to the Government of Canada and several provinces, has created a wedge in terms of the expectations of Quebec and English-speaking farmers regarding the appropriate responsibilities of governments with respect to securing farmers' incomes. In addition, as revealed in the discussion below on trade policy, the close partnership between the UPA and Quebec governments can give the organization strong incentives to go its own way, outside the umbrella of the CFA.

Besides its lack of a stable and secure independent financial base and its heavy reliance upon member organizations for finances and policy expertise, the CFA has also been plagued by organizational competitors. An early rival was the National Farmers Union. From the 1930s onward, it had organizations in the three prairie provinces. It later expanded to British Columbia and Ontario as well. Although the NFU operated mainly in the provincial sphere and had no permanent staff in the national capital, it did provide an alternative vehicle for farmers wishing to engage more directly, and often more militantly, in farm politics. More recently, alliances of non-member commodity groups have been the CFA's major competitor.

Despite its organizational limitations, the CFA emerged after 1940 as the most credible voice of Canadian farmers. It built up a close, cordial, and trusting relationship with officials in the department of agriculture, one fostered by the stability in office of both the CFA's president and the deputy minister of Agriculture. It met annually with the federal cabinet to outline the main problems facing Canadian farmers and its proposed solutions. It avoided confrontation, believing that non-partisan cooperation was more effective (Dawson, 1960). Its quiet lobbying, although criticized by more militant farmers who abandoned it for the National Farmers Union, was instrumental in establishing early pillars in the model of state assistance by 1960: a price stabilization program that supported the prices of Canada's most important commodities, and a monopoly agency to market prairie wheat, barley and oats. The establishment of the Canadian Wheat Board, with its operations financially guaranteed by the Government of Canada, provided prairie grain growers with a guaranteed annual initial payment as well as equity in pricing and delivery opportunities.

Other important pillars of state assistance were secured with the aid of the National Farmers Union and following public protest and demonstrations. The creation of a national system of dairy supply management in the late 1960s came following repeated demonstrations on Parliament Hill by thousands of Quebec and Ontario farmers and their provincial farm union leaders. In the early 1970s, legislation to allow supply management in other sectors was passed, and led to national marketing agencies in the egg and poultry sectors. Through a combination of production controls, administered prices and import controls, these national marketing agencies assured producers of dairy, egg, and poultry products a profit on their enterprise. After 1976, largely because of the intense efforts by CFA organizational members in prairie Canada (the wheat pools and provincial federations of agriculture), the Western Grain Stabilization Act supported and stabilized the prices of a basket of prairie grains.

A Privileged Relationship with the Canadian State - or Not?

How can one best characterize Canadian national farm interest groups' relationship with the Canadian state down to the 1980s, before the domestic and international context of Canadian agricultural policy shifted dramatically? Was it a privileged relationship in the sense that access translated into the influence the CFA sought? The answer would appear to be No.

In 1967, Helen Jones Dawson compared the CFA and the British National Farmers' Union (NFU). Discovering that the British NFU enjoyed much superior organizational resources and policy capacity to the CFA, she concluded that it also exercised more influence over agricultural policy. Whereas in Britain, the NFU was recognized as *the* single voice of farmers, in Canada there were two general farm organizations that did not always agree, and several commodity organizations acting on their own. The financial resources of the CFA paled besides those of the British NFU, as did the size of its expert staff and its technical capacity. In terms of policy influence, Dawson observed a striking difference between the informal nature of the CFA's relationship with government officials as compared to the NFU's guarantees of formal input into and influence on British agricultural policy. Canadian farmers' membership on advisory committees, Dawson concluded, added up to much less influence on farm policy than it did in the United Kingdom, in part because Canadian governments paid less attention to these committees but also because Canadian farm organizations lacked the expertise to make substantive contributions. The "flavour" of the relationship between civil servants and the CFA in Canada was much different from that between civil servants and the British farm organizations, concluded Dawson (1967, p.457): 'It is much less stratified–there is no concept at all, as in Britain, of the "opposite number"....'. Further, 'the British organizations, particularly the Farmers' Union, speak of carrying on "negotiations" with government. This word is not used in the literature on the Canadian farm organizations'.

The CFA itself supported Dawson's analysis. In 1969, at the Canadian Agricultural Congress, the President of the CFA was critical of a government-commissioned Task Force Report struck to advise on future agricultural policy guidelines, arguing it did not recognize that governments have a responsibility for the welfare of farmers. And it chastised the Canadian government's failure to take farmers' views adequately into account in formulating agricultural policy. President Charles Munro argued for 'improved consultation and improved consultation procedures' that 'represent real breaks with tradition'. Producers, he said, needed to be informed of the consequences of courses of action which the government was considering '*before* final decision-making'. He attacked existing procedures, by which governments received the views of farmers before 'retiring into private deliberations of which the farmers will be informed of the results in due course'.

This critique, which signalled considerable dissatisfaction with the outputs that resulted from access, was based on the view that agricultural policy should be left to governments and farmers. The CFA opposed a recommendation by this same task force for the formation of a new national advisory council to the minister of agriculture that would include the CFA, the NFU, councils to be created that would represent major commodity sectors, as well as agribusinesses and trade associations (Federal Task Force on Agriculture, 1970, p.300). The CFA rejected the idea of a broad all-industry advisory structure. It argued that 'the interests of the two will often not be identical' and further, 'on many subjects the primary interest involved will be that of the farmer, and the agri-business role in a policy-making process in such areas would be inappropriate'. The CFA adopted a similar position in the late 1970s, when the Government of Canada attempted to devise a Food Strategy for Canada. At a conference to which the Government of Canada had invited over 400 representatives of all sectors of the food system – producers, processors, distributors, retailers, consumers, and the input sector – the CFA sought to make it 'unequivocally clear' that 'farming is the farmer's business' (Canadian Federation of Agriculture, 1978). As CFA President Dobson Lea phrased it:

> We will not accept decision-making, consultative, advisory or representational systems where non-farm representatives are invited to be the vehicle through which the government is advised on farmer's business.

Accept it or not, inclusion of a broader array of actors and interests into agricultural and food policy-making became the norm from the mid-1980s onward.

The National Farmers Union: National in Name Only

In many ways it is a misnomer to label the National Farmers Union (NFU) a *national* farm interest group. Neither its size nor the geographic scope of its membership warrant the label. The NFU's influence on Canadian agricultural policy is definitely secondary to that of the CFA and much inferior to that of many commodity groups. Even so, on selected policy issues it has historically made a difference, most often in concert with the CFA.

The current National Farmers Union dates from 1969 when farmers' unions in Saskatchewan, Manitoba, Ontario, and British Columbia merged. They were later joined by members of farmers' unions in Alberta and the Maritime provinces. The NFU appealed then, as it does today, to small and medium-sized family farms worried about structural trends in agriculture that threaten their way of life. To preserve the family farm, the NFU has advocated more radical policies than the CFA, including government intervention to ensure farmers receive the cost of production for their commodities. It has also opposed government policies geared toward rendering farmers more competitive through consolidation of farm units and adoption of technological advancements. These positions have put it at odds with the neo-liberal philosophy of Canadian national governments over the past 35 years.

The NFU is a direct membership organization of farm families. With an estimated 10,000 members, the NFU represents far fewer Canadian farmers (4 per cent) than the CFA, and indeed fewer farmers than do some commodity organizations. In three provinces – Quebec, Manitoba and New Brunswick – the NFU is disadvantaged by provincial legislation which requires farmers to pay dues to provincial farm federations that belong to the CFA. Plagued over its life by inadequate financing and debt, the NFU has recently experienced an increase in membership as a result of legislation in the province of Ontario which accredited the NFU as one of three farm organizations eligible for a dues checkoff. Besides its precarious financial situation, the NFU's major representational handicap is that it lacks representation in Quebec, the home of 12 per cent of Canadian farmers and the best organized on a provincial level.[7]

The NFU has a democratic organizational and decision-making structure. Family farm members are organized on a local basis, then local organizations are grouped into district level organizations, which, in turn, are united into regional bodies. Member delegates and officers meet annually to pass policy resolutions and select a national Board of Directors. The Board of Directors is the NFU policy-making body between conventions, and the Executive, its administrative arm. The annual convention establishes NFU policy by a majority of those voting. All policy resolutions approved by the National Board, a regional convention, or a district convention are eligible for presentation at the annual convention. Members have policy input at the lowest, local level; all resolutions they approve are eligible for presentation to the district convention.

The NFU operates with a slim administrative and professional staff. The total number of paid full-time staff in all NFU offices numbers between six and twelve, of whom the vast majority are administrative officials. Its budget is small –

in 'the hundreds of thousands of Canadian dollars' – and, like the CFA's, overwhelmingly reliant upon membership dues. Its limited financial resources require the NFU to rely heavily upon volunteer work by its officers and members for policy development and recruitment of new members. In addition, it draws on the informational resources of coalitions critical of neo-liberalism, of which it is a member, to produce excellent analyses of the increasing concentration of firms in the farm input (fertilizer, fuel, machinery), retail, and transportation sectors.

Unable to afford professional recruiters, and persuaded in any case that this recruitment method would not be effective, new members are brought into the NFU principally by personal appeals on the part of existing members, meeting face to face across the kitchen table. They are retained through a mixture of incentives, including, in some regions, discounted tax advice and access to fertilizer and fuel supplies at bargained rates. However, those who join the organization seem to be attracted less by material benefits and much more by the opportunity to be a part of a community of shared values that includes a commitment to preserving the family farm.

In recent years, the NFU has been less inclined to engage in protest politics – sit ins at legislatures, tractor demonstrations blocking traffic into provincial capitals – and is as likely now to use conventional lobbying channels. It forms alliances with non-farm and other farm groups on policy by policy basis. Like the CFA, the NFU is officially non-partisan. Nonetheless, it is ideologically closer to the New Democratic Party (NDP). When the NDP forms the government in Saskatchewan or Manitoba, the NFU's influence is arguably greater than when either the Liberal or Conservative Party does. Its influence in the national capital is limited. It is, however, an important reinforcing support for commodity groups and the CFA on selected issues like orderly marketing in the export grain sector and supply management in the dairy and poultry sectors.

Post 1980: New Actors, New Issues in the Agri-Food Policy Community

New actors and issues injected themselves into the agricultural policy community just as the farm community itself was becoming more organizationally fragmented. Among these new actors were specialist commodity organizations representing cattle, grains, and oilseeds producers and which are philosophically committed to a greater role for market forces in Canadian agriculture. Governments played a role in this phenomenon. In 1969, the federal Liberal Government provided public funding to a new organization to represent the grain industry, mounting a direct challenge to the prairie pools and the CFA. The Alberta government subsidized two new organizations representing western wheat and barley growers in the 1970s. The birth of the Palliser Wheat Growers' Association and the Western Barley Growers Association, when coupled with the fact that the second largest grain cooperative company did not belong to the CFA, seriously undermined the CFA's capacity to speak for prairie grain farmers. With the organization representing Canadian cattlemen also outside its umbrella, the CFA's representational credentials in prairie Canada were particularly weak.

Just how weak the CFA was, and how disastrous this state of affairs was for its consensus building capability, was fully revealed in the Crow debate of the early 1980s. This debate unfolded when the government of Canada decided to end an 80-year old statutory obligation on Canadian railways to transport grain at fixed and low costs to farmers. The prairie community was torn over whether the Crow rates (named after the Crows Nest Agreement that had established the rates in 1897) should end, and, if they did, who should bear the cost of higher freight rates. Prairie livestock and grain producers were pitted against one another, driving a deep wedge inside the provincial farm federations that were the CFA's members. Its organizational members at odds, the CFA retreated to the sidelines, leaving its member prairie wheat pools and the National Farmers Union to battle it out against a coalition of oilseed, cattle, and grain commodity groups. The former were adamant that increases in railway freight rates not come at farmers' expense, while the latter were willing to accept higher freight costs to producers. An eleventh hour alliance between two CFA members–the Saskatchewan Wheat Pool and the Quebec UPA–secured an outcome (government payments to the railways) that avoided the worst case scenario for the wheat pools and the NFU. (Skogstad, 1987, chapter 6)

The costs to the CFA of the acrimonious Crow debate lingered well into the 1990s. The provincial farm federations in Saskatchewan and Alberta, faced with the impossible task of reconciling the disparate interests of their members, dissolved shortly thereafter. Their death left the CFA without representation from these two provinces throughout the remainder of the 1980s and well into the 1990s.

Dealing with Fiscal Deficits and Internationalization in the 1980s and 1990s

The second factor that has caused the agricultural policy community to open up – and indeed to warrant the new label, agri-food policy community[8] – is the emergence of new issues and policy goals linked to developments in the domestic and international political economy. Domestically, large and growing fiscal deficits and public debt made government expenditure transfers to producers vulnerable. These concerns interlocked with worries about the competitiveness of the Canadian economy, including its agricultural economy. If the model of state assistance and market intervention that had led to both costly expenditure programs and market inefficiencies was to be weakened and even dislodged, state officials realized that opening up the agricultural policy community to opponents of this model was necessary.

Accordingly, as Canada pursued regional and global liberal trade agreements in the 1980s and early 1990s, new political actors – most notably agribusiness representatives and commodity groups supportive of liberal markets – were brought into consultative and advisory forums. The same phenomenon characterized the process of domestic policy reform that was designed both to bring Canadian agricultural programs into conformity with the terms of international trade agreements and to curb government deficits. The latter exercise was dubbed *Growing Together* and was intended to implement a new vision of a *'more market-oriented agri-food industry'* and *'a more self-reliant sector* that is able to earn a reasonable return from the market place' (Agriculture Canada, 1989). It outlined several new directions for change that included farmers assuming the primary responsibility for variations in their income and changes to supply management to make it more market responsive (Agriculture Canada, 1989).

The policy debates engendered by the negotiation of liberal trade agreements and *Growing Together* severely tested, and more than once found wanting, the consensus-building capacity of the CFA. As one of a plurality of groups competing for influence, the CFA strategy shifted between concertation – deliberation and bargaining with state officials behind closed doors – and confrontation. Confrontation is its fall-back strategy, resorted to when quiet diplomacy fails. The NFU's opposition to liberalizing trade agreements, like the FTA and NAFTA, on the grounds that these agreements threaten food sovereignty and small producers, has left it on the margins of trade policy discussions, but not on other policy debates that ensued.

Negotiating Trade Agreements: The Politics of Accommodation[9]

The Canadian government's decision to pursue liberal trade agreements – with the United States (1989) and under the auspices of the GATT during the Uruguay Round (1986-93) – presented a major challenge for both it and the CFA.[10] That challenge was how to reconcile two sets of interests. The first were those of grain, oilseed, cattle and hog farmers, concentrated in western Canada, who were dependent on export markets for almost 50 per cent of their farm cash receipts (Agriculture Canada 1989: 15). An international agreement that removed tariffs and non-tariff barriers and allowed market forces to dictate commercial transactions appealed to them as it did to the Mulroney Conservative government which had swept to office in 1984 with a strong base in western Canada. The other set of interests were those of dairy, poultry and egg producers, concentrated in central Canada and producing under a system of supply management that included import controls. A liberal trade agreement that removed this protection was obviously much less attractive to these farmers since their profitability rested on a protected domestic market. The Mulroney Progressive Conservative government understood the need to assuage their concerns; it had secured office in 1984 by unprecedented success in capturing Quebec seats. The national government's over-riding political imperative was therefore to find a way to accommodate the interests of both outward- and inward-looking farm groups.

To that end, it created an elaborate machinery to receive industry input into its trade policy position. Part of this machinery was the Sectoral Advisory Group on International Trade (SAGIT), on which the CFA sat, as did some of its members (including the UPA), and representatives of agribusiness and commodity groups. The SAGIT was not to be up to the task of reconciling the differing interests within the agricultural sector. And the CFA was sorely tested, as well, when positions within the farm community became polarized. This polarization did not show up during the negotiations on the Canada-US Free Trade Agreement because both Canada and the US were anxious to protect 'sensitive' sectors (like supply management) and excluded them from the terms of the Agreement. It reared up with a vengeance, however, during the multilateral Uruguay GATT Round. The CFA's internal brokering efforts led it to call for a 'balanced position' that would simultaneously open markets for western Canada's export commodities while maintaining domestic protection for the supply managed sectors. The Canadian government accepted the CFA's best effort as its agricultural trade position.

But this negotiating position of maximum liberalization for some agricultural products and minimum change for others quickly drew criticism from champions of both the export- and domestic-oriented sectors. Each feared that their interests would be jettisoned when Canada was forced to abandon what many perceived to be an untenable position. Grain commodity groups, including the CFA member Prairie Pools, united in the Canadian Agricultural Policy Alliance, had the support of Conservative provincial governments in Alberta and Saskatchewan who publicly criticized the government's 'balanced' trade position. The UPA and its leader, Jacques Proulx, built a strong alliance with the Quebec government and international farm groups to defend the family farm from globalization and market liberalism. Proulx denounced what he perceived to be an inadequate CFA lobbying campaign on behalf of supply management and Canadian farmers, and threatened to withdraw the UPA from the CFA. Although he later retracted this threat, which other senior officials in the UPA never endorsed,[11] Proulx distanced himself from both the CFA and its provincial farm organization members. With its members either going head to head or not talking to one another, CFA leaders found themselves on the margins of the internal struggle within Canada's farm community to shape Canada's agricultural trade position. This was not true of their members, including the Ontario Federation of Agriculture and the UPA, who took to the streets of Montreal, Ottawa and Brussels to keep their government's feet to the fire in protecting Canadian farmers from the excesses of market liberalization. If the CFA's 'balanced position' remained the Government of Canada's position throughout the Uruguay Round, it was in part because of this mobilization effort. But it was also because this position was the one that best accommodated the political base of support and ambitions of the governing Conservative Party by preventing it from having to choose one over the other.

The conclusion of the Uruguay Round precipitated further policy debates as reforms to a number of agricultural programs were needed to bring them into conformity with the Agreement on Agriculture.

Eliminating Export Grain Subsidies: Policy Reform by Government Fiat

The WTO Agreement on Agriculture required a 36 per cent reduction in the value of export subsidies. This stipulation meant that the government payments to railway companies that had replaced the abolition of statutory freight rates in 1984 (and which meant that farmers absorbed a portion but not the full costs of exporting grain) had to be reduced by this amount. Rather than keep to the 36 per cent requirement, the Government of Canada completely eliminated the subsidy – which had reached as high as C$720 million per year – in the 1995 budget. It did so without formally consulting farm groups and as part of a government-wide fiscal restraint exercise. Farmers were compensated with a one-time payment of C$1.6 billion 'but the true value of the lost benefit was three to four times that amount' (Schmitz *et al.*, 2002, p.173.) Farmers now pay more, and in some cases substantially more, to ship their grain. The governments' rationale for not formally consulting farm organizations like the CFA was that the industry was 'consulted out' from the earlier 1980-84 debate and wanted the government to take action (Skogstad, 1998, p.43). Record high grain prices at the time mitigated farm organization protest.

Revising Farm Income Safety Nets: From Corporatism to Adversarial Pluralism

The CFA and other farm organizations have been involved virtually continuously in the redesign of farm income safety nets – income stabilization and support programs – since the late 1980s when the Canadian government first put farmers on notice that they would have to be 'more self-reliant' and earn 'a reasonable return from the market place' (Agriculture and Agri-Food Canada, 1989). In the early 1990s, a task force that included the CFA, commodity groups and government officials was mandated to devise new income support programs. It functioned much like a corporatist policy network; that is, farm organization representatives were equal participants with government officials in formulating the new programs for the grains and oilseeds sector (Coleman and Skogstad, 1995). These new programs proved financially unsustainable and were also at odds with the parameters for domestic support programs in the WTO Agreement on Agriculture. Subsequently, a National Safety Nets Advisory Committee was struck to obtain the input of the farm community on income support programs, including their periodic revision. The President of the CFA has chaired this advisory committee and CFA representatives make up half of its membership, the remainder coming from agri-business and other commodity groups. (The NFU has refused to participate since the early 1990s initiative.)

Evidence suggests that the advisory committee falls short of the corporatist arrangement that accompanied the early 1990s reform of income safety nets. Successive leaders of the CFA have complained publicly that the advice of the Safety Nets Advisory Committee has been ignored by federal officials. In 2002, the CFA President accused the Agriculture Minister of breaking his promise to engage with farmers in a 'full partnership' on the design of a new framework to manage farm income risks. He suggested that the Minister's determination to proceed, despite farmers' opposition, posed 'a real danger that the relationship between governments and the industry will be jeopardized and will be undermined irreparably' (Friesen, 2002, p.14). The CFA went directly to the Prime Minister to complain about the agriculture minister's behaviour.

When concertation via advisory committees fails, the CFA, the NFU and commodity groups have little recourse but to fall back on conventional lobbying. Such was their strategy in the late 1990s when low international prices and climate-induced low yields, combined with rising input costs (fuel, machinery, fertilizer), caused grain, oilseed, and hog growers' profits to vanish. Existing income safety nets (described above) failed to compensate farmers sufficiently for their losses. Acting in tandem, the farm lobby proved capable of building a broad coalition that included business organizations whose fate is closely tied to the well-being of the farm community, political parties of all persuasion, and provincial governments. Two prairie premiers personally petitioned the Prime Minister, the opposition parties launched emergency debates on agriculture in the House of Commons, parliamentary agriculture committees held hearings and issued reports recommending more government assistance, and the rural caucus of the governing Liberal Party concurred. This impressive show of support succeeded in securing ad hoc, income disaster assistance programs, and caused government transfers to the farm community to rise quite dramatically. Even so, while the outcome revealed the power of the farm lobby to evoke multi-party support for its cause, the effort that had been necessary was also a reminder that Canadian farmers enjoyed no special relationship with the federal Liberal government.

The Fate of the Canadian Wheat Board: A Cleavage too Wide to Bridge

The integration of the Canadian and American agri-food industries and markets, pursuant to the implementation of free trade agreements with the US in 1989, and extended to Mexico in the North American Free Trade Agreement in 1994, deepened existing cleavages in Canada's prairie community over the role of the single desk export marketing agency, the Canadian Wheat Board. Philosophically opposed to the Canadian Wheat Board's monopoly over the export sale of barley and wheat, a minority of prairie grain and oilseed producers have chafed at what they perceive to be lost marketing opportunities and lost profits by their inability to sell their products freely into the US market. Their complaints go back to the 1980s but gathered steam in the 1990s when commodity groups representing wheat and barley growers grew emboldened by support from the Alberta Government and the then governing Conservative Party. The minister in charge in the Mulroney Conservative Government abolished the Wheat Board's monopoly over barley exports in 1993 – a move that was quickly challenged by three prairie wheat pools and eventually overturned by a Canadian court. Determined to end the Wheat Board's monopoly, commodity groups championed a 'dual market' in which the Wheat Board would be one export seller alongside private grain dealers.

In the mid-1990s, their criticisms reached crisis proportions, when individual farmers illegally circumvented the Wheat Board's authority and launched a court challenge to the Wheat Board's monopoly. In this fractious situation, the CFA aligned itself with the defenders of the Wheat Board as did the National Farmers Union. It fell to the federal minister in charge to resolve the discord. He brokered a compromise which gave farmers more control over the operations of the Wheat Board but left its export monopoly powers intact. The retention of the Wheat Board's monopoly was a clear victory for the two general farm organizations – but one that could as readily have been a defeat had another minister in another (Conservative) government been in charge.

The foregoing represent the key debates over the past twenty years that implicated the state assisted model of agriculture in Canada. They show the difficulty of building policy consensus in Canada's pluralist agri-food policy community. Alliances across national farm interest groups, commodity groups, agribusiness, and provincial governments are vital. As in other OECD countries, agricultural practices have become more salient for constituencies that have not historically been part of the agri-food policy community. The licensing of genetically engineered crops and foods, food safety, and the sustainability and protection of the environment from industrialized agricultural practices have brought public interest groups representing consumers and environmentalists, as well as globalization critics, into the agri-food trade policy community. The CFA and the NFU have taken distinct substantive approaches to these issues and the threat posed to farmers' centrality in agri-food policy making by the controversy each has aroused.

Biotechnology Policy

The position of the Canadian Federation of Agriculture and that of the Government of Canada have been closely aligned on biotechnology policy. Both endorse the licensing of GM foods and crops solely on the basis of available scientific evidence demonstrating their health and environmental safety. Both also oppose mandatory labelling, worried that it would drive up costs to the producer and invite retaliation from the US which does not label GM products. By contrast, the NFU called for a moratorium in 2000 on the production, importation, distribution and sale of GM food pending determination not only of their human health and environmental effects, but also consumer acceptance, technology ownership and farmer profitability. It supports mandatory labelling of food products that contain GM ingredients, and has called for segregation programs to isolate GM and non-GM crops. Unlike the CFA which has participated in government-industry discussions around the regulation of biotechnology products, the NFU has boycotted these endeavours. Along with environmental organizations, it refused to participate in the consultations of the government advisory body that sought input on improving the regulation of GM foods, arguing the Canadian Biotechnology Advisory Committee is dominated by proponents of biotechnology.

The NFU's position puts it in agreement with the majority of the Canadian public, who want mandatory labelling of GM products. Despite a concerted campaign for mandatory labelling undertaken by environmental organizations and a broad based anti-globalization group, the Canadian government has supported voluntary labelling by the industry – with little political backlash to date.

Food Safety and Environmental Protection

Unlike in other (European) countries, the issue of food safety has not appeared on the agri-food policy agenda because of a regulatory failure to assure the public that its food supply is safe. Policy here has been anticipatory – recognition that consumer concerns were increasing – and driven significantly as well by trade considerations: namely, the need to harmonize Canadian food safety standards with those in the US in order to ensure full access to that vital market. (Approximately two-thirds of Canadian agri-food trade is with the US.) The CFA and farm commodity groups have been drawn into a close partnership with federal and provincial governments, who have provided the funding and technical assistance, to develop commodity-specific on-farm programs consistent with international HACCP (Hazard Analysis Critical Control Point) principles. HACCP programs oblige farmers and food processors to take a greater measure of responsibility for food safety. The CFA and NFU have endorsed these endeavours, no consumer-producer rift has opened up, and the agri–food industry remains in control of the food safety policy agenda.[12]

Although province are the most important order of government for regulating the environmental effects of agricultural practices, the national government does regulate pesticides and toxic substances, assesses the environment effects of projects involving the federal government, and is responsible for international environmental agreements that impact on trade. On all these issues, the CFA's over-riding concern has been to minimize the cost of environmental regulations to producers and to ensure they are not put at a competitive disadvantage by discrepancies between Canadian regulations and international (especially American) legislation. Thus, for example, it has lobbied hard to ensure that Canadian farmers have access to the same pesticides approved in the US. (The NFU, by contrast, has promoted a low or no-chemical input agriculture.) The CFA has not always succeeded in securing its environmental policy goals, principally because it is the environment ministry, not that responsible for agriculture, which is responsible for most of these matters. It opposed Canada's signing the Cartagena Protocol on Biosafety, an agreement endorsed by the federal Minister of Environment, but since then has successfully persuaded the Government of Canada not to ratify it until a number of questions relating primarily to its costs to producers and its negative effects on trade are cleared up.

Limiting State Retrenchment and Checking Market Liberalism

How have Canadian farm interest groups fared in dealing with the challenges in the late twentieth and early twenty-first century presented by domestic fiscal restraints, government goals of a more market-oriented sector, and regional and multilateral trade agreements? The verdict is that farm groups as a whole have not fared badly. Liberal market reforms have been checked. And although governments have indeed privatized more responsibility for income stabilization to Canadian farmers, they have not withdrawn expenditure support to levels as low as those in some other countries.

The signal in *Growing Together* that supply management systems would be made more market responsive did entail changes to the internal working of dairy, egg, and poultry marketing boards. Reforms weakened producers' dominance in the implementation of supply management plans while strengthening government supervisory powers (in poultry supply management) and enhancing the influence of non-producer interests like processors, further processors and consumers (Skogstad, 1993). However, regulated marketing in these sectors has not been eliminated and producers of supply managed commodities are still largely protected from foreign competition. Although the WTO Agreement on Agriculture opened the borders to minimum levels of imports, tariffs on imports above these amounts remain high (Schmitz *et al.*, 1996). In addition, as noted above, reforms to the operations and management structure of the Canadian Wheat Board did not extend to its monopoly powers over prairie wheat and barley exports.

Table 9.3 Canadian and provincial government agri-food sector expenditures, selected years ($C thousands)

Year	Total	Income Support
1985-86	4717	626
1988-89	6927	1686
1991-92	9145	1982
1995-96	5533	789
1999-00	5245	1614
2000-01	5751	2251
2001-02	6206	2590

Source: Agriculture and Agri-Food Canada, Strategic Policy Branch

State assistance in the form of public expenditure support is a story of greater retrenchment. Government (consumer and taxpayer) transfers to Canadian producers dropped significantly over the decade of the 1990s. Whereas taxpayer and consumer transfers to Canadian farmers comprised 34 per cent of farmers' gross receipts over the period 1986-88, by 2000-02, they accounted for only 19 per cent (OECD, 2003). This decline is consistent with the trend in all OECD countries, and is in keeping with the requirements of the WTO Agreement on Agriculture. However, it represents a more dramatic decline in Canada than in OECD countries as a whole, the United States and the European Union. Government expenditure support declined most in the grains sector and led to farmers bearing more of the cost of stabilizing their net returns.[13] Table 9.3 demonstrates provincial and federal government spending on income support and stabilization dropped from the record high levels of the late 1980s and early 1990s to less than C$ one million in 1995-96 before rising dramatically in the late 1990s and early twenty-first century. This upsurge will level off with the implementation of the new Agricultural Policy Framework which puts a cap on federal and provincial government spending and requires farmers to pick up a bigger share of the costs of stabilizing their incomes.

Summary and Future Challenges

The Canadian experience suggests the need to be leery of any cross-national generalizations about the historically privileged role of farm interest groups, the linkages between encompassing farm interest groups and effective policy making, and the 'irrepressible' forces of globalization. The politics of agricultural policy making cannot be reduced to simple assertions to the effect that encompassing farm organizations are a pre-requisite to both influential agrarian representation and effective policy-making (where the latter is interpreted to mean policy making that anticipates problems and addresses them). This premise may well be true in single-order governments. However, in multi-level governance systems like Canada's, where legally and financially powerful governments, with their own discrete goals for agriculture, exist at both orders, a peak farm association is difficult – perhaps impossible – to construct. Moreover, it may also be less determinative of policy outcomes. Where agricultural policy making is a matter of two orders of government, the interests and goals of governments figure large in policy outcomes. Farm interest groups can both gain and lose in this institutional setting. Further, if Canadian agriculture never fell wholly under a paradigm of state assistance, it was not simply because of the CFA's limitations as an encompassing peak association. It was also in part because some export-oriented commodity sectors preferred to take their chances with the laissez-faire market.

Has effective agricultural policy making in Canada been stymied by the pluralistic chaos that often seems to characterize Canadian agricultural politics? Likely. Many observers of Canadian agricultural policy, most of them agricultural economists, lament what they perceive to be a long history of ad hoc, reactive policy making in response to the latest crisis. Whether Canada suffers from this phenomenon to a greater degree than other countries is not clear. Nor is it evident how much the dearth of anticipatory policy making should be blamed on the weak organizational development of the farm community, rather than gaps in state policy capacity, some of which are the consequence of having to coordinate policy making across two orders of government.

Looking ahead, what does the record of Canadian farm interest groups and their relations with the state suggest for the future? On the one hand, the CFA as the premier national farm interest group has shown considerable resilience over its 70 year lifetime. It has brought the voice of Canadian farmers to bear in the nation's capital and had considerable influence on policy issues on which farmers in all regions and commodity sectors share interests. And its membership base is more encompassing today than it was for much of the 1980s and 1990s. The NFU's achievements are more limited and issue specific.

On the other hand, significant challenges, some originating at home, others driven by developments in the international political economy, confront the Canadian farm community and its farm organizations. At home, farm numbers continue to decline and the wedge between profitable and not-very profitable farmers persists. The depopulation of rural Canada[14] and the need to travel further to obtain a second job, combined with the concentration of retail and public services in the fewer and fewer urban centres (Stabler and Olfert, 2002), makes imperative an effective rural policy. Canadian governments have recognized the need to shore up off-farm employment opportunities and rural services, but the sums invested to date are small and the results unclear.

The decline in the economic significance of commodity production, relative to food manufacturing, shifts bargaining power and political influence ever more to agri-business. Most of the one in seven Canadian jobs attributed to the agri-food sector are located off the farm, upstream in the farm input supply sector or, more often, downstream in the food manufacturing, retail and distribution sectors. Concentration in these sectors not only impairs farmers' economic bargaining power. It also makes it harder for farm organizations to ensure that the interests of farmers are not subordinated to those of agri-business. To avoid that, the CFA will need to put a high priority on building alliances with agri-business and other segments of the food chain.

The international political economy presents other challenges. Liberal trade agreements and market integration have lent legitimacy to, and strengthened the resolve of commodity groups championing freer markets. Philosophically conservative governments in a number of provincial capitals espouse the market liberalism discourse that accompanies globalization. To the south, Canada's most important trading partner maintains continuous pressure for Canada to align its policies more closely with its own. Considerable harmonization of technical regulations and some public policies (relating to food safety, genetically modified products) has already occurred. For national farm groups like the NFU and the CFA, the challenge is to mount strong arguments as to why and how Canada can avoid succumbing to convergence pressures that are not dictated by international law but driven but by power politics. To date, national governments have concurred with that objective.

The current Doha Round of international trade negotiations brings not only new opportunities – to level the playing field vis-a-vis producers in other countries whose governments support them more – but also risks to national farm interest groups. To date, the united trade position which the CFA crafted across its export- and domestic-oriented member organizations has been the trade policy of Canadian negotiators. However, a new alliance of export-oriented interests is urging the Canadian government to abandon its trade policy position of support for orderly marketing systems, such as supply management and the Canadian Wheat Board. The Canadian Agri-Food Trade Alliance (CAFTA) is pressing for Canada to adopt a position of liberal trade across the board. It is still a relatively young organization – having been formed in early 2001 – and has only one full time staff member and a small budget. Nonetheless, CAFTA's members include producer organizations, processors, marketers and exporters from the major trade reliant sectors in Canada. Together, they are said to account for almost 80 per cent of Canada's agriculture and agri-food exports; 500,000 jobs in production, processing and marketing; and more than half of Canada's farm cash receipts.

To enhance their likelihood of maintaining state support for agriculture during the Doha Round, both the CFA and NFU have formed alliances with like minded groups in other countries. The NFU is a founding member of Via Campesina (Peasant Way/Road), a network of almost 70 organizations in over 30 countries opposed to free trade agreements. It is also a member of the Council of Canadians, a broad-based coalition that includes labour unions and which takes credit for helping to defeat the proposed Multilateral Agreement on Investment and stalling the launch of the Doha WTO Round. For its part, the CFA is a member of an international coalition of farm groups in Europe, Asia and North Africa which is committed to fair and equitable world trade rules.

        In conclusion, the Canadian experience suggests caution in attributing cataclysmic effects to regionalizing and globalizing developments in the international economy. Canadian agriculture underwent significant structural change in the postwar period through to 1970 – well in advance of the current globalizing era – and at the very time policies consistent with the state assistance model were being put in place. The farming community has certainly faced new structural pressures as a result of the globalizing and regionalizing political economy, but these stem principally from the reduced pricing bargaining power of producers as upstream and downstream agribusinesses consolidate into fewer and fewer entities. The resulting inferior bargaining power of producers in the pricing system promises to be a crucial issue for national farm organizations and an important future test case of their cohesion, resilience and policy influence.

Notes

[1] Increasingly, the three territorial governments are also party to intergovernmental agreements.

[2] Source: www.ats-sea.agr.ca/supply/e3314.pdf; Agriculture and Agri-Food Canada (2001).

[3] Average farm size varies across provinces. In Saskatchewan, for example, the home of the largest (grain) farms, the average farm was 519 hectares in 2001, a 35 per cent increase since 1981.

[4] Commercial farms have revenues over C$100,000. Small and medium-sized farms have revenues between C$10,000 and C $100,000. The remaining 34 per cent of farms are hobby firms which account for 1 per cent of production and are totally dependent on off-farm income.

[5] The Canadian Federation of Agriculture reported the average farm family's annual income was $53,435 in 1995, as compared to an average non-farm family's income of $55,247. See http://www.cfa-fca.ca/english/agriculture_in_canada/farm_structure_and_finance.html.

[6] Provincial farm federations in Canada's ten provinces are members or associate members, as are commodity groups representing producers of grain, oilseeds, milk, eggs, poultry, fruits and vegetables, hogs, and sugar beets.

[7] Although the Quebec farm union adheres to much of the NFU's philosophy regarding state responsibility for agriculture, it was a member of the CFA before the NFU came into existence in 1969 as a national organization. By then, the UPA leaders had established a good working relationship with the CFA and saw little to gain by joining the upstart farm union.

[8] In 1993, Agriculture Canada, the ministry responsible for agriculture, was re-named Agriculture and Agri-Food Canada.

[9] This discussion draws on Cooper (1997, chapter 7) who uses the term "politics of accommodation" to describe Canada's negotiating position during the Uruguay Round.

[10] Besides wanting to give a competitive kick to the Canadian economy, the FTA with the US was motivated by the desire to put an end to US non-tariff trade barriers that Canadian commodities, including agricultural products, had experienced with increasing frequency in the 1980s.

[11] Senior UPA individuals stated in interviews that Proulx's withdrawal threat was never seriously considered, and did not have the support of other UPA leaders.

[12] Following the discovery of a single cow infected with BSE in Alberta in 2003, beef consumption in Canada went up, not down.

[13] The OECD (2003) reports Canadian PSEs over the period 1985-89 for wheat, beef and veal, and milk were 50.2, 19.6 and 78.2, respectively; for 1995-99, they were 13.6, 11.2, and 57.6 for these same commodities.

[14] Epp and Whitson (2001, pp.xix-xx) attribute this phenomenon in part to government policies, and in particular the withdrawal of government services like the closing of post offices, schools, and rail lines, as well as the scaling back of medical services. Rural and small town Canada's population share of the total Canadian population was 22 per cent in 1996. See http://www.cfa-fca.ca/english/agriculture_in_canada.

References

Agriculture Canada (1989), Growing Together: A Vision for Canada's Agri-Food Industry. Ottawa.

Agriculture and Agri-Food Canada (2001), The Agriculture and Agri-Food Sector: Minister's Forum. June 18. Ottawa.

Bowlby, Geoff and Michael Trant (2002), 'Agricultural Employment and Productivity Trends, Observations and Measurement Methods', Presentation to the International Working Group on Agriculture Seminar on 'Perspectives for Agricultural and Rural Indicators and Sustainability', available on OECD website.

Canadian Federation of Agriculture (1978), Statement of Dobson Lea, in Government of Canada, Report on the Proceedings of the National Food Strategy Conference, Ottawa, February 22-23. Ottawa.

Canadian Federation of Agriculture. (2003), Standing Policy. Available at: www.cfa-fca.ca.

Coleman, W. D. and Skogstad, G. (1990), 'Introduction' in W. Coleman and G. Skogstad (eds.), *Policy Communities and Public Policy in Canada*, Copp Clark Pitman, Toronto.

Coleman, W.D. and Skogstad, G. (1995), 'Neo-Liberalism, Policy Networks, and Policy Change: Agricultural Policy Reform in Australia and Canada', *Australian Journal of Political Science*, Vol. 30, pp.242-63.

Cooper, A. F. (1997), *In Between Countries: Australia, Canada, and the Search for Order in Agricultural Trade*, McGill-Queen's University Press, Montreal and Kingston.

Dawson, H. J. (1960), 'An Interest Group: The Canadian Federation of Agriculture', *Canadian Public Administration*, Vol. 3, pp.134-49.

Dawson, H. J. (1967), 'Relations Between Farm Organizations and the Civil Service in Canada and Great Britain', *Canadian Public Administration*, Vol. 10, pp.450-470.

Epp, R. and Whitson, D. (2001), 'Writing Off Rural Communities?', in R. Epp and D. Witson (eds.), *Writing Off the Rural West: Globalization, Governments, and the Transformation of Rural Communities*, Parkland Institute and University of Alberta Press, Edmonton, pp.xiii-xxv.

Friesen, B. (2003), Testimony to the Standing Committee on Agriculture and Agri-Food, House of Commons. Ottawa. February 20. Available on line:

http://www.parl.gc.ca/InfoComDoc/37/2/AGRI/Meetings/Evidence/AGRIEV16-E.HTM.

National Farmers Union (2001), Policy Statement of the National Farmers Union. Saskatoon, Saskatchewan.

National Farmers Union (2003), 'Safety Nets and the Future of the Family Farm in Canada'. A report to the Minster of Agriculture as part of consultations on the Agriculture Policy Framework. January 23. Available on the NFU website: www.nfu.ca.

OECD (Organization for Economic Co-operation and Development) (2003), *Agricultural Policies in OECD Countries: Monitoring and Evaluation 2003: Highlights*, OECD, Paris.

Schmitz, A., de Gorter, H. and Schmitz, T.G. (1996), 'Consequences of Tariffication', in A. Schmitz, G. Coffin, and K. A Rosaasen (eds.), *Regulation and Protection under GATT*, Westview, Boulder, pp.37-50.

Skogstad, G. (1987), *The Politics of Agricultural Policy Making in Canada*, University of Toronto Press, Toronto.

Skogstad, G. (1993), 'Policy Under Siege: Supply Management in Agricultural Marketing', *Canadian Public Administration*, Vol. 36, pp.1-23.

Skogstad, G. (1998), 'Agriculture and Agri-Food Canada: Program Review I and II', in P. Aucoin and D. J. Savoie (eds.), *Managing Strategic Change: Learning from Program Review*, Canadian Centre for Management Development, Ottawa, pp.39-69.

Stabler, J. C. and Olfert, M. R. (2002), *Saskatchewan's Communities in the 21st Century: From Places to Regions*, Regina, Saskatchewan, Canadian Plains Research Centre.

Wilson, B. K. (1981), *Beyond the Harvest: Canadian Grain at the Crossroads*, Western Producer Prairie Books, Saskatoon.

Wilson, B K. (1990), *Farming the System: How Politicians and Producers Shape Canadian Agricultural Policy*, Western Producer Prairie Books, Saskatoon.

PART IV
CONCLUSION

Chapter 10

Conclusions:
The Fate of Groups in a
'Globalizing Era'

Darren Halpin

Introduction

This edited collection examines the challenges confronting agricultural interest group organizations in western developed nations at the beginning of the 21st century. The book is particularly concerned with those groups that make a claim to be general in coverage and national in focus. The prominence of these types of groups as important state 'partners' in post-war agricultural development has served as a benchmark against which to make some rudimentary assessment about how they are faring in what has been referred to as a 'globalizing era'. The preceding chapters have reviewed the contemporary challenges facing groups in Western Europe (Denmark, France, Germany, Ireland, United Kingdom, Spain), North America (USA and Canada) and Australasia (Australia). This concluding chapter provides a review of key findings.

Caution is called for when making generalizations about interest groups across western nations. As Wilson reminds us, the comparative study of interest groups is a particularly hazardous exercise (1990, pp.17-23). Not only do the 'home' political systems of groups differ, but the political culture of groups, the emphasis on density and concentration in group systems, and the tactics used (legislature versus bureaucracy as target) vary significantly. The purpose of this concluding chapter is not to explain each and every difference or distinguishing feature in the national cases but to examine how groups fare in the contemporary environment by focusing on the dynamics that create a challenging contemporary environment for these groups and the factors that contribute to decline and resilience. This is approached by asking how the contemporary environment reshapes or disturbs the conditions that underpin partnerships. The evidence suggests that global change has reshaped the conditions that structured historical partnerships, altering the posture of the state towards policy goals, changing the organizability of the farm base and expanding the capacities required for groups to prove valuable. The overall argument is that groups seem to do best – are most resilient – when they can retain or create conditions that approximate those of historic 'partnership'. In some cases this resilience can be put down to the minimal change in these historic conditions, while in others it is the establishment of these conditions in a new form. Overall the posture of the state to globalizing pressures, and the flow on effect this has on group-state relations, proves to be one of the decisive factors in group decline and resilience.

A Narrative of Historic 'Partnership'? Looking Through the Rear View Mirror

As intimated in the introductory chapter, general agricultural interest groups rose to scholarly notice largely on the strength of their roles as 'partners' to the governments of western nations, mostly during the post-war period of agricultural development. Like any group-state 'partnership', these relationships were built on mutual exchange. Farmers are said to have exchanged control over what they produced, who they sold it to and how much they received, in return for state guarantees of a livelihood and price stability. This exchange was sustained by a certain dynamic and milieu. At its most basic level, the partnership relied on broad community support for state assistance to agriculture, which was forthcoming mostly on the basis of shared concerns about food security but also export income generation. It was also nourished by broadly held community sympathy towards the inherent value, even virtue, of a vibrant agricultural sector. It further relied on the state finding a confluence between its policy aims and the desires of the farming community, along with a view that 'partnership' was a useful tool for achieving policy ends. The involvement of farmers in such a partnership relied on them viewing the controls and governmental surveillance they allowed themselves to be subjected to as justified by the degree of benefit they gained from state support.

The realization of partnership is said also to have relied on strong general agricultural interest groups, but also sometimes commodities based groups. General agricultural groups involve members regardless of commodities. As such, they address the entire spectrum of issues related to farmers in their nation. This encompassing nature leaves them prone to conflicts, splintering and internal dispute. While the propensity for internal faction and dispute is the central weakness in their organizational design their capacity to resolve these disputes, and accept the policy wins alongside the losses, underpins their value to the state. Their capacity to resolve conflict and enforce unity, along with their ability to provide valuable agricultural expertise and information, made these types of groups suitable partners in the post war era.

This narrative of 'partnership' provides a point of comparison for contemporary analyses of national groups; and we confront this issue in the next section. However, in deploying this narrative we first need to gauge how generalizable it is.

The Nature of 'Partnership'

In the European context, Moyano-Estrada (1995, p.351) has argued that the discourse of partnership reflects northern and central European experiences, where farm organizations,

> ... were able to develop independently from political parties and consolidate their organizational structures in the context of agricultural modernization policies. In such contexts, the close relationship between the state and farmers' unions was remarkable. Being recognized as partners by the state, they accepted the role of guiding the process of reducing the agricultural population by legitimizing the selection of good farmers and the exclusion of the rest.

By contrast, Moyano-Estrada argues that processes of agricultural modernization in southern European nations were not the product of 'an internal partnership between the state and organized interest groups', but the result of 'favourable international economic conditions in the 1960s' and a change in the 'composition of political elites' (1995, p.351).

This variation is clearly borne out in the contributions to this volume. The French, Irish, UK and Danish chapters flag the historic basis of close group-state partnerships, and the importance of the capacity of national groups in maintaining such partnerships. The Spanish contribution highlights a different pathway, with groups constituting relatively new features on the political landscape, and lacking the developed organizational features of their northern counterparts. The chapters in this volume from outside Europe illustrate further that partnership – at least northern and central European style – was not fully replicated in other regions. As Skogstad notes (this volume), early Canadian groups never approached the peak nature of the British groups, and their early involvement with the state was sporadic and lacked the structure of that in the UK. In the US, Wilson (this volume) explains that partnership was associated with the 'new deal' policies that emerged from the depression years. The process favoured the AFBF, but other groups were soon admitted into the process. In Australia, 'historic' partnership involved commodities based groups operating in isolated clientelistic relations, securing assistance in the pre war era and consolidating it in the post war era. As Halpin (this volume) notes, a general national group emerged in the late 1970s not to secure assistance through partnership, but to participate in a form of 'bargained consensus' whereby they joined a broad coalition of interests in promoting the end of industry wide protection and assistance and the reform of the broader economy.

National and General? The Historical Evidence

The narrative of 'partnership' (pursued in the introduction) assumes that groups were *typically* dominant, general and national. But, as both Moyano-Estrada (1995) and Ball and Millard (1986) have noted, groups that were involved in post-war partnerships, however defined and constituted, may well have been involved in national level public policy but were not always national or general. The German

DBV and the British NFU are, according to Ball and Millard, the clear examples of systems with one 'monopolistic' group, but they are nevertheless the exceptions and not the rule (1986, p.135). The chapters in this book illustrate the different origins of the agricultural interest groups we find prominent today. The French and British chapters focus on groups with direct continuity from the period of post-war partnership. Others, like the Australian chapter, focus on groups that had their genesis in fragmented commodity and regional groups. Still other cases, like Canada and the US, show how several groups continue to persist, each claiming a national voice but representing members with a distinctive commodity or territorial complexion. In these cases, the prominence of each group tends to fluctuate, contingent in part on the party political complexion of sub-national and national governments. Overall, the salient point is that one should not arrive at conclusions about the *contemporary* fate of groups based on an assumption that groups *historically* were always monopolistic and group systems organizationally well developed.

While there is a necessary need for caution in endorsing narratives that generalize across historical periods and national cases (see Skogstad this volume), this 'partnership' narrative serves a useful purpose. Regardless of the precise composition of the 'partnership' in each national case, historically some semblance of a pact between farmers and the state around processes of agricultural modernization is evident; albeit that the times, triggers and the shapes of farmer organizations, understandably differ.

The Contemporary Group Environment

In the introductory chapter, based on the review of relevant literature, it was established that the fate of groups partially rested with the constitution of the group environment. The group environment was said to be decisively shaped by the strength of three key trends; trends which it was anticipated would unpick, or at the least disrupt, the pattern of partnership and of general agricultural group prominence in the post war period. It was posited that the regionalization and globalization of agricultural governance, challenges to agricultural exceptionalism and policy paradigm change would remove the premise for exchange which structured the group-state partnerships, hence changing the group logic of influence. Similarly, it was surmized that agricultural restructuring would reduce the organizability of the farming constituency, hence undermining the stable base of general groups. This would force a change in the logic of membership of such groups.

From a review of the literature regarding these trends the theses of resilience and decline were constructed. The purpose of these theses was to characterize the manner in which changes in these three trends shape the group environment, disturbing the dynamics of post war partnership, and challenging groups to modify logics of influence and membership.

It was not expected that the environment in any one case study would replicate resilience or decline, and this is precisely what the case studies illustrate.

These three trends are not packaged together in any of the national cases in a way that replicates either the theses of decline or resilience. Indeed, most cases illustrate an environment constituting elements of both. Listing off or reciting how each case study nation manifests the three trends is not going to reveal levels of challenge inherent in the contemporary environment. For example, a conclusion down this pathway would read something like, cases exhibit both strong and weak policy change, strong and weak challenges to agricultural exceptionalism, and strong and weak patterns of agricultural restructuring.

In understanding the challenges the contemporary environment presents to groups, a better approach is to examine the impact these changes have had on the key conditions that supported historic partnership. That is, it is more productive to look at how the conditions that support partnership are redefined in a globalizing era.

The Shape of Partnership in a 'Globalizing Era'

The cases in this volume illustrate that contemporary conditions are somewhat different from those that prevailed in the post war era. In understanding the challenges presented by this change, one approach is to look at how the threshold levels for partnership shape up in a globalizing era. As referred to in the introduction, this volume adopted a framework developed by Schmitter and Streeck (1981, 1985) which presents groups as facing ongoing challenges with respect to organizing their constituency and exerting policy influence (logics of membership and influence). The changes in the values, interests and collective identity of the members create challenges in settling upon a logic of membership, while the opportunities and challenges offered by the group's political environment (principally the state) guide the logic of influence. In terms of looking at points of change, these two logics provide a neat set of categories. It is possible to restate the way that contemporary conditions have shaped a) the policy objectives of the state and hence its receptiveness to partnership (and by extension a group's logic of influence), b) the degree of organizability of the farming constituency (and by extension, a group's logic of membership) and c) the capacities required of a group to render it valuable. Each will be examined in turn.

A Receptive State (Logic of Influence)?

The state's receptiveness to working with groups is likely to be a defining feature in the way groups go about influencing public policy. Historically the state's participation in partnerships with groups was founded on three factors; i) the confluence of farmer and state aims, ii) a political climate to legitimate aims of partnership, and iii) the mechanism to facilitate partnership (for example, a dedicated state administrative structure). So how do these conditions present themselves (and do they differ) in a globalizing era?

As Skogstad makes explicit in her chapter, one needs to be cautious in endorsing strong themes of globalization and of its catastrophic impacts on national sovereignty and, by extension, of domestic policy processes. As all chapters illustrate, the economic processes of liberalization, championed as they often are through intergovernmental institutions (regional and international), are heavily influenced by national agendas and imperatives. Of course, some nations are better placed than others in influencing these international and regional agendas. While this volume does not pretend to adjudicate on the overall debate on globalization, it is possible to conclude that the orientation of national governments to market liberalization proves decisive in structuring the environments that groups participate in. Nation states confront a tension between domestic imperatives and international commitments. As one US commodity group observed as it entered WTO disputes over domestic assistance, 'This dispute highlights the difficulty associated with any nation designing farm policy to serve domestic goals while meeting international trade commitments' (farmonline, 2004).

The first element of any partnership is a good fit between the aims of farmers and those of the state. In a 'globalizing era', confronted with economic global change, and mindful of the associated economic and political costs of adjusting to change, nation states clearly have a number of strategic policy choices. As Harris (1993, p.31, p.39) argues nation states can i) resist change, ii) pursue international coordination of economic polices, and iii) accept changes and adjust to them. They can resist encroachment of the international system, and often do so in response to the domestic economic and political costs associated with change. Insulating the domestic economy from the impacts of such change confronts international pressure for a trade liberal response. As such, the capacity to resist that pressure is typically reserved for a few large states, like the US, or collections of states, like the EU, that can subsidize producers, hence transferring the costs to less developed nations and/or smaller nations. Second, nation states can seek international coordination. Large states may use such opportunities to seek to impose their domestic agendas on others, while smaller states seek collaboration in mutually advantageous outcomes. Finally, nation states can accept and embrace change, opening up the domestic market to global change. The latter option is most often pursued by smaller nations. The choice between these options is no doubt informed by a subjective judgment about the likelihood that trade liberalization will occur. It is further shaped by domestic concerns such as the cost of farm support, the export exposure of a country's agricultural sector and the size of its domestic market.

In the case studies there is evidence of all these approaches. Policy paradigm change may have taken place in all cases reviewed, but the extent of change is variable and the impact is uneven. Yet it does tend to adhere to the calculus set out above. Australia has progressed further down the path of liberalization and domestic deregulation, with Canada further behind. The direction of change may look the same but its motivation in some cases is remarkably different. Whereas liberalization in Australia has an ideological thread, arguably fitting into an overarching 'philosophy of government', in Canada reform has been based on budgetary rationale. Progress was promising in the US, with a Republican dominated congress in the latter half of the 1990s, but as Wilson (this volume) explains, a drop in world prices and farm incomes saw it wound back almost immediately. The retreat from a trade liberal paradigm was confirmed in 2002 with the Farm Security and Rural Investment Act (2002). The evidence from the EU is quite complex. It illustrates the diversity in the type and nature of change and its varied impact on group-state relations, even within the overarching discipline provided by the EU and CAP. There tend to be pro and anti CAP reform camps, which generally (but not exclusively) accord with whether a nation is an exporter and/or a net winner from CAP payments.

For groups in nations that can resist change, the US and member states of the EU, the substantive basis for partnership may remain. That is, the aims of farm policy may not have shifted very far. However for other groups, particularly in Australia, the aims of the state are substantively different from the developmental approach of the post war era and groups need to adapt to this.

The second and third elements of any partnership involve a *politics* and *mechanics* of partnership. The *politics* of this partnership relate to the degree of agricultural exceptionalism ascribed to by the general public, which is important for legitimating programs that are expensive for taxpayers or raise food prices. The *mechanics* of such a partnership require a certain degree of state capacity. That is, the state must also have segments of its administrative apparatus (at least in part) dedicated to the agricultural sector so as to make a reliable and identifiable partner for groups, with the ability, knowledge and expertise to push forward an agreed agenda.

As evidenced by the case studies, in a globalizing era there is an overall deterioration in the politics and mechanisms of partnership, driven by challenges to agricultural exceptionalism. In terms of *mechanics*, all nations examined in this volume, with the exception of the UK, retain a dedicated agricultural ministry.[1] While it is the exception in this book, the UK experience reflects similar patterns of change in Germany, where the Ministry for Consumer Protection, Food and Agriculture was recently established. However, as Grant (this volume) notes, the jury is still out in relation to the significance of this administrative remodelling. Potentially more important in terms of state attitude is the *politics* of partnership. Overall assistance levels and the 'special' provision of services and infrastructure are being reduced or substantially cut back. The attentiveness of the state to agricultural policy matters reflects both the decline of farm numbers and the contribution of agriculture to national economies (in terms of GDP and direct employment). The evidence is more varied in terms of public support for agricultural exceptionalism. Agriculture is under siege in the UK, on the back of food scares and concerns about environmental impacts, while rural and countryside issues emerge on the agenda (see for example Greer, 2003). This is of less significance in other EU and non EU nations. This book also finds that the policy process is more open and less exclusive across most cases, as environmental, consumer and agribusiness interests have become more active and organized. Where the cost of agricultural programs has an impact (or too great an impact) on the national budget, main line departments, like treasury, are drawn into the mix. However, policies related to agricultural assistance remain less scrutinized in cases, like Ireland, where the budgetary impact is positive, and where the agriculture and related agri-food industries are key components of the domestic economy.

Where groups operate with clientelistic departments and supportive publics, then the *mechanics* and *politics* of partnership are more easily preserved. Consequently, the insider and responsible group strategy historically pursued by farm groups is more likely to be supported and groups are less likely to come under competition from other interests.

An Organizable Constituency (Logic of Membership)?

In ascertaining the contemporary challenges to groups, the impact of the group environment on the organizability of the farming constituency is critical. It is generally conceded that the logic of membership of a group is structured by the homogeneity or otherwise of the membership base. As emphasized in the introduction, and is reiterated in many chapters, farming constituencies have always been diverse. For example, each nation, with perhaps the exception of Australia, tends to have a split between small/family farmers and more commercially orientated farmers, even if they are not expressed as a separate group but subsumed within the same organizational structure. However, in the introduction it was hypothesized that contemporary agricultural restructuring would increase this diversity, create tensions between the winners and losers and disrupt organizability.

In all nations agriculture is undergoing significant restructuring. Farm numbers are dropping rapidly and have done so for some time. Farm sizes are generally increasing and production is concentrating in the hands of a smaller proportion of producers. Nations such as Canada report a shift away from specialization, while others like Denmark and the United Kingdom report increasing specialization. In some cases these changes have been rather recent and rapid, such as in Australia, and can be linked to domestic policies associated with global change. However, in most cases, change is brought about by background effects of technological change and cost/price factors, with policy change merely acting upon existing trends. Perhaps one of the most significant changes is the general trend towards off-farm income which means that many farmers are no longer reliant on agriculture for the bulk of their income. Such a shift implies a shift in identity, both in terms of how farmers see themselves and how society views farmers.

For all groups, this overall trend points to more difficulty in spanning already divergent memberships, expressed in terms of economic and ideological cleavages.

Group Capacity

In the post war era, groups were valued because of their capacity to resolve conflict and enforce unity, along with their ability to provide valuable agricultural expertise and information. They pursued insider strategies and accepted that compromise was necessary and that wins would come alongside losses. The contemporary environment suggests that the capacities required of groups to provide a similar role are much expanded.

While the expectations that groups would retain the capacity to bridge internal divisions remains, there is no doubt that the demands on groups have expanded in a globalizing era. A simple thought experiment illustrates the general point. Most groups in this volume historically developed elaborate secretariats, staffed by well educated experts that in most respects matched bureaucratic structures. There were departments for most large commodities and for general areas like trade, economics and the like. What would a secretariat have to look like today?

Evidence supports that groups are forced by and large to be spread more thinly. The increasingly large range of issues upon which groups have input into, alongside the expansion of venues (multi-level governance), create a complex policy terrain. The technical productive and assistance issues preoccupying groups in the post war era were clearly complex. However, the sheer breadth of issues has multiplied. Groups now have to have input on diverse areas such as rural community decline, GM technology, global trade negotiations, plant breeding, food safety and quality assurance. The expertise required to stretch across these issues is expensive and, indeed, one could not imagine many groups having the resources to maintain expertise across all areas. The degree of technical competence is simply beyond such groups, particularly given declining membership bases and the reliance on member subscriptions for financial resources. Although, as Skogstad points out (this volume), there is a division of labor between groups organized at national and supra national levels that enables some groups to match heightened complexity.

Evidence of Decline and Resilience: The Fate of Groups

The first conclusion one can draw from this volume is that, if nothing else, farm interest groups claiming a national presence and a general coverage continue to survive in a 'globalizing era'. That they survive beyond the cases we have examined is evidenced by the fact that both the International Federation of Agricultural Producers (IFAP) and the Committee of Agricultural Organisations in the European Union (COPA) remain dominated by national level general agricultural organizations (see lists in Appendix 1 and 2). Survive they might, but at the start of the 21st century what condition are they in? That they remain speaks for their survival, but not to what extent their survival can be characterized in terms of decline and resilience.

Amidst this environment the evidence in this volume provides ample justification for concluding that groups face challenges, show evidence of decline, but are by and large resilient. Most groups are influential beyond the small economic and numerical base of their membership. They retain a commitment to an insider form of activity and orientate themselves to generating general and national positions on national farm and related policy areas.

An important indicator of resilience is the extent to which a group retains its shape and function as a national general agricultural interest group. Compared to the groups systems of the post war era, at the start of the 21st century we find reversing trends in terms of monopolistic group structures and cohesive group systems. In the UK and France, for example, we see fragmentary tendencies, with dominant post-war groups finding themselves sharing the representative space with competitor and complementary groups. While in Australia, Spain and Denmark we see unification and rationalization of structures as strong tendencies. But as Wilson notes, we should be careful in seeing these tendencies deterministically as constituting historical trajectories. Indeed, as the US evidence reveals, 'partnership' and strong group development may emerge and then reverse over time: there is no inevitability. But keeping in mind the historical starting point of most groups (earlier this chapter), the case studies illustrate that groups in Ireland, Australia and Denmark are perhaps more resilient, than say those in the UK and France. The former three cases are groups that have enhanced or maintained organizational unity, operate without competitors and are generally accepted as the voice of farmers in their nations. The latter two, however, show signs of enhanced competition and that their commitment to insider strategies and political activity are waning. Compared to historical conditions groups in Spain, Canada and the US remain largely stable.

In venturing an explanation as to why some groups are more resilient than others one could be tempted, say on the strength of the Australian case, to conclude that 'Nations with trade liberal policies foster resilience'. Such a policy change could be expected to remove the central basis for group interactions with the state (i.e. bargaining assistance levels). However, it is precisely these issues that are typically divisive amongst the membership of general groups. A trade liberal turn means issues such as price are resolved by market, and not political, forces. This seems a plausible argument, however this confronts a second conclusion, based say on the Irish case, that 'state assistance delivers resilience'. In the Irish case groups and the state form a common cause in pursuing CAP funds for the nation. This, along with the technical nature of the CAP, binds groups to the state.

These observations and conclusions deny any straightforward explanation that *individual* trends drive group resilience and decline. But, it is argued, that they can be reconciled and synthesized by recognizing that group resilience and decline is best explained by the net sum or confluence of these trends working together. That is, groups prove most resilient when and where they can replicate or continue the conditions that support partnership amidst global change.

While generally groups appear, much as Coleman (1997) predicted, remarkably resilient, explaining this resilience is the subject of the balance of this chapter.

Towards Explaining Resilience and Decline: Approximating 'Partnership' in the 21st Century

One of the overall conclusions of this volume is that groups are more resilient where they operate in an environment that supports their effort to i) renew group-state relations while retaining general community support for agriculture, and, ii) establish a stable membership base that provides resources and can be effectively represented. Further, they prove more resilient when they can approximate the expanded capacities required in the contemporary era. In this section we review this thesis citing examples from the book.

Finding Common Ground with the State

At the outset of this book it was surmized that policy paradigm change to trade liberalization, globalized and regionalized governance structures, and challenges to agricultural exceptionalism, would be decisive in establishing the character of the contemporary relationships between states and groups. Moreover, stronger shifts would lead to decline and more modest shifts to resilience. It has been found, however, that state receptiveness to groups is a more complex matter, and that groups seem resilient under both strong and weak versions of change across these trends.

As established earlier this chapter, the receptiveness of the state in a 'globalizing era' hinges on establishing a confluence between state and farmer interests and rebuilding and retaining the *politics* and *mechanics* of partnership. The evidence in this book supports the conclusion that those cases where groups are resilient manifest such conditions while groups less resilient operate in an environment where these conditions are substantially diminished. Let us take a few illustrative examples.

Contemporary partnership in Australia is embedded in an acceptance by the NFF that the overall policy agenda is about international competitiveness, facilitating global trade liberalization and macro economic reform in the domestic economy. There is a certain inevitability surrounding the approach to global economic integration in countries, like Australia, which disarms forces that may wish to reverse a pathway to international trade liberalization and associated domestic de-regulatory reforms. Its agricultural sector is heavily reliant on exports. It has a small domestic market and it is unable to sustain the taxpayer and consumer costs of protectionism. The real debate in countries like Australia is not over the direction of the approach to liberalization of world trade, but about the posture of the national government to compensating or softening the impact of operating in 'corrupt' global markets. These background conditions no doubt emboldened the NFF in its liberalizing agenda.

Of course, partnership can also emerge around shifts other than to trade liberalism. In the EU the basis of exchange between state and groups is in optimizing national positions with respect to CAP negotiations. Net winners from the CAP neutralize any internal domestic debate about the value of agricultural support and remove the influence of treasury departments. (e.g. Ireland, France, Denmark). Here the contrasting examples of Ireland and the UK illustrate the general point.

The UK is the only nation in this volume that is not a net exporter but that also supports agricultural trade liberalization and CAP reform. This is explained by the cost of support to taxpayers as it is a net loser from CAP. While this explains public and treasury scrutiny of CAP matters, it also highlights that the domestic politics of this partnership are as crucial as the economics. In the UK, perhaps more than any other case, agricultural exceptionalism in all its forms is under sustained challenge. Successive food safety scares, concerns over environmental impacts from intensive farming, and the keen interest in 'preserving' rural communities, have all weakened the grip that agricultural interests have had over agricultural policy more generally in Britain. Moreover, the reorganization of the dedicated agricultural department has potentially weakened the clientelistic interface for the NFU. These factors aside, the general support for liberalization is also explained by the strength of neo-liberal values and ideologies among elites. The UK case also illustrates that the general national policy making style has a bearing on the acceptance of groups and partnerships as valuable in policy making. The UK approach seems to be shifting to support outsider activity which places pressure on insider groups to abandon such logics of influence.

As Greer (this volume) highlights, the case of Ireland demonstrates the opposite dynamic. Ireland is a net winner from the CAP. As such, agricultural interest groups and government find common cause in extracting the maximal amount of money from Brussels for Ireland. This removes the treasury from deliberations over support, leaving dedicated agricultural departments and farmer unions to plot the best strategy for CAP negotiations. The absence of any significant food safety scares, and the absence of high profile concerns about environmental impact, serves to reinforce the value of agriculture to the national identity. This agricultural exceptionalism in the values and sentiment of the broader public has served to buttress the partnership established around the economic calculus about the national interest.

In terms of a receptive state, somewhat surprisingly it is evident that two ends of the policy change spectrum provide the most promise for group resilience. On the one hand, resilience is supported where there is good continuity between the type of partnership in the post war period and that prevailing at the start of the 21st century. Ireland is a good example of this situation. On the other hand, Australia provides an example where the 'inevitability' of trade liberal shifts has created a joint basis for a new partnership aimed at international competitiveness. However, it is important to recognize that those partnerships founded on extracting national benefits from the CAP are highly vulnerable, as their longevity relies heavily on the nature and shape of future CAP reform. For example, renationalization of the CAP would likely mean a higher burden on national treasuries. One would expect this to heighten domestic pressure for reform in cases like Ireland.

A general finding of this volume is that groups tend to do best – are most resilient – where the state's strategic policy agenda can be aligned with the agenda of farmers and where the politics and mechanics of partnership can be reproduced. Of course, the real issue is when and under what conditions they 'can' be aligned. In this respect, the evidence is that they *can* be aligned where the politics of partnership make state support for agriculture electorally palatable, where financial/economic considerations make alliances functional for the state, where the farm interest group is able to exercise a stable insider approach to policy making and where farm leaders adopt a similar definition of the problems and solutions facing agricultural policy.

Keeping the Constituency Together

At the outset of this book it was argued that agricultural restructuring would likely interrupt the organizability of the farm base. While the pattern of agricultural restructuring may be reasonably common across cases, the impacts on organizability are quite diverse.

As speculated about in the introduction, the most obvious impact of restructuring has been the decline in constituency size, with a requisite impact on electoral and systemic power. Although, as Wilson noted (this volume), electoral power often extends beyond the farm vote, which can compensate for any decline in farm numbers. A related impact is that the resources of groups, financial at least, have been reduced as most rely on membership subscriptions for income. In Denmark and the UK a period of specialization has apparently raised debate about the logic of commodity versus general organizations. But conflicts do extend to less tangible differences, such as ones around ideology and values referred to by Moyano-Estrada (this volume) and by Halpin (this volume).

Almost all groups suffer from high (unrealistic?) expectations from their memberships, which are evidenced by numerous and repeated calls for internal reforms and for stronger emphatic 'outsider' actions by group leaders. While this internal dissent is common place amongst general groups, it is particularly severe during patches of rapid restructuring as part of challenges to existing levels of state assistance and trade liberalization processes. Members become dissatisfied with the immediacy of gains (conflict over insider strategies) as amply demonstrated in Grant's discussion of the UK (this volume). This affects the logic of membership, particularly in groups that are the sole or monopoly representative group for a nation. However, it may be less problematic where a group system comprises of two competing groups, as in Canada. As Skogstad notes (this volume), the more respectable group can largely ignore those farmers who demand renewed state assistance and protection. This is because these farmers are a shrinking component of farming (it is they who are leaving farming), the state is not interested in meeting their demands, and the competing group represents these members.

The cases in this volume show that some groups demonstrating resilience in the contemporary environment exhibit rapid restructuring while others show slow restructuring. This suggests that the exact impact of change on organizability is complex. Logically one may have surmized that diversity would straightforwardly reduce organizability. Indeed, Moyano-Estrada argues that 'Diversity is a characteristic of farmers' unions in the European Union and the current process of agricultural restructuring makes such diversity even more pronounced' (1995, pp.353-4). Somewhat counter intuitively, those countries with a very stable and simple commodity structure seem to have found their groups increasingly less able to bind their constituency together. One explanation may be that groups organizing an agricultural sector with a diverse structure are less prone to being pulled apart because the size of any subgroups is never sufficient for them to go it alone or to disregard other subgroups. Similarly, external policy changes that may adversely affect one sub-sector are never likely to destabilize the entire group and can be productively separated off and managed in dedicated committees or councils. Let us look at a few examples.

The French example is perhaps the clearest in terms of the vulnerability of groups with two large component member groups. The French case demonstrates well the way in which the CAP can render 'everyone a winner' (livestock and cereal producers), hence resolving potentially damaging internal conflicts. But attempts to reform the CAP, specifically the move to area based payments, threatens to destabilize this mechanism for enhancing organizability. By contrast, Denmark's strong export orientation means its farmers are largely agreed that trade liberalization is desirable, so long as other nations do likewise. The same could be said for Australia, with most industries being export focused.

Change can also bring with it opportunity. For instance, as Grant notes (this volume), the rump of the British NFU membership, which intermittently demands outsider action and return to state subsidy, is considered to be one of the biggest liabilities for the group. This is a similar phenomenon across most countries where there is a dominant group committed to partnership and an insider strategy. Restructuring is generally assumed to remove the less viable of farmers, those who are most often actively advocating state assistance and outsider activism and who are less likely to be group members. As such, the organizability of farmers may actually be enhanced by restructuring. Evidence of this dynamic is found in the Australian and Canadian examples.

The evidence in this volume supports the conclusion that the contemporary environment has not so much created new problems in relation to organizability but exacerbated existing ones or rendered them less manageable. Difficulties in organizability derive from several cleavages that are, in most cases, long standing but exacerbated under contemporary conditions. These include, export versus importing sectors, cereal versus livestock producers, winners and losers from restructuring and small versus large farmers. Thus, we find that organizability is not so much adversely affected by restructuring per se, but where this acts to emphasize even splits along these cleavages. The relationship between farm restructuring and organizability is contingent not on whether there is change *per se*, but whether the farm constituency has become narrower or more diverse in its base.

Capacity Deficit?

It has been established that contemporary conditions by and large demand more of agricultural interest groups. That is, the capacities required to render groups 'valuable' in the 21st century are harder to achieve. Two of the main capacities are resolving conflict and creating unity, and the ability to provide valuable expertise and information. On both scores most groups show a capacity deficit, albeit groups in environments that support these capacities appear more resilient.

In terms of the capacity to provide expertise and information, evidence in this volume shows that in some cases groups may no longer be the sole, or even one of the central, sources of information and technical advice for departments considering agricultural policy issues. This threatens to unpick at least one of the important threads binding groups and state. Most groups cannot employ and retain dedicated experts on diverse areas such as rural decline, GM technology, trade negotiations, plant breeding, food safety, etc. Even groups that appear more resilient than most, such as the Australian NFF, find that consultants and academics are the key source of data and advice to government, even in areas like foreign trade and marketing where groups have traditionally been key players. The explanation for the capacity gap is that both the financial resources of groups have by and large declined at precisely the same time as the number and complexity of issues has increased.

Interestingly, those groups organized as federations tend to find themselves in resource (staffing and budget) terms much weaker than many of their member organizations. This is certainly the case for the NFF in Australia and the CFA in Canada; although the weakness of the CFA is to some extent balanced by the financial strength of some provincial groups that benefit from a compulsory fee system. Unitary organizations tend to have a larger staff as they cannot rely on the resources of member groups and receive all, rather than a slice, of the member subscription income. One can also reasonably assume that superior economies of scale are achieved inside unitary structures. Obvious exceptions to this association between federal structure and under resourcing would be the AFBF in the US and the French FNSEA. Groups for the most part obtain the vast majority of their funding from membership subscriptions. One exception is in Spain where between 50 per cent and 70 per cent of group income is derived from government payments. This partly explains the viability of three national groups in Spain. Daugbjerg (this volume) noted that Danish Agriculture has significant levels of group income aside from member subscriptions which makes it less vulnerable to shifting farm structures. Several nations (eg. Australia and Canada) have statutory systems of levy collection on commodity sales, which are used to fund commodity organizations (which in turn are member organizations of national and/or general groups).

As we may have expected given the overall decline in farm numbers amongst developed nations, membership numbers of the groups examined in this book are in a long term pattern of decline. The reliance on membership subscription for income in combination with the shrinking size of their constituency highlights a point of vulnerability common to all groups in terms of financial resources. The impact on expertise and information provision capacity is highlighted above. However, interestingly, membership density, the percentage of potential members who are actual members, is generally stable – if not rising – among groups. This is largely due to membership levels dropping at a slower rate than the overall farm population. This hints at an emerging stability in some national farming structures which could provide a more certain membership base.[2] It also establishes that the representativeness of groups, itself an important capacity, may be on the rise in most nations.

The representativeness of groups in terms of membership density is one thing, but unity of purpose and unity of organization is quite another. In terms of unity, the structure of contemporary group systems and of individual groups varies enormously. In some nations, such as Australia and Denmark, the agricultural interest group system includes all the groups affiliated with a dominant peak or umbrella group. Interestingly, these groups developed into monopolistic peaks in the last two decades, with the NFF doing so explicitly to lobby for trade liberal change. This suggests that, at the very least, group development may not be hindered but in fact assisted by global change. Yet, in some cases, most notably the US, Canada and Spain, the agricultural interest group system implies a more complex range of discrete organizations that may be in varying levels of cooperation or competition with one another. Interestingly, it is the two groups that have a direct continuity with the post war period, the French FNSEA and the NFU in Britain, that have developed significant signs of disunity. The United Kingdom presents an interesting case, where quasi federalist developments mean that 'devolved' administrations create new centers of power, particularly pertaining to agriculture. These enhance the strength of groups such as the NFU Scotland. Indeed, one could argue that the contemporary UK has no peak agricultural interest group, just one for each sub-national region (albeit that the NFU coordinates action at the national level and for the purpose of European level activity). No simple explanation can account for this diversity across cases. Nations like the US, Canada and Spain, all with vastly different farm sector sizes, are able to support two or more national general farm interests groups. Recalling Daujgberg's earlier comment, less calculable variables, like tradition and internal rivalries (personal and ideological), would seem to best account for both the resistance to unity and the prevalence of group divisions. But it is important to remember that unity does not require organizational amalgamation. Indeed, the Irish case shows how groups largely mimic each other's approach, acting as one voice, if not being organized in one group.

There is no doubt that managing diversity is increasingly difficult, as the previous section highlighted. As referred to earlier, farm interest groups that attempt national and general coverage are, by definition, going to manifest significant internal diversity. Their value as partners for the state, and their capacity to generate representational resources, relies on resolving, or at least managing, this division. In systems with two or more groups this division can be manifested in patterns of group joining. However it is also managed in more subtle ways. In terms of organizational structures, these have (and largely continue) to be managed through allocating councils, committees or sections to relevant commodity or regional sub-groups. In federated structures, like the Australian NFF and Canadian CFA, state groups look after state issues, commodity groups after commodity issues and the federal body all other generic issues that span commodities. While this makes for an unwieldy and resource hungry approach, it does tend to effectively manage division from federal bodies. In unitary structures, like the British NFU, commodities have dedicated committees to pursue issues of singular interest. As Roederer-Rynning (this volume) argues, groups tend also to develop 'recipes' which they deploy to manage the inevitable internal divisions or cleavages within their groups. The Australian case highlights the role played by the rhetorical framing of farm elites in 'disciplining' members. Amidst rapid process of agricultural restructuring and associated socio-economic hardship for large sections of the farming constituency, the NFF deployed a clever campaign constructing the decline of farms as a 'natural' part of becoming farm businesses and a competitive sector. In the case of the French FNSEA, the CAP itself has resolved tensions between cereals and livestock producers. However, the danger in external forces being a defining feature of such 'recipes' is that they are apt to change, which renders groups vulnerable.

Finally, groups are generally valuable to the extent that they can adhere to an insider strategy of influence. However, we find that groups are under more pressure to adopt the outsider or protest and single issue strategies of their competitors. It is not that outsider activity has not always been a standard part of the repertoire of farm interest groups. Rather, the outsider activity has become detached from its tactical place as a buttress to insider negotiations and increasingly viewed as a legitimate stand alone strategy. This is most pronounced in the British example.

Dealing with Challenge: Adaptation and Transformation

The review above highlights a varied, nevertheless challenging, environment for contemporary agricultural interest groups. However, as Daugbjerg notes (this volume), groups are not the result of rational processes of organization building but often the result of historical tradition and compromise between political and economic interests. Group structures may make more sense if we assumed they were designed under a rationale of 'making do' rather than one of 'optimization'. As is apparent in many cases in this volume, while groups often seek to engage in efforts at organizational design these are often thwarted by the dictates of tradition and internal conflicts. As Moyano-Estrada (this volume) emphasizes, the environment does not determine or dictate group resilience and decline: endogenous factors and group agency must play a part. We cannot read off resilience on the weight of the group environment alone nor expect that groups will seamlessly transcend perturbations in that environment. Environments may present challenges and opportunities, and shape the likelihood of the success of any responses, but how do groups respond to them?

Adaptation

The evidence in this volume is that by and large groups have been active in generating strategies to adapt to new state priorities which suggest new logics of influence and changes in organizability which suggest new logics of membership. Further they have also made attempts at reducing the capacity deficit.

The biggest challenges for groups in terms of finding common cause with the state arises where public support is waning, programs are costly to the national purse and where forces for trade liberalization have threatened to disrupt the purpose of group-state negotiations. In many cases groups are responding to contemporary challenges to agricultural exceptionalism and policy change by trying to create or tap new sources (some may say pretexts) for exceptionalism. Groups are trying to adapt messages that legitimate support to farmers, formerly based on post war concerns of food security, to contemporary 'public interest' concerns such as environmental care and rural development. Although, most recently, exceptionalism has been justified in terms of protecting domestic consumers from risks to food security associated with 'global terrorism', for example in the US and UK. As discussed in a previous section, where and when the general public comes to support these arguments there is a good prospect of renewing a base for partnership.

While exceptionalism may be revived, or maintained, there is no doubt that the policy process is more competitive than in the post war period. In terms of adaptation to the pluralization of policy networks we notice an overall increased use of coalitions with other societal interests. For example, the Australian NFF and the French FNSEA, to name but two, have both pursued cooperation with environment and consumer groups. There is, however, little evidence of transnational activity beyond coordination of their national activities with other agricultural groups on a basis that reflects trade alliances. For example, EU agricultural groups organize through COPA and CPE (in addition to operating as own account actors), while third nations organize under the banner of the Cairns Group Farm Leaders. What is perhaps more surprising is evidence from most nations that groups are complicit in acting to alter the policy image in other nations through alliances with transnational non-farm interests. For example the NFF in Australia is involved with consumer and green groups in US and Europe. The NFU in Canada and the CPE in Europe, have been involved in Via Campesina, which Skogstad (this volume) describes as 'a network of almost 70 organizations in over 30 countries opposed to free trade agreements'. French groups have become involved with EU consumer and environment groups. However, consistent with Braithewaite and Drahos (2000) we find that national agricultural interest groups remain predominantly domestic territorial actors. That is, they focus their energies on representing a constituency that is rooted in the specificity of a nation state's boundaries; albeit, they often do so through regional and international vehicles such as COPA and IFAP.

In terms of addressing organizability, many groups have found that reduced farm numbers has hit it more financially than representationally. The reason is that the homogeneity of group membership is in many cases enhanced by the natural attrition of those producers that were typically difficult to organize or who demanded benevolent state action. But, of course, what may to observers appear as an emerging homogeneity can be perceived very differently on the ground. And there is much evidence that groups face splintering and internal dispute along ideological, commodity and regional cleavages. In the face of this shifting organizability, there is weak evidence that some groups have entertained altering the scope of their membership and/or rebranding themselves; although this is often linked with measures to increase group income and financial resources, which are dealt with below. For instance, the FNSEA in France is trying to incorporate the policy territory of competitors in environment area (integrate environment and production agendas). The NFU has apparently rebalanced its mix between policy and market activities, accentuating the latter. Grant (this volume) highlights the British NFUs belief that many members require and see value in service provision and marketing assistance than in 'insider' lobbying.

Most effort has gone into the more immediate task of rectifying capacity deficits. This is perhaps understandable given it is an area where groups have a more direct level of control and influence. In this respect, there is evidence of some specific strategies.

In almost all cases, there is an emphasis on working towards group unity. All chapters refer to significant rationalizations in the number of groups and the creation of umbrella groups. Even in Spain, with three national groups currently, these groups are themselves the outcome of a significant level of prior rationalization. In terms of creating a single encompassing group, efforts in Australia and Denmark have been successful. UK efforts to formally merge Welsh groups to the NFU structure, and similar merger attempts in Ireland, have been unsuccessful. Nevertheless, the key point to recall is that these efforts persist and the issue of unity is a constant theme for these groups. The Australian case shows that even with the unification and then rationalization and professionalization in the 1980s, it is still looking at forming a unitary style body to reduce costs.

An important group capacity is unity, or at least the appearance of unity. Each group has approached the emergence of splinter groups and internal dissent in a unique way. For the British NFU, the battleground has become the internal electoral process, as rebels see election results as evidence of an unresponsive organization. It finds itself under pressure to renounce its commitment to an insider role and take more emphatic militant and protest action. Grant argues that the NFU will survive, attracting small members for services but remain the voice of larger viable farmers. In Australia, rebel commodity groups have also sought forms of direct election as a way of circumventing elites who seek to retain an orderly transfer of power. However, more generally, the NFF has pursued a neoliberal form of ideology to govern their own group, claiming they are there to create an environment within which members survive (or otherwise) according to individual ability. This tends to create social relations that mitigate against politicized dissent and create a renewed focus on individual business assistance and education rather than structural policy issues and assistance levels.

What most groups face is a significant reduction in financial resources. This has hampered attempts to address the increasing number of issues along with the sophisticated nature of the policy debate. Where groups rely heavily on member subscriptions the most common response has been to stop the slide of members with Olsonian style selective material incentives, such as access to discounts, advisory services or legal/business advice. The second element has been to expand the membership base. In the UK, the NFU offers a form of associate membership to non-farmers, with estimates that this non-farm group outnumber the actual farm members. This serves a dual purpose of adapting to a diverse constituency by offering services to satisfy small farmers while pursuing policies that reflect the interests of the larger farmers. Some member groups of the NFF in Australia have done the same or offered associate memberships to additional family members.

Transformation

In terms of transformation, there is not a great deal of evidence that national general groups are being replaced as the dominant means of farm interest organization. Although there are some pointers of how things may develop. In Denmark, this has been taken to a new level whereby agriculture forms part of a larger umbrella agri-industry group, *Danish Agriculture*. Daugbjerg notes that this has not led to a diminution of farmers' interest or power. However, as Grant notes, a similar proposal in the UK for a Trade Union Congress type group for British agriculture has had cold water poured on it given its potential to reduce the clout of the NFU. Some member groups of the NFF in Australia have adopted a broader rural group approach, but this is really more of a membership expansion exercise than an attempt to create a truly integrated rural interest group. Moyano-Estrada, in his discussion of the UPA and COAG, draws attention to the role that the ideology of the group has to the way it views forming logical alliances and membership expansion. These groups take a horizontal (countryside) rather than a vertical (agribusiness) perspective and, as such, look for coalition building and alliances accordingly.

Industry Associations and Global Change

Agriculture has often been a canvas to make more general points about public policy and the role of interest groups in modern political life. The findings presented in this book could also hold some important insights that may inform more general debates in the discipline and beyond. Two seem most pertinent. Firstly, it contributes more generally to the debate about the fate of industry associations in a global era. Secondly, the fate of such groups is particularly relevant and instructive given the growing debate over the significance of groups in national strategies for reforming and adapting industry sectors to retain competitiveness in a globalizing era. These implications are briefly reviewed and considered below.

In terms of gleaning lessons for the general literature, the findings in this volume loosely accord with Coleman's argument (1997) (see introduction to this volume); that groups have a high degree of sticking power, particularly those with longstanding histories of partnership with the state. The evidence in this volume is that groups persist, and indeed, in most cases show remarkable resilience (they have not been overtaken by other groups and are still the central agricultural interest organizations). Perhaps the most significant finding is that those groups operating in a domestic policy environment where trade liberal policies are orthodoxy, like Australia, are particularly resilient. On this basis alone, one could venture that any suggestion that global change, and its related domestic policy and industry restructuring trends, spells the decline of groups is overstated. Instead of resting on the impact of global change, this volume has put forward the proposition that groups are more resilient where and when they can renew longstanding or establish new grounds for partnership with the state, enhance organizability through the adjustment 'out' of marginal producers/firms, and address endogenous capacity deficits. Of course, it is for others to explore how this specific finding emerges in other industry sectors. But one could expect these conditions to be harder to achieve where industries are polarized in two or three large sub-groups and where industry adjustment is slow (undermines organizability and cohesion), where the industry does not have wide spread community support or is unpopular (undermines politics of partnership), where the state has little expertise in that industry sector (undermines mechanics of partnership) and where the goals of the industry are diametrically opposed to those of the state.

Another key finding in terms of the fate of groups is that, however resilient they may be, agricultural groups are by and large found to exhibit i) diminishing endogenous capacity (financial and research) and ii) a heavy reliance on external forces for achieving cohesiveness, unity and political relevance. This finds groups in a vulnerable position, with their ongoing resilience either resting on future agricultural policy reform, mediating public opinion or on the ability of groups to rationalize structures and fundraise to meet escalating financial resource demands. This finding does seem to resonate with more general findings about the declining ability for large general and national groups, in particular unions and business associations, in the 21st century.

The second issue, as Coleman noted, was not only whether industry groups would persist or be resilient, but that the associational forms of governance, like group-state partnership, would survive global change. He supposed that the state's receptivity and the stability of the politics surrounding partnership were apt to change along with global change. While there is much disagreement, even differences between the contributors to this volume, about the role of groups in public policy, the desirability of peak groups pursuing 'anticipatory' policy, and the importance or otherwise of forms of partnership (however loose) between groups and the state, the conclusions in this book should prove of interest to those involved in these larger debates.

From two related standpoints the contemporary role of groups in a global era would seem tenuous. Strong versions of the globalization thesis support the idea that the shift of sovereignty upwards, sideways and downwards, necessarily shifts the conduct of politics away from the nation state. As observed in the introductory chapter, much emphasis has been placed on INGOs and transnational social movements on the strength of this strong globalization thesis. Similarly, those who see globalization as the freeing up of economic relations and the deregulation of national economies, find support for the public choice view that groups are unhelpful impediments to the dominance of market forces. From this view domestic industry groups are successful to the extent they extract rents from government as a form of compensation for global change. It follows that weak groups mean strong states and, in a neoliberal policy environment, strong and undistorted markets. The contributions to this volume suggest reasons to be much more circumspect about strong arguments about globalization and negative impact on the role of groups. There is plenty of evidence to support a thread in political science that has nation states as authors of their own destiny, albeit in a globalizing era.

There is a thread in the literature that would in some senses revive the meso-level neocorporatist role of groups in governing national industries. Weiss (1998, pp.4-5), for instance, has persuasively argued that state capacity (the ability to 'transform' or 'upgrade' industry sectors in the face of global change) in a globalizing era will become a defining feature of a nation's competitiveness and that groups-government relations are crucial in generating this capacity. Most importantly, though, she points out that the ability to cut protection and subsidy is one half of the challenge, the other component is the ability to re-skill and rebuild those businesses and industries that remain for international competitiveness (Weiss, 1998, p.21).[3] In the Australian context, Marsh (1995) asks why groups are not used more consciously by government in achieving industry revitalization and economic competitiveness rather than viewed as inevitably selfish only interested in 'subverting the national interest'. This conclusion suggests a reconnection with the corporatist literature of the 1980s, and the emphasis on groups and governments as partners for growth. Indeed, this literature has had somewhat of a contemporary revival (see Rhodes, 2001).

While this volume cannot resolve issues like the importance of partnership to national competitiveness, it has explicitly addressed the issue of the contemporary fate of groups and their capacity. Clearly there is no point advocating the role of group-state relations as a driving force for national industry sectors achieving global competitiveness if groups are simply incapable of serving as reliable partners. In this respect the findings have some import for informing these debates. The poor capacity of many groups, their struggle for financial resources, the decline in staff expertise and information gathering and analysis, undermines the ability of such groups to make an autonomous contribution to public policy. This suggests that the state needs to be proactive in fostering group capacity if it wishes to harness groups in any kind of partnership. Of course, these arrangements also require state capacity, which is another issue again. While this has not been explicitly addressed in this volume, some chapters show that it is weakened by the generic processes of hollowing out. The conclusion here is that much more attention needs to be put into establishing the capacities required by groups, and how to enhance these capacities, if progress is to be made in pursuing associational governance in the 21st century.

Final Remarks

If one were to venture an overall message from this collection of national cases, it may be that the group environment in the 21st century does not create a plethora of new and unique challenges that undermine groups, but that changes in the environment exacerbate existing challenges, those arguably inherent to general group structures, in ways that destabilize groups. Further, the character of the contemporary group environment cannot be said to be singularly defined by processes reasonably captured by the term globalization. The promotion of liberalization and global economic integration, and forms of regional and international governance, has recast and shaped domestic conditions (both in relation to groups strategies of influence and membership organization) that in turn create challenges, but also opportunities, for groups. While this marks a globalizing era as distinct from the post war era of national modernization and development, we have identified other factors that also play an important part in contributing to the character of the group environment and which are more or less loosely (if at all) connected to globalizing processes. Here we refer to the level of public support for agriculture, domestic policy change and patterns of agricultural restructuring.

Amidst this change, the chapters in this book illustrate that agricultural interest groups with a national scope and general coverage survive. The challenges confronting groups, however, are not always new. Indeed, for the most part global change seems to work on and sometimes exacerbate longstanding weaknesses or vulnerabilities in these types of groups. Nevertheless, these challenges destabilize and disrupt often longstanding patterns of behaviour and understanding that characterized both policy making activity and the organization of farming constituencies.

Without too many exceptions or derogations it is possible to say that agricultural interest groups confront an environment whereby there is growing pressure for trade liberalization and associated reforms to domestic polices of support; where the general public increasingly scrutinizes and challenges taken for granted farming practices and their impacts on the environment, rural development and food safety; and where competition from other organized interests is heightened (including consumer, environment and agri-business). They do so as groups that typically rely on membership subscriptions (except Spain) and have a shrinking potential membership base (but often with rising densities). In the face of an environment that contains many of the drivers of decline, groups illustrate a remarkable degree of, as Coleman noted, 'sticking power'. They have adapted, by and large, to conditions that reduce resources, shifted the venue and level of competitiveness of the policy process, and where members see their individual market competitiveness as important, alongside, but in addition to, traditional state assisted public policy concerns. The environment is an ever changing one and a number of possibilities, albeit very divergent ones, suggest points that may further unsettle the picture we have assembled. The challenges documented here will become greater should we see additional trade liberalization, the rise of anti-globalization forces and the rise in the activism of the 'global south' as they seek to reset international trade agendas.

Of course, change rarely presents only challenges alone. And in this volume we can identify opportunities presented by global change. Perhaps most apparent is the potential for agricultural restructuring to remove marginal farmers and hence create a more organizable, if not smaller, agricultural constituency.

Groups that proved most resilient are those that operate in an environment that supports both state receptivity and organizability, and where capacity is demonstrable. As we can see, this approach to explanation reconciles the apparently contradictory conclusions that groups in a state assisted and trade liberal environment, and those with rapid and slow farm adjustment, appear resilient.

The opportunity exists to examine the resilience and decline of similar groups in developing nations, in addition to national industry associations in other sectors. Such research will inform not only debates about the fate of groups amidst global change, but also broader debates about the role of groups and associative governance in assisting states to develop global competitiveness.

Notes

[1] While many departments may remain agriculture departments, both in name and responsibilities, it is important to recognize that many explicitly frame policy issues with respect to 'food' policy rather than 'agricultural' policy.

[2] Other factors are also at play. For example, the 90 per cent density for Denmark can be explained in part by the way in which new farmers, when purchasing a farm business, are brought into contact with the advisory centers run by Danish Agriculture. The value of this advisory service is that it keeps membership turnover very low and provides a unique point for recruitment.

[3] See Coleman and Chiasson (2002) for this approach applied to the activities of French farm groups.

References

Ball, A. and Millard, F. (1986), *Pressure Politics in Industrial Societies*, Macmillan, London.

Braithwaite, J. and Drahos, P. (2000), *Global business regulation*, Cambridge University Press, Melbourne.

Coleman, W.D. (1997), 'Associational Governance in a Globalizing Era: Weathering the Storm', in J.R. Hollingsworth and R. Boyer (eds.), *Contemporary Capitalism: The Embeddedness of Institutions*, Cambridge University Press, Cambridge, pp.127-53.

Coleman, W.D. and Chiasson, C. (2002), 'State power, transformative capacity, and adapting to globalisation: an analysis of French agricultural policy, 1960-2000', *Journal of European Public Policy*, Vol. 9(2), pp.168-85

Farmonline (2004), 'US Cotton disputes Brazil's case', www.fw.farmonline.com.au, accessed 14/5/04.

Greer, A. (2003), 'Countryside Issues: a Creeping Crisis', *Parliamentary Affairs*, Vol. 56, p.523-42.

Harris, S. (1993), 'The International Economy and Domestic Politics', in I. Marsh (ed.) *Governing in the 1990s: An Agenda for the Decade*, Longman Cheshire, Melbourne, pp.30-55.

Marsh, I. (1995), *Beyond the Two Party System*, Cambridge University Press, Melbourne.

Moyano-Estrada, E. (1995), 'Farmers' unions and the restructuring of European agriculture', *Sociologia Ruralis*, Vol. 25(3/4), pp.348-65.

Rhodes, M. (2001), 'The Political Economy of Social Pacts: "Competitive Corporatism" and European Welfare Reform', in P. Pierson (ed.) *The new politics of the welfare state*, Oxford University Press, Oxford.

Schmitter, P.C. and Streeck, W. (1981), 'The Organisation of Business Interests. A Research Design to Study the Associative Action of Business in the Advanced Industrial Societies of Western Europe', International Institute of Management, Berlin, Discussion paper IIM/LMP 81-13.

Schmitter, P.C. and Streeck, W. (1985), 'Community, market, state – associations? The prospective contribution of interest governance to social order', *European Sociological Review*, Vol. 1(2), pp.119-138.

Weiss, L. (1998), *The myth of the powerless state: governing the economy in a global era*, Polity Press, Cambridge.

Wilson, G.K. (1990), *Interest Groups*, Basil Blackwell, Oxford.

COPA, COGECA and CPE: Three Pillars of Farm Interest Group Systems in Europe

Eduardo Moyano-Estrada and Cristina Rueda-Catry*

Introduction

In the European Union (EU), farm interest representation is channeled through three supranational organizations. Two of these, the COPA (Committee of Professional Agricultural Organizations) and the CPE (Coordination Paysanne Européenne), group together national farmers' organizations from the 25 Member States that make up the EU today, while the third, the COGECA (General Confederation of Agricultural Cooperatives), encompasses national federations of agricultural cooperatives.

Since their creation in the late 1950s, the COPA (1958) and the COGECA (1959) have come to be recognized as official mediators by the European Commission, allowing them to play a key role in the sectoral advisory committees and hold an almost exclusive monopoly on farmer interest representation in the EU for over thirty years. The CPE, founded later in 1986, was not to be acknowledged as a valid mediator until 1991 through a decision taken by the European Commission recognizing the plural nature of farm interest group representation in Europe. Since then, these three organizations have been actively engaged in the CAP process through representatives, which are appointed to agricultural advisory committees.

The aim of this paper is to present the most important features of these supranational organizations, their historical trajectory, ideological discourses, models of organization and strategies for collective action concerning European issues. Appendices Two, Three and Four provide a list of the different national associations that form part of these organizations after the recent EU enlargement to include 25 countries.

The COPA and the COGECA: The Social Construction of the CAP

The Historical Context

The creation of the COPA and the COGECA ran parallel to the establishment of a common agricultural policy between the six Member States that made up the European Economic Community (EEC) at the end of the 1950s. Prior to this event, farm interest representation was achieved in each country through national farmers' unions with diverse social and ideological characteristics and distinct historical trajectories. These included organizations based on the Catholic tradition (Coldiretti in Italy, Boerenbond in Belgium or the CNJA in France), those of lay or socialist inspiration (the Italian Allianza Contadina, the French MODEF or the Belgian UPA) or more liberal organizations with a clear professional orientation (the FNSEA in France, the NFU in England, the CGI in Italy or the DBV in Germany). Through all of these organizations, European agriculture of the fifties recovered its rich trade union heritage following the devastating effects of totalitarian regimes (which had imposed obligatory membership in corporative systems) and the Second World War. At the supranational level, two associations existed at that time: the FIPA (International Federation of Agricultural Producers), which was founded in 1947, and the CEA (European Confederation of Agriculture), founded in 1948. These two associations represented the European political and agricultural elite's old desire to create forums for debate regarding agricultural issues. However, they did not act as a unifying force for the different national farmers' organizations given that a common European agricultural policy in which to participate had not yet come into force.[1]

The opportunity to create a European structure to represent the interests of farmers from the six founding states of the EEC came about following the signing of the Treaty of Rome in March 1957. At this point the governments of the then FRG (Federal Republic of Germany), France, Italy, Luxembourg, The Netherlands and Belgium decided, among other things, to establish a common agricultural policy that would permit the participation of a wide range of national farmers' unions.

Articles 38 to 47 of Title II of the Treaty of Rome established, in a very precise manner, the implementation of a common policy concerning agriculture, setting out three main objectives. These included a social objective (to achieve fair incomes for farmers), an economic objective (increase food production, stabilize and harmonize agricultural markets) and a political objective (work towards European integration). The Treaty, however, did not clarify the content of the future CAP, leaving this matter up to an intergovernmental conference to be held in the coming months. Similarly, the manner in which the agricultural organizations were to participate in the CAP process was left open by the Treaty. Nonetheless, during the Conference held in the Italian city of Stresa from 3-12 July 1958 and presided over by the then vice-president of the European Commission Sicco L. Mansholt, the Ministers of Agriculture of the six founding states met, inviting representatives of each country's agricultural organizations and the CEA and FIPA to participate as observers.

The weeks following the Stresa Conference were marked by intense coordination and close contacts between national leaders of the agricultural organizations supporting the CAP process. The leaders soon came to realize that in order to be recognized as mediators in the newly formed institutions, they had to organize themselves into representative structures at the European level. Ruling out the CEA and the FIPA as the basis for these structures (given that they included organizations from countries that did not belong to the recently created EEC), and taking advantage of the legal vacuum that existed in matters of representation, they opted to create a new structure of representation open to any national organization interested in forming part of this European project that met with the unanimous approval of the participating members.

Thus, on September 6, 1958, the leaders of 15 national agricultural organizations from the six founding states of the EEC decided to found the COPA (Committee of Professional Agricultural Organizations). It was established as a European structure to represent the following organizations:

- *In France*: the Fédération Nationale des Syndicats des Exploitants Agricoles (FNSEA), the Centre National des Jeunes Agriculteurs (CNJA), the Asamblée Permanente des Chambres d'Agriculture (APCA) and the Confédération Nationale de la Mutualité, la Coopération et le Crédit Agricoles (CNMCA).
- *In Germany*: the Deutscher Bauernverband e.V. (DBV).
- *In Italy*: the Confederazione Nazionale dei Coltivatori Diretti (Coldiretti), the Confederazione Generale dell'Agricoltura Italiana (Confagricultura) and the Federazione Italiana dei Consorzi Agrari (Federconsorzi).
- *In Belgium*: the Belgische Boerenbond (BB), the Allianza Agricole Belge (AAB), the Federation Nationale des Unions Professionnelles Agricoles (UPA) and the Fédération Wallone de l'Agriculture (FWA).
- *In the Netherlands*: the Koninklijk Nederlands Landbouwcomité (KNL), the Katholieke Nederlandse Boeren- en Tuindersbond (KNBTB) and the Nederlandse Christelijke Boeren- en Tuindersbond (NCTB).
- *In Luxembourg*: the Centrale Paysanne Luxemburgeoise (CPL).

All of these organizations had already strengthened their ties through international agricultural conferences organized, prior to the Second World War, by the International Agricultural Congress (CIA) founded in 1889 (see endnote 1) and later by the above-mentioned CEA (European Confederation of Agriculture). This paved the way for a common project of agricultural representation at the European level. At the same time, Catholic-based organizations of young farmers led by the French CNJA founded the CEJA (European Council of Young Farmers) in 1958. Hence organizations with a wide range of social characteristics and ideological stances contributed to the creation of the COPA: a combination of Catholic-based family farmers' organizations and large farmers' organizations that were fully integrated into the markets and the agri-foods *filiére*, namely the FNSEA in France, the Confagricoltura in Italy or the DBV in Germany. For one reason or another, all of these organizations accepted the agricultural policy model proposed by the EEC – including market regulation and granting of aid to farmers – thereby contributing to its social legitimization. However, other organizations that made up the associative panorama of Europe in the fifties (i.e. the Allianza Contadina in Italy or the MODEF in France, both of which had close ties to the communist parties in their countries) did not take part in the creation of the COPA as they were opposed to the process of EEC construction, and more specifically, to the agricultural policy model set out in the Mansholt proposal.

Following COPA's model, six national federations of agricultural cooperatives from the six member states of the EEC became organized at the European level through the creation of the COGECA (General Confederation of Agricultural Cooperatives) on 24 September 1959. The founding members of this umbrella organization included the following federations:

- *In France*: the Confédération Française de la Cooperation Agricole.
- *In Belgium*: the cooperative branch of the Belgische Borenenbond.
- *In Germany*: the Deutscher Raiffeisenverband e.v. (DRV).
- *In Italy*: the cooperative branch of the Federaconsorzi.
- *In Luxembourg*: the cooperative branch of the Central Paysanne Luxembourgeoise.
- *In the Netherlands*: the Nationale Coöperatieve Raad voor Land- en Tuinbouw (NCR).

Thus, by the late 1950s, the ground was laid for the European interest group system; a system in which the duties of each associative structure (the former CEA and FIPA, and the new COPA, COGECA and CEJA) were to become ever more specialized. Indeed, a new protocol signed between them in 1971 granted the COPA authority to act as the main representative body for farmers, while the COGECA was designated to represent the cooperatives in EU institutions. It was likewise established that the CEA would be in charge of the social issues of agricultural policy (forestry, farmers' social security, professional training, problems faced by rural women, etc.), the FIPA would represent European farmers at the international level, and the CEJA would be responsible for issues concerning young farmers.

In 1962, the COPA and the COGECA created a joint secretariat. This structure, which continues to remain in place today, has permitted both organizational structures to hold a de facto monopoly of farm interest representation in Brussels by controlling access to and participation in the advisory committees until 1999.

The Expansion Process

Since their creation, the COPA and the COGECA have expanded on six occasions in consonance with the different EU enlargements to include the farmers' unions and the agricultural federations of the new Member States. Hence in 1973, the National Farmers' Union of England and Wales (NFU) of the United Kingdom, the Danish corporative body Landbrugsraadet (which includes the DH and DL organizations) and the Irish Farmers' Association (IFA) joined the COPA. Later, the Greek organizations PASEGES and GESASE joined COPA in 1981 as did in 1986 the five Spanish organizations UPA and COAG, CNAG, CNJA and UFADE (these three last organizations merged and created ASAJA), and the Confederaçao dos Agricultores de Portugal (CAP). In 1995, the COPA opened up its doors to very liberal organizations from northern Europe such as the Swedish Lantbrukarnas Riksförbind (LRF) and the Finnish organizations Maa-Ja Metsatalous Tuottajain Keskusliito (MTK) and Svenska Lantbruksproducenternas Centralförbund (SLC). That same year an agricultural chamber representing farming sector throughout Austria: the Austrian Präsidentenkonferez der Landwirschaftskammern Österreichs (Prako), also became a member of COPA. Today the COPA comprises national organizations, all of which have a general role, as no sectoral organizations have been admitted.

The COGECA, on the other hand, encompasses federations of cooperatives from the new Member States, bringing the number of its members to 17. Unlike the COPA, in which each country is represented by several organizations to reflect the existing plurality in the sphere of farmers' unions, each country's agricultural cooperatives are usually represented in the COGECA by a single national federation (with the exception of Italy which has three).

The fifth and most recent enlargement of May 2004 is by far the most far-reaching in terms of both its size and political repercussions. Indeed, on 1 May 2004, ten new countries joined the EU: Hungary, Poland, the Czech Republic, Slovenia, Slovakia, Estonia, Lithuania, Latvia, Cyprus and Malta. Two years earlier, on 12 September 2002 in Copenhagen (Denmark), the COPA and the COGECA contributed to the process of EU enlargement by signing protocols with agricultural organizations from the 10 new Member States, as well as organizations from Bulgaria and Romania (candidate countries for accession in 2006); allowing these farmers' organizations to gradually become integrated into the COPA-COGECA structure.

The EU enlargement of 2004 to 25 countries will raise the number of COPA's member organizations from 43 to 63, and from 17 to 24 in the COGECA; a change that is quantitative and qualitative alike. The integration of these new organizations will no doubt bring about significant changes that will lead to a greater diversity of agricultural models in Europe as it has meant the incorporation of complicated mechanisms of national representation inherited from the era of communist collectivization and the way toward economic liberalization adopted in these countries (see list of the COPA and COGECA members in Appendices Two and Four respectively).

Organizational Structure

The joint secretariat of the COPA and the COGECA has its head office in Brussels where some 47 people are employed, including a team of 15 interpreters and translators who ensure that all the organization's documents (agreements, common positions, press releases, reports, etc.) are translated into five working languages of COPA and COGECA: French, Spanish, Italian, English and German. The working budget for the secretariat amounts to 4.5 million Euros annually and is funded solely through contributions made by its member organizations, be they farmers' unions or federations of cooperatives. The members of the advisory groups are, however, reimbursed by the European Commission for travel expenses from their country of origin to Brussels, thus constituting an indirect form of funding for the European structures of representation as both the COPA and the COGECA take advantage of these trips to hold working groups.

The targeted actions undertaken by COPA and COGECA may vary, depending on the stage which the EU decision-making process has reached. At an early stage, the COPA and COGECA's participation in the CAP decision-making process is partly achieved through the presence of their representatives on these advisory committees. This is completed with the very close relations between the European Commission services and the staff of the COPA and COGECA's common Secretariat, especially on technical issues. The decision-making bodies of the COPA and COGECA (the *Presidia*) meet monthly, and on those occasions often meet Members of the European parliament, Agricultural Ministers and members of the European Commission (specially Commissioners related to agriculture, trade, budget, health and consumers affairs, enterprise). But the most important targeted actions undertaken by COPA and COGECA, once the Commission has agreed on a proposal, is the one dealing with the Agricultural Council (the EU body composed of the Agricultural Ministers from the Member States). Before each Council meeting (once a month), where the decisions are taken, the Presidents of COPA and

COGECA meet the Council President and discuss openly the issues that will be decided during the ministers meeting as well as transmitting the position of COPA-COGECA. Members of the Agricultural Council are also periodically approached, mainly via written submission, with the common positions of the COPA-COGECA.

The different national delegations of the agricultural organizations maintain close, albeit non-official, ties with the European Commission members through a sort of feedback process. Furthermore, the DG AGRI (Directorate-General of Agriculture) staff members are frequently invited to participate in conferences held by the agricultural organizations in their respective countries, thus creating useful support networks to carry out their lobbying activities in Brussels. In spite of the weak role played until now by the European Parliament's Agricultural Commission in formulating the CAP, the COPA-COGECA has worked actively with such a commission, using it as a 'sounding board' for farmers' demands. However, following the Treaty of Maastricht, the European Parliament has taken on an increasingly important role through the establishment of a co-decision procedure for consumer protection, public health and environment related issues. Following the project to develop a European constitution, the co-decision procedure will, certainly, also be extended to CAP regulations, meaning that the COPA and the COGECA will be even more interested than before in lobbying this EU institution.

In addition to the activities channelled through the COPA-COGECA structure, the majority of national farmers' unions and national federations of agricultural cooperatives have their own staff in Brussels, lobbying before civil servants of the European Commission or members of the European Parliament to gain rapid access to information concerning regulation and directive proposals with a view to influencing their content before they are finally passed.

The CPE: An Alternative Farm Representation Structure

For over four decades, COPA and its member organizations have been the sole farmer representative at the EU level. Due mainly to unresolved disputes with other organizations from their own countries, some farmer organizations remained on the sidelines of the official system of farm interest representation in the EU. In contrast, the hegemony held by the COGECA has not had the same effect on the cooperative sphere. As mentioned above, this is due to the fact that the representation of agricultural cooperatives at the European level has been channelled through one federation per country (Italy being the only exception with three federations) that groups together practically all cooperatives of each country.

The effects of this exclusion (or self-exclusion) were felt in the early days of the COPA, in a stage (the middle sixties) marked by an ideological stand off between its member organizations (mainly those having a Catholic or professional orientation) and organizations that were critical of the project to construct a common agricultural policy (mainly socialist-based organizations oriented towards defending small farmers). Later, when political confrontation gave way to other types of differences arising from questions related to the content of the CAP, certain associations were excluded for reasons having to do with the domestic life of each country; differences which were manifested in the heart of the COPA vis-à-vis vetoes by organizations to block the entry of rivals (this is exactly what happened in the eighties when the French liberal FNSEA vetoed the socialist CNSTP, or when the Catholic Coldiretti vetoed the Italian social-communist Confcoltivatori).

These dynamics of exclusion gradually led to the establishment of a critical sector which would, over time, intensify their contacts and coordinate their actions of protest. This eventually culminated in the creation of alternative platforms. The crisis of the European productivist model, its environmental implications, the problems of mountain farms and the successive CAP reforms, led these critical organizations to consolidate their positions and strengthen their structures of representation. Finally, at a meeting held in Madrid in 1986, 27 of these national organizations established, under the leadership of the French Confédération Nationale Paysanne, what is known today as the CPE (Coordination Paysanne Européenne).

Since then, the aim of the CPE has been to promote a new European agricultural policy based on four pillars: to maintain the agricultural population (by acknowledging the importance of farmers in the revitalization of rural areas); to curb the process of farm concentration (by preventing the disappearance of family farming); to promote environmentally sound sustainable agriculture (by controlling the negative effects of the intensive model of production) and rural development (by promoting the diversification of activities and multi-functionality). The ideological stance taken by the CPE in this regard was grounded in a serious reflection on North-South relations, leading many of its member organizations to take part in international platforms supporting alternative agriculture (i.e. the Via Campesina) and some of its most prominent leaders to make their demands known publicly through the media, namely the renowned French peasant leader José Bové.

Since 1999, the CPE has been officially recognized as an interlocutor by the European Commission, providing it the opportunity to participate alongside (in the group of producers and cooperatives) the COPA, the COGECA and the CEJA in the agricultural advisory committees. This recognition has meant that the CPE now forms part of the official system of farm interest representation, giving rise to a more formal structure within the organization itself. In fact, some of the proposals put forward in the CAP incorporate principles upheld by the CPE, namely the implementation of agri-environmental programs (through contractual mechanisms for the granting of public aid to farmers) or the support of alternative forms of agriculture. Thus, the integration of the CPE into the official system of farm representation can be said to be a reflection of some changes occurring in the CAP and the recognition of the social and economic plurality in the European farming sector.

Today, the CPE includes 18 member organizations coming from the European countries (some of them are not Member States of the EU, like Norway or Switzerland) (see list of members in Appendix Three). The majority of these organizations are national structures (like the German ABL, the Belgium FUJA and VAC, the French MODEF and Confédération Paysanne or the Portuguese CNA), although some of them are regional organizations (like the three Spanish: the UAGR coming from La Rioja region, the EHNE from the Basque Country and the SLG from Galizia). Finally, some members of the CPE are social movements and peasant platforms (like the Italian Foro Contadino).

Participation in the Agricultural Advisory Committees and Others Strategies of Collective Action

The Stresa Conference, referred to earlier, included in its final resolution a point that expressed satisfaction with the European Commission's intention to 'maintain (...) close and continual collaboration with professional agricultural organizations'. The Economic and Social Committee of the then EEC asked the European Commission in 1960 to 'bring together producer, trade and workers' organizations as well as consumer associations at the European Economic Community level in a advisory committee' to enable them to take part in each of the agricultural bodies and funds associated with the CAP.

In response to these demands by the Member States and representatives from social and occupational groups, the European Commission set up the first advisory committees in 1962, one for each agricultural or livestock sector regulated by a common market organization. Thus, two of the first advisory committees were created: one for the cereals sector and another for wine-growing products (Commission Decision, Official Journal no. B072 of 8/8/1962). In these early committees, fifty percent of the members were farmers' representatives designated by the COPA-COGECA, while the remaining 50 per cent was made up of representatives from the food manufacturing industry, trade, farm workers and consumers. The objective of these committees was to issue non-binding recommendations on regulation and directive proposals submitted to them for consultation by the European Commission; a function that has been maintained and enlarged in accordance with the implementation of new common market organizations. Likewise, non-sectoral advisory committees were set up to issue opinions regarding the CAP's horizontal measures (i.e. structural, agri-environmental or rural development policy).

In addition to carrying out the tasks assigned by the European Commission, the agricultural advisory committees have contributed to the development of a participatory democracy at the EU level by allowing various interest groups, with an interest in the CAP, to express themselves politically. At the same time, the agricultural advisory committees have been a rich source of information for the European Commission staff when devising regulation and directive proposals. They have brought the complexity and diversity of European agriculture to the EU sphere. Furthermore, the agricultural advisory committees have constituted an excellent training ground for the leaders of national agricultural organizations who have been able to acquire experience in negotiating at the European level and become familiar with the complex technical language of the CAP.

Since 1962, the advisory committees have undergone successive reforms. The most recent took place in May 2004 (Commission Decision of 23 April 2004, OJL, p.50) and reflected the CAP reforms of 1999 and 2003, as well as the EU enlargement. Following this reform, the advisory committees have come to be called 'agricultural advisory groups' to distinguish them from the *management committees* and the *regulatory committees* (both composed of civil servants designated by the governments of the EU Member States) and the *scientific committees* (that are made up of experts from the European scientific community).

In 1999, in an effort to allow new social and occupational groups such as ecological organizations to take part in this process, the European Commission agreed to enlarge some of the agricultural advisory committees. This includes the committees on oilseeds and protein crops, sugar, rice, energy crops, milk, beef and veal, pigmeat, fresh fruit and vegetables, olives and derived products, forestry and cork, organic farming, rural development, and agriculture and the environment. Within the framework of this reform, and in line with the recognition of the social and economic diversity and plurality of European agriculture, the CPE was invited to participate and now has a representative on most of the agricultural advisory committees. Currently, there are 30 consultative/advisory groups. Many of them are sectoral committees (linked to common market organizations) while others are non-sectoral ones (linked to structural, agri-environmental or rural development policies). On the most important sectoral advisory groups the COPA-COGECA representatives maintain half of the seats.

These advisory groups have been key to the development of agricultural organizations in Europe as they have permitted the agricultural sector to maintain and strengthen the privileged position it holds before the European Commission; a position that provides them access to information, rather than allowing them to exert any real influence. The role of the advisory groups has also been a crucial factor for the development of trade, industry, workers, consumers and environmentalist

European organizations, because they reimburse members of the national organizations for their travel expenses to Brussels. Most European organizations, and particularly the COPA and the COGECA, take advantage of these committee meetings to meet on a regular basis to discuss and negotiate the consensual European positions, which are the basis of the ideological discourses. During these preparatory meetings, the delegates exchange deeply about the market and production situation in each country.

Nevertheless, the collective action of the European agricultural organizations is no longer led by the work of the sectoral advisory groups. The main reason is that the CAP is no longer a market policy which needs information from operators to be managed correctly. Since the 1992 CAP reform, market mechanisms are not determinant of producers' income (with the introduction of the direct payments) and so the sectoral advisory groups lose their principal aim. Recent changes in the CAP (2003 Reform), leading to total decoupled aid, increase this trend as the common market organizations are reduced to sole intervention mechanisms.

These changes in the CAP have led to the development and reinforcement of the relations of the COPA-COGECA with the other socio-economic representatives of the *filière*, which are directly and indirectly related to the farming sector (food chain organizations, NGOs from civil society, etc.). These contacts take place through the advisory groups as well as through frequent bilateral contacts, common collective action strategies, participation at general assemblies, etc.

In parallel, the increasing number of EU regulations and directives concerning food and the environment, has led to the creation of new bodies, such as DG SANCO (Directorate-General for Consumer Affairs) and DG ENVIRONMENT, as well as advisory and scientific structures such as the European Food Agency (where the COPA and the COGECA are members of the board). The European agricultural organizations have also become active in other *fora*, as for example the "Dialog with civil society" initiative carried on by DG TRADE.

Conclusions

The COPA, the COGECA and the CPE form the three components upon which the European system of farm representation is built. The two first structures (the COPA and the COGECA) emerged parallel to the CAP process, and in the past, they were an important element of the construction and the implementation of this policy. The CPE has gathered together a wide range of groups, social movements and farmers' organizations that, on the margins of the official system of representation, had been taking a critical stance against the CAP, manifesting their vigorous opposition to the expansion of a homogeneous model of agriculture and a uniform farm profile.

In view of the development and consolidation of a European system of farm interest representation, the question arises as to whether or not this system has replaced the national systems of representation. Given that the sovereignty of national governments on matters of agriculture has been transferred to the EU institutions, there is no doubt that, in terms of agricultural policy, the sphere of farm interest representation has become *europeanized* to such a degree that we could think that national spheres have lost their importance. Thus it should come as no surprise that the COPA, the COGECA and the CPE act as genuine *European* organizations before the EU institutions, since the national organizations have delegated in them to formulate their CAP discourse and define their claiming strategies.

Nonetheless, if we look more closely at how the three pillars of the system (COPA, COGECA and CPE) function and participate in the CAP decision-making process, a different conclusion is reached. In practice, these European structures of representation (especially the COPA and the COGECA) behave as bureaucratic superstructures whose aim is to try maintaining its role as legitimate interlocutors with EU institutions and to manage the participation of each country's associations in the advisory committees. In fact, the position held by the member national organizations of the COPA-COGECA and the CPE in such committees is not the result of a previous strategy of supranational coordination, but the construction of a consensual position of national interests. This explains the presence in Brussels of numerous technical staff from the different national farmers' organizations and the intense lobbying activities that each undertakes within these European representation structures and in an autonomous manner (independently of the COPA, COGECA and CPE) before the EU institutions (especially before DG AGRI and the European Parliament). In addition, the fact that the governments of the different Member States are important actors of the decisional process and are given a wide margin to implement the CAP in their countries explains why the existence of a common European agricultural policy has not diminished the role of national systems of representation, but has instead reinforced them. Thus, we cannot speak of a European system of agricultural representation, constructed as a network, but rather a European partnership structure that coexists alongside the autonomous presence of national systems of representation in carrying out the CAP process.

Notes

[*] Cristina Rueda-Catry has a PhD in Rural Sociology from the University of Nanterre (France). She has worked on the farm interest group system at the European level. Her doctoral thesis was on discourses, attitudes and strategies of Spanish farmers unions before the entry of Spain in the EU.

[1] As Lagrave (1993) says, the International Agricultural Congress held in Paris during the World Expo of 1889 set the first precedent for the CEA. This international congress was held every two years, bringing together some one thousand participants, among them farmers, agronomists, scientists, university professors, journalists, members of parliament and representatives of agricultural organizations. Most of the papers given at the conference focused on the agricultural crisis occurring at the turn of the century, its causes and measures to overcome it. During the congress and at Jules Meline's instigation, the then Minister of Agriculture in France, the CIA (International Agricultural Conference) was established with the commitment to continue holding international meetings on agricultural issues. During the Second World War, the work of the CIA was interrupted. Once the war ended, and at the initiative of the British National Farmers' Union (NFU), a new umbrella organization known as the International Federation of Agricultural Producers (FIPA) was founded in 1947, which included professional agricultural organizations from the English-speaking and Commonwealth countries. In response, the CIA decided to change its name to the European Confederation of Agriculture (CEA) in order to defend the interests of European farming on the international stage.

Appendix Two

List of COPA Members

Web sites provided where available: Correct as at June 2004

AUSTRIA
- Präsidentenkonferenz der Landwirtschaftskamme Österreichs (PKLWK)
  www.pklwk.at

BELGIUM
- Boerenbond Belgiche (BB)
  www.boerenbond.be

- Federation Wallone de l'Agriculture (FWA)

CYPRUS
- Panagrotikos Farmers' Union

CZECH REPUBLIC
- Czech Agrarian Chamber (Agrárni Komora Ceské Republiky)(CAC)

- Agricultural Association of the Czech Republic (Zemedelsky Svaz Ceské Republiky) (AACR)

- Association of Private Farming (Asociace Soukromého Zemedelství) (ASZ)

DENMARK
- Landbrugsraadet
  www.landbrug.dk

- De Danske Landbrug

ESTONIA
- Estonian Chamber of Agriculture and Commerce (Eestimaa Põllumajandus-Kaubanduskoda) (EPKK)
  www.epkk.ee

- Estonian Farmers Federation (Estimaa Talupidajate Keskliit) (ETKL)
  www.taluliit.ee

FINLAND

- Central Union of Agricultural Producers and Forest Owners (Maa-ja Metsätalous Tuottajain Keskusliitto) (MIK)
  www.mtk.fi

- Svenska Lantbruksproucenternas Centralförbun (SLC)
  www.slc.fi

FRANCE

- Assamblée Permanente des Chambres d'Agriculture (APCA)
  www.paris.apca.chambagri.fr/apca/default.htm

- Fédération Nationale des Syndicats d'Exploitants Agricoles (FNSEA)
  www.fnsea.fr

- Confédération Nationale de la Mutualité, de la Coopération et du Crédit Agricoles (CNMCCA)

GERMANY

- Deutscher Bauernverband e.V. (DBV)
  www.bauernverband.de

GREECE

- Confédération Panhellenique des Unions des Cooperatives Agricoles (PASEGES)
  www.paseges.gr

- General Confederation of Greek Agrarian Association (GESASE)
  www.gesase.gr

HUNGARY

- Hungarian Chamber of Agriculture (Magyar Agrárkamara)
  www.agrarkamara.hu

- National Federation of Agricultural Co-operators and Producers (Mezögazdasági Szövetkezök és Termelök Országos Szövetsé) (MOSZ)

IRELAND

- Irish Farmers' Association (IFA)
  www.ifa.ie

ITALY

- Confederazione Nazionale Coltivattori Diretti (COLDIRETTI)
  www.coldiretti.it

- Confederazione Generale dell'Agricoltura Italiana (CONFAGRICOLTURA) www.confagricoltura.it

- Confederacione Italiana degli Agricoltori (CIA) (ex Confcoltivatori) www.cia.it

LATVIA
- Latvian Farmers Federation (Latvijas Zemnieku Federäcia) (LZF)

- Association of Latvian Statutory Societies (Lauksaimniecibas Statütsabiedribu Asociäcija) (LSA)

- Farmers' Parliament (Zemnieku Saeima) (ZSA) www.ltn.lv/~zsa/index

- Latvian Rural Support Association (Latvijas Atbalsta Asociäcija) (LLAA)

LITHUANIA
- Lithuanian Farmers' Union (Lietuvos Ükininku Sajunga) (LUS) www.lus.lt

LUXEMBOURG
- Centrale Paysanne Luxembourgeoise (CPL)

MALTA
- Malta Agriculture Lobby (MAL)

NETHERLANDS
- Land- en Tuinbouw Organisatie Nederland (LTO Ned) www.lto.nl

POLAND
- National Union of Farmers' Circles and Agricultural Organization (KZRKIOR)

PORTUGAL
- Confederaçao dos Agricultores de Portugal (CAP)

SLOVAKIA
- Slovak Agricultural and Food Chamber (Slovenská Pol'nohospodárska a Potravinárska Komora) (SPPK) www.sppk.sk

- Union of Farmers and Agrarian Entrepreneurs of Slovakia (Zurol'nikov a Agropodnikatel'ov Slovenska) (ZRAS)

- Association of Landowners and Agrarian Entrepreneurs of Slovakia (Zdruzenie vlastnikov pödy a Agropodnikatelòv Slovenska) (ZVPA)

SLOVENIA
- Chamber for Agriculture and Forestry of Slovenia

SPAIN
- Asociación Agraria-Jóvenes Agricultores (ASAJA)
  www.asaja.com

- Coordinadora de Organizaciones de Agricultores y Ganaderos (COAG)
  www.coaginforma.com.

- Unión de Pequeños Agricultores (UPA)
  www.upa.es

SWEDEN
- Lantbrukarnas Riksförbund (LRF)
  www.lrf.se

UNITED KINGDOM
- National Farmers' Union of England and Wales (NFU)
  www.nfuonline.com

- National Farmers' Union of Scotland (NFUS)
  www.nfus.org.uk

- Ulsters Farmers' Union (UFU)
  www.ufuni.org

The COPA's Member Associations from Other Candidate Countries

BULGARIA
- Bulgarian Farmers' Association (BFA)

- Central Co-operative Union (CCU)

- National Union for agricultural Co-operatives (NSZK)

- Bulgarian Chamber of Agriculture

ROMANIA
- National Union of agricultural Producers in Romania (Uniunea Nationala a Producatorilor Agricoli din Romania) (UNPAR)

Appendix Three

List of CPE Members

Web sites provided where available: Correct as at June 2004

AUSTRIA
- Österreichische Bergbauernvereinigung (ÖBV)
  www.bergbauern.org

BELGIUM
- Front Uni des Jeunes Agriculteurs (FUJA)
  www.cjef.be/OJ/FUJA.htm

- Vlaams Agrarisch Centrum (VAC)
  www.vacvzw.be

FRANCE
- Confédération Nationale Paysanne

- Mouvement de Défénse de l'Exploitation Familiale (MODEF)

GERMANY
- Arbeitsgemeinschaft Bäuerliche Landwirtschaft (AbL)
  www.abl-ev.de

ITALY
- Foro Contadino
  www.altragricoltura.org/forocontadino

- ARI

NETHERLANDS
- Kritisch Landbouwberaad (KLB)

NORWAY
- NorskeBonde- og Småbrukarlag (NBS) (Norwegian Farmers' and Smallholders' Union)
  www.smabrukarlaget.no

PORTUGAL
- Confederaçao Nacional da Agricoltura (CNA)

SPAIN
- Sindicato Labrego Galego (SLG)

- Euskal Herriko Nekazarien Elkastasuna (EHNE)

- Unión de Agricultores y Ganaderos de la Rioja (UAGR)

SWEDEN
- Nordbruk
  www.nordbruk.org

SWITZERLAND
- Uniterre
  www.uniterre.ch

UNITED KINGDOM
- FFA
  www.ffa.org

EUROPE
- Mouvement International de Jeunesse Agricole et Rurale Catholique (MIJARC-Europe)

Appendix Four

List of COGECA's Members

Web sites provided where available: Correct as at June 2004.

AUSTRIA
- Österreichischer Raiffeisenverband (ÖRV)
  www.raiffeisenverband.at

BELGIUM
- AVEVE-Boerenbond Belgische (BB)

CYPRUS
- Panagrotikos Farmers' Union

CZECH REPUBLIC
- Agricultural Association of the Czech Republic (Zemědělský svaz České republiky)

DENMARK
- Danske Andelsselskaber
  www.danskeandelsselskaber.dk

ESTONIA
- Estonian Farmers Federation (Eestimaa Talupidajate Keskliit)

- Estonian Co-operative Association (Eesti Ühistegeline Liit)
  www.eca.ee

FINLAND
- Confederation of Finnish Cooperatives (PELLERVO)
  www.pellervo.fi/finncoop/

FRANCE
- COOP DE FRANCE (ex CFCA)
  www.coopdefrance.coop/sites/cfca/

GERMANY
- Deutscher Raiffeisenverband (DRV)
  www.raiffeisen.de

GREECE
- Confederation Panhellenique des Unions des Cooperatives Agricoles (PASEGES)
  www.paseges.gr

HUNGARY
- Association of Hungarian Producers' Sales and Service Co-operatives (Magyar Termelői Értékesítő és Szolgáltató Szervezetek/Szövetkezetek Együttműködése)

IRELAND
- Irish Cooperative Organisation Society Ltd (I.C.O.S.)
  www.icos.ie

ITALY
- Federazione Nazionale delle Cooperative Agricole ed Agroalimentari (CONFCOOPERATIVE)
  www.confcooperative.it/

- Associazione Nazionale Cooperative Agricole (ANCA-Lega)
  www.ancalega.coop

- Associazione Generale Italiana Cooperative Agricole (AGCI/AGICA)
  www.agci.it

LITHUANIA
- Lithuanian Farmers' Union
  www.lus.lt

LUXEMBOURG
- Centrale Paysanne Luxembourgeoise (C.P.L.)

MALTA
- Malta Agriculture Lobby (MAL)

NETHERLANDS
- Nationale Coöperatieve Raad voor Land- en Tuinbouw (NCR)
  www.cooperatie.nl

POLAND
- National Union of Farmers' Circles and Agricultural Organizations (KZRKIOR)
  www.kolkarolnicze.pl

PORTUGAL
- Confederaçao Nacional dos Cooperativas Agricolas e Credito Agricole de Portugal (CONFAGRI)
  www.confagri.pt

SLOVENIA
- Co-operative Union of Slovenia (Zadružna Zveza Slovenije) (ZZS)

- Chamber for Agriculture and Forestry of Slovenia (Kmetijsko gozdarska zbornica Slovenije) (KGZS)

SPAIN
- Confederación de Cooperativas Agrarias de España (CCAE)
  www.ccae.es

SWEDEN
- Federation of Swedish Farmers (LRF)
  www.lrf.se

UNITED KINGDOM
- Federation of Agricultural Cooperatives Ltd. (FAC)

Other Candidate Countries

BULGARIA
- Bulgarian Farmers' Association
- Central Co-operative Union Central Co-operative Union
- National Union for Agricultural Co-operatives
- Bulgarian Chamber of Agriculture

ROMANIA
- National Union of Agricultural Producers in Romania (Uniunea Nationala a Producatorilor Agricoli din Romania)

Associated Members

CYPRUS
- Pancyprian Farmers' Union (PEK.)
- Union of Cypriot Farmers (EKA)
- Pancyprian Farmers Union (AGROTIKI)

HUNGARY
- Hungarian Peasants Association (Magyar Parasztszövetség)
- National Association of Hungarian Farmers' Societies and Co-operatives (Magyar Gazdakörök és Gazdaszövetkezetek Országos Szövetsége) (MAGOSZ)

LATVIA
- Latvian Agricultural Co-operatives Association Latvijas Lauksaimniecības kooperatīvu asociācija (LLKA)

LITHUANIA
- Association of Agricultural Co-operatives Žemės ūkio kooperatyvų Asociacija "Kooperacijos kelias"

MALTA
- APEX Organisation of Maltese Co-operatives

POLAND
- Federation of Agricultural Producers' Union (FZPR)

- Samoobrona Agricultural Trade Union

- National Council of Chambers of Agriculture (KRIR)
  www.krir.pl

- National Co-op Council (KRS)

- National Union of Agricultural Employees (OJCZYZNA)

- Federation of Agricultural Employers and Landowners Union (FZPR)

- 'Solidarnosc' Farmers Unions

SLOVAKIA
- Association of Agricultural Co-operatives and Companies (Zväz poľnohospodárskych družstiev a obchodných spoločností SR) (ZPDaOS)

Appendix Five

List of IFAP Members

Web sites provided where available: Correct as at June 2004

ALGERIA
- National Chamber of Agriculture of Algeria

ARAB REPUBLIC OF EGYPT
- Central Agricultural Co-operative Union
  www.cacueg.org

- IFAP Egyptian National Committee

ARGENTINA
- Sociedad Rural Agentina
  www.ruralarg.org.ar

AUSTRALIA
- National Farmers' Federation
  www.nff.org.au

AUSTRIA
- Austrian Committee for Agriculture and Forestry
  www.praeko.at

BANGLADESH
- Surjamukhi Sangatha (SMS) -Women Farmers Organization of Bangladesh

BELGIUM
- Boerenbond (BB)
  www.boerenbond.be

- Federation Wallone de l'Agriculture

BÉNIN
- Féderation des Unions de Producteurs de Bénin (FUPRO)

BRAZIL
- Brazilian Confederation of Agriculture and Livestock (CNA)

CAMBODIA
- Cambodia Farmers' Association for Agricultural Development

CAMEROON
- Chambre d'Agriculture, de l'Elevage et des Forets

CANADA
- Canadian Federation of Agriculture (CFA)
  www.cfa-fca.ca

COLOMBIA
- Federacion Colombian de Ganaderos (FEDEGAN)
  www.fedegan.org.co

- Sociedad de Agricultores de Colombia
  www.sociedadagricultores.org.co

- CECORA

- FEDEPANELA

CORMOROS ISLANDS
- Syndicat National des Agriculteurs Comoriens

COSTA RICA
- Mesa Nacional Campesina

CÔTE D'IVOIRE
- Association Nationale des Organisations Professionnelles Agricoles de Côte d'Ivoire

CYPRUS
- Cyprus Turkish Farmers Union

DEMOCRATIC REPUBLIC OF CONGO
- Syndicat de Défense des Intérêts Paysans

DENMARK
- Landbrugsraadet
  www.landbrug.dk

FINLAND
- Maa-Ja Metsatalous Tuottajain Keskusliitto (MTK) (Central Union of Agricultural Producers and Forest Owners) www.mtk.fi

- Finn Coop Pellervo www.pellervo.fi/finncoop/index.htm

FRANCE
- Assemblée Permanente des Chambres d'Agriculture http://paris.apca.chambagri.fr/apca/default.htm

- Centre National des Jeunes Agriculteurs www.cnja.com

- Conféderation Française de la Coopération Agricole www.cooperation-agricole.asso.fr

- Conféderation Nationale de la Mutualité de la Coopération et du C.A.

- Fédération Nationale de la Mutualité Agricole

- Fédération Nationale des Syndicats d'Exploitants Agricoles www.fnsea.fr

- Fédération Nationale du Crédit Agricole

GERMANY
- Deutscher Bauernverband e.V. (DBV) www.bauernverband.de/

GREECE
- Confédération Panhellenique des Unions des Cooperatives Agricoles (PASEGES) www.paseges.gr

GUINEA
- Fédération des Paysans du Fouta Djallon www.paysansdufouta.org

ICELAND
- Baendasamtôk Islands www.bondi.is/landbunadur/wgbi.nsf/key2/index.html

INDIA
- Farmers' Forum

- National Institute of Agriculture

IRELAND
- Irish Farmers' Association (IFA)
  www.ifa.ie

ITALY
- Confederazione Nazionale Coltivattori Diretti (COLDIRETTI)
  www.coldiretti.it

- Confederazione Generale dell'Agricoltura Italiana (CONFAGRICOLTURA)
  www.confagricoltura.it

- Confederacione Italiana degli Agricoltori (CIA) (ex Confcoltivatori)
  www.cia.it

JAPAN
- Ja-Zenchu
  www.e-zenchu-ja.org

- National Chamber of Agriculture

- National Council Farm Policy Organisation

JORDAN
- Jordan Farmers' Union

TAIWAN
- Taiwan Provincial Farmers' Association
  ww.tpfa.org.tw

TUNISIA
- Union Tunisienne de l'Agriculture et de la Pêche (UTAP)
  www.utap.org.tn

TURKEY
- Union of Turkish Chambers of Agriculture
  www.tzob.org.tk

UGANDA
- Uganda Co-operative Alliance

- Uganda National Farmers' Association

UNITED KINGDOM
- National Farmers' Union of England and Wales (NFU)
  www.nfuonline.com

- National Farmers' Union of Scotland (NFUS)
  www.nfus.org.uk

- Ulsters Farmers' Union (UFU)
  www.ufuni.org

URUGUAY
- CNFR

- Cooperativas Agrarias Federadas–CAF.
  www.caf.org.uy

U.S.A.
- National Farmers' Union
  www.nfu.org

ZAMBIA
- Zambia Co-operative Federation Ltd.

- Zambia National Farmers' Union

ZIMBABWE
- Commercial Farmers' Union
  www.samara.co.zw/cfu

- Zimbabwe Farmers' Union

Index